A DIFFERENT ROAD TAKEN

Critical Studies in Communication and in the Cultural Industries

Herbert I. Schiller, *Series Editor*

A Different Road Taken: Profiles in Critical Communication, edited by John A. Lent

Consumer Culture and TV Programming, Robin Andersen

Marketing Madness: A Survival Guide for a Consumer Society, Michael F. Jacobson and Laurie Ann Mazur

Public Television for Sale: Media, the Market, and the Public Sphere, William Hoynes

Counterclockwise: Perspectives on Communication, Dallas Smythe (edited by Thomas Guback)

The Panoptic Sort: A Political Economy of Personal Information, Oscar H. Gandy, Jr.

Triumph of the Image: The Media's War in the Persian Gulf—A Global Perspective, edited by Hamid Mowlana, George Gerbner, and Herbert I. Schiller

The Persian Gulf TV War, Douglas Kellner

Mass Communications and American Empire, Second Edition, Updated, Herbert I. Schiller

FORTHCOMING

The FAIR Reader: An Extra! *Review of Press and Politics in the '90s,* edited by Jim Naureckas and Janine Jackson

Monopoly Television: MTV's Quest to Control the Music, Jack Banks

Communication and the Transformation of Economics: Essays in Information, Public Policy, and Political Economy, Robert E. Babe

The Social Uses of Photography: Images in the Age of Reproducibility, Hanno Hardt

Introduction to Media Studies, edited by Stuart Ewen, Elizabeth Ewen, Serafina Bathrick, and Andrew Mattson

Invisible Crises, edited by George Gerbner, Hamid Mowlana, and Herbert I. Schiller

The Communications Industry in the American Economy, Thomas Guback

Hot Shots: An Alternative Video Production Handbook, Tami Gold and Kelly Anderson

A DIFFERENT ROAD TAKEN

Profiles in Critical Communication

edited by

JOHN A. LENT

WestviewPress
A Division of HarperCollins*Publishers*

Critical Studies in Communication and in the Cultural Industries

All photographs appear courtesy of John A. Lent, except photograph of James D. Halloran, which appears courtesy of James D. Halloran.

Published in 1995 in the United States of America by Westview Press, Inc., 5500 Central Avenue, Boulder, Colorado 80301-2877, and in the United Kingdom by Westview Press, 12 Hid's Copse Road, Cumnor Hill, Oxford OX2 9JJ

Library of Congress Cataloging-in-Publication Data
A different road taken : profiles in critical communication / edited by John A. Lent
p. cm. — (Critical studies in communication and in the cultural industries)
Contains interviews with Dallas Smythe, George Gerbner, Herbert Schiller, James Halloran, and Kaarle Nordenstreng, bibliographies of their works, as well as discussions of their importance and comments on critical communication in general by ten other specialists.
Includes bibliographical references.
ISBN 0-8133-1635-9 — ISBN 0-8133-1636-7 (pbk)
1. Mass media criticism. 2. Mass media scholars—Interviews.
I. Lent, John A. II. Series.
P96.C76D54 1995
302.23—dc20 95-262
CIP

The paper used in this publication meets the requirements of the American National Standard for Permanence of Paper for Printed Library Materials Z39.48-1984.

10 9 8 7 6 5 4 3 2 1

For those few brave ones
who wander down different roads
in search of truth, justice, and new ways

Contents

PART FOUR
JAMES D. HALLORAN

PART FIVE
KAARLE NORDENSTRENG

1

Introduction

JOHN A. LENT

Critical Scholarship: Problems of Definition and Scope

One word in the communication lexicon that needs some boundaries is "critical." Applied to a variety of areas of communication studies, "critical" takes on the meanings, among others, of "crucial," "perilous," "serious," "negative," and "pertaining to criticism" (as in reviews). Thus, one might hear that a critical (crucial) area of communication research is agenda setting, or that the field is in a critical (perilous) state, or that such and such scholar is *just* being critical (negative). Obviously, these usages do not reflect what we mean by "critical" here.

Courting accusations of paranoia, I am tempted to say that the word has been coopted by "mainstream" communication scholars (much in the same way that advertisers "stole" the words and phrases of various revolutionary movements to serve their own ends), who, by doing so, make it appear that they are amenable to critical scholarship, although they continue to produce works in support of the establishment and status quo.

Robert McChesney, after crediting gains made in critical communication scholarship during the past decade, went on the say that the legacy of the field has been one of "promise unfulfilled." His premise for that conclusion relates to the way "critical" is used. In his view, "Arguably, we are heading toward the point where the term *critical* may lose its bite and simply refer to bounded areas of study or methodologies, its links to movements for radical social change buried beneath so much academic rigamarole" (McChesney 1993:98–99). McChesney said that existing critical communication scholarship was way off course, if by

---

I wish to thank Rose L. Lent and Judi Walsh for helping to transcribe the tapes of the five interviews.

"critical" one means "an explicit skepticism toward dominant institutions (including the university), ideologies, and social relations and an implicit commitment to a more democratic, egalitarian, and humane social order" (McChesney 1993:98).

This definition of "critical" could serve well as the basis for this book. My own way of thinking of critical communication does not differ greatly—an in-depth analysis of the strengths and weaknesses of dominant communication institutions, processes, and artifacts, with the intention of arriving at solutions, guidelines, and policies that benefit the masses, not the power brokers.

Critical communication scholarship, defined in either of these ways, faces some huge roadblocks as the university and the more general scholarly community are increasingly subordinated to big business interests. In the United States and some other countries, universities have become big businesses: administrators are attracted from business schools or industry, students are thought of as clients, the instruction workforce is downsized while the administrative bureaucracy is greatly augmented, programs and courses are determined by tuition money generated rather than intellectual curiosity or societal needs, and faculty members' worth is gauged not necessarily by teaching or research ability but by their expertise at writing successful grants and getting "on side" with those in power.

Because journalism/communication schools are directly connected to an industry, these faculty are asked to draw on print and broadcast corporations for funds, hardly the breeding grounds for critical scholarship. In some cases, professors are enticed and encouraged to do research that supports industry's needs; in most instances they are implored to prep students uncritically for survival in the media. Those who deviate, who use critical approaches, are apt to be labeled negative influences and pay the price at merit, promotion, and tenure time.

But not all the fault rests with the dominant institution, the university. The field of critical communication scholarship itself has some of its own dirty linen that needs washing. For whatever reasons, but usually those pertaining to money, some critical scholars have become highly paid consultants and employees of repressive governments, suffocating conglomerates, and fundamentalist religious groups. At other times, certain ideas of a critical strand find their way into, and are used by, the very entities they were meant to attack. McChesney reported that two conferences he attended had papers that discussed the use of cultural studies "methodologies" to help advertisers "improve" message effectiveness and that a major advertising agency in Chicago uses a seminal cultural studies work to train advertisers on how they might better influence consumers (McChesney 1993:101). Other problems in critical communication research relate to the mobility of scholars, their efforts to justify the field of study, and the insularity of the research itself.

Often, when serious scholars who have started critical programs, courses, and communities leave an institution because of frustration or better opportunities elsewhere, their creations are folded or remodeled by mainstream faculty. Not very many communication programs have more than one "critical" person who can carry on the legacy in such situations. Mobility is a factor with some less serious faculty members who weave in and out of critical scholarship to suit their mood or the academic fashion of the day.

As with any new field, critical communication scholarship has tried to justify its existence. Usually, manifestations of this are the setting up of barriers to admission and the coining of a different vocabulary of often incomprehensible and irrelevant gobbledygook. None of this bodes well for the field, and it would seem that critical scholars would not follow the highly structured, institutionalized route they meant to replace or modify, but they do.

McChesney discussed the insularity, which he said manifests itself in three ways: a "shocking ignorance of the entire tradition of critical social and political thought over the past 200 years"; a preponderance of "the most hackneyed notions about the histories of the various social movements" of the same period; and a myopic perspective that omits critical scholarship in "other disciplines and from the broader left intellectual community" (McChesney 1993:99–100).

Not only are critical (and mainstream, for that matter) communication scholars unaware of the rich tradition in "critical social and political thought," but they also do not know what preceded in "critical journalistic" work. Surely, Upton Sinclair's self-financed and self-produced indictment of the press, *The Brass Check*, rates as critical scholarship, as do the works of George Seldes, A. J. Liebling, and Heywood Broun. They wrote about concentration of power in journalism, the big business–oriented press, publishers who "covered up" stories to serve their own, or their advertisers', interests, and the exploitation of reportorial labor. Yet, we see very little indication that critical communication scholars have read these works, much less recommended them to students. The result is that critical scholars, much like their more conservative colleagues, work under the illusion that they have made a revolutionary discovery, when actually they have carried on the next phase of a long-standing critical tradition.

Objectives and Dimensions of *A Different Road Taken*

The idea for this book came to me in the earliest years of the 1980s. At the time, the institution where I labor had one of the strongest critical communication faculties anywhere, made up of Dallas Smythe, Vincent Mosco, Janet Wasko, Dan Schiller, Tran Van Dinh, myself, and a few others.

Listening to Dallas and Tran swap personal yarns, it struck me that critical communication scholars had some fascinating stories that needed to be shared and that the history of the field could be documented through those same stories. I wondered what factors and influences prompted these scholars to take a different way, what hardships—even indignities—they had endured for doing so, what in their view, their major contributions were, and what trends, directions, and problems for critical scholarship they envisioned. In fact, these became the main areas of inquiry in the subsequent interviews.

In my estimation, five individuals stood out then for their international recognition, their immense productivity, their taking the field of mass communication into new directions, their criticism of mass communication agencies and research, and their interconnections. Each had a number of characteristics that merited his inclusion: Dallas Smythe, development of the first political economy course, criticism of media economics, new information technology, and mainstream social science research; George Gerbner, television and violence studies, multidimensional theoretical models of the communication process, cultural indicators work; Herbert Schiller, media/cultural imperialism, mind management, corporate takeover of cultural expression; James Halloran, violence and television, criticism of Western social science and communication research, new information technology; and Kaarle Nordenstreng, global television flows, international communication diplomacy, and international ethics for journalists.

The first interviews were conducted with Smythe and Schiller when we attended the First Canberra Conference on International Communication in late 1986. Halloran and Nordenstreng were interviewed during the International Association for Mass Communication Research assembly in Bled, Yugoslavia, in August 1990, and Gerbner at the same assembly two years later in Guaruja, Brazil. The interviews stretched over this long period mainly because I did not have funds to make the trips specifically to record these stories and because the interviewees were not always available when I was. The interview structure was purposely flexible, and interviewees were given an opportunity to edit transcripts.

By the time interviews were completed, other attempts had been made to chronicle the development of critical communication study or to profile critical scholars. David Barsamian, in *Stenographers of Power: Media and Propaganda* (1992), interviewed seven media critics (Noam Chomsky, Ben Bagdikian, Alexander Cockburn, and Michael Parenti among them) on the role of media in constraining democracy, but these interviews did not provide much insight into the development of a critical communication tradition. In a 1989 monograph in German, Jorg Becker provided intellectual portraits of thirty critical communication researchers; sixteen were from Germany and the other fourteen hailed from ten other countries. Among the latter were B. Agrawal, N. Garnham, C. Hamelink, K. Jakubowicz, W. Kleinwächter, W. Melody, B. Pavlic, H. Schmucler, S. Splichal, and T. Szecskö. Each profile in this volume includes an abbreviated c.v. and a description of the person's most important work in a bibliography. Additionally, three of those interviewed for *A Different Road Taken* have been honored with their own Festschrifts—Schiller (Becker, Hedebro, and Paldan 1986), Smythe (Wasko, Mosco, and Pendakur 1993), and Halloran (Hamelink and Linne 1994).

Lai-si Tsui interviewed Schiller (1991) and with Closepet interviewed Gerbner (1992) for a series in *Media Development.*

Although the five interviews form the foundation of *A Different Road Taken,* contributions by ten other critical scholars provide insights into the work of the interviewees and the present and future roles of critical communication. Each of the five featured scholars was asked to name researchers or practitioners who could either capture the essence of and critique their work or discuss trends, problems, and directions of critical communication research. In nearly every case, the top two individuals suggested by the interviewees readily accepted the challenge to write a critique, although each approached the task in a different way.

In looking at Smythe's work, Robin Mansell singled out elements central to his process of doing social science research, his critical and materialist methodology. She allowed Smythe's views to come out in copious quotes—on what social scientists should do, on definitions of concepts, and on how he helped forge the tools of the social scientist.

Michael Morgan divided Gerbner's work into three areas: development of multidimensional theoretical models of the communication process, cultural indicators, and the Cultural Environment Movement. Because of his own bias for cultivation analysis, Morgan devoted considerably more space to this aspect.

Lai-si Tsui listed the major themes of Schiller's writings as mind management, corporate takeover of cultural expression, electronics and economics for crisis management, cultural imperialism, transnationalization, impact of new information technology, and recognition of transformations in capitalism. She showed how Schiller changed his thinking over the years and used this review as a base to raise issues central to the political economy debate.

Tamás Szecskö analyzed Halloran's work in television and violence, his crusade against conventional research, his promotion of relationships between researchers and communicators, and his support of critical research, delineating in the latter between policy-oriented and policy research. Additionally, he lists Halloran's fifteen commandments of critical research.

Balancing the successes and failures and good and bad points of Nordenstreng's theoretical and practical work, Wolfgang Kleinwächter treated his global television flow study and *National Sovereignty and International Communication* book, as well as his active and, at times, behind-the-scenes role in international communication negotiations and his attempts to design an international journalistic code of ethics.

The contributors who analyzed the field of critical communication studies were instructed to build their essays around five broadly stated questions: (1) How has critical research in communication changed since it was conceived about a generation ago? What has changed and what has remained constant concerning research problems and issues, theories, and research techniques and approaches?

(2) Do you believe that critical research in communication has advanced during the past generation, and if you do, what has brought about those advances? (3) What are the impediments to carrying out critical research in communication at governmental, institutional (including your own), funding agency, professional organizations, or other levels? (4) Where is critical research in communication heading? What do you think are the major issues that critical researchers in communication must consider? and (5) How and why did you decide to take the route of the critical researcher in communication? What personal and professional experiences influenced you?

Thus, the book is organized into five parts, each representing one of the interviewees and including a profile, interview, analysis of this work, and critique of the field of critical communication studies. A bibliography of the works of the interviewees, which they contributed, completes the book.

Commonalities of Featured Scholars

Smythe, Gerbner, Schiller, Halloran, and Nordenstreng line up rather consistently in a number of areas. This can be written off as a coincidence or explained by the interconnections among them.

For example, Smythe, Gerbner, and Schiller were at the University of Illinois at about the same time: Smythe recruited Gerbner, and Schiller went to Illinois when Smythe left. The International Association for Mass Communication Research also played a role in connecting them. All five—Smythe to a lesser extent—had official roles in IAMCR for most of the Halloran administration (1972–90).

Invariably, two or more of them participated in various UNESCO meetings, probably beginning with the 1969 policy session in Montreal, attended by Smythe, Halloran, and Nordenstreng. Although Schiller was not present, fifty copies of his *Mass Communication and American Empire* were there at the request of Nordenstreng. In some cases, they collaborated on books: Nordenstreng and Schiller on two editions of *National Sovereignty and International Communication*; Schiller and Gerbner (with Mowlana) on the Gulf War; and Nordenstreng and Gerbner (with Mowlana) on the *Global Media Debate.* Smythe had a role in Nordenstreng's (with Varis) television traffic flow book and wrote the foreword to Schiller's 1969 *Mass Communication and American Empire.* Schiller returned the favor in Smythe's *Dependency Road* more than a decade later.

Looking at the backgrounds of these five scholars, a number of commonalities are apparent. The poverty of the Depression, fascism, World War II, and, in its aftermath, the U.S. military occupation of Germany, changed the thinking of four of them. Nordenstreng, born about a generation later than the others, talked of the influence of the "crazy years of the late 1960s." Seeing the "Okies" and "Arkies" mishandled in California and hearing of the fascism of the Spanish Civil War in the 1930s changed Smythe's life, whereas Gerbner obviously was affected by Nazi fascism, volunteering for dangerous military missions during World War II. Schiller recounted his father's not being employed full time for a decade during the Depression and his own "real social science education" as a member of the U.S. military government occupation of Germany as heavy influences, and Halloran mentioned the poverty of the Depression.

In the forefront of their careers, all served in government or in military capacities. Smythe distinguished himself in numerous state and federal positions, culminating with his appointment as chief economist of the Federal Communications Commission. Gerbner advanced through the ranks from private to first lieutenant in the U.S. military, Schiller served in the U.S. military government occupation of Germany, Halloran put in two and one-half years with the RAF Special Duties ("playing rugby and cricket most of the time") and was secretary of the government-sponsored Television Research Committee in his early career, and Nordenstreng headed audience research at the governmental Finnish Broadcasting Company.

For varying amounts of time, all were in leadership roles in university programs. Gerbner, Halloran, and Nordenstreng were much more closely associated with university administration. Gerbner did the bulk of his work while dean for twenty-five years of the Annenberg School of Communication in Philadelphia; Halloran, most of his as director of the University of Leicester Centre for Mass Communication Research; and Nordenstreng as head of journalism at the University of Tampere. The support and prestige of these home bases obviously enhanced their careers. Halloran talked about his vice-chancellor's help and the freedom from teaching duties that he and his fellow staff members enjoyed for a decade, and Nordenstreng acknowledged he was permitted to retain his professorship at Tampere while assuming the rigorous schedule demanded of him as International Organization of Journalists president for fourteen years. Smythe chaired departments at Simon Fraser University and the University of Saskatchewan for a total of twelve years, and Schiller, on two occasions for about three years, coordinated the communication program at the University of California, San Diego.

Smythe, Gerbner, and Nordenstreng worked in media-related institutions, although Smythe was an economist rather than a journalist. Gerbner, on the other hand, was a reporter, critic, and assistant financial editor of the *San Francisco Chronicle* and editor of the occupation forces newspaper in post–World War II Vienna. Nordenstreng became the Finnish Broadcasting Company's youngest reporter, serving in radio at age fifteen. Later, he directed the company's audience research unit.

Political and social activism was a key element of the interviewees' lives. All have spent considerable time disseminating their ideas concerning social consciousness and change at academic conferences, supranational organizations' and governmental hearings and meetings, and public fora. Before his FCC assignment, Smythe investigated and testified on behalf of workers, seeking fair wages and decent labor conditions, and much later helped start the Union for Democratic Communication. Gerbner's activism took many forms—antifascist activity as a teenager in Hungary, paratrooper and intelligence service during the war, editorship of the newspaper of the Independent Progressive party of California, and establishment of the Cultural Environment Movement. Early in his career, Halloran lectured for the Workers Education Association and worked in a prison. He carried out many commissioned research projects in conjunction with the mass media and was nearly solely responsible for revitalizing the IAMCR as a home for critical and other scholars. Believing one must be action oriented yet critical, Nordenstreng has worked closely with media personnel in the Finnish Broadcasting Company and International Organization of Journalists on research, training, and professionalism projects. His career has taken him into active roles in domestic and international communication policy, Finnish foreign policy, and UNESCO work, including negotiations concerning the Mass Media Declaration.

If only one word were allowed to explain the career choice and advancement of each of these individuals, it would be "chance." There is no hesitation in using the words "chance" and "accident" in these interviews. It was chance that Smythe won an essay contest at age fifteen that motivated him to go into economics, chance that Gerbner's mediocre grades were changed by the principal so that he could attend university, chance that a journalism instructor at John Muir College left abruptly and Gerbner took his job, discovering teaching as a career, and chance that Halloran became a critical scholar when after two years of teaching extramural classes he thought he had exhausted all he knew but was persuaded by his students to return and teach sociology of mass communication. Halloran chalks other milestones in his life to chance—the publication of his first articles and first book, his appointment as secretary of the government committee to study the influence of television on children, and his joining the IAMCR. Repeatedly, Nordenstreng credited his success to a "combination of accidents" and "good luck and chance . . . sense of accidental," including his year's stay in the United States during the radical 1960s and his position in a well-to-do institution (the Finnish Broadcasting Company) that "just happened to be on its way to the left." Schiller benefited from some fortuitous situations, one of which was escaping the normal academic processing in graduate school, allowing him to go his own way. Chance, according to him, was also responsible for his being in high-level situations while very junior and observing the reconstruction of the political economy of Germany in the 1940s. His conversion to the communication field happened by chance when Smythe left Illinois and Schiller took over his political economy of communication course.

All interviewees cited examples when they were either ignored or given a difficult time for taking a different road. Smythe faced the indignities of an FBI investigation for activity in the American League for Peace and Democracy, House Un-American Activities Committee (HUAC) interference with his University of Illinois appointment and a less than forthright intervention by his boss, Wilbur Schramm, a minuscule pay increase during eight years at Illinois, and some difficulty getting published in U.S. journals. Gerbner was subpoenaed by the California HUAC to testify regarding the superintendent of schools for whom he edited a newsletter and subsequently was told at the last moment before deadline that he no longer had his government job. He said he has been isolated to a certain degree because of his criticism of the mainstream. Schiller and Halloran agreed that their early critical work was not so much opposed as it was ignored. Even today, according to Schiller, he is not likely to be invited to universities by senior faculty or significant leaders in the field. Schiller's landmark work, *Mass Communication and American Empire,* almost did not see print after eight or ten publishers rejected the manuscript; it was eventually picked up by an obscure New York publisher. At his university, Schiller said he was treated as a nonperson and for ten to twelve years went without a promotion or a wage increase. The press universally condemned Halloran's early books, which showed journalism's warts and all. He told how in the early days of the Leicester center there were direct and indirect attempts to block the research, suppress the results, and generally distort the work being done. Nordenstreng was stigmatized by the Finnish media as a hostile force, especially after becoming IOJ president.

Despite their varying approaches, topics of interest, and presentation styles, these scholars come close to agreement on some subjects. One is the all-encompassing and all-powerful impact of capitalism on mass communication. Smythe thought we need to interrogate the systemic character of capitalism as related to communication, asking the question, How do media serve capitalism? For forty years, Gerbner hammered home the subtle forms of media as a profit-making business. He warned that storytelling was being controlled by a small group of conglomerates concerned only with making money and, in recent years, told Eastern Europeans that uncritical acceptance of commercial control of media means "mortgaging the socialization of their children to global conglomerates." (Closepet and Tsui 1992) Schiller has produced work on mind management and the industrial-military complex of the capitalist West and corporate takeover of all forms of culture. He has pointed out in every way possible that the program of the media is to selfishly promote capitalism. Halloran is also critical of media primarily concerned with making profits for the few.

Another topic that has been a favorite among these scholars is the way conventional mass communication research is conducted. An aspect of this research that has caught their attention involves types of questions and how they are asked.

Smythe said he was not against the use of mathematical and statistical tools in research but insisted that they be used to attack questions stated correctly. Although he himself was forever asking questions, Smythe related how in his early audience research he let the people talk about television without posing any questions to them. Gerbner favored another tact—instead of asking people what they thought of television, he said we should simply ask what they *thought.* Halloran's major complaint of Western researchers was that they failed to ask the right questions: "If you ask silly bloody questions, you get silly bloody answers. If you're statistically sophisticated, that statistically compounds the stupidity of the answers that you get" (Bingham 1976:18).

The bibliographies of these five scholars attest to their long-term commitment to promoting critical research and challenging conventional theory and methods, most often those emanating from the United States. One of the most vociferous denouncers of U.S. conventional research is Halloran, who said that after his 1964 visit to American mass communication scholars, he did not know precisely what to do in research but he knew what not to do. He does not spare adjectives in describing what he sees coming out of the United States: "sterile, positivistic, behaviouristic, causal, psychologistic, media centered, pseudoscientific, essentially conservative, unquestioning, status quo maintenance." Upon his return from the United States in the 1960s, Nordenstreng condemned what he found among American communication researchers. Essentially, he and Halloran criticized U.S. conventional research for its lack of thinking and doing and its overemphasis on counting. Schiller seldom engaged in methodological debate, shunned the use of quantitative research techniques, and insisted on analyzing and confronting the dominant power structure through "empirically informed and passionate" work. Gerbner, as Morgan and others pointed out, has been difficult to figure out. At times, his work seemed to be the antithesis of a critical perspective, but it must be remembered that he used empirical techniques for critical purposes. Gerbner always felt a need to support his arguments and conclusions with publicly credible, repeatable evidence. He has been known to make caustic statements about how research is done, as evidenced by a quote made during the interview for this book: "The tendency of some theorists to become abstruse, involved in ideological terminology or to quibble about 'proper' methodology is inhibiting research, and it's a waste of time."

Some Personal Reflections

Editing this book has made me reflect on my own life and career. For example, as I listened to Schiller talk about growing up in poverty during the Depression, my mind harked back to my own youth in a desolate village in western Pennsylvania.

A worked-out coal-mining town, East Millsboro was made up of four rows of virtually identical, wood-frame company houses, usually unpainted and unshingled, and mounds of gray, smoldering—and therefore stinking—slag pulled from the earth's underbelly by a previous generation of coal miners. There was a post office, which also served as the general store, a school with four rooms, in three of which three teachers taught us all subjects from first through eighth grades, and one to three bootlegging joints, depending on whether the miners (who worked in adjoining towns) were on strike. Because these were the days when John L. Lewis, head of the mine workers' union, was bolstering the wages and benefits of miners by confronting the coal companies and, in some cases, the federal government, invariably they were on strike. Many of my relatives were miners, but most of the men on my father's side of the family worked as railroad maintenance employees. They were placed in those jobs by my grandfather, who was the foreman. When the railroad hired him as a laborer in 1903, it Anglicized and simplified his Italian name (Zinghini) first to Lan, and later to Lent. My father started tamping ties and laying rails in his early teens, and when he retired about fifty years later he told me he had never wanted to be a railroader; his ambition had been to be a mechanic. My grandfather and one of my uncles also put in more than fifty years each on the railroad.

The townspeople of the coal fields suffered not only economic but also cultural and educational deprivation; books and new ideas were in even shorter supply than food. The fatalism endemic to traditional, closed-in societies was all too evident, as was the helplessness miners felt in relation to the dangerousness and tenuousness of their jobs. Despite—nay, because of—all this, I felt I picked up some useful characteristics living there, such as an empathy for the downtrodden, resourcefulness, perseverance, honesty, and a detachment from institutions (which later grew into a distrust of them). The latter came naturally in East Millsboro; there were so very few institutions.

I finished my undergraduate and master's degrees in journalism at a time when journalism students were expected to be skeptical in dealing with the powers-that-be. In 1960, I began teaching and serving as director of information at a technology institute in the coal-bearing hills of West Virginia. I found the people there exploited, as they had been in my hometown, by corrupt governments and the chemical and coal companies that dotted the Kanawha Valley. Two years later, I entered the doctoral program in communication at Syracuse University, about the time media magnate Sam Newhouse donated $15 million to build a monument to himself—the Newhouse School of Communication. Although I finished all course work for the doctorate after two years, I did not don an orange cap and gown. In the interim, I had written a critical manuscript about the Newhouse empire, which the Newhouses tried to keep out of print by intimidating the publisher and threatening me with a legal suit. I learned many years later they had actually met with the district attorney's office in Manhattan with the intent of bringing legal action.

The book never went very far because the Newhouse press shunned it. Libraries in Newhouse newspaper cities (New Orleans and Syracuse come to mind) refused to make it available, and university deans (two of them) friendly to Syracuse University Communications Dean Wesley Clark wrote scathing reviews that included outright lies and went far beyond fair comment. The publisher, who worked on partial subsidy, did not work up much of a sweat promoting it. At one point before publication, the publisher actually broached the idea of us selling the manuscript to the Newhouses and forsaking publication, which I refused to do.

My Ph.D. did not advance either as my potential committee members gradually abandoned Syracuse University (not before purchasing copies of my book and placing them in the university library against the wishes of the dean) and after I wrote Clark a very strong letter informing him I would not allow him to see the Newhouse manuscript before publication.

In 1964–65, while in the Philippines on a Fulbright scholarship, I witnessed the deep-seated colonial mentality that affected all areas of society, including the mass media, studied the oligarchic nature of the media industry, participated in what were probably the first development journalism sessions anywhere in the world, and observed the unique problems of Third World journalism. I wrote about all this even before we had names to categorize such phenomena as media imperialism and development communication.

For the following five years I moved about, teaching in small colleges and universities in West Virginia, Wisconsin, West Virginia again, and Wyoming. I had two occasions to use a favorite line from an e.e. cummings poem—"There is some shit I will not eat"—in letters of resignation, brought about because of reactionary stands concerning civil rights. One was at Marshall University, where Journalism Department Chairman Bill Francois and I organized Freedom and Racial Equality for Everyone (FREE), with the intent of helping African Americans obtain jobs, housing, and equal rights. The cummings line had much use that year as I pulled it out again when I resigned in protest from the University of Wyoming, only five or six weeks into my first semester there. The impetus was the football coach's "firing" of fourteen black players after they had asked to wear black armbands as a mark of protest while playing Brigham Young University, an institution operated by the Mormons, who at the time had a discriminatory policy concerning African Americans. I stayed on for the rest of the school year, teaching my classes, writing for and eventually coediting a successful weekly underground newspaper, *Free Lunch: Where the Effete Meet to Eat,* and actively participating in the antiwar movement. The latter led to a frightening nighttime confrontation with the National Guard and police during a demonstration after the Kent State massacre. It's no wonder that Nordenstreng's comment in this book about the influences upon him of the "crazy years of the late 1960s" piqued my interest.

About this time, I began doing research on Caribbean mass communications, considered a very obscure topic that not many scholars took seriously or lent much importance. I discovered patterns of cultural enslavement and dependency relationships that were more ingrained and overpowering than those I had witnessed in the Philippines, for a large chunk of the Caribbean was still colonized.

In 1970, I pursued the Ph.D. again, this time at the University of Iowa. Braving, as we all did, the asinine politicization of the faculty, which seemed split nine to six between so-called sophisticated researchers (mostly positivist-empiricist) and those labeled traditional, I finally snagged the degree in 1972. Immediately after, I went to Malaysia as the first coordinator of the new program in communication at Universiti Sains Malaysia, thus fulfilling my vow to leave the United States after Nixon's 1968 election.

Listening to Malaysian scholars, interviewing media personnel, participating in national and regional development communication workshops and seminars, and observing the fragile relationship between the media and the authoritarian government, I added to my knowledge about mass communication problems in the Third World.

When I returned to the United States in 1974 (incidentally, in time to celebrate Nixon's fate as a result of Watergate), I used some of those perceptions in a paper Nordenstreng accepted for the IAMCR assembly in Leipzig. Titled "Four Conundrums," it identified as key problems of Third World mass communication (1) making mass media economically and culturally practicable for developing nations, (2) having media better serve the interests of the masses, not just elites and white collar groups, (3) resolving the conflict between press freedom and development journalism, and (4) designing mass media theory and research appropriate to the Third World. Nordenstreng used portions of the talk in his own IAMCR keynote address that year. He told me later that the "Four Conundrums" paper was useful to Non-Aligned Countries Movement delegates the following year as they drew up their media statement. Throughout the 1970s, I spun a number of larger articles out of this paper and in the late 1980s updated and packaged them as a book manuscript. At separate times, both MARA Institute of Technology in Kuala Lumpur and the Asian Mass Communication Research and Information Center (AMIC) in Singapore agreed to publish the book but backed off because of what they perceived as critical comments about media in Malaysia and Singapore. AMIC actually set the book in type before dropping it.

For the past twenty-five years, I have written on many areas germane to critical communication—media ownership, cultural imperialism, press freedom, women and media, New International Information Order, impact of new information technology, transfer of conventional social science theory and methodologies to the Third World, transnationalization of communication, Third World media, and popular culture.

One final aspect of these interviews that hit home to me concerned comments by Schiller and Smythe about the academic isolation engendered when one is critical of dominant institutions (especially the university) and theories. Through a combination of insularity brought about by my colleagues and myself, I work alone, except for occasional collaboration with the many doctoral students I supervise. This is not necessarily to complain, for, like the eminent Caribbeanist Gordon Lewis, I believe research and scholarship are lonely pursuits.

REFERENCES

Barsamian, D., ed. (1992). *Stenographers of Power: Media and Propaganda.* Monroe, ME: Common Courage Press.

Becker, J., ed. (1989). *Positionen der Kritischen Sozialwissenschaft. Informations—und Kommunikations-technologien.* Stuttgart: KomTech.

Becker, J., G. Hedebro, and L. Paldan, eds. (1986). *Communication and Domination: Essays to Honor Herbert I. Schiller.* Norwood, NJ: Ablex.

Bingham, R. (1976). "If you ask silly bloody questions, you get silly bloody answers." *Campaign* (February 27):1–18.

Closepet, R., and L. S. Tsui. (1992). An interview with Professor George Gerbner. *Media Development,* 1:42–45.

Hamelink, C., and O. Linne. (1994). *Mass Communication Research: On Problems and Policies. The Art of Asking the Right Questions in Honor of James D. Halloran.* Norwood, NJ:Ablex

McChesney, R. (1993). Critical communication research at the crossroads. *Journal of Communication,* 43:4 (Autumn):98–104.

Tsui, L. S. (1991). An interview with Professor Herbert I. Schiller. *Media Development,* 1:50–52.

Wasko, J., V. Mosco, and M. Pendakur, eds. (1993). *Illuminating the Blindspots: Essays Honoring Dallas W. Smythe.* Norwood, NJ: Ablex.

PART ONE

DALLAS W. SMYTHE

Dallas W. Smythe, Canberra, 1986 (Photo by John A. Lent)

Dallas W. Smythe

Born:	1907, Regina, Saskatchewan, Canada
Deceased:	September 6, 1992, Langley, British Columbia, Canada
Education:	A.B. (Economics), University of California, Berkeley, 1928; Ph.D. (Economics), University of California, Berkeley, 1937
Employment:	
1980–92	Professor Emeritus, Department of Communication, Simon Fraser University, Burnaby, British Columbia, Canada
1989 (July–December)	Distinguished International Scholar, Centre for International Research on Communication and Information Technologies, Melbourne, Australia
1988 (Fall)	Visiting Professor, Department of Communication, University of Hawaii, Manoa
1987 (Spring)	Visiting Professor, Department of Communication, Ohio State University, Columbus
1976–87	Professor, Department of Communication, Simon Fraser University
1980–82	Professor, Department of Radio-TV-Film, Temple University, Philadelphia, Pennsylvania
1974–76	Chairman and Professor, Department of Communication, Simon Fraser University
1973–74	Visiting Professor of Communications, Third College, University of California, San Diego
1969–73	Chairman, Department of Social Studies, Chairman, Administrative Committee, Communications M.A. Program, Professor of Economics, University of Saskatchewan, Regina, Canada; Professor Emeritus from 1973
1963–69	Chairman, Division of Social Sciences, Chairman, Administrative Committee, Communications M.A. Program; Professor of Economics, Acting Chairman of

	Departments of Anthropology, Geography, and Sociology, University of Saskatchewan
1948–63	Research Professor of Communications, Institute of Communications Research and Graduate College, University of Illinois, Urbana; 1948–57, Professor of Economics; 1957–63, Chairman, Committee on Graduate Study in Communications
1953–56 (Summers)	Visiting Professor, University of Southern California.
1951 (Summer)	Visiting Professor, Claremont College, Claremont, California
1943–48	Chief Economist, Federal Communications Commission, Washington, D.C.
1942	Principal Economist (labor), Division of Statistical Standards, Bureau of the Budget, Washington, D.C.
1938–41	Senior Economist, Wage and Hour Division, U.S. Department of Labor, Washington, D.C.
1937–38	Economist (agriculture), Central Statistics Board, Washington, D.C.
1934–37	Extension Specialist in Agricultural Economics, College of Agriculture, University of California, Berkeley
1933	University Fellow, University of California, Berkeley
1931–33	Assistant in Economics, University of California, Berkeley
1928–31	Teaching Fellow, Economic History, University of California, Berkeley

Other Service

Committee on International Telecommunications, American Branch, International Law Association, 1978; Secretary, Communication Study Group, International Peace Research Association, and Manager, Clearing House for Materials on Transnational Communication, 1977; Consultant, Canadian Radio-Television Commission, Ottawa, 1975; Consultant, Department of Transportation and Communications, British Columbia, 1973–74; Consultant, Department of Communications, Manitoba, 1973; UNESCO Panel of Experts in Communications Research, 1971–73; Executive Committee, International Association for Mass Communication Research, 1970–73; Panel Member, Canadian Society of International Law (on communications satellites), 1970–73; Chairman, Communications Satellite Section, IAMCR, September 1970; Consultant, Department of Communications, Ottawa, 1969–70; Participant for Canada, Meeting of Experts on Mass Communications and Society, UNESCO, Ottawa, August 1969; panel on International Telecommunications Policy, American Society of International Law, September 1968–73; Witness, Kefauver Sub-Committee on Monopoly, U.S. Senate, 1961; Study Commission on the Role of Radio, Television, and Films in Religion, National Council of Churches, 1958–60; Consultant, Centre International d'Enseignment Superieur du Journalisme de Strasbourg, November, 1959; Consultant, Royal Commission on Broadcasting in Canada (Fowler Commission) 1956–57; Consultant, Joint Committee on Toll Television, 1955; Consultant, Communications Research Project, Broadcasting and Film Commission, National Council of Churches of Christ, 1951–55; Director of Studies, National Association of Educational Broadcasters, 1948–53.

Research

Recipient of grant from Canada Council ($12,000) for study in China, Chile, Yugoslavia, Japan, Hungary, and United Kingdom, 1971–72

Editing, Publishing

Consulting and Contributing Editor, *Journal of Communication,* 1972–92; Editorial Board, *Communication* (University of Iowa); Advisory Committee, Sage Annual Series in Communications Research

Awards and Honors

Distinguished International Scholar, Centre for International Research on Communication and Information Technologies, Melbourne, 1989; Visiting Distinguished Scholar (Australia), British Council and Australian Vice-Chancellor's Committee, March–May 1977; *Illuminating the Blindspots: Essays Honoring Dallas W. Smythe* (Ablex, 1993).

2

Interview with Dallas W. Smythe

CONDUCTED BY JOHN A. LENT
CANBERRA, AUSTRALIA,
DECEMBER 4, 1986

What, in your background, steered you in the direction that you have gone?

Okay, I was born in Regina, Canada. My father was a hardware merchant in town, fairly prosperous. It was a small city then of about forty thousand. He'd never gone beyond ninth grade in school. He had to go out and get a job to support his mother because his father had died, left the family pretty destitute. This was in St. Mary's, in Ontario, and he'd learned the hardware business and eventually had his own hardware store in Regina. During World War I, he was very successful. It was a time when farmers were selling wheat and buying everything, and he did pretty well. He married my mother, who was a nurse from Caledonia, near Hamilton, in 1906. He was a Presbyterian, but he wasn't working very hard at it. She was the Church of England type and a little more devout than he. And I guess religion had a good deal to do with my early childhood. I remember I was taught to pray at night before I went to sleep. I stopped doing that by the time I was about ten or eleven. But we weren't devout in any particular church. We didn't go to church very often. I didn't read the Bible much. I didn't understand it, except the New Testament, which the family was pretty fond of. We used to read the passages in the New Testament that have the ethical principles of Christianity very clearly stated. You know, treatment of the poor, the formula for primitive socialism is in there. I guess that made an early imprint in my mind.

I was an only child, and rather a pampered one, prone to bronchitis. I nearly died in the flu epidemic of 1918—the whole family nearly died. Afterwards, they sold the property in Regina to move to a healthier climate. My parents were very unsophisticated people, and looking back, it was funny because they didn't know where to go. They had two possibilities. One was advice from the medical doctor who had treated us during the flu epidemic, who said, "The Isle of Pines is a good place to go." They didn't know anything about the Isle of Pines, except it sounded great. But they didn't know anybody there and that was an inhibiting factor. On the other hand, my father had had a childhood friend who had gone off to Pasadena and become a jewelry store clerk. He got in touch with that friend, who replied, "Oh sure, it's a great place to live, and do you want me to rent you a house and have it all ready for you?" We moved down there.

There I was, twelve years old in Southern California when there was only a two-lane highway connecting Pasadena to Los Angeles, meandering between the orange groves. There was no smog, it was beautiful, God, it was beautiful there then. So I spent my high school and junior college years in Pasadena. A pretty benign environment. Dad got a job as manager of the Humane Society in Pasadena. He didn't have a big income. We had a modest house. But, well, it was a good life we had. I was an overprotected child and suffered from being an only child, and I resented it. I had a delayed adolescent revolt.

When I was in high school, I was an average student in my last year. I took a course in "Principles of Economics" in high school from a young man, Earl Davis, who had just graduated with an M.A. from Michigan. He was a good teacher. He really got to me with the basic classical theory of economics. I did well in the course, and at the end of the course, he handed me a leaflet that he'd just received from the Simons Saw and Steel Corporation in Fitchberg, Massachusetts. They were sponsoring a national essay contest on "Sharing Our National Income." One thousand dollars, first prize; five hundred dollars, second; and a bunch of subsidiary prizes of one hundred bucks. Earl Davis asked me if I'd like to write an essay and submit it. Why not? He thought it was a good idea, and I said, "Can you help me?" He said, "I'll give you some reading, but you're on your own—it's your essay." So I got hold of all the essential stuff on income sharing. There was a strong social justice component to that literature in the first quarter of the century in the United States. T. N. Carver and other men were worried about the possibilities of too extreme a polarization in the distribution of income. It was a reflection of the "Progressive Movement," from the 1890s to 1914. I wrote about forty pages, double-spaced. I was about fifteen by this time. I typed it myself and I shipped it off, and forgot about it in due time.

About a year later, I was coming back from an intercollegiate tennis match (I was in junior college by this time), and my mother was all excited. She said, "You have a letter here from Fitchberg, Massachusetts." It contained a check for a hundred bucks and told me I had won a prize. Well, that did a lot psychologically for me. The hundred bucks wasn't much, although it would be the equivalent of about a thousand now. But it really was a stimulus reward situation for my effort in economics. I thought, maybe I've got something here.

I didn't know what I was going to do with my life. My father had originally thought we'd go into the hardware business, and I'd be the son in "Smythe &

Son," and that was okay with me when I was a kid. But he never saw the possibility realistically of starting the hardware business in Southern California; the market was already dominated by a few big companies. He wisely decided not to compete with them. So, what in the hell *was* I going to do? My first hunch was I'd want to be a lawyer. This is going to really sound absurd to you. My faculty adviser said okay, then I'll recommend that you take Latin because lawyers ought to know Latin. It was ridiculous, I now realize. It's hard to imagine, but he said, there are a lot of Latin phrases in the law. So he signed me up in a strictly liberal arts program and so I took Latin. I got a 3 in Latin (1 was the top grade, 2 was next, 3 was just above failing, and 4 was failing). I saw him a year later and he said, "Too bad about that. I guess you're not fitted for law, how about engineering?" He steered me into algebra and plane geometry, where I had two more 3s. When I saw the adviser a year later, he said in effect, So much for engineering. This time it was, "How about majoring in commerce? How's that sound?" I said okay. I thought of my father and that maybe I could make it in the business world. So I finished off my high school curriculum studying things like business English and salesmanship. I was manager of the campus bookstore and a little merchant and all that stuff. So there we were: in Pasadena Junior College, where my courses were liberal arts. I played on the football team and the tennis team and I had a pretty good life in the summertime. The beaches were beautiful, I played the trumpet in the band, and we traveled in big red cars over the interurban railway they used to have all over Southern California to go to the games.

I didn't do much dating, I was a very shy kid. Then I fell in love with the woman that I eventually married, my first wife—she was from Santa Monica. I met her in a band—went down for a summer job at the Pacific Palisades, which is where Reagan lived before he became president. As a result of meeting Beatrice Bell, I decided to go to UCLA for my advanced work. I went to UCLA as she did, for one year—that was my third year. My grades were about a B average, as I had in high school. I made the honor society, but just barely. They were mediocre at UCLA.

For my fourth year, I decided to go up to Berkeley and break away from my family. I went up there, lived in a rooming house, and worked at a service station and played in the university band. I really worked hard in classes. My grades at UCLA were B average but in Berkeley I was lucky to have some good teachers. California was good in economics at the time—for my kind of economics. It wasn't mathematical, it was institutional and historical. I got an A in everything that year as a senior.

Bee had come to Berkeley a year after I did. So we were living together for a year before we got married, which was a very shocking thing to do in those days. Then in 1928, when I graduated, I decided to come back and get a master's degree and teaching credential and teach in junior colleges like the man who first taught me economics. It seemed like a pretty good life.

In the fall of 1928, I went to the adviser for masters people. He was a man I'd done very well with in his course in marketing. He said, "What do you want to do with graduate work?" And I said, "I thought I'd get a masters and teach in a junior college." He said, "Why that?" I replied, "It seems like a pretty good thing to do. Why, what else should I do?" To his next question, "Did you ever think of getting a Ph.D.?" I said, "Well, do you think it's realistic for me to think of that?" He said, "Why not?" I said, "If I'm going to get a Ph.D. in economics, shouldn't I get a master's first?" He said, "Why?" I said, "If I'm to get a Ph.D., wouldn't it be wise to learn how to teach?" To which he replied, "Don't you think if you get a Ph.D. in economics that you will by that time know how to teach?" I didn't argue with him. The answer might have been, "Not necessarily," but I wasn't going argue with the guy. So he said, "Well, I think you really ought to go directly for the Ph.D. and forget the master's degree. If you want a job, one of the teaching assistants didn't show up this last week for a job in economic history. If you want to see about it, go over and see Flügel. You just had a course in economic history and you got a straight A in it." So I went over to see Flügel, and the next week I was meeting tutorials and was in a Ph.D. program.

This was the beginning of the Depression. I was old enough to vote. By this time, I was an American citizen and my first vote was cast for Herbert Hoover in 1928. I was an unthinking innocent conservative, much like you find in the Corn Belt. Not like you'd find in New York or then in Wisconsin.

The man who was most influential on me intellectually and probably had more to do with everything else I did in later life than anyone else was the professor who taught economic history that I really worked for in the next five years. He was Melvin M. Knight, a brother of F. H. Knight. But this was an entirely different man from him. This was an economic historian who had been around the world a great deal. He had been an ambulance driver in the French Red Cross during World War I and captain in the Romanian army after World War I. He had gotten a Ph.D. in biology at Columbia, supporting himself by teaching ancient history at Barnard at the same time—a delightful man. M. M. Knight was radical in the best sense of David Hume. He wouldn't take anything for granted. He was a skeptic; he disliked the "automatic" Marxists with their simplistic structural determinism, but he wasn't hostile to anyone who was a Marxist either.

You learn as much or more from your fellow students as you do from faculty as a graduate student. I was lucky to be in the seminar in contemporary economic theory with N. Gregory Silvermaster. He was a Soviet Marxist economist, a bit older than I. He had come over in 1918, just after the revolution, to make propaganda in San Francisco to discourage American longshoremen from loading ships to supply the U.S. Army, which was invading the Soviet Union at that time. He'd stayed on in the Bay Area, teaching philosophy at St. Mary's College—a Roman Catholic college—and he married a daughter of one of the tsar's last foreign ministers. A nice combination—this Marxist communist and this noblewoman. They made a wonderful pair. But anyway, he was in this seminar, taught by Leo Rogin, who was an excellent economic theorist, the critical kind, not the neoclassical type. In conducting the seminar, Rogin was fairly laid back and let the students do a lot of talking. Silvermaster didn't do much talking, but when he did it was extremely insightful, and Rogin respected him and called on him a good deal for comment.

That was the kind of intellectual influence that began to move me. Then, there were three big events in the mid-1930s that shaped my political orientation and decided where I was going to be headed. One was the fact that a San Francisco longshore strike took place in 1934. The National Guard was brought in and shot down a bunch of those strikers who were picketing on the docks. That was over the issue of corrupt hiring practices versus the hiring hall, and Harry Bridges was the leader of the striking union. That really demonstrated the realities of class struggle in a way that no amount of reading did.

Secondly, I finally ran out of appointment eligibility for teaching assistantships after five years. I haven't mentioned my thesis, which took me seven years to write. I'll tell you about that in a minute. So I had to get a job to support myself because I wasn't a T.A. anymore. I got one as an agricultural economist in the College of Agriculture, Agricultural Extension Division, where I knew slightly John K. Galbraith, who later said he didn't then consider himself competent enough to get into the economics department but he was good enough to get into the agricultural graduate program (according to an article he published either in *Harper's* or the *Atlantic Monthly* in about 1984). In that job, I was going around the state of California educating the farmers about the annual economic outlook for their crops: dry edible beans, oranges, grapefruit, lemons, dates, wheat, barley, hops, etc. I was supposed to be an expert on all these things. In relation to writing those outlook reports, I had to go to Washington once a year to consult in the Department of Agriculture to get national forecasts of supply, demand, and prices for these crops. This work took me around the state in the 1934–37 Depression years. John Steinbeck's *The Grapes of Wrath* tells the story about the drought-driven farmers from the Midwestern states who were forced off their land and fled to California. I saw those "Okies" and "Arkies" who were getting kicked around in California by the Associated Farmers. Their little shantytowns were being burned down by the sheriffs; they were being chased, and anyone who tried to organize these Anglo-Saxons from the Midwest was blacklisted and the sheriff's office passed the word on through the network of Associated Farmers—the same groups I had to meet in my job. This was pretty sickening to see. It made me furious. And that reinforced what I'd learned in the longshore situation.

The third big event that radicalized me was the Spanish Civil War. I didn't volunteer to go with the International Brigade. I had a friend who did. I felt guilty about that, but I didn't. He was Bob Merriaman, who had been a teaching assistant at Berkeley and he became the chief of staff of the Abraham Lincoln Brigade.

But that bit into me very deeply, so when 1936 came, I was not voting for Roosevelt, I was voting for Earl Browder as I also had in 1932. I never did vote for Roosevelt until 1944, at a time during World War II when the New Deal was fading away and he needed support. I had moved a long way from the callow fellow who voted for Hoover in 1928. I was ready to be a political activist as soon as I could finish my Ph.D. thesis.

My thesis was a monster. The East San Francisco transit system had been built up by an amalgamation of little street railways that had once been horse-car railways. Then they also developed an interurban Key System, it was called, which ran ferries across the bay, and electric trains connecting with the ferries and fanning out to Oakland, Berkeley, San Leandro, Hayward, and Richmond. The integrated company had been promoted by the man who developed 20 Mule Team Borax, F. M. Smith. He built himself a big mansion in East Oakland near the lake and he had his private railroad car. He imitated J. P. Morgan and, like him, had a large steam yacht. He had great ambitions to control the urban and interurban railways all through central California, and he organized the United Properties Corporation—it was going to own railroads, water companies, and land. The parts of his empire would all grow by stimulating each other. They didn't call it synergy in the twenty years before 1914, but that's what he aimed to practice. He got overextended; his creditors clipped his wings; the San Francisco banks formed a protective committee to take care of their interests in his assets. That was the last he saw of his dream. The creditors' committee reorganized the thing and squeezed out some of the water during World War I, but not enough to make a viable company, and so the successor company went broke about five years later, which was about 1920, and that new company squeezed out more of the water so that the old holders of junior bonds were now common stockholders, and the original common and preferred stockholders were wiped out. Well, the man that the investment bankers put in to run this shrunken company was a homegrown intellectual from Scandinavian stock, Lundberg was his name. He'd never gone beyond grammar school and he read Thornstein Veblen and smoked twenty large cigars a day for pleasure. He had gotten acquainted with Stuart Daggett, the professor of transportation at Berkeley. I had studied with him and was fascinated by transportation so I wanted to do my Ph.D. thesis in that field with him as my thesis adviser. This was probably connected with the fact that the trains were very glamorous in that period and that I'd grown up in western Canada, where the trains were our main connections to anywhere and everywhere. But here I must backtrack a bit to my qualifying examination in 1931.

In those days, the qualifying examination was three hours of oral examination on six fields: economic theory, history of economic theory (these three [Dallas only gave two] were required of everyone), and three others, in my case, transportation and public regulations; money, banking, and foreign exchange; and marketing. It was an ordeal that I prepared for very, very carefully. After I got through that easily (after it, I could say that I enjoyed it), Daggett said, "About your Ph.D. thesis—you've been interested in street railways (I had done a little term paper for him on that subject) the president of the Key System has told me he would be willing to open his files to any competent student who wanted to go down and study the history of that sad story. Do you want to go down?" So I went down. Lundberg gave me an office and said, "You're welcome to use anything, see anything in the place. There is only one condition: When you have had it accepted at the university, will you give me a copy?" He called in his vice-president and chief engineer (Stranberg) and told him to give me all the facilities, and for the next five years what I did was to sift all the company files. I read the minutes of board meetings, I read the officers' correspondence, its history of bad labor relations, reports to the stockholders, the accounting reports and previous reorganization documents, and the litigation that had gutted the company. So I wrote, eventually, a 650-page thesis on the corporate history of the properties, integrated with an analysis of land economics and the relations of real estate speculation to the development of the East Bay area and its transit system. I had about three theses in one. I never forgave Daggett for letting me do too big a thesis—it was much too big. The final examination was easy, Lundberg received his copy of the thesis, and I learned much from doing it that I have been grateful for ever since. It was never published in whole or in a part.

By the time I was finishing the thesis, I was planning what to do after I got the Ph.D. The Depression had lifted and most of my friends were going to Washington to get jobs, but I didn't have any contacts in Washington, except for Mordeicai Ezekiel, who was Henry Wallace's economic adviser in the early days of the Triple A. Ezekiel visited the Berkeley campus in September 1936. He visited our Extension Service and I invited him out to the house for dinner and we had a great time with him. He was interested to hear that I had walked through the passenger train I had used to return from an Eastern trip a few weeks earlier and given all the passengers slips of paper and asked them to indicate their preference as between Roosevelt, Landon (the Republican candidate), and the mass party candidates in the current campaign. The poll showed Roosevelt with a big lead. When I dropped him at his hotel, he said, "When you finish your thesis, let me know and I will help you get a job in Washington." So by the time I got the thing finished in October 1936, I was in Washington for one of these Outlook Conferences and I called him about eleven o'clock in the morning and said, "Dally Smythe from Berkeley." He said, "Are you finished with the thesis?" I said, "Yes." "Are you here for the Outlook Conference?" "Yes." "Come into my office." So I went in and he sat down and he called the executive secretary of the Central Statistical Board, which now is the Division of Statistical Standards in the Budget Bureau, but then it wasn't an independent agency. Morris Copeland, a really fine institutional economist who used to be at Cornell, was then the executive secretary. Ezekiel set up a lunch date for me with Copeland. At lunch with Copeland

and two of his senior staff, about the first thing I said was, "I think you may have me here under false pretenses. I'm not a statistician. I'm an economist, not a statistician, and you call this place the Central Statistical Board." Copeland had an evil glint in his eye as he said, "That's fine. We don't want statisticians. We want economists." So he proceeded to give me the equivalent of an oral examination in economics for the next hour and a half over lunch, taking me back to the history of economic theory and economic history—and I passed all right. Then they gave me the job. So I went to Washington to work for them.

No sooner did I get there in March 1937 than the Spanish Civil War came to a boil, and the question of the embargo on the shipment of arms became a public issue. I took the initiative in organizing a unit in the first CIO union in the government. The unit was the Central Statistical Board. We only had five members in the union, but we had a little local of five members. I also taught a course in principles of economics in 1938 at the Federal Workers' School (CIO). There I met Danny Driesen, the legislative representative of the American Communications Association (CIO) in Washington. He and his colleagues in ACA became my close friends. I went to a union meeting of the local representatives, and there I met a guy who said—we got chatting about the Spanish Civil War and he said—"Hey, I want you to come to a meeting tonight. We are organizing a branch of the American League for Peace and Democracy, the purpose of which is to lift the embargo by public pressure and education. Mrs. Roosevelt is among our members, and Secretary of the Interior Harold Ickes, . . . a lot of good people." So I did, and I ended up that evening being elected vice-president of the Washington branch. Well, we had a number of public meetings with distinguished foreign speakers; we raised money; we leafleted; we petitioned—it was a good baptism in political action. All the CIO unions were members, plus many outside unions—altogether we represented millions of people. We had a newspaper; we were very active. Then the following summer the original House Un-American Activities Committee was formed under Martin Bies. The first witnesses they called attacked the American League for Peace and Democracy, and they named me and seven others from the Washington branch as the ringleaders in this nefarious activity. This was 1938. So I became a PAF, a premature antifascist, as we were called after Pearl Harbor to the security agencies. I was investigated by the FBI—and that really confirmed in me a radical position. I wasn't going to get kicked around by these people. I just was stubborn. I never joined the Communist party, but I thought of it. In fact, at one time I suggested to some friends in the party that maybe I should do so. By this time, I was in a pretty senior position in the government, and they said, "It's too dangerous. Too many FBI stooges in the senior echelons of the party. Even if you want to, we wouldn't let you." So that's how I got into my ideological space.

Now, how did I get into the communications part of my life? That isn't at all difficult to understand. My first job at the Central Statistical Board was covering the Department of Agriculture for questionnaires in that area. We reviewed every form on which information was collected. Would it duplicate other questionnaires? Was it technically competent? If it was, it got our seal of approval. I did that for a year and a half. Then the Wage and Hour Division Law was passed in 1938, the Fair Labor Standards Act, and I had an opportunity to move to the Economics Division in that organization. By this time, I'd become a senior economist when I took that step. I was among the first people to work in that division, and I was involved in very interesting work there—litigation work helping our lawyers establish the interstate character of certain activities, which would confirm our jurisdiction, like newspapers. It testified in the *Dallas Morning News* case involving news reporters and their other employees, including the boys who delivered the papers. They tried to say they weren't engaged in interstate commerce. We analyzed the source of the paper physically and the source of the news and distribution of the finished product and proved they crossed state lines. We won our case against them after a two-week trial in the U.S. District Court in Dallas, in which I testified as an expert witness.

I testified in cases involving the Atlantic Coastline and the reasonable cost of housing, etc., provided by the company to maintenance of way people. There was a provision in the law that said an employer running a company store or providing housing could claim as part of the minimum wage (then 25 cents an hour) the reasonable cost to the employer of providing these things. I had to gather the information from the company's books and from the workers to prepare myself as an expert witness as to determining what was the reasonable cost. The trial in the Atlantic Coastline case was in Raleigh, North Carolina, and we got half a million dollars' restitution for the workers and a consent decree there. I did a similar study of a textile mill in Union Point, Georgia, which we also won. A third case was a frightening Cypress logging operation at Holopaw, Florida, near Orlando, which was run as if it were in South Africa. The company "disappeared" some of the witnesses we had interviewed and lined up to testify after they had testified. A very rough trial took place in Baton Rouge, where the head offices of the company were. The judge was one of Huey Long's appointees, and the whole thing was a farce. He found for the company on all matters of fact, thus giving no effect to my testimony on the facts, including pictures of the decrepit shacks and working conditions. He found for us in all matters of law. Appeal courts will not review the facts before the trial court so we couldn't appeal and the company didn't have any interest in appealing because under that decision they had not broken the law. So it was a huge bust as far as we were concerned. Well, I did that sort of work in many other cases (red caps in railway stations, insurance agents, etc.) for three years, and then came Pearl Harbor.

When war came, I wanted to get back to Central Statistical Board, which was by this time the Division of Statistical Standards in the Bureau of the Budget. There I would be closer to the action in connection with the war. So in 1942 I rejoined the staff of the Division of Statistical Standards as a principal economist. This time, instead of working the agriculture beat, I was now working the labor beat. So when the war agencies came along, I was the guy who advised the budget estimates' people as to how big a research staff was needed for the War Manpower Commission, the War Labor Board, the Maritime Labor Board, and the labor aspects of the War Production Board and the Board of War Communication. The study I made of telegraph messengers showed that their earnings averaged nine cents an hour. In doing it, I interviewed the officers of Western Union and the Postal Telegraph companies and the AFL and CIO unions in the industry. As a result of this study, the newspapers got 25 cents an hour.

The same left-wing friends in the American Communication Association that I had made in the original government union period were still close to me. While at Wage and Hour, the study I made of the telegraph had familiarized me with the basic economy of the telegraph and telephone industries. Danny Driesen was informal liaison between the staff of the Board of War Communications and me. Through him I learned how badly the FCC needed me. They didn't know anything about labor, and they were having problems with deferments of technical workers in telecommunications industry and selective service. They were about to have strike problems, they needed liaison with the War Labor Board, etc. There was about to be a merger of Postal and Western Union, and that would create labor problems. The question was, did I want to be the chief economist initially to work on labor and after the war to take on any economic problems that came along, and I agreed. Through my union friends, I met the chairman of the FCC and moved to the new job. So I became a communications economist instead of a labor man, instead of an agriculture man. This was in 1943.

I was chief economist until July 6, 1948, when I resigned to go to Illinois. As my friends put it, I was about the last New Dealer to leave Washington with his scalp still on. The ones who stayed beyond me got 'em taken off by the new un-American inquisition. I went to Illinois, thanks to Harvey Magdoff and to Bob Heller, who was about to become the first vice-president in charge of TV at CBS. The day after that happened, one of these tabloid papers in New York ran a column saying, "Heller's been a secret Communist . . . now he's vice president of CBS in charge of television." Before the next weekend had come, Heller had resigned that job and gone to Mexico City. My job at Illinois was a split between commerce, where I was the professor of economics, and research professor in the Institute of Communications Research.

Schramm was the director of that center then?

Yes. It was just being formed. The idea was it would have a lot of split appointments. I would be the guy for economics; we hired Charlie Osgood for psychology the next year. They never did get anyone for political science or sociology. My relations with Schramm were soured even before I showed up to begin teaching.

Why?

Because the House Un-American Activities Committee had a staff man who sent a letter attacking me to the Superintendent of Instruction of Illinois, who was ex officio on the Board of Governors. He then challenged my appointment after I already had a legal contract. In those days, the president could make an appointment, but he then submitted it to the Board for information. When this happened, President Stoddard was organizing UNESCO in Paris—he was working on that for Truman at this point. So they put my appointment on hold and rechecked with all my referees and sent them copies of the letter from the HUAC. The letter charged me with being responsible for the FCC's refusing to turn over fingerprints of radio operators to the FBI when they had requested it. It's true that the FCC did refuse this, but that all happened two years before I got to the FCC. They accused me of having a black secretary, which was true; the first one in the commission, which was true; and of getting her pregnant and paying her hospital bills, which was not true, unfortunately, because she was very beautiful and I was flattered by the lies, but it wasn't true. Then they had awful things to say about me, like I was a friend and associated with Commissioner Clifford Durr, whose brother-in-law was Hugo Black, the notorious civil libertarian on the U.S. Supreme Court. I was reputed to have been one of the authors of the "Blue Book," which was obviously inspired by Moscow, because it intended to try to limit commercial advertising on radio. My referees were an amazing gang. Charlie Denny, a former chairman of the FCC, who by this time was vice-president and general counsel of RCA; Frank Stanton, who was vice-president of CBS at this time; Paul Lazarsfeld; Larry Fly, who had been the chairman who had hired me at the FCC; Cliff Durr. They all sent me copies of their replies.

Schramm never had the decency to show me the HUAC letter or any of this correspondence, and Schramm tried to get me to stay away from the campus. He was afraid the thing would blow open if it ever got any publicity, and he wanted it not to blow, at least until Stoddard got back and could take responsibility. I was damned if I was going to give them a technical basis for saying I violated my contract, so I showed up in plenty of time to meet my classes, and Schramm nearly had a hemorrhage when he saw me. By this time, Stoddard had returned to Urbana. He phoned the attorney general, having been refused a copy of my FBI file by J. Edgar Hoover. He wanted to see it for himself. He got hold of Tom Clark, who was the attorney general, and Clark said, "I'll get back to you." When he called back, he said, "I now have Smythe's file on my desk. I've looked it over and there's nothing in it which would bar him from holding high public office." So Stoddard wrote a memorandum to this effect and reported this to the board, which then confirmed my appointment. The bottom of the memorandum about this says, "All copies of this are to be destroyed." Schramm put a copy of this in my file, which he never showed me. Eventually, he left and went to Stanford and his secretary gleefully turned my file over to me.

The incident soured my relationship with Schramm. As he put it when he broke the news to me that my appointment had been put on hold, he had no idea there was anything in my past that would bring this about. He was surprised and shocked, and yet when Howard Bowen (dean of Commerce) and he took me to the Urbana Lincoln Hotel after they had me out for interviews and offered me the job, I said, "Before you get serious about it, you should know that I was a member of the American League for Peace and Democracy and I was a member of the Washington Cooperative Bookstore." Schramm had replied, "Oh, that wouldn't worry us at all if that came out." I said, "In an election year 1948 with J. Edgar Hoover having a big fight with Commissioner Durr, you're telling me this isn't likely to blow up. I think you're optimistic; it very well may." And he said, "Well, we wouldn't worry about it." Howard's reply was, "If you were shown to be a member of the Communist party, it might be a little sticky, but nothing short of that would bother us." So I said, "Okay, you're warned now." So they went ahead and made the offer and I accepted it.

About 1979 I obtained my FBI file under the Freedom of Information Act. In it there appears that in the summer and fall of 1948, Schramm was in the role of informer to the FBI. A check with *Who's Who* revealed that Schramm had been consultant and adviser to the intelligence agencies of the U.S. military, the OSS, and the CIA over the period from 1942 on. I have great respect for Howard Bowen but none for Schramm.

You stayed on at Illinois until 1963?

My salary began at $8,000 in 1948, and was $8,600 a year eight years later—to show you how generously they treated me. A $600 increase over eight years.

What other types of harassment or ill feeling were directed your way during that time? With that type of start, you must have felt somewhat isolated.

No, I made a lot of compatible friends there, and there were good people in economics, and I found them in all parts of the faculty. I became the secretary-treasurer of the AAUP chapter on campus. I didn't have any complaint about the collegial relationships apart from the immediate environment with Schramm.

During this time, 1948 to the early 1960s, do you feel that you were teaching communications from a critical viewpoint?

Yes, I was.

What types of courses were you teaching?

I was teaching the political economy of communications course.

That early?

Yes, I began it in 1948.

That must have been one of the first.

It was, as far as I know, the first anywhere. I must admit, as I look back on it now, my approach was kind of simple-minded and the literature I had available was very limited. But I would use the report on the special telephone investigation that the commission made to Congress, and the students and I would analyze it, and we'd take a critical look at regulation and that sort of stuff. Broadcasting was easy to be critical about and I was critical about it.

Were others in other universities or institutes teaching communications from a critical viewpoint?

Not in communications or journalism departments, but yes, there were a few in other departments, such as Fearing in film at UCLA, Newcomb in psych at Michigan, and Horace Grey in economics at Illinois.

Were there any others at Illinois?

No. You know Schramm, Peterson, and Siebert were writing *Four Theories of the Press* and glorifying the American system, and that was the standard line in the journalism faculty there. . . . No, there weren't any people in the communications field. I was very lonesome when we were taking a critical perspective. There was Charles Siepmann at NYU in broadcasting. I can't think of anyone else that I would call critical. They were all teaching administrative theory stuff.

From that time on—when you were teaching political economy at Illinois—how do you feel that the field of critical analysis of communications was developing? When do you feel it really started to take hold? What were some of the factors that brought it about? Who were some of the people?

The way you put the question implies that it has become very substantial. I'm not sure how substantial it is yet. I must admit I was impressed when I went to Hawaii to the ICA (International Communication Association) meetings in 1985 to find ten or more younger people who were fairly critical, if somewhat naive, but certainly far more critical than my generation had been thirty years earlier. That, I think, was the fallout from the Vietnam War more than anything else. The youth protest movement against the draft was a major factor, too—that's what I mean by Vietnam. I think that was what generated this and the general imploding of the American empire and the corruption manifesting itself throughout; that's what has stimulated the growth of critical analysis. Vietnam was a major factor.

So you're saying then that this probably happened in the late 1960s and early 1970s.

Yes.

What were you writing from the 1940s to the 1960s that would be of a critical nature?

Well, I think offhand the first serious article I wrote of a critical nature was published in *Public Opinion Quarterly* in about 1950. It was called "A National Policy for TV?" and I analyzed the commercial nature of the polity. I raised questions as to the opportunity for educators to get in on the ground floor for TV and pointed out the lack of economic support for education to make it possible through regular budgetary channels. I suggested the same elements that were eventually put together in the educational TV network, that there would be federal grants. That, I think was the first obviously critical thing I did. In the 1950s, the best area for my critical work on broadcasting was with the national level of the Churches of Christ. Everett Parker, Dave Barry, and I did a large study, based at the Yale Divinity School, on *The Television-Radio Audience and Religion,* in which my critical method was used with content analysis and nondirected interviews with sample surveys where the authors actually did and analyzed the interviews. (Harper, 1955) This work was linked with seminars and lectures on the cold war, where I found the most open discussions of ideological issues among theologians in the mainline Protestant churches.

I also published a monograph, *The Structure and Policy of Electronic Communication* (University of Illinois Press, 1957; republished in Michael Kittross, *Documents in American Telecommunications Policy,* vol. 2, Arno Press, 1975), in which I first explored the political economy of the radio spectrum. Then in the field of theory, about 1952, I wrote a piece called "Some Observations on Communications Theory," first published in *Lo Spettacolo* (in Italy, for lack of a U.S. publisher), which was then reprinted several times; it is in *The Sociology of Mass Communications* (Denis McQuail, ed, Penguin, 1953). There, I really teed off on scientism and stupid applications of what was thought to be scientific method. I really blasted them. I originally published that in 1953. In 1951, I wrote "The Consumer's Stake in Radio and Television," where I first formulated the "blind spot" argument about audience members' work for advertisers (*Quarterly of Film, Radio and TV,* vol 6). That was the old *Hollywood Quarterly,* which used to publish a lot of my stuff before it went out of business. That was a journal published at UCLA, edited by Franklin Fearing, who was a very good social psychologist who hated the cold war, and he himself was a victim of McCarthyism. He wasn't directly attacked, but he was certainly boxed off and pinned down in corners.

How did you fare under McCarthyism?

I never was openly attacked. As I told you, I nearly lost the job at Illinois before it began, but after that settled, I didn't hear any more about it. Of course, I was smart enough not to be disappointed when I didn't get any grants from the Ford Foundation to go off to the Middle East to do surveys of attitudes toward the Voice of America, like somebody I know. But I didn't want that anyway. I didn't have any foundation support from anyone in that sense. You could say I suffered a little. I did—I should mention that . . . although I'm not sure whether it could be called critical research . . . when the monitoring studies were done, which were originally intended to be the predicate for the grant of, for the . . . well, let me begin this way. I was asked to be the director of research for the National Association of Educational Broadcasters when it was a collection of college radio broadcast organizations. I served in that role for a couple of years and then the question came up of television allocations and the possibility—thanks to the freeze on licensing new stations until the difficulties with the original allocation of station assignments could be corrected—of having the commission reserve some frequencies for educators' use. That hearing was to begin in January 1951. So we had an NAEB board meeting in the Waldorf Astoria, about the 25th or 26th of December 1950. Sy Siegel was the president. He was the director of WNYC, the New York municipal broadcasting station, and himself a commander in the U.S. Navy. He was always a staunch friend and supporter of mine. Telford Taylor, the deputy war crimes prosecutor at Nuremberg, was our general counsel at this time. He had been the general counsel at the FCC who, with Fly, hired me there. There were about eight or ten of us. Well, we had a discussion on "how can we support a recommendation for reserving channels for education?"

You can say it's a good idea to have educational stations, but how can we prove it with hard evidence? Taylor looked across the room and said, "Dallas, you know about content analysis, don't you." I said, "Sure." He said, "You did some at the FCC, didn't you." "Yes." "How about you organizing a content analysis of commercial TV so we could show the FCC how lousy it is?" Well, we kicked it around a bit and agreed it was a great idea. We would monitor New York television for a week. We would classify all the programs, and we would get this evidence ready by the 20th of January. Mounting the whole thing and getting the whole thing done would be a big job. Then George Probst—oh, this is so funny—you'll be amused by it. George Probst was the manager of the University of Chicago's Round Table program, and he obviously knew about my FBI file, although I never told him about it. He began by suggesting maybe it would be a good idea to have codirectors on this project. Taylor said, "I don't know why Dallas can't do it alone." Well, when others watching George

Probst got the signals, they all began to side with him. Probst wanted Don Horton, an anthropologist, to codirect the study. Well, Horton was, at that time, in the Anthropology Department at the University of Chicago. He was at the meeting because he was interested in this, too. I had never seen him before. He'd worked for the CBS Research Department. With that industry experience, Probst obviously thought we would have some ideological insurance. So it was suggested that Don be my colleague on it. It was all right with me; I didn't oppose it. So that's the way it went.

So we did the monitoring. I got the monitors; we printed the forms; we wrote instructions; I rented sets from Zenith television; I got Western Union to provide their large sweep second hand clocks; I got stopwatches for everybody; I got aspirin bottles; we called in the press. We wanted to milk it for all the public relations value we could. We rented two large rooms in the Waldorf on about the twentieth floor and had this operation going there and Sy Siegel came and called in the press. There was a story with pictures on us in *Time* magazine. You know, it was really big stuff.

When we finished the actual monitoring, we had to do the editing and tabulating, and by this time we were so fed up with the food in the Waldorf we were glad to get out, and besides it would be cheaper to move out. You see, Don and I had gone to New York thinking we were going for a one-day meeting at the Waldorf. We didn't have money for a four-week trip. Nor enough clothes. We had to charge everything to the rooms. When the monitoring was done after ten days, we moved to the Algonquin Hotel. You know what the Algonquin was famous for besides having been a hangout for Hemingway? Excellent food. We got a much cheaper suite over there for our editing and tabulating and ordered food up. We still had no money. My salary at the time was pitiful. I was paying alimony. My wife and I were living on less than three thousand bucks a year.

One day, we were busy editing away and the waiter, at lunch time, came. We phoned down for the waiter to send up the menu so we could see what was on for the day to order lunch. I remember the menu featured "lobster mexicaine" and the waiter looked at us and I said, "Don, go ahead and order." He said, "Oh, if I could only go out and order a plain milkshake and a peanut butter sandwich, I'd be so happy. I mean, I have no money." Gorgeous food in the place. Anyway, we got it all done. We bundled it into the train, went down to Washington, got it printed over the weekend, and submitted it. The industry seemed off balance from our data, our presentation, and the big publicity we had generated. They didn't know how to cope with this in cross-examination. There was no character assassination attempt on either Don or me. It was a great success, and our testimony was substantially accepted by the commission and the educational channel reservations were established. Eventually, the educational television system was established. Maybe this was critical research, I don't know. This was in 1951.

We repeated it in Los Angeles and Chicago later in the year to make certain that the pattern of programs we found in New York was general. It was. We did similar studies for three successive years in New York and it was all published. I wrote it up for *Public Opinion Quarterly.* Oh, I forgot to finish off the story. The funny part about Probst in the fireproofing of this venture was that a year later the House Un-American Activities Committee held hearings in Chicago. And who do you suppose appeared as a voluntary witness to confess that he had been a Communist? Don Horton. He had been a Communist when he worked for CBS. And they asked him to name names and he said, "Well, look, I took the initiative in coming to you. I'm not going to name names. I am telling you I was a Communist. That's all I'll tell you." Then they let him off. He was pretty decent about it. He just had been scared to hell.

You mentioned some of your articles. Did you have any trouble getting published?

Oh, yes! This article on some observations on economic theory—on communications theory—I mentioned earlier that I couldn't figure out where to go to get it possibly published in the United States. I'd heard about *Lo Spettacolo* in Italy. They had it translated and published in Italian, and in it I really criticized Joe Klapper, who had done a study for the Rockefellers on the effects, and I had a mimeograph copy of it and it was a perfect target. I saw Klapper at a meeting soon after it appeared, and he said, "Dallas, my Italian isn't very good. Could you give me the English version of the paper you published in Italy?" I said, "Sorry Joe, I should have thought of that. I owed it to you to do that."

So you had to get it published in Italian?

Yes. Then the *Audiovisual Communications Review* published the English version, and that was picked up and published by Denis McQuail, as I said earlier, and it's the first chapter in his book.

Did you try to get published in Journalism Quarterly or similar journals?

I didn't try *Journalism Quarterly* because I figured they'd turn me down, until I knew I had something they couldn't turn down. I waited till 1959, when I wrote a piece on the "Political Economy of Communications" and sent it to them. I knew it was so solid they wouldn't have much chance to turn it down. They printed it. Then I put in another one a couple of years later. I only published twice in *Journalism Quarterly.* I didn't like it.

The only book I had a hand in writing in the 1950s was the one I referred to earlier, involving religion. Everett Parker, Dave Barry, and I did this New Haven study of the effects of TV and motion pictures—the mass media—on religious aspects of people's lives. We called it *TV-Radio Audience and Religion* (Harper, 1954). We did content analyses. We applied modified versions of the F scale from Adorno's *Authoritarian Personality* to the analysis of the characters we interviewed. We did extensive in-depth interviews. I had designed the technique in 1949 in an exploratory study I did in Illinois. Using the Rogerian therapy technique.

Carl Rogers?

Carl Rogers, yes. You know the method. "So you have problems with your wife . . ." Each question is a paraphrase of the last thing the other guy said with a question mark. You know, it worked wonders. I'd go in with a tape recorder and set it up and let them listen to their voices, and they let the kids listen to their voices, and they'd all chatter and then they'd settle down. Soon they'd say, "What do you want to ask? You made the appointment, here's the whole family sitting around." And I'd say, "Well, we're interested in studying the relations of people to the mass media. There's television, radio and motion pictures, newspapers, magazines and books. We'd like to know what you like about these things and what you don't like about them, how they relate to you, and that's all there is." And I shut up. They'd look at each other and they'd look at me and say, "Don't you want to ask any questions?" And I said, "I'd rather you just talk about it in any way you see fit." That was very interesting to see who would open up—whether the daddy would, or the mommy would, or whether the kid would. It was fun playing this game, and with only one or two exceptions out of about forty interviews we did there, the interviews lasted two or three hours, and they almost invariably ended with an offering of coffee and cake and cookies. They're so grateful to you that you came and gave them a chance to talk.

Of course, there's a big interview bias, and I recognize that. But having done all this, I didn't know what to do with it in 1949. How are you going to analyze this stuff except impressionistically? I was trying to be scientific. Then Parker, Barry, and I did the book, and it was really a good solid job.

I did a monograph in 1956 called *The Political Economy of Communications*, which was published by Mike Kittross in volume 2 of his *Documents in American Communications Telecommunication Policy.* It's the study of political economic aspects of the telephone and telegraph and the radio spectrum. That's where I really began to formulate a theory about the radio spectrum. I was talking about it this afternoon [at a communication conference in Canberra].

Then, of course, you did Dependency Road in 1981.

I wrote the blindspot article because I got irritated with my old friend Harry Magdoff, the coeditor of *Monthly Review.* When [Herbert] Schiller went to Amsterdam, I retired from Regina and went to San Diego to be a visiting professor in his place for one year, 1973–74, and they gave me money for a lecture series. One of the people I invited in was Harry Magdoff. I wanted him to talk to our students about Marxist theory in relation to communications. When I invited him, he said, "Well, Dallas, I don't know anything about communications." And I said,

"I really think you do, Harry, if you ever let your mind address the question." So he came anyway. He never got around to talking about communications. He just talked about Marxism. Afterwards he said, "How'd I do?" And I said, "You gave a splendid talk on Marxism and you gave me a title of an article I'm thinking of writing." He said, "What's that?" And I said, "'Communications, the Blindspot of Western Marxism'; you just proved it. You lectured a whole hour and a half and you never mentioned the word 'communications' at all." And he said, "I guess that's right."

So I wrote the article, which I then tried to get published in the *Journal of Communication,* and they wouldn't touch it in its then form. So I revised it and sent it to a new journal in Canada called the *Canadian Journal of Political and Social Theory.* They grabbed it and published it. Shortly after, when that article came out, I had a visit from a guy from McLelland and Stewart, their college sales manager. He said, "That's an interesting article you did on 'Communications, the Blindspot of Western Marxism.' Why don't you blow it up into a book?" That's how *Dependency Road* got written. It was done inside of fifteen months. It didn't require much—well, I had to refer to sources to document some things that I couldn't remember the sources on, but it was not a synthetic job where I piled up material and added it up. It was an analytical job. But when I'd finished it and phoned the man at McLelland and Stewart in Toronto, he'd been fired because of American competition. So I had to use an American publisher, Ablex.

When you left Illinois, you went back to Canada?

Yes.

Why did you leave the United States?

It was on the heels of the Cuban missile crisis. My wife and I had been active in the peace movement during the 1960s, and we concluded at that point that we might get just as blown up in Canada as the United States. We probably wouldn't avoid it. But at least we wouldn't be raising our children in the interim in this country. We couldn't stand it anymore. She's from North Carolina and she was fed up. And we were scared.

I went up there at my own expense and made a round robin inspection trip of the western Canadian universities to see what opportunities were there. They were just looking for a man to head the social sciences at this new university in Regina, and I fit in. So they hired me. That happened to be where I'd been born. I made a big circuit.

How long did you stay at the University of Regina?

Ten years. I've been at Simon Fraser for twelve years. I haven't spent more than ten to fifteen years in any one place since I was born.

We haven't talked about Simon Fraser and the type of program that you developed there.

I didn't develop anything while I was there. It was a holding operation while the thing began to shake down bureaucratically. I inherited six or seven people who were castoffs from different parts of the university, which put them together and said, "You make a communications department." There were a couple of educational psychologists, there was a guy from communications arts who didn't know anything else. There was a composer—full professor—of music. Well, at the time they hired me, they also had Lee Thayer. But he resigned within a couple of months, went out to be a farmer in New England.

You seem to have a knack for fomenting action. For instance, your action proposal today at this conference. And I remember in—when was it?—1980, that you helped start the Union for Democratic Communications. Can you spend a little time talking about your motivation for starting UDC?

Well, I guess I've always been a political activist. I try to apply what I can learn in theory to practice, and I don't miss opportunities if they look promising—that looked like a possibility. I overestimated the political maturity of the organizing group so I faded into the background because of the way it was handled by the people that took over the thing just after we got it started. So . . .

But that was your idea?

By no means. Some eight or ten people had somewhat similar ideas at the same time. The formative meetings were held at Temple University.

I was at the first one in the basement of the Unitarian Church in Philadelphia. Earlier, we talked about critical communication. You said that was assuming that it was developed or had gotten started. What do you see the role of critical communications study right now? Do you see it going downhill?

Well, I think it's perking along. I don't think it's going downhill. I don't think it's going uphill very much. To answer that question, I have to deal with the larger question of what are the prospects of there being a general theory of communications. There's never been one yet. The salience of this question occurred when I was arguing with George Gerbner in Urbana in about 1958. He said that a general theory deserving and getting respect was feasible in the near future. I argued that it would probably be a hundred years before it would be realistic to talk this way. I don't think we're ready. For one thing, we can't begin to comprehend the scope of the things that are involved in communication. The notion that communication science is transdisciplinary is an illusion—a pretense. Economics isn't, in any significant way, comprehended in it. The same is true for art. I'm sure philosophy isn't, nor physics, chemistry, biology, history, archeology, anthropology, astronomy, and geology. I think it is obvious that an acceptable general theory of communication must make sense as applied to the problems faced in *all* the fields of knowledge.

My friend Bill Livant may have given us the key to a general theory of communication. He suggests that information and communication are two aspects of one ontological process. Information may be looking at it structurally, and communication may be looking at it as motion in time-space. And that is fascinating—if you just begin to play with that notion. But to deal with that, and to elaborate it, will take you into all areas of knowledge. When we get that far, we will need to deal also with the relation of images to the things of which something is an image. In other words, quite simply, the difference between images and reality. But until one can begin to grapple with the full range of knowledge, I don't think we're in a position to talk about a grand theory. For much the same reason, on the method side, I don't think that we're in a position to talk about the positive aspect of critical theory. Until then, I think critical theory is going to be a catch-up game. Just like I'm going to say tomorrow [at the Canberra conference], as far as the peace movement is concerned it's a catch-up game. We seem to be running as fast as we can to stay in the same place, because the thing we're trying to catch up with seems to run faster than we do.

Besides working on these theoretical aspects, what do you see as some of the areas that would need more work in critical communications? If you were to advise young Ph.D. students right now, what would be some of the dissertation topics you would suggest?

The thing that comes immediately to my mind is, again, an analysis of the relation of the historical records that are all around us to the problems we now face. I'm referring, really, to the area that you have been specializing in in your life and which I'm late in getting a handle on. I'm referring to the traditional societies. They are the remnants of neolithic society that have been pushed off in the corners and exploited, smashed, or exterminated, bypassed and forgotten by the pirates who've seized the desirable property in the world. Therefore, I now urge students to focus on the values that originated in the local communities of paleolithic peoples in what is now Africa, Asia Minor, East Asia, Southeast Asia, and Central America, which underlie the traditional societies of the Third World. The approach is via the ideological aspects of the values embodied in traditional rituals, social organization, and intragroup relations. In such a context, the intrusion of Western "technology" has disastrous effects on the indigenous social organization and its autonomy. I think the work of Armand Mattelart, his wife, and their collaborators is extremely timely and important.

In this sense, the paper I did on "Needs Before Tools" is probably one of the most important things I've tried to do. I think we've got to begin to look at the proposition that civilization and the history of civilization is the negation of the virtues of an ecologically viable, classless society, which was the neolithic one. We've been trying to justify, to ourselves, a class-based exploitative system, and calling it civilization. I think we've been exactly inverting the significance of civilization's relation to prehistory. I think that the most important thing students can do now is to begin to reconcile the present characteristics of these remnants of the neolithic-style culture with the process by which they have been and are now being smashed. I think this way we'll begin to understand better what's wrong with us in the so-called civilized world. I think we've been . . . we're about to be consumed by the corruption that we spawn with the classes we've inflicted. The craft of historians grew out of the fact that when neolithic social organization was replaced by "civilization" with its class structure resting on the power of the few to control the many by military force, the collection of taxes from the many required for the first time somebody to keep records of who paid the taxes and who didn't. So you had scribes. This is the beginning of "history," and the glories of the kings who hired the scribes. So it's been a biased enterprise from the very beginning, some six thousand years ago.

What would be some other dissertation topics or areas?

I can think of a hundred in this one alone. I mean, go around the world and try to select out (I'm sorry if I just seem to be evading you there)—I'd go around and see if I couldn't select the types of stages by which the civilizations found the weak spots in the neolithic cultures and moved in and smashed them. I think it would be very important to detect the strategies with which they were defeated. It seems to me from the standpoint of understanding where we are, we'd better find out how we got this way, and we'd then be better able to deal with where we are. Well, this is the thing that, at the moment, seems to me of the most importance. As I say, I've been playing with this matter of the theory of information, and I hope to write something on it. I'm not much interested, at this stage in life, in supervising people in doing things like content analysis or descriptive studies of what's happening in Ontario on educational TV, or that sort of thing. At my age, I don't like to repeat work I did earlier. I think somebody has to do that work in order to give students a chance to learn how to use the tools of the trade, but I'm going to ask to be excused. (This seems like an accidental end for the interview.)

3

Against the Flow: The Peculiar Opportunity of Social Scientists

ROBIN MANSELL

Communication policy debates . . . encapsulate all the contradictions in the world.

—D. W. Smythe

Just two years after Dallas Smythe joined the University of Illinois Institute of Communications Research, he observed that the innovation of a social phenomenon of major proportions was under way (Smythe 1950a:461). In one of his first published articles in *Public Opinion Quarterly,* he confronted broadcast television, arguing that "it is the peculiar opportunity and responsibility of social scientists to evaluate" just what those proportions might be. Dallas Smythe was well seasoned in the processes of policymaking, having spent the period from 1943 to 1948 as the first chief economist at the Federal Communications Commission (FCC) in the United States. There, he had observed the transformation of his own work, which had spelled out the public service responsibilities of broadcast television licensees, in the FCC's "Blue Book." The responsibilities that licensees would be required to bear regardless of their private interest in profits accruing from their use of the radio frequency spectrum that appeared in the FCC document had not gone nearly far enough to define the scope of their public interest responsibilities.

The author wishes to thank Bob Everton, Richard Hawkins, Michael Jenkens, Bill Melody, and Rohan Samarajiva for their helpful comments on an earlier draft of this chapter.

The search for ways of giving preeminence to the public interest in the face of enduring contradictions between this and the interests of private capital was to be a central theme throughout Smythe's life. In the early 1950s he recognized that without action, the social, cultural, economic, and political potential of innovative communication technologies would not be realized. He understood, too, that communication policy would help to shape the uses of successive generations of communication technologies. As he noted in 1950, "Policy decisions on these issues will be made, whether we make them consciously or unconsciously" (Smythe 1950a:471).

Smythe was concerned with the implications of the pervasiveness of communication and the technologies that support it. His focus shifted between analysis of mass media (radio and television broadcasting) and telecommunication (telegraphy, telephony, and advanced information services). Always, he was concerned with the interaction of knowledge, whether labeled as educational product, ideology, or propaganda, with change in economic and political institutions, and with the determinants of innovation in technical artifacts such as satellites, the terrestrial telecommunication infrastructure, and the hardware, software, and program marketed to businesses and consumers. The "consciousness industry," the "invisible triangle" (broadcasters, advertisers, and audience members), the "MCIC" (military-civilian-industrial-complex), and the "C^3I's" (command, control, communications, and Information) were at the heart of Smythe's efforts to construct a political economy of communication (see Smythe 1986b, 1977b, and 1989).

This chapter was commissioned before Dallas Smythe's death in September 1992. The editor of this volume had requested a synthesis of key themes and issues in his work. There were many possible approaches to this challenge. For example, one could extract key concepts and trace their evolution through time. One could offer a synthesis of major segments of work on issues such as management and control of the radio frequency spectrum, or one could take on the "blindspot" debate and tackle the utility of Smythe's "audience commodity" thesis. I have chosen to do none of these. The substantive arguments embedded in Smythe's work will be accessible for analysis by communication scholars in the decades to come.

Instead, I have chosen to concentrate on elements that seem to have been central to Smythe's process of doing social science research. Completing this chapter in October 1992, I feel that those of us who knew Dallas Smythe have special responsibility to convey some part of his commitment to the realization of the "potential of humanity on this Earth" (Smythe 1987:10). One expression of that commitment was echoed in his struggle, through the application of social science methodologies, against the flow of the systemic exigencies of the capitalist system. This chapter highlights features of Smythe's critical and materialist methodology.

Wherever possible, I have used his own words to capture the enduring questions and issues that guided his inquiries. My aim is to offer a provocative synthesis that, regardless of superficial changes in communication technologies, can point to how we might continue to uncover the *principal contradictions* in social, political, and economic life.

In April 1992, during two days of discussion with Dallas Smythe, I was privileged to hear of his work on communication theory during the last several years of his life. He questioned me on my knowledge of recent works in psychology, computing science, anthropology, biology, physics, and a range of other physical and social sciences. I put to him my plan for this chapter and asked whether one could explore all the manifestations of contradiction at the same time as he appeared set to do. He smiled enigmatically and offered to give me a critique of a draft of this chapter. That can no longer be done. Nevertheless, it is my belief that Smythe's legacy must influence us to look critically and constructively at just how we use society's scarce resources to undertake research on the central contradictions in communication theory and practice.

As C. E. Lindblom observed, "Whatever distinctions between belief and feeling or between cognition and affect may be drawn, probing or inquiry has to be recognised as, among its other aspects, an inquiry into one's reactions of love, hate, revulsion, sympathy, admiration, or horror, among many other possibilities, as one actually experiences the many aspects of social life" (Lindblom 1990:31–32). Smythe ascribed Lindblom's early stance with regard to political change in the past several decades to the *administrative* research category.[1] But in his more recent work on *Inquiry and Change,* Lindblom began to reexamine the process and practice of social science inquiry. He moved closer to a *critical* perspective, no longer regarding social science as an *objective* science.[2] He wanted to "call attention to thinking that is engaged in real-world problem solving, to the relation, consequently, between thinker and the world thought about, and to the open-ended and exploratory quality of thought . . . to the interplay between thought and action as part of the process of probing or inquiry itself" (Lindblom 1990:35).

Subsequent sections of this chapter highlight ways in which Smythe sought to engage in the process of probing and action. We begin with some observations upon what he thought social scientists should do. This is followed by illustrations of how his definitions of concepts were instrumental in forging the methods and tools of the social scientists. These, in turn, shed light on how socioeconomic inquiry can be oriented toward critical analysis of communication processes and their implications for both the powerful and those with relatively less power to make change.

What the Social Scientist Might Do

One of the first questions Smythe asked as he took up his academic post at the University of Illinois was, "What kind of world will be born through the midwifery of our new and more powerful communications tools?" (Smythe 1950c:51). Here his concern was the implications of television technology. But the question is no less relevant to high-speed, digitally distributed data processing networks or any of the more recent technical configurations for mass or point-to-point communication. Smythe noted in the 1950s, "We have observed how aural radio served the fascist revolution of Nazi Germany and in Italy. So it is that there is a growing apprehension that TV may be misused, and a growing feeling that a new national policy for its use needs to be developed" (Smythe 1950c:51).

Investigation of the institutions of national and international policy and their particular forms became central to Smythe's social science inquiry. In his earlier works, there was sometimes a flavor of technological "determinism." For example, in "The Structure and Policy of Electronic Communication," he stated his purpose as being to consider "the degree of integration of communications agencies in organisation and practice which the technology of electronic communications *has forced* within and between nations" (Smythe 1957c:7; emphasis added). In 1960, we find a reference to the "communications revolution," a concept he would later deride.

> On the material side of life the most conspicuous feature of the cultural context of the mass media in the last two-and-a-half centuries is the development of techniques for using non-human resources to serve human needs for goods and services. . . . Embedded in the stream of scientific discoveries in the last century and a half was the source of the mass media of communications. These were discoveries in fundamental aspects of electronics, optics, mechanics, and chemistry. . . . The use and the effects of all of these developments according to the policy of the particular forms of organisation which operate them add up to the *communications revolution.* (Smythe 1960a; emphasis added)

Despite the language of quasi-determinism, in his research on specific issues within the communication field, Smythe had a much more nuanced approach. This was to become more and more clearly articulated throughout his life. For example, in 1972 the relevant questions for research with regard to the technical artifacts of communication would focus on the complex relations between technical artifacts and social processes and, particularly, on the types of social (and economic) relations that could be expressed through public and private institutions: "How does this artifact predispose or educate people to a particular ideological/political view of life? From what sort of social relations does this artifact arise? Is there a social as distinct from individual need for this artifact? What sort of artifact is appropriate to a particular ideological/political view of life? What changes in social relations would be necessary in order, e.g., to produce artifacts most appropriate to socialist culture? And so on" (Smythe 1972b:13).

During the 1980s, Smythe made his priority for inquiry in communication research absolutely clear: to expose through critical research the articulation of political and economic power relations as they were expressed in the institutional relations embedded in technology and the content of communication in all its forms. In 1988, Smythe would conclude, "The power to control communications and the flow of information is the basis of political power as well as of the possibility of realizing the potential of humanity on this Earth—if we don't stupidly blow ourselves away first. Communication policy debates therefore encapsulate all the contradictions in the world" (Smythe 1987:10).

By the beginning of the 1970s, Smythe was deeply engaged in the formulation of an international research program within the UNESCO context. His paper, "Toward Goal-Oriented Critical Research for Communications Media," stated: "In the accelerating pace of technological/development, must we not distinguish between administrative decisions (which always raise the Eichmann problem of obedience to authority) on the one hand, and critical decisions, on the other hand, and *make places for the latter explicitly in our institutional processes* (as "cultural ombudsmen")?"(Smythe 1970b:8; emphasis added). Thus, the social scientist was firmly planted in the process of institutional change and could do no less, from Smythe's vantage point, than to actively engage in that process. Of course, this left considerable room to argue over just how this was to be done and with what effect on both the researcher and the world of political and economic decisionmaking. Nevertheless, this was a challenge that would stand "against the flow" of much of the mainstream administrative research tradition in the United States, Canada, and internationally in the decades of the 1950s onward.

From the 1950s, too, Smythe had an aversion to what he called idealist or administrative research. He recognized all too well the pitfalls into which social scientists fall when they do not engage with the social processes they choose to study. In 1957, he observed that "the 'eggheads' have been easy to seduce" in their assessment of the likely transformations in the United States media industries as a result of early proposals for the introduction of pay television (Smythe 1957b). He went further to describe the "propensity of intellectuals to condemn indiscriminately free TV programs as 'vulgar' without, in many cases, bothering to watch them enough to know what they are like" (Smythe 1957b). He also had little time for the "linked propensity to accept naively as an escape from 'commercialism' the vaguest promises of 'culture' made by the pay TV promoters" (Smythe 1957b). This was what he proceeded to do with regard to the advent of satellite communication, integrated services digital networks, and numerous other communication technologies. This task was a major part of Smythe's political economy of communication.

The Design of Policy Research

If these were some of the central questions underlying Smythe's *critical* research agenda, to what extent did he conclude that the theory and practice of social science could provide relevant insights? In part, Smythe believed that relevant inquiry depended upon the creation of collective institutionalized processes to generate conditions under which appropriate research designs and researchable propositions would emerge. In the early 1970s, he argued that IAMCR (International Association for Mass Communication Research) could provide a context for the *design* of research in the international communication field (Smythe 1972b).

Smythe was well aware that communication research had yet to yield serious consideration of such methodological issues. In a paper presented to the 1972 IAMCR/AIERI conference, he argued:

> The fact that communications research until now has not given such a *design* serious consideration and that communications research tools may be inadequate now to cope with this design may be admitted. But at that point the challenge stands clearest: *Let us develop the necessary tools and use them.* If it be suggested that the task I am suggesting has never been done and is beyond man's capacities at this point in time, I must remind you that in principle the task has been done. . . . The famous Querelle des Anciens et Moderns which went on intensively in France for more than a fourth of the 17th Century was just such an analysis and sorting-out of the arts and handicrafts under the impact of the Renaissance on the previous medieval culture. Indeed, the Renaissance as a whole amounted to a *cultural screening* of medieval culture which was necessary if modern capitalist structure were to have coherence and identity, ideologically/politically speaking (Smythe 1972b:13–14; emphasis added).

As far as the extant tools of the social scientist were concerned, Smythe had recognized that "social science . . . was heir to the naive notion of science's apoliticalness developed in the nineteenth century" (Smythe 1971a).[3] But he knew that then, as today, "any commitment of resources, whether material or personal, in the context of the real world obviously has a dialectical political consequence—either in some fashion to support or to change the ongoing social system, or to clarify or obfuscate political issues, or both. As Mark Twain asked, '*Who are you neutral against?*'"(Smythe 1979b:104; emphasis added).

Openness to an eclectic array of social science methods was to characterize all of Smythe's work. His concerns about the misuse or abuse of the tools and methods of social science were profound. He considered the growing potential of quantitative empirical methods to provide misleading answers to misstated questions a problem no less serious than the inclination of some *critical* researchers to suggest that simply by using qualitative methods they would avoid the pitfalls of the *administrative* traditions in the social sciences. Smythe had grappled with the problems of statistical analysis when he undertook the first content analyses of television broadcast stations in the 1950s (Smythe 1948–49, 1950a, 1950b, 1951b, 1952; Smythe and Campbell 1951). Prior to this, he had believed that there was hope that techniques would be devised for analyzing the relationship of television to the dynamics of the "need-value systems within the personality . . . in contrast to the simple cause-and-effect logic with which early communications research was often concerned" (Smythe 1952:26). After completing a pilot study in 1950, he said that "progress in the preceding decade in the social sciences—especially in psychology—should by this time have placed us in a position to formulate significant hypotheses regarding the effects of a new technique such as TV. The author [Smythe] now blushes for his professional naivete in this respect" (Smythe 1950b:1).

Smythe's work spoke to the methodological issues rather than to sterile debates over method. In 1954, for example, he observed that "neither in the social nor the physical sciences can the validity of information be tested by whether it is 'an established fact.' . . . This fallacy is the essence of scientism" (Smythe 1954, cited in Samarajiva 1993). For Smythe, the question of "data" interpretation in the light of evidence from history, sociology, political science, and economics had to be considered. In the 1956 introduction to his comprehensive study of "Canadian Television and Sound Radio Programmes" for the Royal Commission on Broadcasting, he was to write:

> The data here presented are objective and, within narrow limits of variance, such as would result from the efforts of other persons who followed the same procedures as were used in these studies. Because the resources of the social sciences for dealing with content analysis are limited . . . there should be a clear understanding of the scope of the questions which are answerable from these studies. *They provide no categorical answers to many questions which are important yet with which social scientists are presently unequipped to deal* . . . the reader will find no evaluation of the "effects" of certain kinds of programmes . . . a fully satisfactory discussion of the data would *interpret them in relation to their causes, if not also to their effects . . . it would require examination in detail of the network and station structure as well as operations and programme policy in relation to the detailed findings on programmes.* (Smythe 1957a: xiii–xiv; emphasis added)

The lesson was not simply the underresourcing of social science inquiry into the development of the cultural industries. It was that any empirical inquiry would not be satisfactory in the absence of the political, economic, and cultural context in which it was undertaken. These experiences and observations did not mean that Smythe eschewed the empirical methods available to the social scientist. He was not "antiscience," nor was he opposed to the use of mathematical and statistical tools. Instead, at least in the early 1970s, he welcomed these tools. But he said, "I want them to be used to attack questions stated correctly—that is, I want them to be used to pursue questions that are framed in a realistic policy context. Far from being value free and nonpolitical in their application around the world, the great bulk of what passes for social science today is culture-bound and highly political in its consequences both in its home country and in other nations" (Smythe 1971a:104).

Smythe argued that the proper task of the social scientist was to contribute to the task of building *socialist realism.*[4] He wanted to borrow from *capitalist realism* the

> idea of an appropriate institutional form for the conduct of the dialogue over the review of capitalist culture and the development of the necessary new modes of socialist culture. . . . An appropriate institutional form for the conduct of the dialogue over the development of socialist realism would be different from the elite-based academies used in the development of capitalist realism. For socialist realism to develop consonantly with its own ethic, it would probably require an institutional form for this purpose that involved the effective participation of everyone—a nice dialectical problem, to *design a specialized institutional form for public decision-making.* (Smythe 1979b:108; emphasis added).

Pragmatically, Smythe sought to understand the institutions and policies which mediate all forms of *cultural realism* and, perhaps more importantly, to entertain the notion that local, national, regional, and even international institutions could be *designed* in such a way as to maximize the likelihood of more beneficial communication processes and structures.

Lest this characterization be taken to mean that Smythe adhered to a dualistic perspective on communication technologies, that is, a view in which the positive or negative features of innovations in technical systems depend simply upon the uses to which they are put, it must be recognized that his methodology sought to explicate contradictions in socioeconomic and political relations. Such relations were embedded in, and endogenous to, all systems of cultural phenomena—from technology to institutions to information products. There could be no naive opposition of positive or negative solutions in the development and use of communication technology. Instead, he saw a continuous dynamic struggle for control characterized by the changing structure of innovation, assimilation, and rejection of technological artifacts and information.

Mainstream administrative social science suggested that "science is pure; it exists in a rarefied vacuum (as far as real world pressures are concerned) and is value free. . . . Science is or ought to be ecumenical. . . . Satellites (or TV or cassettes) are neither good or bad; it depends on what they are used for." Smythe, however, would argue that "this naive view is unreal, substantially untrue and mischievous" (Smythe 1971b; Mattelart and Siegelaub 1978:171). From the early 1970s, Smythe worked toward the elaboration of a theory of communication that would redress the inadequacies of the administrative theory and practice he observed around him. Whereas references to critical research had been much in evidence in his earlier work, the word "critical" became a synoptic means of referencing particular theoretical and methodological approaches.[5]

> Some day, I predict, communications theory will take a grand definitive form. It will be a large theory which comprehends the historical scope of man as a message system using animal. It will explicitly recognise the context in which message systems originate, exist and are transformed into qualitatively different systems. This context will involve the functions of institutions of all kinds (from the family and tribe to world organisations) which use such message systems. To get significant communication theory the problem must be formulated correctly. A correct formulation must be historical in the sense of incorporation of a theory of history. A correct formulation must at the threshold recognise that the scientific study of message systems is not the private preserve of psychologists . . . rather it is a matter central to the natural scientist, the specialist in the humanities, the specialist in the fine arts, the social scientist (among whom I class the historian). And finally, a correct formulation of the problem will be set in a critical framework in which the nature of theory itself is also subject to continual critical scrutiny. We are a very long way from now having even a first approximation to a first draft of an adequate theory of communication. But the first step is to address ourselves to the problem. As the Chinese say, in order to walk 5,000 miles, it is necessary to walk the first mile. (Smythe 1971b:175–176)

It is not the purpose of this chapter to debate the realism of the theoretical agenda that Smythe set for himself. He was unable to complete his contribution to this agenda. Colleagues and friends wondered whether such a work could have been completed. Nevertheless, the threads of this agenda, and those within his earlier work, which culminated in the 1981 publication of *Dependency Road: Communications, Capitalism, Consciousness, and Canada* (Smythe 1981a; see also Smythe 1960a, 1962b, 1977a, 1984b), provide signposts to the ingredients of a continuing program of *critical* communication research.

Critical Communication Research

Smythe's *critical* research methodology had at its core the need to interrogate the systemic character of capitalism as it was expressed through the means and structures of communication. As he observed, "if . . . one ignores capitalism's systemic character, then inevitably the historical process will appear to be powered by one of the following: conspiracy, 'innocent accidents' or chaos" (Smythe 1979c). It is one thing to call for a deepening of such a perspective; it is quite another to develop the conceptual apparatus. A combination of concepts was elaborated to stimulate questions that Smythe retained at the forefront of his work.

First, and perhaps foremost, was the priority given to the definition of approaches to problem areas. By *administrative* researchable problems, Smythe generally referred to "how to market goods, how to improve the efficiency of media operations, etc." (Smythe 1974). By *critical* problems, he meant "research addressed to macro institutional structures and policies" (Smythe 1975:37) and at the "'micro' level, how to conduct psychotherapy and how to study rumors"

(Smythe and Van Dinh 1983:118). Second was the need to consider the mass media or any other institutionalized form of communication in terms of their relation to power and in terms of "an overall theory of who wins and who loses in the real world power struggle." Smythe cautioned that to do otherwise was to undertake research programs where the categories of argument and the research projects would "multiply toward infinity, defying effective synthesis. . . . The purpose of the exercise becomes the continuation of the exercise" (Smythe 1981c:219). Next, in the light of his emphasis on institutional change, was the need for a definition of institutions, which he defined as "those patterned social relations which humanity has developed to perform specialized functions which not everyone can perform for her/himself" (Mayer 1984:21).

If institutions were to be regarded as the sites of power struggles, then policy would need to be considered as one expression of those struggles. Smythe defined policy as "nothing but one way of doing things chosen from among various possible ways. Whether we are always aware of it or not, in this vast complex country of ours [the United States], a way of handling such a thing . . . is worked out, although most of the population, and indeed most persons in the learned professions, may not share consciously in the working-out process" (Smythe 1950a:474).

In the analysis of power relations embodied in institutions, it was also necessary to find a means of expressing the dialectical nature of contradictions within these relations. To do so, Smythe argued in terms of the *political* character of science and technique. He suggested that "science and technique necessarily involve *choices* of problems to be studied and knowledge to be put into practice and that such *choices* arise out of and are conditioned by, as well as affecting in turn, the on-going social structure of power relationships" (Smythe 1971b:172). In the 1960s, Smythe's contribution on this aspect of a research agenda was captured in a volume entitled the *The Struggle Against History.* Here he observed:

> Today, as in all of man's history, the central issue for the bulk of the world's population is the essential means of survival . . . and the prospect of their children's children developing into the human maturity which would be marked by self-respect and respect for the human animal. Modern science and technology offer the possibility of meeting this central issue. The agenda for the bulk of the world's population is therefore headed by the problems of so organizing social relations and so using science, technology and social resources as to meet this elemental objective. (Smythe and Wilson 1968:59–60)

To work within this framework, careful attention had to be given to the definition of "technology." In 1974, Smythe would argue that "technology is the fruit of social systems, embodies their consciousness, values and policies, and tends to reproduce them wherever it is carried regardless of juridical issues as to private versus worker legal title to property" (Smythe 1974:37). By the early 1980s, technology for Smythe had become one of several myths that needed to be critically interrogated:

> The term "technology" is a myth. But it has some very material constituents. Its makeup consists of the following ingredients. One part is bureaucracy (in both the private and public sector) which like the emperor's nobles and lackeys is following orders. The second part is science which is being taken over increasingly by the third part, capital. The fourth part is tools and machines created by engineers. The fifth part is ideology, which provides the raw materials with which the sixth part, propaganda, seeks to mold public opinion to accept the myth. (Smythe 1984b:212)

Smythe had concluded that to focus on the technological tools and artifacts, as so many pundits of the "information society" and the "communication revolution" were doing in the *administrative* research tradition of the 1970s and 1980s, "and ignore the institutions which use them is to embark on technocratic adventurism" (Smythe 1977b:201).

Smythe's longstanding commitment to analysis of both the institutional structure and the content of communication led him to give consideration to a definition of information. In early 1981, he defined information as "marks of relationships" and asked whether languages, art, science, news, advertising, data banks, and the like should be treated as aggregations of such "marks of relationships."[6] He went on to inquire, "Are hierarchical human organisations and professional expertise . . . the forms in which information as marks-of-relationships are organised in dialectical struggles?"(Smythe 1981b:6). This was the relevant question awaiting consideration from a *critical* research perspective. It was one that he argued that analysts such as Frank Peers, Anthony Smith, and Jeremy Tunstall had chosen to ignore (Smythe 1980, 1981b, 1979c).

From this perspective on information, Smythe was able to envisage a political economy that would distinguish between different types of information in their resource and commodity forms. For example, in 1983, he observed, "We need a politico-economic analysis of information which *inter alia* distinguishes what might be called environmental or 'new' information (Landsat photographs of wheat fields in Saskatchewan), from partially processed information (World Bank analysis of the wheat market in the world) and end-product information (e.g. money or executive summaries of economic conditions including wheat market information used to make decisions on World Bank loans to a particular country)" (Smythe 1984b:213–214).

The implications of the commoditization of information and its peculiar characteristics as resource and product had been taken up by economists including D. M. Lamberton and W. H. Melody several years before. Lamberton had defined information economics as analysis of the "processes by which information and knowledge is produced, diffused, stored and used" (Lamberton 1971:7). Melody had observed that "the functioning of society depends upon information and the efficient and effective communication of it among society's members. In the broadest sense, the social, cultural, political and economic institutions in any society are defined in terms of the characteristics of the shared information within those institutions" (Melody 1981:C7-5 to C7-9). But Smythe was to go much further by insisting that "the so-called 'information age' rests on the treatment of information as the crucial factor of production for the operation of the innovative/capital intensive system which is current monopoly capitalism" (Smythe 1986b:71).

Smythe called for studies focusing on research and development in the "Military-Civilian-Industrial-Complex (MCIC) engine which powers capitalism today," and he suggested that the relevant economic and political theories would require reconsideration.[7] A major task for critical research was to "describe the institutional nodes which today comprise the MCIC engine, and to show how they are integrated by communication. So tightly do these institutional nodes interpenetrate that it is difficult to conceptualize them as discrete components in the overall nodal matrix" (Smythe 1986b:67).

Smythe observed in 1986 that neither his own work nor the work of other colleagues within the communication research field had produced a "Marxist/critical theory" that was sensitive to the need to resolve the "principal contradiction between monopoly capitalism and life-continuing modes of social organisation and policy" (Smythe 1986b:71). Neither he nor they had adequately dealt with the ways in which innovation in the military sector was responsible for the origination of political and economic institutions relevant to the civilian population. Research on innovation processes and the *linkages* between the military and civilian sectors had been under way for some time with respect to other technologies, but little of this had filtered through to the *critical* communication literature at the time Smythe was writing.[8]

It was these conceptual definitions that informed Smythe's major work on the *consciousness industry.*[9] But in those writings where he developed many of his ideas with respect to the *audience commodity* and related themes, the foregoing context was all too often implicit and deeply embedded. We can now briefly highlight two facets of Smythe's work on the mass media of communication that were major ingredients of his *critical* research methodology.

Cultural Screens and the Audience Commodity

We begin as before with a definition, this time of *culture.* For Smythe, "culture . . . must be thought of as an aspect of a social process. Not as discrete things, objects or skills" (Smythe 1985:9). From his earliest studies of the broadcast industry, there were close synergies between his views on the determinants of the cultural apparatus of an economic system and the role of media content in the education process. For example, in 1951, Smythe observed that "the educational program would be designed to help the viewer to organize himself, to order his relations with other individuals, and with social groups ranging from the family to the human race, past and present" (Smythe 1951a:125).

This kind of programming stood in contrast to what he later elaborated as the commodity form of mass-produced, advertiser-supported communication:

> The bourgeois idealist view of the reality of the communication commodity is "messages," "information," "images," "meaning," "entertainment," "orientation," "education," and "manipulation." All of these concepts are subjective mental entities and all deal with *superficial* appearances. Nowhere do the theorists who adopt this worldview deal with the commodity form of mass communications under monopoly capitalism on which exist parasitically a host of sub-markets dealing with cultural industry.
>
> I submit that the materialist answer to the question—What is the commodity form of mass-produced, advertiser-supported communications under monopoly capitalism?—is audiences and readerships. . . . The mass media of communications are *simultaneously* in the superstructure *and* engaged indispensably in the last stage of infrastructural production where demand is produced and satisfied by purchases of consumer goods. (Smythe 1977a:2–3)

This set of observations and their elaboration generated much consternation among the *social science* community, not least among those who felt that Smythe was arguing for a choice between a theory of economic process and a theory of ideology. Smythe claimed that this had not been his intent, rather he was arguing that "commodities as well as ideas carry ideological meaning" and that "at the job matrix there is ideological instruction and at the household matrix where income-spending decisions are made, commercial messages or mass media output are to be considered in relation to the role of the audience as a do-it-yourself marketing agent and reproducer of labour power" (Smythe 1978:121; see also Murdock 1978, Livant 1979).

Smythe's perspective had evolved from the early 1950s, when he had first asked what the product of the U.S. mass media was. Then he had answered, "In the first place there is the group of products and services which relate to the receiving sets. . . . In the second place there is that product known as station time, and sometimes as audience loyalty . . . which stations sell to advertisers. . . . But it is not that simple. What is sold is *a program for the audience* (in whose continuing loyalty the station management has a vital interest), and *the probability of developing audience loyalty to the advertiser*" (Smythe 1951a:110).

Although the language had changed and there are still today reverberations of arguments as to just what Smythe meant to achieve in exposing the *blindspot*, there are deeper legacies of a methodological nature. The first is the fact that Smythe was discontented by extant received theory, whether it arose from longstanding historical respectability or more recent revisions to mainstream and critical/Marxist thought. He challenged all students of the cultural industries to subject theory to critical scrutiny. Second, he was not concerned only to address his "critical/Marxist" colleagues. Thus, for example, he noted with a major dose of ire, "the neoclassical economists' illusion that consumers make decisions based on marginal utility and opportunity costs is a monstrous fraud" (Mayer 1984:24).

Third, although it is arguable as to whether he succeeded, Smythe sought new concepts that would bridge the material or structuralist and ideological or cultural approaches to communication. As he put it some time later in 1986, the concept of *audience power* was integral to his analysis of the dialectical struggle in which the consciousness industry is resisted by people and their older institutions. It was also part of his critical research agenda that was to "grasp the size of the reorganisation of policies and structures which is required" if popular resistance has the potential to take back the hegemony which the consciousness industries had seized over the past century (Smythe 1986a:7). These arguments were very much in line with Smythe's earlier observation in 1963: "While the monolithic inertia of our mass media in these [unacceptable] directions is frighteningly powerful, we can take heart from the realization *that no concentration of institutional power has ever been eternal or immune to change*" (Smythe 1963b, and in Goodman 1964:470; emphasis added).

It was also in the context of a commitment to institutional change through both theory and practice that Smythe developed the related concept of *cultural screens*. As far as this author is aware, he never fully applied this concept directly to the development of local or domestic media policy;[10] however, it was intimately linked to his arguments concerning the cultural realism of any given system of political and economic relations. By "cultural screens," Smythe referred to the aspects of a culture or system that serve to protect its cultural realism against extracultural disruption, whether they be the protective features of a particular language or restrictions on movement of people or things (Smythe 1971a:100). Cultural screens were the name given for "a dialectical struggle over the terms of national development—the interest of which class it should serve" (Smythe 1981a:236).

For the full utility of this concept as a methodological construct to emerge, it is necessary to consider the gestation of the idea. The context initially was a debate in the late 1960s as to how best to institutionalize and control the proliferation of telecommunication and broadcast satellites (see Smythe 1958, 1960d, 1961b, 1965, 1967, 1961c, 1960c, 1960b, 1961a, 1962a, 1964, 1966, 1970a). Smythe had noted that communication satellites exemplified the highest stage of development of the relationship between the power of the national state, its institutions, and their existence within a context of "world-ecological organisation" (Smythe 1969).[11]

As early as 1969, Smythe had referenced H. I. Schiller's call for *cultural embargoes,* which would forbid the intrusion of satellite signals originating within a foreign country. He observed that this would be "a neat trick if it could be accomplished."[12] Smythe's understanding of the real underlying processes of institutional change called for a more nuanced approach.

Smythe had the benefit of close observation of the way in which the Canadian government had been unable to impose an embargo through the use of technical standards on the influx of television broadcast signals into Canada from the United States in 1949. As Peers had reported it, the Canadian Department of Transport had decided by 1949 to adopt the same television standards as the United States. Any other approach would have been perceived by the policymakers of the time as the erection of a "television curtain." Despite the fact that other countries such as England, France, and Germany had erected "electronic curtains," which could be bypassed at gateways with transcoding of signals for selected rebroadcast of foreign programs, the Canadian government had not felt able to do so.[13] Why, Smythe reasoned, would the political and economic sanctions created by similar embargoes in the face of international satellite communication be any different from this experience?

Nevertheless, as always, Smythe's research methodology led him to seek the principal contradiction in the real world of international communication. This he argued was "between the processes based in the mature market economies which exercise cultural domination on the rest of the world's peoples, on the one hand, and on the other hand institutional structures and policies with which the world's poor peoples . . . are increasingly able to *screen* themselves from such domination" (Smythe 1979a:1). The resulting concept of "cultural screens" was not to be regarded as an impermeable wall: "a screen is to a degree permeable" (Smythe 1979a:1). As with much of his conceptual apparatus, Smythe situated his concept of cultural screens within a much broader historical context. For example, in 1963, he noted that, "In principle the sort of cultural screening called for has been practiced by mankind for many millenia. The perpetuation of languages is a cultural screening device. . . . Traditional cultural artifacts, services and institutions embody a particular world view held by a people and serve to transmit and protect it against foreign ideological intrusions" (Smythe 1973:21–22).

Thus, in practice, Smythe's search was for new and complementary means of creating the space for the management of social or self-control that had been characteristic of an era before the advent of the widespread diffusion of electronic modes of communication. This aspect of Smythe's work was never developed more fully, and he often asked why "nobody appeared to have taken up the idea." By focusing upon power as articulated in the relations between nation-states, he tended to overlook the dynamics of change within international institutions and the nation-state. Indeed, the role of other socioeconomic communities often disappeared completely. However, in the concept of "screens," there is an indirect link, particularly with work by *critical* researchers who are tackling institutional mechanisms for handling the "crisis of control" over personal information generated by electronic transactions and the ways in which communication is mediated in "electrospace."[14] Here the dynamics of the social and economic structuring of boundaries, as well as the permeability of boundaries or "screens," is an essential issue for critical exploration.

If it was the opportunity of the social scientist to advocate the erection of cultural screens in the international communication domain in the 1960s and 1970s, there would need to be innovations in the ways in which political and economic power was mediated by institutions. It is to Smythe's remarks concerning the viability and formation of appropriate international (and, by extension, local, national, regional) institutional forms that we now turn.

Design and the Policy Institution

The political economy of institutional *design* was pervasive in Smythe's work. Much of Smythe's attention to the design of institutions was devoted to the management of the radio frequency spectrum. He believed, as Hardin argued, (1968:1243–1248) that when common property is excessively used to pursue individual private interests, the "inevitable result is to impair or destroy the capacity of the common resource to serve the interest of the whole society—including the private 'market' interest" (Smythe 1989:133–134).

Smythe argued that an *ecological view of communications* would show that "for more than half a century man has enjoyed a few of the benefits of world government without hardly noticing it. The radio spectrum is public property . . . the use of the radio spectrum has been regulated since 1906 by international conferences, now known as the International Telecommunication Union" (Smythe 1963a:17).[15] But when he examined the characteristics of the International Telecommunication Union and other related United Nations organizations in the 1960s, he concluded:

> If there is no appropriate international organization or policy to plan for, yes and even to administer, this use of everybody's property—the radio spectrum—in space—which itself appears hopefully also to be everybody's property—then the world faces the probable extension of cold-war rivalry into the development and aggressive use of this technology. As things now stand, the first power to begin extensive use of space satellites will initiate the malevolent cycle. The second power would then try to outdo or at least equal the first with a rival satellite broadcast service and so on. (Smythe 1960d:23)

For our purposes, whether "star wars" eventuated in the absence of such an organization is not at issue. The methodological point concerns how one assesses the role and purpose of social science research at junctures when governance systems are in a state of political flux and transformation. In 1966, Smythe answered:

> Policies conducive to freedom of information and regional and world organizational development are currently frustrated by national state considerations. There are many roads to an ecologically organised world. Regional and world government will rest on community, communications and public opinion. A UN-based broadcast satellite operation is proposed. Also a UN-based information service to supplement present wire services. . . . Presently there is a void in the world's technology precisely in the area of world communications institutions. They simply do not exist in terms relevant to the technical problem. (Smythe 1967:11–12)

What Smythe argued was absent in discussion of satellite communication issues was analysis that focused on "the organisational and policy implications of a continuing process of accommodating the technical possibilities of communications systems . . . within the assignable bands of the radio frequency spectrum" (Smythe 1972a). Later he would give considerable thought to the management of the radio frequency spectrum at the national level (Melody and Smythe 1978, 1979, 1980).

The challenges to world governance structures, especially in the communication field, are at least as widespread in the 1990s. Today we see increasing rivalry among transnational corporations and some governments being expressed not only through the International Telecommunication Union, and the GATT, but also through a host of regional standard setting organizations (Hawkins 1992:339–353). It is also clear that the "internationalization" of the whole complex of cultural industries and the information and communication technologies (military and civil) is creating severe problems for the protection of the "commons" in which all social actors have an interest.

As Smythe put it in 1960, "As social scientists, we would seem to have a special responsibility and interest to study and to advise concerning the means by which the institutional lag may be reduced to limits which will permit human survival, not to mention the enjoyment of the fruits of our technology and social organisation in a world where, as Einstein remarked, everything is changed except our ways of thinking" (Smythe 1960d:35).

Yet how many social scientists are encouraged to tackle these fundamental issues in the political economy of relations between technical and institutional change in the 1990s? There are only a relatively few sites of activity that encourage social scientists to analyze and advise from what Smythe might have regarded as a *critical* perspective. The different phases of Smythe's career and work hold lessons as to how to uphold the precepts of social science inquiry and, at the same time, to engage in real world processes of decisionmaking.

Conclusion

Smythe contended that in an "age of information technology" there is a continuing challenge to formulate the genuine needs of people before technical artifacts and institutions are designed to try to satisfy those needs:

> In the age of information technology, nothing is more important than to identify and formulate the genuine needs of people before tools are applied to try to satisfy those needs. . . . Since the mid-1970s a spate of studies has grappled with these questions by focusing on the problem of production. But these studies leave the definition of the production context to the individual researcher. Industry structure, enterprise rules of thumb, new hardware and software, licensing changes, organisational roles, etc., pop in and out of the research "contexts." . . . Consequently, people's needs no longer unambiguously precede their awareness of tools; rather the contrary is true especially in the core area. (Smythe 1985:8–9)

With regard to international control of satellite communication, Smythe raised the question, How can or should special geographic interest groups and nations protect their interests in communication satellite services in the Western Hemisphere? The answer seemed obvious. He suggested that they *bargain* for them (Smythe 1972a:13). He was also favorable toward appropriately designed training programs, especially for those with relatively few resources to engage directly in the bargaining process in the International Telecommunication Union and other fora.

This then is our last clue to Smythe's methodological agenda. If institutional change is dynamic and continues alongside innovations in all aspects of the technical, social, economic, and political spheres, then new opportunities for *bargaining* must be expected to arise. It is the peculiar opportunity of the social scientist to be prepared to assist in that process of bargaining. To do so, *critical* social scientists must be armed with the methodological tools on offer in the 1990s. These will never fully meet expectations and "needs," just as they failed to meet Smythe's expectations in the 1950s and later. The reasons for this cannot be addressed here. Suffice it to say that much can be done if the community of social scientists remains attuned to the lessons of Smythe's *critical communication research* agenda. This should not be taken as advocacy of the need to rigidly apply his concepts or his methodology. As Smythe himself commented, "Like methods used in ordinary life, the method of science is to define the job, to study it, to try to do the job, and to analyze and synthesize the results of the trial. The process is known as observation, experiment, analysis (taking apart) and synthesis (putting together again)" (Smythe 1971b:171).

NOTES

1. Personal discussion with Dallas Smythe, 1980. The context was a discussion on Lindblom (1977), which extended to include Lindblom and Cohen (1979).

2. See Lindblom (1990). On page 102, Lindblom cited Smythe's *Dependency Road* in connection with acknowledgment by social scientists of the "long-term effects of constantly repeated messages." In this chapter, no attempt is made to address whether social inquiry should be considered a "science." Nevertheless, a critique of positivist orthodoxy is implied.

3. See also *Lo Spettacolo,* 22 (January–March 1972):1–18.

4. The concepts of socialist and capitalist realism were linked to Smythe's concept of *cultural realism,* which referred to the context of the arts and sciences in any social system. Cultural realism meant the central values of the system as expressed in its artifacts, practices, and institutions. These were the central values that provided the rationalization that informs and is implicit in the relations of the components of the system. See Smythe (1979b:100).

5. Whether Smythe's synoptic use of *critical* research embraced "Marxist" and "institutional" theoretical traditions was, and undoubtedly will continue to be, the subject of some debate. Personal communications with Dallas Smythe and review of material for this chapter have led the present author to conclude that the question eludes a simple yes or no answer.

6. Smythe may have been influenced by arguments such as those presented by G. Bateson. For example, "in a strict sense, therefore, no data [information] are truly 'raw,' and every record has been somehow subjected to editing and transformation either by man or by his instruments" (Bateson 1972:xviii).

7. "Relevant theory" here refers to work by Herbert Schiller, Armand Mattelart, and Dan Schiller. Smythe gave as examples H. Schiller (1981), Mattelart (1979), and D. Schiller (1982).

8. See Kaldor (1981). For general review, see Weston and Gummett (1987) and Woodhouse (1985). For a later work, see Gummett and Reppy (1989).

9. "Through its penetration of the work institutions, the military, and all other major institutions, the integration of computer-type information into the 'communications' institutional complex seems fully to justify christening the whole sprawling communications institutional complex consciousness industry." See Smythe (1974:374).

10. This concept would have been applicable to the struggles of ethnic groups and other political formations within the nation-state in their efforts to gain success or control of the mass media of communication.

11. Smythe used this term to refer to communication technology development, which he argued provided the mainstay of power of the national state and its symbiotic institutions and within world organizations that functioned in an integrated way (1969:54).

12. Smythe noted that H. I. Schiller was correct in stating that a developing nation, faced with "communication diplomacy" from the West and determined to pursue its own development program nevertheless, would be well advised to adopt a policy of cultural embargoes designed to protect its own programs through maintaining some "social distance" between itself and the West. See Smythe (1969:63).

13. See Smythe (1980). Smythe used the term "electronic curtains" to reference a quotation from Alphonse Ouimet: "Any other standard . . . would have erected a television curtain between Canada and the United States." Cited by Peers in Smythe (1980:19).

14. See Samarajiva and Shields (1992) and Ruggles (1992). Samarajiva argues correctly that "electrospace" and "electronic space" are quite different. The former is a way of depicting the radio spectrum; the latter concerns social space as constituted by humans. Insofar as the technical applications of "electrospace" are socioeconomically constructed and this human activity structures and constrains the environment constituted as "electronic space," there are important connections that can be explored. "Electronic space" is a concept derived from the work of E. Goffman and others (see Goffman 1963). Smythe attributed the term "electrospace" to W. R. Hinchman (1969), cited in Smythe (1984a:274).

15. "Ecology" referred to "the science of the relation of living organisms to their development." Smythe (1963) cited Huxley, who argued, "The beginnings of ecological politics are to be found in the special services of the United Nations Organization . . . all these are . . . concerned with the ecological problems of the human species" (1963:6–7).

REFERENCES

Bateson, G. (1972). *Steps to an Ecology of the Mind.* New York: Ballantine Books.

Goffman, E. (1963). *Behavior in Public Places: Notes on the Social Organization of Gatherings.* New York: Free Press.

Goodman, P., ed. (1964). *Seeds of Liberation.* New York: Braziller.

Gummett, P., and J. Reppy, eds. (1989). *Relations Between Defence and Civil Technologies.* Dordrecht: Kluwer.

Hardin, G. (1968). The tragedy of the commons. *Science,* 162:1243–48.

Hawkins, R. (1992). The doctrine of regionalism: A new dimension for international standardization in telecommunications. *Telecommunications Policy* (May–June):339–53.

Hinchman, W. R. (1969). Use and management of the electrospace: A new concept of the radio resource. IEEE International Conference on Communications, Conference Record, Boulder, Colorado (June):13.1–13.5.

Huxley, A. (1963). The politics of ecology: The question of survival. Occasional paper. Santa Barbara, CA: Center for the Study of Democratic Institutions.

Kaldor, M. (1981). *The Baroque Arsenal.* London: Andre Deutsch.

Lamberton, D. M., ed. (1971). *The Economics of Information and Knowledge.* Harmondsworth: Penguin Books.

Lindblom, C. E. (1977). *Politics and Markets.* New York: Basic Books.

———. (1990). *Inquiry and Change: The Troubled Attempt to Understand and Shape Society.* New Haven: Yale University Press.

Lindblom, C. E., and D. K. Cohen. (1979). *Usable Knowledge.* New Haven: Yale University Press.

Livant, B. (1979). The audience commodity: On the "blindspot" debate. *Canadian Journal of Political and Social Inquiry,* 3:1 (Winter):91–106.

Mattelart, A. (1979). *Multinational Corporations and the Control of Culture.* Atlantic Highlands, NJ: Humanities Press.

Mattelart, A., and S. Siegelaub, eds. (1978). *Communication and Class Struggle: 1. Capitalism, Imperialism.* New York: International General.

Mayer, H. (1984). Capitalism, advertising and the consciousness industry: Dallas Smythe. *Media Information Australia* (February):20–25.

Melody, W. H. (1981). The economics of information as resource and product. In *Pacific Telecommunications Conference, Papers and Proceedings,* edited by D. J. Wedemeyer, pp. C7-5–C7-9. Honolulu: Pacific Telecommunications Council.

Melody, W. H., and D. W. Smythe. (1978). Opportunity cost and radio spectrum allocation: A study of the feasibility of applying the opportunity cost concept to the spectrum allocation process. Report for Department of Communications, Ottawa.

———. (1979). Economic analysis of radio spectrum licence fees: The microwave band. Report for Department of Communications, Ottawa.

———. (1980). The level and structure of licence fees in the microwave band. Report for Department of Communications, Ottawa.

Murdock, G. (1978). Blindspots about Western Marxism: A reply to Dallas Smythe. *Canadian Journal of Political and Social Theory,* 2(2):109–19.

Ruggles, M. (1992). Personal information flows and boundaries in the intelligent network. CIRCIT Policy Research Paper No. 28 (July).

Samarajiva, R. (1993). Down dependency road: The Canada–U.S. free trade agreement and Canada's copyright amendments of 1988. In *Illuminating the Blindspots: Essays in Honor of Dallas Smythe,* edited by J. Wasko, V. Mosco, and M. Pendakur. Norwood, NJ: Ablex.

Samarajiva, R., and P. Shields. (1992). Electronic space: Institutional and strategic analysis. Paper presented at the Communication Technology Policy Section, International Association for Mass Communication Research, São Paulo, Brazil, August 16–21.

Schiller, D. (1982). *Telematics and Government.* Norwood, NJ: Ablex.

Schiller, H. I. (1981). *Who Knows: Information in the Age of the Fortune 500.* Norwood, NJ: Ablex.

Smythe, D. W. (1948–49). Television: Position and outlook. *Current Economic Comment* (University of Illinois), 10 (4):15–33.

———. (1950a). A national policy on television? *Public Opinion Quarterly* (Fall):461–75.

———. (1950b). People and television: The natural history of an unfinished study. Urbana: University of Illinois Institute of Communications Research (June).

———. (1950c). Television and its educational implications. *Elementary English* 27 (January):41–52.

———. (1951a). The consumer's stake in radio and television: Consumer problems in a period of international tension. Fifteenth anniversary report from the Consumers Union. *Quarterly Review of Film, Radio and Television,* 6 (Winter): 109–28.

———. (1951b). A problem in content macro analysis in the NAEB Monitoring Study of New York television. Columbus, OH: Institute for Education by Radio (May).

———.(1952). Civilian TV research: 1952 model. Mimeo. Institutional Media Seminar, New York.

———. (1954). Some observations on communication theory. *Audio Visual Communication Review,* 2:24–37.

———. (1957a). Canadian television and sound radio programmes, Appendix XIV; An analysis by Dallas W. Smythe, December 1956. In *Report of the Royal Commission on Broadcasting*, pp. xiii–xiv. Ottawa: Queen's Printers (March).

———. (1957b). Pay TV: An attempted revolution within cultural industry. *Current Economic Comment* (November):49–66.

———. (1957c). The structure and policy of electronic communication. *University of Illinois Bulletin*, 54:75 (June):7.

———. (1958). American culture in the shadow of the satellites. Address to the Broadcasting and Film Commission, National Council of Churches of Christ (February).

———. (1960a). On the political economy of communications. *Journalism Quarterly*, 37:4 (Autumn):563–72.

———. (1960b). Space satellite broadcasting. *NAEB Journal* (July–August): 71–78.

———. (1960c). Space satellite broadcasting: Threat or promise? *Journal of Broadcasting*, 4:3 (Summer): 191–98.

———. (1960d). Space satellite communications and public opinion. American Sociological Association, New York, August. Published as Monograph 59 University of Illinois Institute of Communications Research.

———. (1961a). Communications satellites. *Bulletin of the Atomic Scientists*, 17:2 (February):65–70.

———. (1961b). The space giveaway: Public benefit or private privilege. *The Nation* (October 14 and 21):242–45, 264–68.

———. (1961c). Testimony before the Subcommittee on Monopoly of the Select Committee on Small Business, United States Senate, 86th Congress, First Session, *Hearings*, August 3, pp. 95–119.

———. (1962a). Considerations on a world wide communications satellite system. *Telecommunication Journal* (September):269–73.

———. (1962b). Time, market and space factors in communication economics. *Journalism Quarterly*, 39:1 (Winter):3–14.

———. (1963a). Change and the mass media of communication. Saskatchewan Farmers' Union, Saskatoon, December.

———. (1963b). Mass media and the cold war. *Liberation*, 8:10 (December):18–23.

———. (1964). On thinking about the effects of communication satellites. American Institute of Aeronautics and Astronautics, Washington, D.C., June.

———. (1965). On the effects of communications satellites, paper no. 9:Communication explosion. Washington, D.C.: George Washington Program of Policy Studies in Science and Technology.

———. (1966). Freedom of information: Some analysis and a proposal for satellite broadcasting. *Quarterly Review of Economics and Business*, 6(3):7–24.

———. (1967). The political and economic conditions of freedom of information. International consultation, World Council of Churches, Celigny, Switzerland, February. Published in *Study Encounter*, 3(1):2–20.

———. (1969). Conflict, cooperation and communication satellites. In *Mass Media and International Understanding*, edited by School of Sociology, Political Science and Journalism, pp. 51–73. Ljubljana. Also published in *Estudios de Informacion*, No. 9 [October–December 1968]:31–73.

———. (1970a). The legal problems of international telecommunications with special reference to INTELSAT, and international legal problems of direct satellite broadcasting. International Law Association Panel Discussion Report. *University of Toronto Law Journal,* 20(3):287–313, 314–332.

———. (1970b). Toward goal-oriented critical research for communications media. "Communications 80," Mass Communication Research and Policy, Hanko, Finland, April. Finnish National Commission for UNESCO and Finnish Broadcasting Company, published as part of *Report,* Helsinki.

———. (1971a). Cultural realism and cultural screens. International Symposium on New Frontiers of Television, Lake Bled, Yugoslavia, June. Published as Realism in the arts and sciences. In *National Sovereignty and International Communication,* edited by K. Nordenstreng and H. Schiller. Norwood, NJ: Ablex.

———. (1971b). The political character of science (including communication science) or science is not ecumenical. Annenberg School of Communication, Philadelphia, February. Translated into Finnish, University of Tampere, 1972.

———. 1972a). The orbital parking slot syndrome and radio frequency management. Conference on International Communication by Satellite, Stanford University School of Law and American Society of International Law, Stanford University, Stanford, California, April 1970. Published in *Quarterly Review of Economics and Business,* 12 (Summer 1972):7–18.

———. (1972b). Reflections of proposals for an international programme of communications research. International Association for Mass Communication Research, Buenos Aires, Argentina, September.

———. (1973). After bicycles, what? Mimeo. Regina: University of Saskatchewan (March).

———. (1974). The role of mass media and popular culture in defining development. In *Der Anteil Massenmedien bei der Herausbildung des Bewusstseins in der Sich Wandelnden Welt,* pp. 367–74. Leipzig: Karl Marx University. Based on a paper presented to the International Association for Mass Communication Research, Leipzig, September 1974.

———. (1975). Agenda setting: The role of mass media and popular culture in defining development. *Journal of the Centre for Advanced TV Studies,* 3(2):37.

———. (1977a). Communications: Blindspot of Western Marxism. *Canadian Journal of Political and Social Theory,*1:3 (Fall):1–28.

———. (1977b). Critique of *The Consciousness Industry* by H. M. Ensenberger. *Journal of Communication,* 27:1 (Winter):198–202.

———. (1978). Rejoinder to Graham Murdock. *Canadian Journal of Political and Social Theory,* 2:2 (Spring–Summer):120–126.

———. (1979a). Issues in international communications: Peoples, commodities and political processes. George A. Miller Lecture, University of Illinois–Urbana, April.

———. (1979b). Realism in the arts and sciences. In *National Sovereignty and International Communication,* edited by K. Nordenstreng and H. Schiller. Norwood, NJ: Ablex.

———. (1979c). Review of *The Media Are American* by J. Tunstall. *Media, Culture and Society,* 1:1 (January):107–14.

———. (1980). Review of *The Public Eye: Television and the Politics of Canadian Broadcasting* by F. W. Peers. *Canadian Journal of Sociology,* 5:1 (Winter):79–80.

———. (1981a). *Dependency Road: Communications, Capitalism, Consciousness, and Canada.* Norwood, NJ: Ablex.

———. (1981b). Idealism and realism in international communications: A review essay, A. Smith, *The Geopolitics of Information: How Western Culture Dominates the World,* and A. Mattelart, *Mass Media, Ideologies and the Revolutionary Movement.* Mimeo (July).

———. (1981c). Rethinking reductionism, review of *Does Mass Communication Change Public Opinion After All? A New Approach to Effects Analysis,* by J. B. Lemert. *Journal of Communication,* 31:3 (Summer):217–20.

———. (1984a). The electronic information tiger, or the political economy of the radio spectrum and the Third World interest. In *Politics of News: Third World Perspective,* edited by J. S. Yadava. New Delhi: Concept.

———. (1984b). New directions for critical communications research. Mass Media and Development Conference, Northwestern University, Chicago, October 14, 1983. Published in *Media, Culture and Society,* 6(1984).

———. (1985). Needs before tools: The illusions of technology. *Media Development,* 23(4):6–17.

———. (1986a). The 1986 Southam Lecture: Culture, communication "technology" and Canadian policy. *Canadian Journal of Communication,* 12(2):7+.

———. (1986b). On the political economy of C^3I. In *Communication and Domination: Essays to Honor Herbert I. Schiller,* edited by J. Becker, G. Hedebro, and L. Palden, pp. 66–75. Norwood, NJ: Ablex.

———. (1987). Freedom is the act of resisting necessity, response to L. R. Sussman. ICASIETAR (Montreal) (April 20):10.

———. (1988). Unsaintly alliance against NIICO. *Democratic Journalist* (March):10–12.

———. (1989). Television deregulation and the public: A critique of V. Farrall's *Impact of Television Deregulation on Private and Public Interests. Journal of Communication,* 39(4):133–38.

Smythe, D. W., and A. Campbell. (1951). *Los Angeles Television.* Ann Arbor, MI: Edwards Brothers.

Smythe, D. W., and H. H. Wilson. (1968). Cold war mindedness and the mass media. In *The Struggle Against History,* edited by N. D. Houghton, pp. 59–60. New York: Washington Square Press.

Smythe, D. W., and Tran Van Dinh. (1983). On critical and administrative research: A new critical analysis. *Journal of Communication,* 33(3):117–27.

Weston, D., and P. Gummett. (1987). The economic impact of military R and D: Hypotheses, evidence and verification. *Defense Analysis,* 3(1):63–76.

Woodhouse, T. (1985). A peaceful economy? Defence conversion and the arms industries in the USA: A survey of recent trends. *Peace Research Reports* (University of Bradford), No. 7.

4

"Critical" Communication Research: New Directions

MANJUNATH PENDAKUR

Critical research in communication is a broad category encompassing divergent methodologies, approaches, and theoretical assumptions. Whereas the Frankfurt School's legacy of pessimistic analysis of modern communications media left a strong impression on New Left critics in the United States, the cultural studies approach to television from the Birmingham Centre for Contemporary Cultural Studies and the political economy approach from the University of Leicester in England broke new ground in critical media research. As John Fiske has noted, "The work of the two centers in Britain is both complementary and contradictory, and each proceeds along its own path in the knowledge of where the other is going. The comparative absence of the political economic perspective in cultural studies is perhaps less disabling in the United Kingdom than it is in the United States" (1989:21)—a perspective with which I agree.

In this chapter, I address the influence of Dallas Smythe in my own research and the directions of my work, along with that of my students who are concerned with "critical" communications research.

Dallas Smythe pioneered a particular variant of critical communications theory, first at the University of Illinois in the United States and then at Simon Fraser University in Canada. Coming from an activist tradition that emphasized policy intervention to check the abuses of state/capitalist power, he distinguished between administrative and critical varieties of research. Administrative researchers approached the study of communications assuming "perfect knowledge" and generally served the needs of its sponsors (corporations, governments, and nonprofit organizations), thereby becoming apologists for the status quo. Critical researchers, on the other hand, situated themselves against the "dominant" and developed their own form of discourse. Smythe drew a sharp distinction between certain tendencies in critical communication theory:

> Critical Marxist theory in communications has the transdisciplinary scope of the social sciences, humanities and arts. It ranges between, at one pole, spastic polemics against the status quo through "criticism," new or otherwise, of literature, drama or art, from a liberal or even anarchistic individualist point of view, to sharp critical analysis of communications phenomena in their *systemic* context. It is this pole where the cutting edge of critical theory exists. . . . And it is to be noted that this definition of critical theory does not require that it be explicitly or even consciously Marxist in nature. It simply requires that there be criticism of the phenomena in their systemic context. (Smythe and Van Dinh 1983:30)

Smythe cast a wide net to include liberal variants of communications research also under the rubric of critical theory, as long as it was sensitive to the question (central to him): How do these media phenomena serve capitalism? It is interesting, however, that Smythe's work is not taught in many of the prestigious universities in the United States and Canada where communication is studied from a "critical" perspective. His book *Dependency Road,* which raises critical questions related to Canada's dependence on the United States, could not be published in Canada. Response from Northwestern University students to Smythe's work, however, has been positive, although they are critical of his assertion that watching television is "work."

Personal and Political

Growing up in a liberal, politically engaged family in India, I was always concerned with the larger questions related to social change. My own professional training and subsequent work in India consisted of making films, some development-related documentaries but most in the mass-oriented cinema in the South. I came to the United States in 1969 to get advanced education in mass communications, for I believed that much could be done with social uses of television technology. What I found in the academy, however, was the narrow (and often narrow-minded) positivism that excluded questions of import to me. Class, caste, race, gender, and other structural barriers to social development (which were to sweep the academic field later on) were not yet of interest to communication scholars at major universities in the United States. I also found that the ideologically constructed "development communication" field and its spokespersons (Lerner, Schramm, Rogers, et al.) were studied at these universities in an uncritical way. When I was going through these introspections (as the academy did not allow them in its curriculum), I ran across an article written by Dallas Smythe on what needs to be done in communication research. It just so happened that Smythe was teaching at Simon

Fraser University by then, just 150 miles from Seattle, where I was living. I decided to visit him, and looking back I see that this changed my whole life.

Dallas Smythe was the exact opposite of the many professors ("experts") I had encountered in my graduate education until then. His silver gray hair was worn long, almost to his shoulders. I remember the crimson jacket he wore that day quite vividly. His first statement after listening to my research interests was, "I don't know a damn thing about India. It is such a complex country that I've never been able to understand it." I knew well that he was genuinely interested in underdevelopment and its relationship to imperialism and neocolonialism. His humility (by then he was nearly seventy years old and was head of the department at Simon Fraser), however, was striking, a signifier of a good teacher for me. I assured him that what I needed to learn from him was his critical approach, which he called the political economy of communication. India, I believed, I could study on my own. He had a good answer to that: "I know Hari Sharma, a Marxist sociologist who writes about India, and if he were to supervise you for a year, we may be able to accomplish our goals." Smythe was very excited about China at that time, and he was studying Mao's works. My broad interests in media and social change perhaps appealed to him.

Another important motivation for me to pursue critical research in the academy was the fact that I had worked as a cinematographer for a CBS-affiliate television station in Seattle for almost three years. My part-time job consisted of shooting and editing news stories for the evening and weekend news. That experience left an indelible impression on me about the structure and function of news in society, the daily routine and the rigors of the production process, and the issues of corporate control over content and form. Simon Fraser's interdisciplinary program allowed me to include such concerns in my academic development, whereas that would have been stifled at the University of Washington.

In the 1960s, Simon Fraser was a hotbed of radicalism. Not only did professors and students organize against the U.S. war in Southeast Asia and Canada's collaboration in it, but they also opened up the whole question of power at the university for popular participation. Closely held decisions by faculty—departmental budgets, teaching assistantships, tenure, promotion, hiring/firing, and so on—were opened to students in some departments. There were student members with voting power on important committees where decisions were made. By the time I arrived to study with Smythe, however, the administration had fired a number of professors in political science, anthropology, and sociology to "cool" the campus.

Racism in the city and on campus was on the rise, and the "targeted scapegoats" in British Columbia were the immigrants from the Indian subcontinent. A few of us from India, Sri Lanka, Bangladesh, and Pakistan got together to organize the South Asia Students Association, the first of its kind on that campus with its primary focus on political education. We did alternative media work and regularly screened critical documentaries on campus that allowed students to discuss issues of poverty, migration, race, class, and gender on a global basis. We also took our media work to unions and churches to have them consider the Asian minorities in a humane way as opposed to the dominant media representations.

My development as a scholar and my work in the community grew in a related, parallel way in this period. It was extremely gratifying to see my two principal teachers—Dallas Smythe and Hari Sharma—come to the many meetings and rallies we organized on and off campus. By doing that, they taught me how to be a good, nurturing teacher.

Working within the paradigm of political economy of communication, which offers tools for inquiring into the institutions, policies, products, and audiences of communications industries, I've attempted to expand its concerns. Political economy is particularly powerful for explaining macro structures and their relationship with larger, global institutions in human society. For example, a great deal of interesting research was done on imbalances in the flow of information by political economists in the 1970s and 1980s that contributed to the UNESCO debates on a New International Information and Communication Order. A large body of work also assesses the power of the media in agenda setting and reproducing capitalist relations.

Critics of political economy point to the fact that although political economists are correct in studying the shifting sands of economic control of media, they cannot simply assume that to be a "sufficient" explanation of cultural and ideological effects (Hall 1980:15). For any ideology to survive, it has to be reproduced on an ongoing basis. Furthermore, challenges to the "dominant" have to be incorporated in the media discourse. Otherwise, the media will have no credibility with their audiences, especially in democratic societies where free choice is a key ideological dimension. Besides, resistance to the dominant ideological formations has been a long-term historical project of people around the world, whether in folklore, song, drama, cinema, or whatever they have at their disposal.

Since it was conceived a generation ago, critical communication research has changed in a significant way to include important questions relating to the text and the audience. Researchers have also been interested in how the media construct the "subject," or the viewer. J. Curran et al. noted this development: "The combination of Althusserian Marxism and semiotics provided the initial impetus for sustained work on media texts. By largely suspending the traditional Marxist concern with the external social and economic determinants of ideology, in favor of a focus on the internal relations of signifying practices, such as film or television, structuralist media research formed the theoretical space within which to carry out detailed textual analysis" (Curran et al. 1982:24). They point out that structuralist studies have moved beyond the Althusserian problematic of ideology embodied in film and television to theorize the relationship of texts to subjects:

"The subject, constituted in language, in Lacanian terminology, is not the unified subject of the Althusserian formulation and traditional Marxist view, but a contradictory, de-centered subject placed across the range of discourses in which he or she participates" (Curran et al. 1982:25).

This may have had something to do with Smythe's 1977 article, "Communications: Blindspot of Western Marxism," which created a transnational debate about audience commodity concepts. Smythe was critical of the structuralists, as well as certain variants of poststructuralist research, because they ignored the economic context in which these commodities were produced and promoted (demand creation). As Morley put it, sophisticated forms of textual analysis arose and important work originated around the question of language and subjectivity:

> Unfortunately, however, it often fell back into an assumption of textual determinacy whereby the subject was presumed to automatically and necessarily "assume the position" preferred by the text, thus seemingly evacuating any need for empirical investigation of the audience. This textual determinism has been questioned recently, however, and in recent years the empirical study of the audience has once more acquired a credible status within this critical perspective. (Morley 1988:26)

Researchers are not only asking what real "people" (defined as interpretive communities of workers, peasants, teenagers, gangs, readers of romance novels) think of what they see and hear but how they deal with media messages that are aimed at them.

Critical Projects: A Convergence

Given these concerns, let me take two areas of study and identify some texts that have gone beyond the traditional political economy approach to media study. In the study of advertising, for example, one finds a substantial body of critical materials. Stuart Ewen (1976) provides a historical account of the development of the institution of advertising in the United States, but he attempts to "read" the messages as well, thereby establishing a connection between the advertisements and the economic/social context. Sut Jhally (1990), on the other hand, elaborates on Marx's concept of fetishism and considers advertising images. Armand Mattelart (1991) examines the twin currents of globalization in contemporary international political economy—accumulation of capital on a world scale and the spread of privatized networks of communication with their attendant advertising imagery. However, none of these scholars examines what audiences "do" with these images/messages.

In the 1960s and 1970s, Herbert Schiller argued the cultural imperialism thesis in an attempt to expose the self-serving doctrine of the "free" flow of information that was practiced by the United States around the world. Schiller and others pointed to penetration by capitalist media technology and program production practices as a "Trojan horse" spreading commercial culture, which was aided by the military and economic might of the United States. Some scholars also pointed out that the spread of commercial culture meant a leveling of national or local cultural production at best and stunted development at worst.[1] What remained a puzzle, however, was that not only did imported media products (American or otherwise) and their forms remain popular, but as alternative media became available (such as CNN and BBC-TV), viewers expressed ambivalent attitudes toward the United States, and, in some cases, were quite critical of its policies.

Although critiques of the cultural imperialism thesis for not being sufficiently nuanced about differentiated audiences and their appropriation and use of media for their purposes have existed for some time, a number of researchers around the world have tried to test it among different audience members. What is lacking, however, is the broad perspective to locate cultural interaction in an ongoing historical process. People make allowances for the "alien" culture within their own. Very often, we find new art forms developing as a result of this intercourse. Take for instance, "Gandhara" art, which emerged in India after Alexander's attempted invasion of the subcontinent. Indian sculpture went through a transformation that combined elements of the Greek and Indo-Aryan styles of the period, and a "new" form appeared. I wonder whether intellectuals at the time thought of this as inflicting "violence" on Indian art; from our vantage point today, it simply appears as an interesting development in Indian art.

My own research has included a more cultural approach combined with political economy in the sense that it attempts to include questions of media consumption contextualized as lived experience. This has evolved gradually, as a process of learning from faculty colleagues and students at Northwestern and addressing some of the critiques of political economy. My department is eclectic in the sense that my colleagues come from both the social science and humanities orientations, and our students' interests include the production/aesthetics of film, video, and computer graphics, as well as institutions and public policy. It is on this background that I have been able to keep an open mind about disciplinary boundaries, an experience that I believe has enriched my own intellectual development.

Instead of resorting to the base–superstructure dichotomy in a mechanistic fashion, Smythe struggled to identify the contradictory process in which humans reproduce themselves. In a number of projects in the last ten years, my students and I have attempted to deal with precisely those contradictions to answer the question, How do people cope with a system of economic/cultural alienation, and what "lived experiences" help us unravel those contradictions? We look not only at the institutional processes of how the media are produced and marketed but also at how they are consumed and with what consequences.[2] Let me outline below some of the projects.

K. R. Kamphoefner (1990) did a study of poor women of Cairo, Egypt, and their responses to the literacy programs offered by the government of Egypt. She learned to speak Arabic and spent more than two and one half years living in Cairo, thereby establishing some trust with a number of women who became her informants. She found that literacy acquisition intersected with a complex web of ideological formations—patriarchy, class, gender, and religion. Her research indicated how these select groups of women made sense of their own desire to improve their lives with what was allowed under tradition, the day-to-day demands of family life, and work.

Kate Kane (1992) was interested in finding out how national advertisers, network television, and manufacturers of feminine hygiene–related products constructed a television discourse that could overcome social taboos and promote consumption. She also wanted to connect such agendas with how audiences read these commercials. She picked a Catholic girls' high school in Chicago and volunteered as a teacher, whereby she taught the students media literacy and rudimentary video production skills. The result has been an inspiring study of how young women can externalize their media knowledge by creating media messages and how the ideology of commercial television, the Catholic school, and capitalism can be made transparent by self-expression.

Sooyen Lee's dissertation project in Seoul, Korea, examines what makes American imported films so popular with Korean audiences. Her study is aimed at developing a critique of "cultural imperialism" by looking at market relations as well as at what Koreans "do" with what they see in American films.

My recent work has focused on India, which introduced national television in 1984. Most of their programming was locally produced until 1991, when unregulated satellite networks emerged to supply CNN, MTV, and other program fare (see Pendakur 1991; Rajagopal 1993). It is too early to tell whether the selective few who can afford to pay for these pay channels will amount to a significant group in terms of studying changing patterns of national cultural identity. What is disturbing and important to study in countries such as India is the rise of fundamentalist political parties and how they have campaigned against this "cultural invasion." Fundamentalists have also been adept at including such progressive ideas as secularism as "Western" and part of this "cultural invasion." They seem to have touched a chord with the majority community (Hindus). Interestingly, these national political struggles manifest in battles over symbols. The demolition of Babri Masjid, a sixteenth-century mosque, by Hindu youth organized by fundamentalist organizations on December 6, 1992, is just such an example of the embattled ground of identity politics.

These developments cannot be seen in isolation from what is going on in Europe and the United States. For instance, the rise of neo-Nazism in Germany, the reactionary forces in Thatcher's England, the attack on minorities in the United States, and the elimination of Muslims in Bosnia are signposts of the new fascistic cultural environment. Research and practical media work need to be done in laying bare the tactics of fascists in various countries.

I have embarked on a long-term project in a village in India to study rural culture and modern communication technologies. Planned as a study of changing social relations and the interventions made by communication technologies in people's lives, it is intended to further innovate appropriate methodological sophistication in the political economy paradigm. Combining elements of cultural anthropology and political economy, I am attempting to get at the questions related to how people in a social system negotiate with cultural technologies. In this case, urban communication systems interface with a rural population. What I am trying to do is to push the boundaries of political economy of communications itself by asking new and different questions about people, places, their identity, and how they make sense and meaning out of an increasingly complex and rapidly changing world. Expressed another way, it is a bottom-up study to see how the "local" is constituted by the "global," how individuals who may or may not be part of a group (caste, class, gender) in a village see themselves and their relationship through their communication practices now that they have CNN (to use it metaphorically!). Scholars in anthropology have begun to combine elements of political economy to inquire into social relations, and, similarly, this project combines political economy with ethnography (see Pendakur 1993).

Where Is Critical Communication Research Heading?

Since critical communication research was conceived about a generation ago, much has been done on the monopolization of the information and communication sector by the advanced industrialized countries (see Schiller 1989; Guback 1969; Mattelart 1991; Pendakur 1990). Excellent work has been done on (mis)representation and propaganda in the dominant Western media (see Chomsky and Herman 1979; Herman 1992; Frederick 1986).

Those issues not only have persisted but may have been compounded in the Reagan and Bush years. Globalization of national economies, the erosion of the nation-state as a power center, and reconsolidation of power in the rich North appear to be the salient features of this new condition. The breakup of the Soviet Union, the end of the cold war between the two superpowers, and the formation of powerful regional trade blocs have dramatically changed the world context. The vibrant debates surrounding the New International Information Order[3] practically ended when the United States and its allies withdrew from UNESCO. The United States refuses to rejoin UNESCO but still plays a king-making role from behind the scenes. It owes millions of dollars to the UN (and its agencies, including UNESCO), which member-states are obligated to pay in order to run the organization. Furthermore, the war against Iraq and selective use of economic and military power to punish some countries and peoples (Cuba, Nicaragua, Palestine) illustrate that the UN has been hijacked by the rich North. I am certain many students of international communication will devote their energies to studying communication as a process of power in the global political economy.

Much more needs to be done, however, in international communication, where dominance is reproduced by way of state or capitalist media and democratization of media is a necessary struggle. The immediate concern for many researchers, especially in different parts of the Third World, is repression of dissenting voices (particularly women) in both state-controlled and capitalist media. Many are also interested in which grass-roots media can be utilized with what consequences for building a consensus around issues of equity, justice, and awareness of human rights.

In the current world situation, where structural adjustment regimes (of the International Monetary Fund and the World Bank) impose privatization dogmas, more research should be conducted on how to create some public space for debate and dissent in the new mediascape that would emerge in the Third World. Researchers need to link up with local, grassroots organizations and artists to make their ideas useful in specific locales. This necessarily will focus scholars' work away from state-centered or supranational projects as were common in the 1970s.

Impediments to Critical Communication Research

The most difficult part of doing critical communication research is getting reliable data from corporations and governments. A cloud of secrecy hangs over much of the meanderings of capital. A scholar who needs to examine corporate decisionmaking on news content, for instance, finds it nearly impossible to gain access to the board rooms. Cultivating productive contacts that will assist in such entry into corridors of power is time consuming and hard. Occasionally, a journalist produces a book that gives us a good look at what happens inside a company; it becomes imperative for critical scholars to use such findings in their work (see Auletta 1991). Interviews with people-in-the-know have always been useful alternatives, although they are not as systematic as being allowed to observe decisionmaking at the board level. Because intercapitalist rivalry is common in any industry, powerful people and institutions often leak information.

Governments are known for secrecy, but the Freedom of Information Act was supposed to have allowed scholars access to data gathered by various government agencies in the United States. However, the Congress and the executive branch have imposed more restrictions over the last ten years, making it harder to get some kinds of data and costlier to access them. Finally, although electronic networks and databases have made it easier to have access to certain types of data that are in the public domain, costs related to using them can be prohibitive.

The nature of the questions that critical scholars ask and the approaches taken to study them are inherently unattractive to big funding agencies. For example, there may be funds available to study why birth control programs are not succeeding in different parts of the world and how to improve the delivery and usage of those technologies, but seldom can we find a sponsor who will encourage the study of how to empower the poor against encroachments on their bodies by the state or other institutions.

With the shock treatment given to UNESCO, ITU, UN Center for Transnationals, ILO, WHO, and so on by the Reagan–Bush regime and their cohorts in Europe, funding for critical scholarship from those agencies has nearly disappeared. What appears as a certainty is that global recession means fewer dollars for academic research in general and for critical research in particular.

Conclusion

This chapter has sketched the influence of Dallas Smythe on my development as a "critical" scholar and the new "roads" my work has taken since I studied with him in the years 1976–79 . Smythe's conception of institutions of power as dynamic and the role of critical research as one of identifying contradictions in order to make life better for all have left a permanent mark on my teaching and research. His concern with people's needs and appropriate tools for solving social problems are constant reminders that academic work does not have to be isolated and codified only for "ivory tower" discussions.

NOTES

1. For a case study of Canada's film industry, see Pendakur (1990).

2. Historians are also increasingly searching for ways to understand the merging of cultural products, social interactions, and politics. Just as there is convergence of political economy and cultural studies in communications, there appears to be a similar convergence of political economy and social history in the field of history. See Lipsitz (1990), Levine (1992), and Kelly (1992).

3. Throughout this book, the authors have referred to this movement variously as the New World and International Communication Order (NWICO) and the New International Information and Communication Order. In most cases, the reference has been standardized to New International Information Order (NIIO).

REFERENCES

Auletta, K. (1991). *Three Blind Mice: How the TV Networks Lost Their Way.* New York: Random House.

Chomsky, N., and E. S. Herman. (1979). *The Political Economy of Human Rights.* 2 vols. Boston: South End Press.

Curran, J., et al. (1982). The study of the media: Theoretical approaches. In *Culture, Society and the Media,* edited by M. Gurevitch, T. Bennett, J. Curran, and J. Woollacott. New York: Methuen.

Ewen, S. (1976). *Captains of Consciousness: Advertising and the Social Roots of the Consumer Culture.* New York: McGraw-Hill.

Fiske, J. (1989). Popular television and commercial culture: Beyond political economy. In *Television Studies: Textual Analysis,* edited by G. Burns and R. J. Thompson. New York: Praeger.

Frederick, H. (1986). *Cuban-American Radio Wars: Ideology in International Communication.* Norwood, NJ: Ablex.

Guback, T. H. (1969). *International Film Industry: Western Europe and American after 1945.* Bloomington: Indiana University Press.

Hall, S. (1980). Cultural studies: Two paradigms. *Media, Culture and Society,* 2.

Herman, E. S. (1992). *Beyond Hypocrisy: Decoding the News in an Age of Propaganda, Including the Doublespeak Dictionary.* Boston: South End Press.

Jhally, S. (1990). *The Codes of Advertising: Fetishism and the Political Economy of Meaning in the Consumer Society.* New York: Routledge.

Kamphoefner, K. R. (1990). A view from the bottom: Women of Cairo view literacy. Ph.D. dissertation, Northwestern University.

Kane, K. (1992). Feminine hygiene commercials: A political and symbolic economy. Ph.D. dissertation, Northwestern University.

Kelly, R.D.G. (1992). A H R Forum: Notes on deconstructing "The Folk." *American Historical Review,* 97:1400–1408.

Lee, S. S. (1993). U.S. popular films and South Korean audiences: A political-economic and ethnographic analysis. Ph.D. dissertation, Northwestern University.

Levine, L. W. (1992). The folklore of industrial society: Popular culture and its audiences. *American Historical Review,* 97:1369–1399.

Lipsitz, G. (1990). *Time Passages: Collective Memory and American Popular Culture.* Minneapolis: University of Minnesota Press.

Mattelart, A. (1991). *Advertising International: The Privatization of Public Space.* New York: Routledge.

Morley, D. (1988). Domestic relations: The framework of family viewing in Great Britain. In *World Families Watch Television,* edited by J. Lull. Newbury Park, CA: Sage.

Pendakur, M. (1990). *Canadian Dreams and American Control: The Political Economy of Canadian Film Industry.* Detroit: Wayne State University Press.

———. (1991). A political economy of television: State, class, and corporate confidence in India. In *Transnational Communication: Wiring the Third World,* edited by G. Sussman and J. A. Lent, pp. 234–62. Newbury Park, CA: Sage.

———. (1993). Political economy and ethnography: Transformations in an Indian village. In *Illuminating the Blindspots: Essays in Honor of Dallas Smythe,* edited by J. Wasko, V. Mosco, and M. Pendakur. Norwood, NJ: Ablex

Rajagopal, A. (1993). The rise of national programming: The case of Indian television. *Media, Culture and Society,* 15:91–111.

Robins, K., and F. Webster. (1988). Cybernetic capitalism, information technology, everyday life. In *The Political Economy of Information,* edited by V. Mosco and J. Wasko. Madison: University of Wisconsin Press.

Schiller, H. I. (1989). *Culture, Inc.: The Corporate Takeover of Public Expression.* New York: Oxford University Press.

Smythe, D. W. (1977). Communications: Blindspot of Western Marxism. *Canadian Journal of Political and Social Theory,* 3:1.

———. (1981). *Dependency Road: Communications, Capitalism and Canada.* Norwood, NJ: Ablex.

Smythe, D. W., and T. V. Dinh. (1983). "On critical theory and the political economy of communications," Unpublished paper (February 22).

PART TWO

GEORGE GERBNER

George Gerbner, Guaruja, Brazil, 1992 (Photo by John A. Lent)

George Gerbner

Born:	August 8, 1919, Budapest, Hungary
Education:	Ph.D., University of Southern California, 1955, USC "Best Dissertation" award; M.S., University of Southern California, 1951; B.A. (Journalism), University of California, Berkeley, 1942; University of California, Los Angeles (Psychology); University of Budapest (Folklore, Literature); Joseph Eotvos Realgymnasium Budapest (First Prize, National Literary Competition)
Employment:	
1989–	Professor and Dean Emeritus, The Annenberg School for Communication, University of Pennsylvania, Philadelphia
1964–89	Dean and Professor, The Annenberg School of Communication
1956–64	Research Assistant Professor, Research Associate Professor, Institute of Communications Research, University of Illinois, Urbana
1954–56	Lecturer, University of Southern California
1952–56	Instructor, El Camino College, Torrance, California
1951–52	Research Associate, Department of Cinema, University of Southern California; educational film consultant and production coordinator; author of television series, Los Angeles County Museum; collaborator with T. W. Adorno in studies in psychodynamics of television drama, Hacker Foundation, Beverly Hills, California
1950–51	Curriculum Assistant, Pasadena City Schools; Director and Editor, Pasadena Education Association
1948–51	Instructor, John Muir College, Pasadena; faculty advisor, college newspaper, yearbook
1947–48	Freelance writer; partner in public relations firm, Hollywood

1946–47	Editor, U.S. Information Service, Vienna, in charge of daily newspaper and news broadcast for U.S. forces in Austria
1942–43	City editor, reporter, feature writer, book reviewer, columnist, assistant financial editor, *San Francisco Chronicle*

Military Service:

1943–46	U.S. Army. Enlisted as private in Parachute Infantry; Editor of regimental newspaper, Camp Mackall, NC; joined Office of Strategic Services; missions in North Africa, Italy, Yugoslavia, Austria, Hungary, Germany; received field commission, Bronze Star award for operations behind enemy lines; honorably discharged as 1st lieutenant

Other Service:

Member, Corporation for Public Broadcasting/Annenberg School of Communications Project Council; Surgeon General's Advisory Committee on Television and Social Behavior; Board of Directors, International Communication Association; International Council of International Association for Mass Communication Research; numerous editorial and advisory boards, including Strategies for Media Literacy (San Francisco); Scott Newman Center Project (Los Angeles); Center for the Study of Commercialism (Washington, DC); *Project Censored* (Sonoma State University); International Advisory Board, Hungarian Television (Budapest); *Reseaux* (Journal of Communication, Technology, Society, Paris)

Research:

Research grant from University of Pennsylvania Research Foundation for an investigation of the communication history of the Russian coup of August 1991, 1992.

Director, study of women, minorities, disabled, and old characters on television, funded by Screen Actors Guild and American Federation of Radio and Television Artists, 1992

Director, study of violence on cable-originated dramatic television programs, funded by National Cable Television Association, 1991–92

Coprincipal investigator, comparative study of U.S. and Soviet television, under a grant from W. Alton Jones Foundation and the International Research Exchanges Board (IREX); principal investigator, comparative study of television in 12 countries, 1987–91

Director, study of women and minorities in television drama, funded by U.S. Commission on Civil Rights, 1991

Principal investigator, study on "Adoption in the Mass Media," under a grant by The Catholic Adoptive Parents Association, Inc., 1988–89

Director, project on "Violence and Terror in the Mass Media," under contract to UNESCO's Division of the Free Flow of Information, 1985–86

Principal investigator, study of alcohol and drug use and the mass media, under contract to National Institute on Drug Abuse, U.S. Department of Health and Human Services, 1985–87

Principal investigator, study of "The American Press Coverage of the Fourth Extraordinary Session of the UNESCO General Conference, Paris, 1982," under a grant from UNESCO's Division of the Free Flow of Information, 1984

Coprincipal investigator, research project, "Religion on Television and in the Lives of Viewers," under a grant from the Ad Hoc Committee on Religious Television Research, 1982–84

Coprincipal investigator, research project, "The Role of Television Entertainment in Public Education About Science," under a grant from the National Science Foundation, 1981–83

Coprincipal investigator, "Aging with Television" and "Aging with Television Commercials," projects designed to measure trends in television content and effects related to aging, supported by grants from U.S. Administration on Aging, 1977–81

Coprincipal investigator, "Cultural Indicators" project, designed to study television content and effects, supported by grants from Surgeon General's Scientific Advisory Committee on Television and Social Behavior, National Institute of Mental Health, White House Office of Telecommunications Policy, American Medical Association, 1972–80

Principal investigator, international collaborative study on the treatment of foreign news in the press of six countries—United States, Great Britain, West Germany, Soviet Union, Czechoslovakia, and Hungary, under a grant by International Research and Exchanges Board, 1971–73

Principal investigator, study of institutional structures and decisionmaking in American television, sponsored by the National Institute of Mental Health, 1971

Principal investigator, study of the portrayal of violence in network television drama, sponsored by National Commission on the Causes and Prevention of Violence and the Surgeon General's Scientific Advisory Committee on Television and Social Behavior, 1968–70

Project director, "A Comparative Study of Films and the Film Hero," funded by a National Science Foundation grant; analysis of personality structure of leading characters in U.S., French, Italian, Yugoslav, Czechoslovak, and Polish feature films, in cooperation with UNESCO and the International Sociological Association, 1964–67

Project director, "Mass Communications and Popular Conceptions of Education: A Cross-Cultural Study," funded by a U.S. Office of Education Cooperative Research grant; study of portrayal and of factors influencing the portrayal of teachers and schools in the mass media of the United States, Great Britain, France, West Germany, East Germany, Poland, Czechoslovakia, Hungary, and the Soviet Union, 1960–64

Investigator, research project on the portrayal of mental illness in the mass media, under a grant from National Institute of Mental Health, 1959–61

Editing, Publishing

Chair, Editorial Board, *International Encyclopedia of Communications,* Oxford University Press, 1983–88; Editor, *Journal of Communication,* 1973–87; Executive Editor, *Journal of Communication,* 1987–91; Coeditor, Oxford University Press "Communication and Society Books," 1985–91; Coeditor, Longman Communication Books, 1981–90; Associate Editor for Communication Theory, *Journal of Communication,* 1966–68; Book Review Editor, *Audio-Visual Communication Review,* 1958–68

Awards and Honors

Excellence in Media Award, International Television Association, 1992; Distinguished Visiting Professor, American University, Cairo, Egypt; Commencement speaker and recipient, honorary degree, Doctor of Humane Letters, Worcester State College, Worcester, Massachusetts, 1992; First Wayne Danielson Award for Distinguished Contributions to Communications Scholarship, University of Texas at Austin, November 1991; Honorary degree, Doctor of Humane Letters, Emerson College, Boston, 1989; "Broadcast Preceptor Award," San Francisco State University, 1982; "Media Achievement Award of Excellence," Philadelphia Bar Association, 1981; "Communicator of the Year" Award, B'nai B'rith Communications Lodge, 1981; Honorary degree, Doctor of Humane Letters, LaSalle College, Philadelphia, 1980; Fellow, International Communication Association, 1979; Fellow, American Association for the Advancement of Science, 1972

5

Interview with George Gerbner

CONDUCTED BY JOHN A. LENT
GUARUJA, BRAZIL, AUGUST 19, 1992

George, tell me about your background, the days in Hungary, your education, your antifascist stands at various times, and your entrance into the American culture. At the same time, discuss the motivating factors that have guided you down a different path in scholarship—factors dealing with personal, institutional, and academic situations.

I was born in Budapest, Hungary, in 1919, during the last real Hungarian revolution, short-lived as it was. I grew up in the 1930s under the rise of fascism, which eventually reached and began to dominate Hungary and began to dominate and oppress much of my own life and thinking. I was educated in a very good gymnasium (high school) in Budapest and became very much involved in Hungarian literature and folklore. I spent probably the most rewarding months each year of my teens in various villages in Hungary, living and working with the peasants and trying to learn their culture, their language, their dialects, collecting folk songs, folk tales. So my first academic interest upon entering the university was folklore and literature. I was fortunate since I was always good at what I was interested in but not in other things, so my grades were far from good enough for entrance into the university, which was a highly selective procedure. But it so happened that my school sent me, on the basis of a schoolwide competition and then a districtwide competition, to a national literary competition. The representatives from each high school—the winners of high school competition—competed for the national prize in Hungarian literature. And it so happened that I won the first prize in Hungarian literature, which led to an amusing incident at the end of our baccalaureate, a week-long examination. The day before that final day of the baccalaureate, the results of this national competition came out and were published in the newspapers.

The principal of our school came to the classroom where the final session of the baccalaureate examination was held and looked at the records and lists of graduating students and looked at mine and said, "They have made a terrible mistake in not recognizing this Gerbner who's so good," and in the presence of everyone, including myself, corrected every one of my grades to an A. That assured my admission to the university. It's one of the series of accidents, if you could call them that, that in many ways provided turning points for my life.

Now my matriculation at the University of Budapest was short-lived. Toward the end of the first year, in the 1938–39 academic year, I was about to be drafted into the Hungarian army. Although I had no particular objections at that time about serving in the army, I had grave objections about serving in the Hungarian army. So, I left the country, and although I had no money, about five dollars, my parents bought a train ticket to Paris. I went to Paris (this was in the spring, I believe, May of 1939). I recall that just while I was on the train into Italy (I was going to Paris through Venice and Genoa, and then the Riviera, and then to Paris), the Italian army marched into Albania. (So we can fix the time by that particular event.)

I arrived in Paris without any money. There is no need now to recount interesting experiences of a penniless Hungarian arriving in Paris. But I did eventually meet some relatives of my parents who lent me the money for a passage to wherever I could go. Now by that time (I have to fill in a few minor details)—I had a half-brother, Laslo Benedek (we have the same mother, different fathers; his father, my mother's first husband, died; my mother remarried and then I was born). He was about fifteen or sixteen years older; he recently died. He was a film director, and by that time he had gone to Hollywood. So my ultimate objective was to come to the United States. It turned out that I could not get a visa to the United States; this was in 1939. The visa list for Hungarians under the American quota was filled for about twenty-five years and I was not about to wait twenty-five years for that visa. So I had to bribe a consulate official to give me a visa to Mexico, which I learned was not unusual; it was pretty much the common practice, and I got a passage on the French ship, *Flanders,* (a wonderful passenger liner) which was, incidentally, sunk in World War II. The only passage open at this time was a first-class passage. So I was traveling first class but had no money, which led to an embarrassment later on of not being able to tip the people who were kindly serving me. I arrived in Mexico on a tourist visa valid for six months.

My stay in Mexico was interesting, rather difficult, because again, I had no money. Within about two or three weeks, I became a guide, a tourist guide, even though I spoke very little Spanish. I was staying in a boarding house where mostly American tourists—particularly, for some reason, American schoolteachers—came in their cars. They knew that I didn't speak good English, so they assumed that I spoke excellent Spanish, which I did not. I offered my services to be their guide in their cars and to take them to places that were "off the beaten path." That was very easy because I didn't know what the beaten path was. So almost everywhere we went—I picked out some places on the map—was off the beaten path. We drove into the main square of a small town or village and I said, "Now we'll stop right here while I go out and make arrangements." I had enough knowledge of Spanish to go to some fairly clean-cut, local native hotel and say here is a group of tourists and how much would it cost. The accommodations were extremely cheap. They were usually clean and dependable and secure, so I would go back to the car and say that everything was arranged. This way I got around Mexico, including Acapulco at a time when Acapulco had only one more or less modern hotel, and I basically had a wonderful time.

At the end of six months, my visa was up and by that time the war had broken out in Europe. I went to the American consulate and said, "I would like to go to Los Angeles where I have a half-brother." About six months before, I had applied for admission to UCLA as a foreign student and I was accepted, but I couldn't get there because I had no American visa. The consul said, "Well, I don't know exactly what to do with you. I'd like to help you, but you know there is an American law that says that if you arrive in an adjoining country to the United States, which could be either Mexico or Canada, you cannot enter even legally or in any way through the border." That is in order to avoid illegal entries, which is a joke, because thousands of people are making illegal entries every week and were then, but anyway, that was the law, and so he said, "My best advice is that you go to Havana which is separated by water. Go to the American consulate there and see what they can do for you." So again, begging and borrowing money for a passage, I went to Havana, went up to the American consulate, told them what the situation was, and the American consulate said, "I don't know exactly how to resolve your situation either, but it's not going to be on my conscience to send you back to Europe—the war is already on, and very clearly, you have no possibility of safely arriving in Hungary, so I'll give you permission to leave Cuba and to go to New Orleans on a ship that's going from Havana to New Orleans and see what they will do with you."

So I arrived in New Orleans. My half-brother had alerted some friends who lived in New Orleans to wait for me in the Port of New Orleans. When I arrived at the port, we were lined up to examine documents but in addition to documents to examine the amount of money that we had with us. I didn't have enough money, so I was taken down to the Customs House. They had a hearing and I was ordered deported. As the hearing was over, a kind soul at the end of the table said, "You know, you can appeal." Nobody formally informed me of any rights. This was a person who had the decency to inform me at least after the hearing was over. So I raised my hand and I said, "Yes, I wish to appeal." That was considered a great nuisance by everybody because they had to sit down again and consider the appeal. Finally they said, "Okay, your appeal goes to Washington. It will take about two weeks. You have to stay here in New Orleans. Do you have any place to stay?" I said, "Yes, as far as I know there are people waiting. I hope they're still waiting for me outside."

I was discharged from this hearing to the custody of these friends, who happened to be the director of the Theatre Le Vieux Carré, a well-known community theater in New Orleans. So I was their house guest. They took me to their home, and there was another house guest staying at the same house, whom I met on my first day in the United States, and his name was Sinclair Lewis. So upon arrival I was a house guest along with Sinclair Lewis, most of whose books I had read in Hungarian, so that was a great experience.

After two weeks, the verdict came back that I could be admitted if I put up a bond of two hundred dollars. That's what this was all about; for only two hundred dollars, which was more in those days than it is today, they would have, without any pangs of conscience, deported me to a totally unknown destination. I cabled my brother, who borrowed two hundred dollars from friends and sent it to me.

I hitchhiked to Los Angeles, entered UCLA, but I was dissatisfied because, before I left Hungary, as I mentioned, I was interested in literature and writing, and the closest to that that I could get, my thought about that was journalism, and UCLA had no journalism, so soon thereafter, I transferred to Berkeley, and journalism.

A little-known fact of recent history is that in 1939 Hungary declared war on the United States, and that classified me as an enemy alien, which was no great problem, except that I had to report once a year. But what that meant was that I could not volunteer or be recruited into the American army.

I graduated in journalism from Berkeley. My stay at UCLA and to some extent even at Berkeley really consisted of trying to sort out my own experiences. The experience of living under fascism, of a certain amount of antifascist activity as much as a teenager can engage in, of knowing great people who sacrificed, struggled, who were jailed, who were martyred, many of whom were Communists, and of becoming very much interested in their lives, in their activities and their cause. My interest in joining the American army also stemmed from that.

After graduation, I got a job on the *San Francisco Chronicle,* where I was working in many capacities on the copy desk as a copy reader, headline writer, reporter, book reviewer, critic, and finally assistant editor, where I think I originated the first consumer column in the country, if not in the world. I was not an economist and not a financial expert, but I knew that during war conditions consumers required a great deal of knowledge about the regulations, the shortages, the quotas, and the various rationing, and I conceived of the idea of writing a column for the consumer about what the consumer needed to know.

Along about 1942, the American army needed men sufficiently to abolish the ban on foreigners, even enemy aliens, so at that point I was permitted to be inducted into the army, which I was. There was one option available. I was determined that if and when I got into the army, I didn't want to do a desk job or whatever I would be doing as a civilian because, you know, I felt that I could contribute to the war effort and to the antifascist effort as a civilian just as well as long as I was writing or editing or doing newspaper work—for that I didn't need the army. So when the inducting sergeant said, "There isn't much choice, but there is only one thing, if anybody wants to join the paratroops, step forward." I almost automatically stepped forward, and he said, "Well, you turn to the left, everybody else turn to the right." I went to the left and I was told to take a train to Fort Benning, Georgia, for paratroop training. So I underwent paratroop training, was assigned to the 541st Parachute Infantry in Camp Mackall, North Carolina.

When I heard that the regiment was about to be sent to the Pacific, I said, "Uh, uh! This is not my destination." So I went to Washington and visited with the OSS (Office of Strategic Services), which was the intelligence arm of the American army, who interviewed me and nodded and said, "Well, goodbye, don't call us. If we need you, we'll call you." In less than two weeks the order came down to my regiment saying, "Private First Class Gerbner report to Washington" at a certain place, which I did, and I was recruited into the OSS in the Operational Group called OG. There were two major field arms of the OSS. One was called OG, Operational Groups; the other one was called SI, Secret Intelligence. I was assigned to an Operational Group, which was a group of about fifteen trained to do small missions—sabotage, blowing up roads, bridges, etc.—and we underwent some training and were sent to North Africa. I had an extended and very pleasant period in Algiers and further training but basically was waiting for a mission.

Soon thereafter came the invasion, the landing in Normandy and Marseilles and so on. At one time we were supposed to go there, but that didn't materialize and we were taken to Italy, where the war was still going on. In Italy, since things went so slowly, I requested a transfer from OG to SI, which was granted, and I was sent to Bari, from Naples to Bari on the other side of Italy, for further training, and on, I believe, January 15, 1945, I parachuted with two others into occupied territory. The two others included one Austrian who was native to the area where we were supposed to land and another American soldier of German extraction, and I was an American soldier of Hungarian extraction, speaking some German, but no other of the related (Slavic) languages.

So on about the 15th of January 1945, the three of us jumped by parachute in what originally was designated to be a target in southern Austria. It so happens that the crew flying us—it was their fortieth (last) mission, and we ran into some flak, some anti-aircraft fire, and I guess, I can't blame them—they decided we were back in the hold, they didn't need us, they just knew that there were three guys who were sitting back there waiting for the target and their communication with us was simply a "green light." When they pressed the button, we were supposed to jump. Well, they pressed the button a little too soon, so they could turn back a little faster, and we landed in very strange territory—across the Drava River, actually in Slovenia, which was a surprise to us. We landed in very mountainous territory instead of a plateau, which was our original designated landing site. So we were separated in the air and never found the Austrian partner.

The other American and I found each other after some searching. We landed in seven feet of snow, in strange terrain. Soon after we found each other, only a few miles from us, all of a sudden the street lights went on, which was a big surprise because we didn't know we were that close to inhabited territory. In fact, we were not far out of Maribor, and at that point we knew that something was very wrong and that the Germans by now were probably after us. So we started climbing the mountain as rapidly as we could, living on our emergency rations that we had in our pockets for about three or four or five days in big snow, occasionally singling out certain farmhouses and going in and asking for food, claiming—this was our cover story—that we were American flyers who had to bail out and asking about the partisans. At first, nobody knew anything about the partisans, but the higher we got—and the language we spoke was German and most of those people in that area, since it used to be part of the Austro-Hungarian empire, did speak it, especially the older people—so as we got higher and higher, they seemed to know more and more about the partisans. One night, they said, "Well, just go to sleep here on the floor and we'll see what we can do." The next morning there was a partisan courier who took us to one of the brigades operating in that area. For the rest of the duration of our stay, we were with the partisans. Germans were retreating from Greece and trying to secure their communication lines against the partisans working in the area and trying to cut off their rail and road transportation. So we were under severe attack. A brigade that started out with maybe 350 or 400 men, at that point, when we joined them, was down to about 60 or 70 or 80. And that kind of struggle for survival lasted, in fact, until VE Day.

When VE Day came, we changed places with the Germans—we went on the roads, the Germans went up to the hills because they did not want to surrender to the partisans, who fought the Germans furiously.

We in the meantime found our way to Trieste, and then back to Foggia in Italy, our headquarters, where we had been reported missing because they hadn't heard from us (through partisan radio) for quite a few weeks. We were sent to a rest camp, a very nice camp in Italy, where, after two days, I was paged and told that rest was over, there was a large army of about 250,000 Hungarians who had fled from the Russians and camped on the Austrian countryside. No one knew who they were, so would I mind going up and finding out who they were and trying to dispose of these people, or at least report what should be done. So I was flown to Salzburg and given all the necessary provisions—a jeep and a jail, which was what I needed. With an American sergeant also of Hungarian extraction, we started to explore the countryside to find out what this was about. We found the Hungarian prime minister, a pro-Nazi politician, his general staff, his high command, his cabinet, and about 250,000 men who were encamped under their command. So I had the privilege of arresting the prime minister under whom I left Hungary and his entire general staff and his high command and of taking them back to Budapest for war crimes trials. I followed some of these trials because soon thereafter I was assigned to the American military mission in Budapest. I was somewhat comforted by the impression that those were real trials; some of these people were acquitted, some of them were convicted, some them were executed, including the prime minister.

During my stay at the American military mission in Budapest, another turning point in my life was meeting my wife. I used to go to the theater, which I liked very much, and one evening I was invited to a party under somewhat false pretenses. I was there to impersonate another American officer, also of Hungarian extraction, for whom this party had been arranged but who was unexpectedly transferred to Vienna and could not attend the party. But only the host knew him. Everybody else knew that there was an American officer coming but didn't know who it was, so they asked me to impersonate this friend of mine whose name was also George, so that's how I attended this party.

Upon arriving at the party I saw this beautiful young woman sitting on a couch and I sat down next to her and, what should I say, I've been sitting there next to her ever since. I said, "I've seen you somewhere before." She said, "Uh ha, I heard that before." And I said, "No, I really saw you on the stage in such and such a play," and I remembered the part, which at least gave me some credibility. At the end of the party, I invited her to join me to go to the American officer's club not too far from there, just for a drink, and maybe a dance, and she said, "Well, I'm not accustomed to coming with two other young men and leaving with somebody else." Thereupon, given no choice, I invited the whole party to come and we all went to the officer's club, and that's how all of this began.

After a few months at the American mission in Hungary, I too was transferred to Vienna to edit a newspaper for the American occupation forces in Austria.

Ilona and I got married and she joined me in Vienna, and after a few months of that, we returned to the United States (to Los Angeles), where I had been registered as a member of the Newspaper Guild waiting for a newspaper job to turn up. While I was waiting, I got a call from the agency where I was registered and they said, "Mr. Gerbner, we don't have the job you are waiting for, but there is something else that came up in which you may be interested, at least temporarily. There is a teaching job in journalism at John Muir"—which was at that time a junior college in Pasadena. "The journalism instructor left abruptly." This was on Thursday. "They need somebody to start on Monday. Would you mind doing that while you are waiting for what you really want?" "Well," I said, "I may as well do it." So I started teaching that Monday. I must say I've been teaching ever since because I discovered something that I had never really—this is another one of those so-called accidents that provides a turning point for one's life—I discovered that indeed, that was what I really wanted. Although I liked journalism, I always felt like a hired hand, basically did what other people told me to do, and I found that as a teacher, and later on as a researcher, I found the style of life, the only style of life I know, in which you don't have to work for anybody else. Basically, you design your own program, and if you're lucky, you can conduct it with a minimum of interference and a certain amount of protection. The protection is never absolute. There is no such thing, but at least you have some claim to independence and freedom.

I started teaching, but I had no certification. In California at that time you could start on an emergency credential, provided that within two years you got the necessary credits and credential. So I started graduate work at the University of Southern California. I got my teaching credential, then I went on to the master's. I wrote the first master's thesis ever, I believe, on education and television. That was completed in 1950, before there was even a national television service.

Then, I entered a Ph.D. program in the only place where communication was taken seriously, and that was in the Audiovisual Department of the School of Education at USC under Professor James D. Finn. He was one of the pioneers in educational technology and in the audiovisual movement. I was fortunate enough to be his student and, later on, his friend, and wrote a dissertation on "Toward a General Theory of Communication." That was simply an attempt to summarize what was written and known about communication in the fields of history, philosophy, social psychology, sociology, and cybernetics. Out of the exploration and that dissertation came what is sometimes called the Gerbner Model of Communication, which has served me pretty well since. So, putting it all together, I came to the conclusion that communication is really where the action is—the political action, the social action, the cultural action.

I was not able to follow my literary interests and my literary career, which led me to publish a book of poetry in Hungary before I left, because literature and poetry are like music. If you don't do it every day, if you don't live in it, if you're not totally into it, you lose it. Being uprooted meant isolation from the language, from everyday practice in the language and its dialects, and its subtleties. I have never been able to recapture that in any language. So partly my circumstances and partly my own interests led me to become more a researcher, an analyst, and social critic of cultural production. This led me, after Pasadena, first to a part-time teaching position while I was a doctoral student at USC; then I was recruited to the University of Illinois by Dallas Smythe. I met Dallas while he was a visiting professor in the summer teaching in the Department of Cinema at USC.

I should come back, I think, to one significant episode. Even before I got my teaching job, while I was still looking for a job in Los Angeles, I became active in political life, as a volunteer worker and editor for a newspaper for the Independent Progressive party, the party that nominated Henry Wallace for president in 1948.

This was the beginning of the McCarthy years, and the California State Un-American Activities Committee came to the city of Pasadena, not so much to get at me—I was small fry—but to get at the superintendent, Willard Goslin, because he committed the unforgivable offense of redistricting the totally gerrymandered school districts of Pasadena in order to alleviate, if not abolish, racial segregation. That must have been a Communist plot, in their opinion, and the Un-American Activities Committee came down to get rid of Willard Goslin. They subpoenaed me because I was appointed to edit a school district newsletter for the Goslin administration. They had me on the stand for about forty-five minutes, asking what I was teaching, asking if it was true (it was) that I showed in my class the documentary film called *Races of Mankind,* based on anthropologist Ruth Benedict's work. They asked me if I was a member of a Communist party. I was not, and said so. Then they excused me without any further ado.

The law in California says, or said at that time, that if you are not notified by the end of the working day on the 15th of May that you have or not been reappointed, you are automatically reappointed. The 15th of May arrived, and four o'clock passed, four-thirty, four-forty-five passed, and I was not notified, so I thought I must have been reappointed. Five minutes before five o'clock, the phone rang from the Board of Education, and someone said, "Mr. Gerbner, we have to inform you that you are not reappointed for the next year." So I lost my job, which was very fortunate, because I got a much better job, but in the summertime—since we just had a child, and I needed a job—in the summertime, I became a research assistant at the Cinema Department at USC. That's how I met Dallas Smythe, who visited there that summer. And Dallas and his wife, Jenny, and the family became friends, and when I completed my dissertation, he proposed my appointment to the Institute of Communication Research, University of Illinois. That's how we arrived in Urbana, Illinois, where we spent eight years, from 1956 to 1964. During that time, I established some of the basic applications of my dissertation ideas and some other ideas about the analysis of the everyday cultural climate of our societies, in the United States, and eventually on a cross-cultural comparative basis.

One of the term papers that Jim Finn asked me to write while I was a graduate student in his class was, "What would you do if you were appointed the dean of a graduate school of communications? What kind of a program would you propose?" Well, in 1964 I was invited to become the dean of the Annenberg School of Communication. There was no faculty and there was no program to speak of. So the first task was to get at least two or three key people with whom jointly we could start building a new curriculum, which we did.

We defined the field of communications as a discipline that is focused on the process of human and social interaction through messages. This is a process that is on the periphery of every other social science discipline but at the center of none. We divided it into three parts: the concern over messages that ranges from semiotics to content analysis; the concern over the relationships between communicating parties, mostly sociological-psychological types of approaches; and, third, the concern over large social institutions that are in the business of producing and distributing messages. We built a strong faculty, established a Ph.D. program in addition to the initial masters' program, and I guess the rest is the history of the school. My own work has developed despite the administrative concerns because, although I was the dean, ours was by far the smallest school at the university, smaller than many departments. The reason we were a school and not a department had to do with the legal terms of the Annenberg grant, and that was purely extraneous but a fortuitous necessity, because it gave us a great deal of independence. A school of about ten to twenty faculty members had the same status as the medical school, the school of engineering, and the school of law, and so we were very independent and successful in trying to implement our own vision of our program, recruit our own faculty, and set up our own criteria and requirements for students. Since much of the administrative work in which I was involved was in my own field, unlike deans who administer a great variety of fields and disciplines, I was able merely to cultivate my own interests and use my own judgment as I worked with our faculty and students on building the school.

My own work then became an extension of a continuing attempt to analyze and try to understand the everyday symbolic environment in which we live and in which we develop our notions and mythologies about life and the world.

I was inevitably drawn into cross-cultural, comparative work because, in order to understand the cultural environment of your own, it's inevitable and necessary to compare it to others. My empirical work was always historically inspired and conceptually guided to test certain propositions about media and society.

More recently, I entered into and launched an activity that attempts to apply the conclusions, or at least the challenges, and many of the dilemmas that I found in my analysis, into a form of citizen action that my colleagues and I call the Cultural Environment Movement. It poses an enormous challenge and requires rethinking cultural policymaking.

George, you have gone a different path. There must have been some penalties over the years that you had to pay for doing that, and also for being politically active at various times. Could you talk about that?

Except for being uprooted from my family and native country, by and large, I've been very fortunate in that penalties were few, far between, and relatively easily remedied, like losing my job in Pasadena and other relatively minor things. The major price that I had to pay is not being able to put it all together in book form, doing mostly fragmentary work that exposed certain aspects of a critical view but never in a totally coherent way. That still remains to be done. As dean for a whole faculty and school, I had to be fairly prudent in expressing personal points of view. So I worked mostly as a researcher supporting conclusions by a great deal of evidence that is publicly and methodologically defensible. It was, in a way, a kind of fortified way of proving or testing propositions in which I was interested. It turns out that it is a very good way because if you get to be too polemical your opinion against anybody else's opinion has no special value. But if you can support your arguments and your conclusions with publicly credible, repeatable evidence, you assume an authority that otherwise cannot be gained.

There have been a few instances of my political interest arousing the ire of more or less powerful academic individuals, even some benefactors, but they were not fatal. As I said, my early experiences under the McCarthy era, and a few incidents, and a certain degree of isolation, and a certain degree of having to rely on one's own like-minded friends and colleagues for collegiality, for critique, and of being known as an analyst and a critic of the mainstream, rather than a part of the mainstream, is a price that I would consider well worth paying.

As to what I consider to be my major contribution—it's hard to say. I'd like to think that my major contribution is still to come in an attempt to synthesize and to put together many of the things that I have done. I am heavily involved in research projects, mostly outside-funded, contractual, or grant type of research projects that have kept me going and kept me extremely busy the past thirty or forty years. So, fighting brush fires and being involved in specific projects, applied to social issues, has in many ways fragmented my work into many parts. As I look at my work, if and when I have the opportunity to put it all together, I think I'll find that they are all organically connected.

How do you feel your research has been used by various sectors, and do you think it has been misused in some cases? Explain some of those. Also, what do you feel, in the field of mass communications studies, have been some of the important changes, let's say, since you began your research career?

Our research has been used in a great variety of ways, including misuse, but most of the misuse, so called, comes from people who have never read it, who read about it from newspaper accounts, or who read about it from other people's critiques, but who have never really taken the trouble to read it carefully. The major misrepresentation has been by the media. My research has always touched some issue of public policy. I am not really that interested in individual behavior. I think that if it were "totally understood" it could be more easily controlled. So I'm satisfied that that is a quest that's beyond, and perhaps should be beyond, our scope of interest. I'm interested in those aspects of culture that are policy governed, are governed by large-scale industrial, social, political interests. And for that reason, when my research gets into the industrial policy area, it is often distorted and used as ammunition for purposes other than those I intended. That is inevitable, but I try to resist or counter it as much as possible.

The best example is our violence research. We analyze violence as a demonstration of power and demonstrate its long-term consequences. There may have been more violent periods than the present, although I am not sure of that, but I'm sure that there has never been an era when every home was drenched with violent imagery. It is mass-produced, happily sanitized, violent imagery with which our children grow up.

When our violence research gets into the media, it is always interpreted in a law and order context. In other words, will it lead to or will it result in imitation, will it result in threats to the established order. The answer to that is yes, but on a relatively small scale. But that is a small price for the enormous pacifying effect of exposure to violence. Exposure to violence cultivates, in most people, a sense of insecurity, a sense of dependence, a sense of demanding protection, and a consequence of being more easily controlled. You make large parts of your population afraid and insecure and say, "Well I can help you and protect you," and you have the best historically developed and tested form of social control that anyone has devised. Media are simply not interested, and if they are, they would not want to look at violence from that point of view, as a way of terrorizing populations. They want to look at it only from the point of view of justifying further repression.

The theory of cultivation is different from effects as a kind of short-term change. Market-oriented communication research came to the conclusion that, well, media are not very effective; they just maintain preexisting ideas, but they really can't change people's ideas. The "limited effects" theory arose. It overlooks the fact that the reason why campaigns to persuade people to change their patterns of thinking and action are so limited is that the everyday cultivation of a consistent orientation is so strong. Those are the real effects of media. They are so strong that they are not easily changed. So I consider our cultivation research a strategic intelligence exercise. That doesn't tell you how best to mount a campaign, but it's going to tell you what you are up against. You're up against a daily long-term cultivation of stable tendencies that large communities absorb over long periods of time and that are not easily changed, unless there is a societal change. So the theory of cultivation has as its target the making of social policy. It demonstrates the difficulty of changing opinion and policy without structural change in society. Academics sometimes interpret this as assuming that there is a passive audience, that they are totally dependent. Of course, there are obvious individual and group differences, and cultivation analysis shows some of them. But it's the long-term continuities and commonalities that determine the formation of public policy, not all the individual variations that some people point to as a way of countering the implications of cultivation theory. I think that these reinterpretations and misinterpretations have a functional value of attempting to defuse or confuse the policy implications of our theories.

What do you feel are the most important changes in the field of mass communications that you've witnessed in the last generation or more? What do you think has changed in the area of critical studies in mass communications?

This is a difficult question to answer because there are so many different strands, and because the temptation and the risk of overgeneralizing from some selected examples are so great. So I approach this question with great hesitation.

On one hand, the study of mass communication and culture has moved to the center of social concerns. On the other hand, the trendy term "cultural studies" was often used to distract from the social policy focus. In many ways, it's a diversion and regression. But that trend has passed and systematic research of the media-dominated, increasingly commercialized, militarized, and globalized cultural environment is becoming the central arena of the national and international struggles for power and privilege and of the resistance to power and privilege and for a more equitable form of society. That the struggle is shifting from older arenas, including military, economic, and political, to the cultural arena. That this is where most of our battles are fought and going to be fought. So we find ourselves center stage, unprepared for our role, unrehearsed in our scripts, and not at all agreed as to what should be done. This is not unusual, especially for critical studies. But there are also very positive developments, such as in critical media literacy curriculum building. There is a demand for communication graduates to teach in liberal arts programs. There is anxiety among parent groups and citizen groups about our cultural environment. Indeed, the liberal arts today include, as an essential part of general education, an analytical view of the everyday cultural environment.

The more academic developments are going in several directions at once—some of them forward, some of them backward. The tendency of some theorists to become abstruse, involved in ideological terminology, or to quibble about "proper" methodology is inhibiting research, and it's a waste of time.

The inclination to look on research that is systematic, that is methodologically self-conscious, that looks at the real world and demands empirical evidence of a systematic and replicable nature as some kind of logical positivism is misplaced. It is both philosophically and historically incorrect. The encounter with the real world has been a liberating force. It liberated thinking from clericalism, from theocratic and other axiomatic propositions that were sacred and therefore not presumed to be available for critical scrutiny. That was the renaissance in art and science. I think it can and should continue to be a liberating force. It has the authority of systematic and representative views of reality behind it. There is no greater authority than the authority to be able to say, "You don't have to believe what I say. This is the way I make my observation. You do it for yourself and see what you find." That to me is the ultimate human authority. Anybody who throws that away because of some misplaced claim of ideological puritanism simply throws away the best political, social, academic, and intellectual tool we have.

All in all, I think communication studies as a systematic critical exercise is becoming more centrally located than ever before. The key question we should ask is not what is respectable to do, what has been successful, what the leaders in the field have done, but simply, Is it right? Does it make any real difference? Would the world be any different if I didn't do it?

6

The Critical Contribution of George Gerbner

MICHAEL MORGAN

For a dozen years, from a modestly staffed war room in Philadelphia, a quiet-spoken, self-possessed man from Hungary has been chronicling the collision of two colossi and explaining the impact of one on the other. The two colossi are the world of television and the world of reality.

—*Philadelphia Bulletin Sunday Magazine*, February 24, 1980

Hungarians Think the Darndest Things.

—Headline, *New York Times Book Review*, January 24 1993

What Is "Critical"?

It is extremely appropriate for the work of George Gerbner to be featured in a volume devoted to critical thinkers in communication. There is a hint of irony in this, in that at some times and in some quarters his theories (and especially his methodological approaches) have been seen as the *antithesis* of a "critical" perspective. This (dare I say) criticism stems from a false assumption, endemic in the 1980s, that the use of empirical research methods was somehow incompatible with the adoption of a critical stance; this presumed dichotomy, happily, seems to be breaking down in current scholarship. What goes around comes around.

I appreciate the helpful comments made by Larry Gross and Nancy Rothschild on an earlier draft of this chapter.

In order to assess anyone's critical contribution, it is first necessary, I suppose, to clarify precisely how one is using the adjective "critical." As Raymond Williams (1976) noted in reference to the related term, "criticism," however, it "has become a very difficult word" to define. To grasp the variety of senses in which the term is used, one has only to thumb through the Summer 1983 double issue of the *Journal of Communication* (edited by Gerbner and Marsha Siefert), devoted to the "Ferment in the Field" brought about by the ascendance of "critical" theories. In recent years, the problem has grown even more complex; the range and diversity of scholarly enterprises that have adopted the term (from law to ethnography to cultural studies, all with different shades of meanings and implications) is such that the label, now almost *de rigueur,* risks losing its meaning altogether.

There is always a temptation to define "critical" by means of opposing it to something else, for example, "empirical," "administrative," or "liberal-pluralist apologia." I will resist this temptation and instead will rely on the traditional (wimpy) strategy employed by at least one Supreme Court justice and numerous presidential commissions when confronted with the need to define "pornography": I know it when I see it. Indeed, it is difficult *not* to see the profoundly critical thrust that permeates George Gerbner's career.

In this chapter, I offer nothing as presumptuous as a full (or "objective") chronicle of his voluminous and varied work. Nor will I address the many specific professional activities and large-scale projects he spearheaded, such as the *International Encyclopedia of Communication* (1988), the numerous international conferences he organized at the Annenberg School, and his long tenure as editor of the *Journal of Communication,* despite the considerable impact all these endeavors have had on the field. I will only attempt to trace a few major highlights, those which I think have made and will make the most significant and enduring contributions to communication theory and research. In particular, because of my own biases and interests, I will emphasize Gerbner's ideas about *cultivation,* but I will also try to illuminate the critical threads that run throughout his writings.

Mesh of European and American Traditions

In 1957, Robert Merton sketched out what he saw as differences between "European" and "American" approaches to social research, the sociology of knowledge, and mass communication. For example, whereas European scholars sought "knowledge," their American counterparts amassed "information." Europeans studied the ideology of social movements; Americans surveyed the opinions of voters. Europeans tackled Very Important Matters in empirically questionable ways, with little concern for "reliability"; Americans brought great empirical precision to bear on trivial issues, with much emphasis on reliability. Europeans, working as lone scholars (presumably in dingy garrets, by candlelight), pondered incomprehensible theories about how ideas emerge; Americans, working in research teams (presumably in labs, wearing white coats), investigated simple models of how to change attitudes and affect behavior. The Europeans could conclude, "At least it's true"; the Americans could claim, "At least it's (statistically) significant." And so on.

These were generalized caricatures even in the 1950s, and although they are perhaps still recognizable today, the geographic distinctions are certainly less sharp than they may have been in the past. Because of historical happenstance, Gerbner was shaped by and trained in *both* traditions, and his work has always embraced both. (As *Newsweek* put it in 1982, his methodology "meshes scholarly observation with mundane legwork.") It encompasses, in some ways, the best of both worlds (which inevitably means it must suffer from some of the weaknesses and excesses of both as well). He understood the special *power* of empirical methods (why else would they be appropriated by powerful groups?), but he was usually able to avoid being *limited* by them.

Gerbner recognized that a general theory could be only partly confirmed by empirical tests derived from it and that, by extension, the failure of specific tests could not fully disconfirm the theory. This is another way of saying that he has never let data get in the way of what he believes, even when the data do not fit the theory. (I leave it to others to determine whether this counts as a virtue or a vice.)

Thus, a vital and lively synthesis of scholarly traditions underlies and informs Gerbner's contributions. This shows up in numerous ways. For example, Merton also claimed that the Europeans took the audience for granted and neglected any systematic analysis of it, whereas for the Americans the audience was uppermost. Also, Europeans were obsessed with broad patterns over the long run, whereas American research was often ahistorical. In all these and other dimensions, Gerbner's work has avoided either extreme. Instead of simply finding some comfortable compromise between them, it has dynamically combined them to forge new ground.

Freedom: Organized Diversity

In 1956, Gerbner wrote, "The structure of freedom is *organized* diversity whether it pleases or not." That statement, I think, pretty much sums up the point of his work. (The emphasis is in the original, and we will consider what it stands for later.) It is possible to identify three major phases in which Gerbner has worked to develop the implications of that statement, in different ways.

First, in the 1950s and 1960s, he developed multidimensional theoretical models of the communication process, in mediated and unmediated forms, and at micro and macro levels. These models both led to and elaborated the concept expressed in that statement. Second, in the 1970s and 1980s, he conducted and directed massive amounts of empirical research, under the aegis of a long-term research program known as the Cultural Indicators Project, focusing on television and devoted to documenting and analyzing the consequences of the absence of this "organized diversity." This work grew out of an earlier series of large-scale content analyses (of confession magazines, film heroes, and others) that were often international in scope, and from several cross-national studies of media institutions. Together, these studies bridged the first two phases. Third, in the 1990s, he has been struggling to mobilize a new social and political movement made up of public groups, unions, and professional and minority organizations and dedicated to the transformation of the cultural environment so that it might someday achieve that diversity and, by extension, become a liberating rather than a repressive force. (If that's not "critical," then what is?)

Gerbner (1990) has noted that "research rarely advances in a straight line," and the thumbnail sketch above may give the impression of a more linear scholarly itinerary than is in fact the case. Nevertheless, as we will see, there has been quite a bit of continuity in his work over the years, and some recurrent guiding themes. In retrospect, his work, for all its diversity, indeed seems to reflect some "natural" and coherent intellectual progressions.

Much of Gerbner's work has sparked controversy. This is fortunate; it would be far worse to be ignored. As he said in a recent interview (Closepet and Tsui 1992), "If nobody screams, you are not doing anything." There were, for example, heated debates in the 1970s with researchers from the television networks over the methods and findings of message system analyses (these debates were mostly, but not entirely, about televised violence). Yet it is safe to say that of all Gerbner's work so far, it is his ideas and the research findings about cultivation that have received the most attention—positive and negative—within and without the academic community.

How influential is Gerbner's Cultural Indicators paradigm? The current (1993) version of the full bibliography of "Publications Relating to the Cultural Indicators Project" runs more than twenty single-spaced pages. Bryant (1986) quipped that studies of cultivation seem "almost as ubiquitous as television itself." Bryant noted that a systematic study of more than 100 "Mass Media and Society" courses in U.S. colleges and universities showed that "cultivation was one of only three topics receiving detailed examination in more than half the courses." Moreover, he argued, "cultivation research is one of the few contributions by mass communication scholars to infiltrate" textbooks in such fields as social psychology and sociology "with some regularity." Clearly, his theories have been the object of considerable attention.

It is not simply the ideas themselves that account for the attention they have received. It is, at least in part, due to Gerbner's skill in "packaging" ideas, in framing them in memorable, and often alliterative, terms (e.g., "risk ratios," or the Three Bs: "blurring, blending, and bending").

The elegant simplicity and obviousness of the idea of cultivation accounts both for what has attracted its adherents and for what has antagonized its opponents. After years of intense theoretical and methodological development, testing, criticism, and refinement, however, it turns out that the cultivation process is in fact neither so simple nor so obvious. That realization has both guaranteed and fueled its continued prominence.

The issues involved in the debates over cultivation analysis have been discussed in overwhelming detail elsewhere and need not be repeated here. Nor will I describe the procedures, assumptions, and findings from the corpus of cultivation studies; that too exists elsewhere (see, e.g., Gerbner et al. 1986, 1994; Signorielli and Morgan 1990). The more important task here is to lay out the general framework of Gerbner's theory of cultivation and how it evolved. In some respects, the "roots" of cultivation have gotten lost in the barrage of charges and counter charges, in the ever widening spiral of conceptual and analytical refinements, and sometimes in hearty doses of theoretical (in Merton's terms, American?) statistical manipulations.

"Cultivation" as a concept did not emerge fully formed. Contrary to the way it is usually presented today (both by some of those doing cultivation analysis and by many of those writing about it), Gerbner's early theoretical arguments about cultivation were vaguer in their empirical implications but more complex and more ambitious in their theoretical scope. Over the years, researchers have, in some respects, increasingly and (probably) unwittingly simplified the notion of cultivation, stripping it of some of its subtler nuances while allowing its methodological and analytical aspects to become almost monstrously complicated and permutated.

The simplified and most commonly encountered version of cultivation says something to the effect that "watching a lot of television makes people afraid." This is the sort of description one might expect to find in the popular press, but all too often it appears in mass communication, sociology, and psychology textbooks as well as in scholarly articles. Indeed, results from cultivation analyses are often erroneously referred to as "cultivation effects," an unfortunately sloppy twist that tends to equate cultivation with the very assumptions, inadequacies, and problems it was designed to go beyond. By stepping back and looking at where the idea came from, it may be possible to reinfuse some of the richness of Gerbner's early ideas and theories into the current debates.

Focus on Messages

Gerbner attempted to alter the nature of the conventional discourse about the social and cultural implications of mass communication. His first struggle was to develop an approach to mass communication that saw it in terms different from those of persuasion and propaganda research and to escape the scientism and positivism of that research. (Later, he applied similar criticisms to experimental work on media violence.) He also argued for the need to dispense with traditional formal aesthetic categories along with conventional concerns about style, artistic quality, high culture vs. low culture, and selective judgments and interpretations. He tried to draw attention to the interplay of the *systems* of messages, in the aggregate, and of the institutional structures that produced them. In almost all of his writings over nearly forty years, he expressed fundamental disagreements with whatever dominant paradigms were currently in vogue. Any assumption, approach, or procedure that seemed widely accepted as the "normal way of doing things" was, by definition, suspect. (Again, if that's not critical, then what is?)

As did many others at the time, Gerbner focused heavily on "messages," but he imbued them with some special characteristics and functions. He acknowledged that messages were the "what" in Harold Lasswell's famous formula, but as early as 1958, he dismissed that conceptualization as "too restrictive and too one-directional for a a general theoretical communications model, or for a framework for critical research." From the start, he sought to develop models of the communication process that distinguished it from other forms of social interaction, and he sought to develop approaches to communication research—cast, importantly, as a form of *basic cultural inquiry*—that were distinct from dominant concerns with prediction and control. He argued that this was, by definition, a critical turn. In doing so, he drew heavily in those days on Paul Lazarsfeld's notions of critical vs. administrative research; in that context, his goal was to free the analysis of media content from the narrow limits of administrative research.

To Gerbner, any message is a socially and historically determined expression of concrete physical and social relationships. Messages imply propositions, assumptions, and points of view that are understandable only in terms of the social relationships and contexts in which they are produced. Yet they also reconstitute those relationships and contexts. They thus function recursively, sustaining and giving meaning to the structures and practices that produce them.

Communication to Gerbner is "interaction through messages," a distinctly human (and humanizing) process that both creates and is driven by the symbolic environment that constitutes culture. The symbolic environment reveals social and institutional dynamics, and *because* it expresses social patterns, it also cultivates them. This, then, is what I think Gerbner originally meant by "cultivation": the process within which interaction through messages shapes and sustains the terms on which the messages are premised.

The *production* of messages then takes on special significance, since the resulting social patterns imply cultural and political power—namely, the right to create the messages that cultivate collective consciousness. With *mass* communication we have the mass production of messages, the cultural manifestation of the industrial revolution. Given the social functions of messages, the mass production of messages and of the symbolic environment then represents a profound transformation in social relationships and power. He summed this up in 1963:

> Message-systems which provide many of the raw materials of our consciousness (and of the terms of our perceptions) have become mass-produced, institutionalized commodities. Bigness, fewness, and costliness in cultural, as in any other, mass production brought centralization of control, standardization of product, streamlined efficiency of technique. These changes meant increasing penetration of influence into many spheres of life and across many previous boundaries of place, time, and social status. (Gerbner 1963:35).

Since messages reflect social relationships, mass-produced messages bear the assumptions of the organizations (although not necessarily of the individuals) that produce them. Early on, he identified as a problem the fact that the major message-producing organizations tended to be profit-oriented, commercial corporations: "Industrial and market conditions and the corporate positions of cultural enterprises . . . implicitly shape the assumptions, contexts, and points of view embedded in mass media products" (Gerbner 1959:269).

Thus, the transformation of message production by the process of industrialization is only part of the story. The more central ("critical"?) point is that message production became dominated by commercial interests. Gerbner quoted Van Den Haag's (1957) observation, "Unless the requirements and effects of industrialization are fully grasped, popular culture does not become intelligible," and then added: "Even more specifically, unless the requirements and effects of a specific system of industrial and market relationships (such as the corporate structure) are fully grasped, mass media content analysis remains superficial" (Gerbner 1958:90). This warning has been lost on all too many of those who have conducted content analyses of media output.

Even in the 1950s, of course, it did not take any unusual gifts of wisdom or superhuman observational skills to realize that the mass media were advertiser-supported, profit-seeking businesses. What Gerbner did was to point out some of the less obvious implications of this arrangement in some new ways and to keep hammering the point home for almost forty years.

"We Are the Stories We Tell"

The key to Gerbner's analysis was to place special emphasis on the cultural process of storytelling. He drew on L. Lowenthal's (1957) notion that "man is born, strives, loves, suffers, and dies in any society, but it is the portrayal of *how* he reacts to these common experiences that matters since they almost invariably have a social nexus." (Presumably, Lowenthal did not mean to imply that these processes did not apply to women, although females certainly figure less prominently in the stories of Western societies.) Some years later, he argued that "whatever else they do, stories confirm authority and distribute power in specific ways. Story-telling fits human reality to the social order" (Gerbner 1986).

Gerbner contends that the basic difference between human beings and other species is that we live in a world that is created by the stories we tell. (I am quoting and paraphrasing rather liberally here.) All living organisms exchange energy with their environments. Many creatures process and exchange information, store impressions, and change their behavior as a result of learning. But only humans *communicate* by the manipulation of complex symbol systems.

Humans therefore uniquely live in a world experienced and conducted largely through many forms and modes of storytelling. Most of what we know, or think we know, we have never personally experienced; we "know" about things based on the stories we hear and the stories we tell. We are, he claims, the stories we tell.

Gerbner identifies three types of stories. There are stories about *how things work,* in which the invisible dynamics of human life are illuminated. These stories are called *fiction,* and they build a fantasy we call reality. There are also stories about *how things are*; today, we mostly call them *news,* and they tend to confirm the visions, rules, and goals of a particular society. And there are stories of value and choice, of *what to do.* These have been called sermons, or instruction, or law; today they are called *commercials.* Together, all three kinds of stories, organically related, constitute culture; they are expressed and enacted through mythology, religion, legends, education, art, science, laws, fairy tales, and politics—and all of these, increasingly, are packaged and disseminated by television.

Gerbner is especially fond of quoting Andre Fletcher of Saltoun (1655–1716), who wrote in a letter to the Marquise of Montrose: "If a man were permitted to make all the ballads, he need not care who should make the laws of a nation." Such a romantic notion is not easily testable by empirical methods, but that makes it no less compelling. Storytelling occupies a crucial role in human existence, and it is being increasingly monopolized by a small and shrinking group of global conglomerates whose attention does not extend beyond the bottom line and quarterly reports to stockholders. Therefore, the world we are inhabiting and (re)creating is one designed according to the specifications of marketing strategies.

A Multidimensional Communication Model

The impacts on those who consume messages and stories are not linear, mechanical, or hypodermic. Because this is a dialectical process (Gerbner 1958), the "effects" of messages are relatively *indirect.* Uncovering aggregate and implicit patterns in mass-produced messages "will not necessarily tell us what people think or do. But they will tell us what most people think or do something *about* and in *common*" (Gerbner 1970). This argument has some affinity to the notion of agenda setting, but it is cast on a deeper and more fundamental level. It is not so much the specific, day-to-day agenda of public issue salience that culture (and cultural media) sets as it is the more hidden and pervasive boundary conditions for social discourse, wherein the cultural ground rules for what exists, what is important, what is right, and so on, are repeated (and ritualistically consumed) so often that they are invisible.

In its earliest forms, then, "cultivation" had little to do with percentage differences between heavy and light viewers in giving "TV answers." Instead, it sought to describe the process by which mass communication creates publics and defines the perspectives and assumptions that are most broadly shared among those publics. In "Toward 'Cultural Indicators,'" Gerbner wrote:

> A message (or message system) cultivates consciousness of the terms required for its meaningful perception. Whether I accept its "meaning" or not, like it or not, or agree or disagree, is another problem. First I must attend to it and grasp what it is about. Just how that occurs, how items of information are integrated into given frameworks of cognition, is also another problem. My interest here centers on the fact that any attention and understanding cultivates the terms upon which it is achieved. And to the considerable extent to which these terms are common to large groups, the cultivation of shared terms provides the basis for public interaction. (1969:139)

Since the symbolic environment gives direction and meaning to human thought and action, cultivation is then the (continuous) outcome of interaction within the symbolic environment, assuring shared terms of discourse and behavior. The cultivation of "shared terms" and "collective consciousness," however, is not to be mistaken for *consensus:* "On the contrary, the public recognition of subcultural, class, generational, and ideological differences and even conflicts among scattered groups of people requires some common awareness and cultivation of the issues, styles, and points of divergence that make public contention and contest possible" (Gerbner 1969:138).

Moreover, cultivation is not in itself the punch line. Again, the point is not so much that it occurs at all (it is, after all, the historic and universal function of all sociocultural institutions and the stories they tell) but that the cultivation of collective consciousness is now institutionalized and corporately managed to an unprecedented degree. As mass communication creates publics, it can also dissolve (or blur and blend?) them. The *critical* point is that the "dissolution of publics into markets for mass media conceived and conducted in the increasingly demanding framework of commodity merchandising is the cultural (and political) specter of our age" (Gerbner 1958). Or, as he put it elsewhere: "The rise of cultural mass production, creating audiences, subjecting tastes, views, and desires to the laws of the market, and inherently tending toward the standardized and the safe rather than the diversified or critical, creates new problems in the theory and practice of self-government" (Gerbner 1959).

A few decades later, the analysis of television's contributions to political orientations (Gerbner, et al. 1982, 1984) only made that statement stronger. These problems, and the challenges to democracy they pose, may not be as "new" as they were in the 1950s, but we do not seem to be any closer to solving them.

In sum, Gerbner's early theories grew from his studies of folklore and literature at the University of Budapest and his studies of psychology and journalism at the University of California. Coupled with influences and arguments drawn from the works of T. W. Adorno, Franklin Fearing, Paul Lazarsfeld, Lowenthal, and others, this provided a unique mix and produced novel and provocative syntheses of these perspectives, culminating in an ambitious and multidimensional model of communication. The model itself (Gerbner 1956) did not really catch on, but its corollary notion of cultivation certainly did, especially as it evolved in the 1970s.

"Three-Legged Stool"

The mid-1970s brought about empirical testing of cultivation and some shifts in the original meanings discussed above—at least in terms of emphasis and focus. Earlier, Gerbner had discussed his "institutional approach" to mass communication as requiring the study of relationships between social structures, message systems, corporate forms and functions, collective image formation, and public policy. When it all came together under the cultural indicators umbrella, it became a three-pronged approach consisting of institutional process analysis, message system analysis, and cultivation analysis. "Cultivation" had thus become a form and technique of operationalizable, empirical analysis.

As it developed, cultivation analysis, put most simply, attempts to determine the contribution that differential amounts of television viewing make to people's conceptions of social reality. The main change from its earlier conceptualization was the incorporation of the empirical assessment of statistical differences in the beliefs, assumptions, and attitudes of light, medium, and heavy viewers. It is not clear from the early writings exactly how this particular strategy developed; compared to institutional and message system analysis, the operational and analytical terms and procedures of cultivation *analysis* were relatively unspecified, and any number of empirical approaches might have emerged. Yet, through Gerbner's collaboration with Larry Gross (Gerbner and Gross 1976), with his work on images of mental illness providing an interim conceptual model, that strategy became synonymous with cultivation analysis.

The trick was to investigate television's contributions to viewers' conceptions without directly asking people about television. Instead of asking people what they thought about television, people were simply asked about what they *thought.* Then, the question of whether or not amount of television viewing made a difference in conceptions could be addressed. This was not a minor methodological departure.

The more elaborated, data-based concept of cultivation was born in a time when over-the-air network broadcasting ruled people's media behavior essentially unchallenged. The term "broadcasting" originally meant to sow seeds at random. In that context, "cultivation" was the perfect metaphor, connoting "culture," which itself has deep etymological implications concerning the practices by which the basic human need for food can be nourished and sustained by means of livestock and agriculture (Williams 1976).

In one sense, and despite its aptness for describing the primary functions of culture, "cultivation" is an uncharacteristically land-based metaphor for Gerbner.

He has often been drawn to *water*-based analogies to describe the "sea-change" of television and its role in redirecting the "flows" and "currents" of cultural "tides" (not to mention the notion of the "mainstream"). Interestingly, in a recent interview (Closepet and Tsui 1992), Gerbner claimed to be unaware of his watery proclivities.

In any case, based on Gerbner's arguments about the cohesiveness of television content, cultivation analysis deals with overall, cumulative exposure to the total world of television. An individual story or program is simply "a drop in the ocean." This emphasis contrasted sharply to most previous research (and public debate), which tended to focus on individual programs, episodes, series, or genres, usually in terms of their short-term "effects" on viewers' attitudes and behavior. Such questions are not "wrong," and such effects are not unimportant; but they do not take into account what makes mass communication in general and television in particular different from earlier cultural media.

As Gerbner (1970) put it, "Most 'effects' research stemmed from theoretical perspectives that did not consider relevance to the mass-cultural process a principal criterion." When "effects" are defined as immediate "change" among individuals, we ignore the unique functions and distinctive features of contemporary mass communication—which means massive, long-term consumption of centrally produced, mass-distributed, repetitive stories among large and heterogeneous publics who never meet face to face and have little in common except the messages they share.

This issue—so central in all of Gerbner's work and at the forefront of many cultivation debates—continues to be important today, perhaps even more so given the spread of VCRs, the impending prospect of 500-channel cable systems, and other new technologies that on the surface appear to offer more "choice" and "diversity." The original premise was that since similarities among different content "types" are more important than their differences, what counts most is overall exposure to and immersion in the world of television. Indeed, it is this global, aggregate, general focus that differentiates cultivation from mere "attitude change" studies. But that's another story.

For now, however, it is worth noting that Gerbner (1966:96) defined the "effects" of communication as "the history and dynamics of continuities, as well as of change, in the reciprocal relationships between social structures, message systems, and image structures." The term "reciprocal" is important here, and is another indication that simplistic S-R (sender–receiver) models of cause and effect are insufficient and irrelevant to the idea of cultivation . A less unwieldy version of this formulation emerged in his "three-legged stool" notion of the relationships among (in effect) social patterns, media output, and public beliefs and ideologies; asking which of the three (i.e., media, culture, society) is the most important is like asking which leg holds up a three-legged stool. In this context, debates over the relationship between base and superstructure, or between materialistic and idealistic explanations for social and cultural phenomena, seem a bit quaint.

Communication is thus neither determinate nor symptomatic but rather an essential cultural nutrient. The critical task is to reveal the dynamics of power in communications and of communications in society, in order to transform them.

Violence and Television

Going back a bit, the "middle ages" were the heyday of the Violence Profiles and the 1972 Surgeon General's report, when an overwhelming amount of research and public attention was being paid to the question of television and violence.

Gerbner saw the problem of television violence in a different way from most others. The message data showed more victims than victimizers: they revealed a clear social pecking order, with some groups (minorities, women, old people) consistently more likely to be victimized. He hypothesized that rather than imitating the acts of violence they see, most viewers might be more likely to identify with *victims*—that rather than disrupting the social order, television violence maintains the status quo by demonstrating and protecting the power of the powerful. By cultivating fear, apprehension, and mistrust, television might contribute to a climate in which demands for security outweigh any remnants of concern about repression and violation of civil liberties. By cultivating "traditional" conceptions of women, minorities, older people, occupations, and so on, television's messages contribute to the maintenance of specific power hierarchies. The connection with the early version of cultivation is that, in both cases, mass-produced messages are seen as fundamental mechanisms of social control.

Violence played a special role in these theoretical developments, both because it was (and is) such a salient public issue and because of the remarkable and consistent frequency with which it is portrayed on television. Stories from mythology to fairy tales to the Bible to Shakespeare have, of course, prominently featured violence. But the sheer amount of violence that television brings into every home on a daily basis is historically unprecedented.

Moreover, what we are awash in (another water metaphor) is entertaining, thrilling, happy violence, quite useful and efficient for solving conflicts, upholding the social order, and demonstrating the consequences of transgression. (I am again paraphrasing liberally.) It is useful for mobilizing massive support for police action at home and for military action abroad, especially when enough of the audience (excuse me; I mean "the public") can be convinced that some "vital interest" is threatened or that some villain (from a Third World dictator to the errant motorist) "needs" to be punished. As a cheap production ingredient, it is useful for the creation of "product" (i.e., television programs) that can be more easily sold to broadcasters in other countries; unlike humor, violence travels well. Most of all, it is useful for delivering to advertisers audiences who are in a "proper" mind set for commercial messages.

The specific, observable, independent contribution of television to conceptions of violence and other issues was assessed by analyses of data from many surveys, comparing responses of heavy and light viewers, other factors held constant.

Other techniques were explored, but cultivation analysis has almost entirely meant the analysis of survey data.

As the data piled up and the reports churned out, Gerbner and his colleagues may have made some overly sweeping claims. The underlying theoretical premises were not forgotten, but there were some gaps between those premises, the empirical data, and the interpretations offered of those data. At the least, they admitted to being (a bit) guilty of "rhetorical excess." In fact, only one or two reports suffered from this "excess," and even there a good deal of scientific caution was expressed (see Gerbner, et al. 1978). Also, the "causality" issue—whether television viewing leads to or is symptomatic of social conceptions—refused to go away, even though it was seen as trivial and irrelevant by Gerbner, and despite longitudinal cultivation data showing an independent influence of amount of viewing on attitudes over time. But by then attention to cultivation analysis was skyrocketing.

Some of the attention took the form of independent replications and confirmations and refinements, but some took the form of (occasionally vituperous) criticism. Some of the criticism was helpful, some mildly annoying, and some beside the point. Some critics lost sight of the theory and became submerged in statistical minutiae. Only later did scholars begin to pay serious attention to the critical and epistemological underpinnings of cultivation theory (e.g., Good 1984).

In a letter to the *Pennsylvania Gazette* (March 1982), TV screenwriters Richard Levinson and William Link bemoaned their feeling that "we and many of our colleagues find ourselves wishing, perhaps in vain, that Gerbner will eventually recognize that people of good will may disagree with him, not because they're misinformed but because they simply think he's wrong." In contrast to this sentiment, Gerbner has demonstrated a willingness (even, at times, an eagerness) to incorporate into his ideas the kernels of truth in the criticisms directed at those ideas, in order to strengthen and advance them. The continuing development and elaboration of cultivation theory is witness to this flexibility.

Still, I have been involved in these controversies for too long and too deeply to claim more than a modicum of objectivity. It seems to me that cultivation came out of the onslaught stronger and clearer than ever—if not quite as simple (For further discussion, see Gerbner, et al. forthcoming).

Internationalization

Gerbner's original ideas and the intense work done in the late 1970s have branched off in dozens of directions. Researchers have examined a variety of conditions and variations of cultivation analysis—mainstreaming, resonance, the roles of cognitive processes, personal experience, selective viewing, perceived reality, new technologies, peer groups and the family, personal vs. society-level conceptions, and so on. Moreover, differences in cultivation patterns among different groups, and in numerous substantive and topical areas, have been investigated (for examples of recent advances in cultivation, see Signorielli and Morgan 1990). Cultivation theory and analysis have continued to develop and progress as new findings and conclusions have further extended and refined the theory.

An especially important outgrowth of Gerbner's work has been the attempt to carry out research in other countries and cultures under the cultural indicators paradigm. The development of cross-cultural, comparative analyses of message systems and cultivation patterns is a major challenge in theoretical, methodological, and pragmatic terms. It provides the opportunity to investigate how relationships between television exposure and conceptions vary according to diverse policies, structures, message patterns, cultures, and audiences.

Again, cultivation means that the dominant modes of cultural production tend to generate messages and representations that nourish and sustain the ideologies, perspectives, and practices of the institutions and cultural contexts from which they arise. It does *not* simply mean that television viewing universally fosters fear, apprehension, sex-role stereotypes, or other related conceptions. If a particular message system (and culture) contains a great deal of (for example) violence, then the media system of that society should cultivate corresponding conceptions; if it does not, then it should not. The fact that U.S. television repetitively portrays (and cultivates) a particular set of images of violence, sex roles, occupations, aging, health, science, social power, minorities, and so on does not mean that other countries' television systems, which may or may not disseminate similar images, cultivate similar views. The fact that most other countries import so much of their programming further complicates the picture.

The early 1980s saw a flurry of attempts to replicate cultivation analysis in other countries, mostly in Western Europe (England, the Netherlands, Sweden, and Germany), Australia, and Israel. More recently, cultivation has been explored in cultural, political, and historical contexts that are more different from those of the United States, such as in Asia (Taiwan, South Korea, the Philippines, and China) and Latin America (Argentina and Brazil). Some of the studies have confirmed general findings from the United States and some have not. (For overviews of these and other studies, see Melischek, et al. 1984; Morgan 1990; Morgan and Shanahan 1992.) Analyses of comparative message and/or cultivation data from Hungary, Japan, Finland, Russia (before and after the collapse of the Soviet Union), and elsewhere are currently in progress.

Some of this international work stemmed from Gerbner's attempt to organize a global project, "Television Around the World," whose purpose was to conduct parallel analyses of television policies, content, and effects with researchers in twenty-six participating countries. A week's worth of programming was videotaped in December 1987 in all of those countries, and much effort was devoted to the collaborative development of research instruments that were comparable but tailored to the specifics of each country. Unfortunately, due to the failure to obtain the funding needed to support such a massive project and to the scarcity of resources in many of the countries involved, the project to date has accomplished far less than originally hoped. Only a few countries were able to complete the analysis of the message data, and survey data for cultivation analysis were collected in even fewer.

The upheavals of old orders and the transition to what is nominally being promoted as "democracy" in many countries in Latin America, Africa, and the former Eastern bloc, place all this in a new context. In many countries, state-run media systems are being privatized and often quickly snatched up by multinational corporations. Veils of oppression are apparently being lifted, only to be replaced by new ones. Gerbner sees the current chaos in such places as Eastern Europe as leading to the resurgence of "neo-fascism, parochialism, and chauvinism." Many cheer the prospect of new freedoms, but Gerbner wants to "warn them of uncritical acceptance" of commercial control of the media, since "they're mortgaging the socialization of their children to global conglomerates" (Closepet and Tsui 1992).

In this context of widespread movement toward "democracy" (often conflated with "capitalism"), the critical implication of "organized diversity" in message production as a means of achieving cultural freedom has only become sharper. To Gerbner, the state is not a benevolent grantor of such diversity; it needs to become a force to promote it, to guarantee it, whereas, in contrast, it has usually worked, complicitly, to obstruct it. As the tyranny of the state is replaced by the tyranny of the market, it is falsely assumed that the *absence* of governmental controls and regulation somehow automatically means diversity and liberation. Although he does not see state involvement or benignly paternalistic regulations as a panacea to the problem of the media, his point is that government has been anything but an innocent bystander.

Cultural Environment Movement

All this brings us, not to the end of the story, but to the next chapter, still largely unwritten. It is a new phase of activism on Gerbner's part, as a political organizer (and occasional op-ed pundit). This chapter is the Cultural Environment Movement (CEM), and it is Gerbner's attempt to take matters a step further, to go from the critique of existing cultural policy to its transformation. It represents a shift from a critique of the practices of cultural industries to an attack on the very system that regulates, deregulates, and protects them. It is about how to turn a research project into a political project.

The Cultural Environment Movement is based on Gerbner's assertion that existing media structures in the United States are beyond the reach of democratic policy making. Since advertising is a tax-deductible business expense, and since the costs of advertising are hidden in the price of the products we buy ("We pay when we wash, not when we watch"), we have taxation without representation. But what can we *do* about it? The question is, How can we work toward a freer, fairer, and more liberating cultural environment? Gerbner has answered, in part: "We must reclaim the rights gained through centuries of struggle and conferred by law, the Constitution, and the basic principles of liberal education and self-government in a democracy. We must mobilize Americans to act as citizens as effectively as commercials mobilize us to act as consumers" (Gerbner 1991).

Through CEM, Gerbner seeks to build a broad-based coalition of media activists; of educational, health, environmental, legal, and other professional associations; of consumer groups and agencies; of women's groups; of religious and minority organizations; and of many other groups and individuals who are "committed to broadening U.S. and world cultures" (Gerbner 1991). CEM wants to have a broader range of voices and interests heard in cultural decisionmaking, to assist grassroots movements in the United States and elsewhere, to promote media literacy and critical viewing efforts, and to support media workers struggling within existing institutional constraints. Most of all, the goal is to put debate over cultural policy on the sociopolitical agenda.

This is a tall order, of course, and one that aims for far more than piecemeal reform. To date, Gerbner's CEM efforts have been directed more toward building a constituency and consolidating a coherent vision for the budding movement than toward specific legislative actions (although the recent passage of a bill, authored by Senator Paul Simon, which allows the broadcast and cable networks and Hollywood producers to develop industrywide standards on violence without fear of prosecution for violating anti-trust statutes, was significantly bolstered by Cultural Indicators' Violence Profiles).

One obvious problem is that "the public interest," historically and ostensibly the guiding principle in media regulation, in practice consists mainly of balancing competing *industry* interests. The "public" component of the interest equation is generally given short shrift by politicized administrative agencies (especially the FCC) and by those in Congress whose reelection campaigns are heavily financed by the various industries. Allowing other voices to be heard, much less making sure that they are heeded, will not be easy to accomplish.

An even more formidable task is to democratize the mechanisms and processes by which program production is funded. Production costs are astronomical; advertisers are more than willing to invest in these efforts, but the idea of federal support is political anathema. This of course serves as the perennial justification for the present system. The few alternatives available have their own problems; PBS's are well known, and the non–commercially supported cable channels (such as pay cable and pay-per-view) do not provide meaningfully alternative content. The problem of the lack of feasible alternatives to the current economic basis of program production is likely to be the major way to dismiss CEM's goals (by both governmental and media organizations), and CEM has not yet reached the stage where it has been able to propose specific, realistic, and workable alternatives that could help to develop the more democratic system it hopes to being about.

CEM may be but a pipe dream, as much "a drop in the ocean" as any individual program or episode, but Gerbner's optimism is not Pollyanna-ish and can give one second thoughts about writing off the movement. As he said in an interview, "To turn things around that almost everybody takes for granted is going to take a long time. And many people will consider it impossible. But then look around the world and see how many things that only five, ten years ago we considered impossible, are now reality. So I would say, if it's impossible, if it seems impossible, it means it's worth doing" (Gerbner 1992).

Gerbner follows this admonition by asking us to remember the slogan of Soviet dissidents of the 1960s and 1970s: offering a toast, they said, "And here is to the success of our hopeless endeavor." Indeed.

A Summation

If there is one central argument in Gerbner's work, it is that the cultural process of storytelling, that most distinctly humanizing phenomenon, is being increasingly taken over by global commercial interests who have something to sell. The traditional functions of the family, the school, the church, and other cultural institutions are being shaped by transnational corporations—a private government run by people nobody knows and nobody elected. Through the nascent Cultural Environment Movement, he hopes to consolidate and strengthen the work of diverse community, professional, and advocacy groups to "take back" the cultural environment, to provide a means of expression for those whose voices and interests do not fit commercial and market needs; that is, to harness the media to promote rather than undermine democracy. "Technological developments in communications hold out the possibility of greatly enhancing culture-power on behalf of existing social patterns—or of their transformation" (Gerbner 1973). In the problem may lie the solution.

Again, "The structure of freedom is organized diversity whether it pleases or not." Whether one embraces or scorns his theories and research, and whether the Cultural Environment Movement succeeds or fails, George Gerbner has made significant, far-reaching, and critical contributions to the field of communication.

REFERENCES

Adorno, T. W. (1954). How to look at television. *Quarterly of Film, Radio, and Television,* 8:213–36.

Bryant, J. (1986). The road most traveled: Yet another cultivation analysis. *Journal of Broadcasting and Electronic Media,* 30:231–35.

Closepet, R., and L. S. Tsui. (1992). An interview with Professor George Gerbner. *Media Development,* 1:42–45.

Gerbner, G. (1956). Toward a general model of communication. *AV Communication Review,* 4:171–99.

———. (1958). On content analysis and critical research in mass communication. *AV Communication Review,* 6:85–108.

———. (1959). Education and the challenge of mass culture. *AV Communication Review,* 7:264–78.

———. (1963). A theory of communication and its implications for teaching. In *The Nature of Teaching,* pp. 33–40. Milwaukee: University of Wisconsin–Milwaukee.

———. (1966). An institutional approach to mass communications research. In *Communication: Theory and Research,* edited by L. Thayer, pp. 92–118. Springfield, IL: Charles C. Thomas.

———. (1969). Toward 'cultural indicators': The analysis of mass mediated message systems. *AV Communication Review,* 17:137–48.

———. (1970). Cultural indicators: The case of violence in television drama. *Annals of the American Academy of Political and Social Science,* 388 (March): 69–81.

———. (1973). Cultural indicators: The third voice. In *Communications Technology and Social Policy,* edited by G. Gerbner, L. Gross, and W. H. Melody, pp. 555–73. New York: Wiley.

———. (1986). The symbolic context of action and communication. In *Contextualism and Understanding in Behavioral Science,* edited by L. Rosnow and M. Georgoudi. New York: Praeger.

———. (1990). Epilogue: Advancing on the path of righteousness (maybe). In *Cultivation Analysis: New Directions in Media Effects Research,* edited by N. Signorielli and M. Morgan, pp. 249–62. Newbury Park, CA: Sage.

———. (1991). Cultural Environmental Movement? What, why and how. Unpublished "Mission Statement" draft.

———. (1992). Interview in *The Killing Screams,* videotape, produced by Sut Jhally.

Gerbner, G., and L. Gross. (1976). Living with television: The Violence Profile. *Journal of Communication,* 26(2):173–99.

Gerbner, G., L. Gross, M. Jackson-Beeck, S. Jeffries-Fox, and N. Signorielli. (1978). Cultural indicators: Violence Profile No. 9. *Journal of Communication,* 28(3):176–207.

Gerbner, G., L. Gross, M. Morgan, and N. Signorielli. (1980). The"mainstreaming" of America: Violence Profile No. 11. *Journal of Communication,* 30(3):10–29.

———. (1982). Charting the mainstream: Television's contributions to political orientations. *Journal of Communication,* 32(2):100–27.

———. (1984). Political correlates of television viewing. *Public Opinion Quarterly,* 48:283–300.

———. (1986). Living with television: The dynamics of the cultivation process. In *Perspectives on Media Effects,* edited by J. Bryant and D. Zillmann, pp. 17–40. Hillsdale, NJ: Lawrence Erlbaum Associates.

———. (1994). Growing up with television: The cultivation perspective. In *Media Effects: Advances in Theory and Research,* edited by J. Bryant and D. Zillmann, pp. 17–41. Hillsdale, NJ: Lawrence Erlbaum Associates.

Good, L. (1984). A critical re-examination of cultivation analysis. International Communication Association, San Francisco, May.

Lowenthal, L. (1957). *Literature and the Image of Man.* Boston: Beacon Press.

Melischek, G., K. E. Rosengren, and J. Stappers, eds. (1984). *Cultural Indicators: An International Symposium.* Vienna: Osterreichischen Akademie der Wissenschaften.

Merton, R. (1957). *Social Theory and Social Structure.* Glencoe, IL: Free Press.

Morgan, M. (1986). Television and the erosion of regional diversity. *Journal of Broadcasting and Electronic Media,* 30:123–39.

———. (1989). Cultivation analysis. In *The International Encyclopedia of Communications,* edited by E. Barnouw, pp. 430–33. New York: Oxford University Press.

———. (1990). International cultivation analysis. In *Cultivation Analysis: New Directions in Media Effects Research,* edited by N. Signorielli and M. Morgan, pp. 225–48. Newbury Park, CA: Sage.

Morgan, M., and J. Shanahan. (1992). Comparative cultivation analysis: Television and adolescents in Argentina and Taiwan. In *Mass Media Effects Across Cultures: International and Intercultural Communication Annual,* vol. 16, edited by F. Korzenny and S. Ting-Toomey, pp. 173–97. Newbury Park, CA: Sage.

Morgan, M., and N. Signorielli. (1990). Cultivation analysis: Conceptualization and methodology. In *Cultivation Analysis: New Directions in Media Effects Research,* edited by N. Signorielli and M. Morgan, pp. 13–34. Newbury Park, CA: Sage.

Signorielli, N., and M. Morgan, eds. (1990). *Cultivation Analysis: New Directions in Media Effects Research.* Newbury Park, CA: Sage.

Van Den Haag, E. (1957). Of happiness and despair we have no measure. In *Mass Culture: The Popular Arts in America,* edited by B. Rosenberg and D. M. White. Glencoe, IL: Free Press.

Williams, R. (1976). *Keywords: A Vocabulary of Culture and Society.* New York: Oxford University Press.

7

Trying to Mix Oil with Water: Fund Raising, Vocationalism, and Critical Communication

JANET WASKO

Personal Reflections

The intriguing world of the electronic mass media captured my fascination and imagination the first time I visited a television studio in Phoenix, Arizona. The year was 1963. It was the year of John F. Kennedy's assassination, civil rights marches, and the slow-burning fuse in a remote place called Indochina.

My visit was to KOOL-TV, where a friend was an assistant puppeteer for an afternoon children's program. Despite the usual Looney Toons and commercials that surrounded the show, it was still *live* television, the kind of exciting and innovative broadcasting that at one time could be found at local stations scattered around the country. It was the dawn of the age of television, and I vowed to take a course in broadcasting the following fall, when I was scheduled to begin my freshman year at San Diego State University.

I decided to become a broadcasting major immediately, but also rather quickly I became one of those broadcasting-film students who couldn't wait to get into the "real" media world—the Industry. I moved north to Hollywood, where I began working in the Network Film Department at ABC. While I shifted from network to station to studio, doing some film editing, but mostly administrative work related to commercial production or distribution, the media business gradually became clearer to me.

Much of it seemed like a waste of talented and skilled people using their talents and skills to sell soap. Of course, some projects were noble and artistic endeavors—the warm, cuddly feelings created by the beautifully executed Eastman Kodak commercials, shot with as much care and attention as a feature film. But then there were the hours and hours . . . no, weeks and weeks, spent by extremely well-trained and intelligent people capturing the precise look on a housewife's face as she ecstatically discovers the wonders of Tidy Bowl Toilet Cleaner—perfectly color-corrected through the skillful work of cameramen, lighting and laboratory technicians, etc. I began to think seriously about other ways that the media might be used.

Educational television. Of course. I returned to finish my degree, convinced that the media resources that seemed so foolishly squandered to sell us potato chips and pet food could be used to educate. Why hadn't I thought of that before?

Yet, confronting the history of educational television and the beginning of the demise of public broadcasting, I began to see why few students even considered a future in noncommercial television. It was boring. Talking heads. Mired in political, bureaucratic, and administrative squabbles. Never enough funding. Insufficient resources. Nixon. Agnew. The liberal East Coast media establishment. Nattering nabobs of negativism.

Yes, it was the early 1970s, and the whole world was watching. The movements that swept the country carried the seeds of revolution, and one of the seeds that took root and grew was a critical orientation to media and communication studies. The questions I found myself asking about communications and mass media led me to that particular movement, to graduate school at the University of Illinois, and to academic positions where it has been possible to continue asking those questions about communication and media resources, trying to inspire others to ask them as well.

My experiences may or may not be typical of many academics, but I share them here because they relate to current concerns I have about working as a "knowledge worker" (Vinny Mosco's term) in a university environment.

The Growth of Critical Communication Research

Critical communication research has grown and expanded during the last few decades. A critical perspective is now far more prevalent in the field than in the days when only a handful of brave, lonely souls challenged established views. Several generations of critical communication researchers, some nurtured by the "founding fathers," others by the founding fathers' students, can be found at universities and colleges across the country. Critical research is now regularly included in established journals, with *Critical Studies in Mass Communication,* which is sponsored by the Speech Communication Association, as a prime example of the influence of critical orientations.

But the road for critical communication scholars has not always been smooth. Challenging dominant power structures is challenging, to say the least, and the intense scrutiny that critical scholars endure in academic settings, plus the typical lack of support for critical research, are only a few of the problems (see Meehan, Mosco, and Wasko, forthcoming).

Several scholars, including some in this volume, have documented the growth of a critical perspective in the field, as well as delineating the varied critical approaches to the study of communications and media. In this chapter, however, I would like to direct attention to a few of the problems that we, as critical communications researchers, face on a daily basis while fulfilling our other duties at the institutions where we work.

Fiscal Pressures, Administrative Answers

Critical approaches may indeed be more acceptable (or at least tolerated) in research circles these days, but for most of us, research is only one part of our job, which includes teaching and administrative responsibilities. It seems to me that it is in these areas where we are more often confronted with problems associated with working in institutions that are legitimated and increasingly funded by the industry(ies) that critical research critiques.

Certainly this is not a novel observation or a new problem. In research terms, we have been aware of this dilemma at least since Paul Lazarsfeld made the distinction between critical and administrative work. Since then, many observers (especially from outside the United States, such as Kaarle Nordenstreng and James Halloran) have noted the predominant professional orientation of communication programs at U.S. universities. As Hanno Hardt observed in his contribution to the Project on the Future of Journalism and Mass Communication Education (the "Oregon Report") in 1987, "For too long journalism educators have paid more attention to the demands of the industry than to the needs of the profession and its role in society. Recently, *checkbook journalism education* has spread without much controversy among the educators, making a mockery of the idea that universities are places for intellectual growth independent of political or economic pressures from outside. As a result some multimedia organizations control journalism programs, creating de facto trade schools in university settings" (*Planning for Curricular Change* 1987; emphasis added).

Some may feel that we have come a long way from the polarization of the critical/administrative labels, and, indeed, some academic programs have backed away from strictly occupational training. Nevertheless, an administrative approach to media education, or "checkbook journalism education," is very much alive and well in a large number of broadcasting and journalism programs across the country. The philosophy expressed rather succinctly by M. Stephens in 1981 is applicable to many broadcast and film programs as well: "Journalism departments are not English literature departments. They are by definition training people to practice a profession." A few years later, Funkhouser and Savage (1987) expressed concern that broadcast graduates were ill prepared for the industry, arguing that educators must play an important role "in preparing students for survival in the broadcast work environment." This sentiment continues to guide countless media programs, or at least is strongly represented by faculty within many communication schools and departments (see Hudson 1987; Roosenraad and Wares 1983).

Indeed, it could be argued that forces at play are pushing toward an even more intense professional or vocational orientation, as fiscal problems and budget cuts in many U.S. educational systems exacerbate these tendencies. In the past few years, budgetary dilemmas have resulted in the actual elimination of a few communication programs, the threat of closure at a number of universities, and drastic cutbacks at most public institutions (see Terry 1993). These moves may strike terror in the hearts of media and communication faculty around the country, but the changing philosophy of higher education funding in many states is perhaps even more insidious. Departments and colleges are increasingly urged to support activities with funds from outside, private sources. Again, this is not necessarily a new strategy for higher education; however, most would agree that the pressure is intensifying. An indication of this trend is the notion of the privatization of public institutions of education—at one time a rare and radical suggestion, but increasingly considered a viable solution to budgetary dilemmas.

Communications departments may be even more susceptible to these pressures than other programs. Although there are well established and respected communications programs in the United States that receive unqualified support from their universities, a more common scenario is a department that is one of the first to be scrutinized when a university's mission is under investigation and budget cuts are looming.

An obvious reason for this is the relatively new status of communication as a discipline and thus the lack of respect from older, more traditional and entrenched disciplines. As we all know, budget chopping is guided by power struggles within the university community, and too often media programs and faculty, despite their popularity and high enrollments, have too little campus clout. This point was reiterated recently by Tim Lyons, who was cited in a recent exchange on one of the electronic networks linking communication faculty: "It always amazed me, the political naiveté of my colleagues . . . , so full of themselves as the purveyors of the discipline destined to rule the university (reminds me of those who think that 'communication' was the sine qua non of a university education) when, in fact English, history, poli sci, the hard and soft sciences, continue to set the political agenda for the running of the university." Although Lyons is referring primarily to his film professor colleagues, the sentiment seems to be just as applicable to other media programs.

Communications and media education has yet another Achilles heel, though, if that is possible. Because journalism, broadcasting, and even film schools can be seen as distinctly linked to an industrial structure in more direct ways than many other disciplines, it is "logical" to many university administrators and some faculty that such programs draw on those rich industry sources, not only for extra funds but increasingly for survival. Fueling this type of logic is the popular notion of an information society, which places communication and information industries at the heart of a revitalized economy. Companies involved with information age developments are perceived to be some of the most profitable institutions in our society (and based on the research of many critical researchers, as well as mainstream scholars, those perceptions are justifiable.)

In addition, many media or communication programs have expensive appetites for specialized resources and equipment, which may sometimes lead "naturally" to direct appeals to industry sources. Thus, in media schools and departments around the country, there is a proliferation of fund-raising drives, endowed chairs, research and equipment grants, plus a wide range of other activities supported by funds from alumni, media industries, and foundations.

As a consequence, it seems that we are experiencing a reinforcement of an administrative orientation to media education. The problem of funding communications schools is ongoing. The Oregon Report noted that "while suffering from hard times, the journalism/mass communication units believe they are even harder hit. For this reason an examination of present and potential outside funding is of considerable importance to the future of the field."

But isn't it logical, again, to expect that as outside funding increases so do the expectations of those funding sources? Consequently, the schools in which we work are even more likely to be driven to provide training programs for media, as well as justifying other activities according to the needs of communication industries. Increasingly in these situations, a university education in media or communication is expected to be occupational training for workers who will compete for the few, often low-paying entry jobs in the media or information business. And why shouldn't the industry expect this type of service? After all, they're paying at least some of the bills.

These trends are propelled as well by the students themselves. Burdened with the enormous costs of a college education, even at public universities, it is not surprising that students seek to maximize their investment, pushing for assurance that their degrees will lead to jobs. This often explains why many of our students accept and embrace our critical orientation in classes, yet ultimately they have practical concerns about their future in a world where jobs are more than often difficult to come by, especially jobs in the competitive and attractive media industries.

In the Belly of the Beast: Working in Occupationally-Oriented Programs

The consequences of these developments are disturbing. In educational programs supported by industry funding, a different mentality often prevails as to the beneficiaries of the educational process. Often administrators reveal these inclinations in referring (in all seriousness) to students as our "customers" or "clients." (I have worked in two different schools where deans have used these specific terms.) But increasingly, in some cases, our "clients" are defined as not only, or even primarily, our students but the media and communication industries for which we serve as training centers and from which we receive important and, increasingly, essential funding. Industry representatives already sit on advisory boards and serve on search committees in some media programs. Too often, deans and endowed chairs are chosen not only for their scholarly attributes but for their ability to liaison with the industry and build external funding sources. If this trend continues, it is not too difficult to envision industry sources becoming far more influential in specific curriculum decisions, hiring policies, and other important components of the educational process. It might be noted that the prevailing attitude of administrators surveyed in the Oregon Report was that there was not enough funding from the media industry and its foundations and that they expected those groups to do more (1987:46).

From another angle, however, it seems that even the primary task of training media workers, if accepted, is doomed to fail. It is extremely difficult for most universities to keep up with industry technology without large budgets or huge endowments from industry sources or alumni. Not every program is as fortunate as the University of Southern California's film school, which has received enormous grants in the past from alumnus George Lucas and, more recently, was the recipient of a donation from Warner Brothers, Hanna-Barbera, and Silicon Graphics to launch a master's degree program specializing in high-tech animation. The arrangement also includes Warners and Hanna-Barbera providing guest lecturers, seminars, and visiting teaching positions. USC's location may be a key advantage to these types of arrangements, but the school deliberately lobbies for these funds, as exemplified by a fund-raising board of Hollywood advisers formed last year to raise $25–50 million.

Other programs are not as fortunate and survive on equipment and resources that are less than state-of-the-art. Thus, typical journalism, film, and broadcasting programs will always be criticized for not being current or up to date, thus limiting the role of such programs to providing basic beginning-level media workers. As Blanchard argued in 1988, "First, we have to reject politely the narrow role assigned to us by the professional media community and the current accreditation process . . . the media professionals would have us teach topical, if not yesterday's skills on ephemeral technology in a passing industrial and personnel environment. While steadfastly singing the praises of 'the liberal arts,' they would limit our priorities to that of entry-level media job prep schools designed to meet every passing need."

These trends have ramifications for our graduate students as well, especially those with critical orientations who seek positions in higher education. Graduate education may actually suffer in schools where undergraduate professional training dominates the time and energies of faculty and staff. It might be possible to argue that the devaluation of research and graduate education may be most prevalent in those programs with the most direct ties and funding from outside media sources, but there are important consequences for all graduates in the communication field. In job searches, beginning Ph.D.'s are increasingly faced with the prospect of having to "fit in" at professional schools, where teaching vocationally oriented courses is the norm. Although these young Ph.D.'s may not always have to justify their critical perspective (although there are certainly instances when this is still a problem), they must show that they are able to serve their "clients"—not only students but the media industry as well.

Naturally, there also are implications for communications research. The administrative call for research supporting the industry's needs will become even more insistent as those industries provide the funding making such research possible. As James Scotton, at the time, dean of Marquette's journalism school, pointed out during the Association for Education in Journalism and Mass Communication's study of journalism education, "In the long run, the hand that feeds doesn't get bitten very hard" (Friendly 1984). It may be more and more difficult for scholars to critique the media and communication professions but much easier to answer an industry representative's plea for more "academercial" research (a term coined by Smith 1983, cited in Bailie 1993), when research equipment (such as computers) and resources (such as research assistance) are funded directly by industry sources.

On the other hand, it might be possible to argue that, despite these potential pressures, it is more often possible to *resist* an administrative or academercial mentality in our research activities. We are a part of a larger university setting, which at best still values research. Often, we are able simply to outpublish other nonresearch-oriented faculty members, thus securing our positions in the larger university community. We also are asking important and relevant research questions emerging from the "real world," thus often our research simply cannot be ignored.

Yet, in the other areas of our jobs—teaching, advising students, curriculum development, and other administrative activities—it is sometimes more difficult to avoid the push toward vocationalism.

Liberating Professional Training

The *professional* training of students in itself should not necessarily be problematic from a critical perspective; we should be eager to prepare people to engage in the communication process. Indeed, if we are true to our arguments for democratic communication, we should be eager to demystify media techniques and encourage such skills that contribute to the notion of critical citizenship and human emancipation. As M. Bailie observes in his argument for a critical production pedagogy for broadcast production courses, "while strictures against emancipatory practices saturate the technological and instrumental discourses of television production courses, the *potential* for resistance and struggle are nevertheless present" (1993). It is encouraging to find new doctorates, such as Bailie and others, attempting to liberate a mainstream, administrative curriculum by turning it on its head. (Another example is a public relations text that is currently being written by a young communications professor from a critical perspective.)

One of the basic tenets of the Union for Democratic Communication, an organization in which many scholars and teachers have focused their critical energies, has been to merge theory and praxis, support alternative communication, and attempt to affect mainstream media. We should not avoid or demean the opportunity to influence students who are excited by the appeal of working in the media and communications business as professional goals. Certainly, from my initial entry into the field of mass communications, I would be the first to understand and in many ways support their motivations. However, we need to insist on a broad-based media and liberal arts education for these students, stressing alternative visions of media and communications technologies beyond the current industry models.

How we go about doing this may vary according to how entrenched an industry/occupational orientation has become at the specific institutions where we work. Of course, the economic and political climate in general will influence our ability to resist pressures toward the privatization of higher education, which has obvious implications for the trend toward private funds for media and communication programs. In other words, we must engage in the struggle to maintain the integrity of the university as an independent institution that contributes to society in a wide variety of ways, not merely molding students into workers. More specifically, in our own discipline and our own professional practice, it is increasingly more urgent for us to recognize that, as academics and scholars who are concerned with changing the current state of the communications and information environment, critical research is only one aspect of our responsibilities.

REFERENCES

Bailie, M. (1993). Toward a critical pedagogy for television production courses in higher education. Ph.D. dissertation, University of Oregon.

Blanchard, R. D. (1988). Our emerging role in liberal and media studies. *Journalism Educator,* 43(3):28–31.

Friendly, J. (1984). Journalism educators debate strategies, technology and ties to the media. *New York Times* (January 23).

Funkhouser, E., and A. L. Savage, Jr. (1987). College students' expectations for entry-level broadcast positions. *Communication Education,* 36(1):23–27.

Hudson, J. C. (1987). Broadcasters want experience, skills and liberal arts. *Journalism Educator,* 41(4):36–38.

Meehan, E., V. Mosco, and J. Wasko. (In press). Rethinking political economy: change and continuity. *Journal of Communication.*

Planning for Curricular Change: A Report of the Project on the Future of Journalism and Mass Communication Education (1987). 2nd ed. Eugene: School of Journalism, University of Oregon.

Roosenraad, J., and D. Wares. (1983). Academics vs. experience. *Journalism Educator,* 38(2):17–18.

Stephens, M. (1981). Don't imitate professionals: In broadcast news training, who's calling the kettle black? *Journalism Educator,* 36(1):49–50.

PART THREE

HERBERT I. SCHILLER

Herbert I. Schiller, Canberra, 1986 (Photo by John A. Lent)

Herbert I. Schiller

Born:	November 5, 1919, New York City
Education:	Ph.D., New York University, 1960; M.A., Columbia University, 1941; B.S.S., College of the City of New York, 1940; *cum laude,* Phi Beta Kappa
Employment:	
1970–	Professor of Communication, Third College, University of California, San Diego
1982–83	Visiting Professor, University of Paris (VIII).
1978 (March–June)	Thord-Grey Visiting Lecturer, Theatre and Film Institute, University of Stockholm
1978–79	Visiting Professor, Department of Communications, Hunter College, City University of New York
1973 (May)	Visiting Lecturer, Universities of Uppsala, Lund, Stockholm and Helsinki
1973 (May)	Visiting Professor, Institute of Communications, University of Tampere, Finland
1973 (September)– 1974 (August), 1975 (April–July)	Visiting Professor, Mass Media Seminar, Institute of the Press, University of Amsterdam
1970–72, 1977–78	Coordinator, Communications Program, UCSD.
1969	Visiting Professor, Institute of Communications, Hebrew University, Jerusalem
1967–68	Visiting Fellow, Institute of Policy Studies, Washington, D.C.
1966–70	Research Professor, Bureau of Economic and Business Research, University of Illinois, Urbana
1963	Ford Foundation Fellow, Regional Faculty Research Seminar of International and Interregional Economics, Brown University

1963–66	Research Associate Professor, Bureau of Economic and Business Research, University of Illinois, Urbana
1962–63	Professor of Economics and Chairman, Department of Social Studies, Pratt Institute, Brooklyn, New York
1961–67	Lecturer, "World Today" Lecture Series, Brooklyn Institute of Arts and Sciences
1960	Associate Professor of Economics, Pratt Institute
1954	Fellowship, Foundation for Economic Education with the Century Federal Savings and Loan Association, New York City
1953–60	Assistant Professor of Economics, Pratt Institute
1950–53	Instructor of Economics, Pratt Institute
1949–59	Lecturer in Economics, College of the City of New York
1941–48	Economist, War Production Board and the Office of Military Government, Department of Labor, U.S. Government (excluding military service, 1942–45)
1940–41	Teaching Fellow in Economics, College of the City of New York

Other Service:

Vice President, 1972–1988, member of International Council, 1988–, International Association for Mass Communication Research; Advisory Board, *American Dialogues,* Los Angeles, 1990–; Advisory Board, Center for the Study of Commercialism, 1990–; external examiner, Universiti Sains Malaysia, July 1987; member, International Consultant Council of *Felafacs,* Federación Latino Americana de Associaciones de Facultades de Communicación Social, 1987–; member, Board of Advisors, Fairness and Accuracy in Reporting, FAIR, 1988–, Board of Judges, *Project Censored,* 1987; Advisory Committee, Edatata Narayanan (EN) Centre for Research and Development and Communication, New Delhi; trustee, International Institute of Communications, 1978–84; external examiner consultant, University of the West Indies, Caribbean Institute of Mass Communication, 1981; President, Pratt Chapter, 1960–61, Secretary, Illinois Chapter, 1966–67, Vice President, Illinois Chapter, 1967–68, American Association of University Professors

Editing, Publishing:

Editor, Westview "Critical Studies in Communication and in the Cultural Industries" series; Consulting Editorial Board, *International and Intercultural Communication Annual,* vols. 13–16, Sage; member, Consulting Editorial Board,

1988–89, *Communication for Peace: Diplomacy and Negotiation Across Cultures,* vol. 14 of the *International and Intercultural Communication Annual,* Speech Communication Association; Board of Advisors, Institute for Media Analysis, Inc., 1986–; Editorial Board, *Critical Studies in Mass Communication,* 1989–; Editorial Board, *Social Intelligence,* University of Stathclyde, Scotland, 1990–; consulting editor, *Communication Yearbook* 9 (1985), 10 (1986); editorial advisor, *International Encyclopedia of Communications,* 1984–88; Editorial Board, *Progress in Communication Sciences* (Ablex), contributing editor; Editorial Board, *Information and Behavior*; International Editorial Board, *Media, Culture and Society*; contributing editor, *Zeszyty Prasoznawcze,* Krakow; consulting and contributing editor, *Journal of Communication*; consulting and contributing editor, *Communication;* editor, *The Quarterly Review of Economics and Business,* 1966–70.

Awards and Honors:

Listed in *Who's Who in America, American Men and Women of Science, Contemporary Authors*; Gold Pen Prize, Los Angeles PEN, best magazine article for 1982 on freedom of information; *Communication and Domination: Essays to Honor Herbert I. Schiller* (Ablex).

8

Interview with Herbert I. Schiller

CONDUCTED BY JOHN A. LENT
CANBERRA, AUSTRALIA,
DECEMBER 1, 1986

What factors or situations in your life—your academic, personal, and professional life—steered you into a critical mold?

Well, let's start with the personal and then we can go to the more general, institutional, academic. Personal, I think, is something that goes well before the period [1960s] we're talking about. It actually relates to the time when I was a college student, and even a few years before that—and that was the period of the Great Depression in the United States and, of course, in much of the rest of the industrialized part of the world. That event was experienced very seriously in my own home. I grew up in a very small family, one in which my father was unemployed from the outbreak of the crisis crash in 1929, and he did not go to a job on a full-time basis until the outbreak of war in Europe in 1939. This spans a whole decade and is also, I think, reflective of what our economy was like. There was the inability to reabsorb working people until the outbreak of the war. You can well imagine that this domestic condition, with all the problems incident to the breadwinner not having any full-time employment for ten years when I was a kid, left very deep impressions and made me have an awful lot of questions about the social order. That doesn't mean I had answers whatsoever. It doesn't mean I had a thought out or even partially organized view of the structure of society. But I do know that I had a lot of feelings that things were really pretty out of control. I would say that was a very powerful, if not the most powerful, force in my youth. You can always point to questions of individual teachers and specific episodes. (I don't want to come up with that now.) After completing my undergraduate education, spending time in the army during World War II, spending time in the military government, and here I would pause again. (Is this what you want?)

Yes, definitely.

Well, another illuminating period of time for me was after World War II. I was still pretty young because I'd gone into the U.S. Army young. I had the opportunity to go back to Europe in a civilian capacity and be a member of the U.S. military government occupation of Germany. That was in the period of 1946–48. At that time I had my college degree and even a master's degree. I didn't have my doctorate, yet this was my real social science education. Everything else I mentioned to you in the past were mostly personal experiences, feelings, intuition, subjectivity.

This period was one in which some very clear social actions and policies were experienced. I was able to be close to important decisionmaking, even though it was at a junior level, because of the kinds of chaos that existed and the types of lapses that frequently occur in large bureaucratic circumstances. I would frequently be in situations where, even though I was very junior, I would be at high-level meetings close to high-level relationships that could never be explained in terms of my own position. Chance would put me there, yet I had an opportunity to see people in important positions or what were regarded as significant positions. How they behaved, who they were, what kind of outlooks they had, and more than any of this, to see the policies themselves. What I was witness to—and I'll just reduce this to a very short summary, because I can spend a long time talking about it—what I saw was the *conscious, the deliberate reconstruction of the political economy of Germany that was achieved in a very short time at the end of the war under the direction of the U.S. military government and the people who were in the U.S. military government.* That reconstruction would make it certain that Germany would have the same monopoly market society—not with all of the political extremes that had developed in the fascist period, but with all of the structures and institutions that had produced the fascist movement and government. So rather than really starting off with a fresh slate, rather than reconstructing Germany in a truly democratic way, there was this facade, this pretense of creating a new Germany. But all of the old institutional structures prevailed. Even now, almost forty years later, and even though we still are hearing about the new Germany, the democratic Germany, should there be any serious rupture and Germany is subjected to strong economic pressures, I wouldn't be too sanguine about the democratic evolution of Germany.

That, in a nutshell, was really the formative set of experiences for me. I saw that almost all of the things that are frequently regarded as "natural," so-called, in quotation marks, "inevitable," "universal," "all of the laws," in quotation marks, of the social order are something far less than that. They are constructs. In a period when there had been this big rupture because of the war and the people overcoming German fascism, there was what you could call something of a socioeconomic political vacuum—how that vacuum was then refilled with the preferred kinds of institutional arrangements that would lead to certain types of outcomes—outcomes in terms of economic activity, in terms of political structure, in terms of social consciousness. It was as close as you can get, I believe, in the social science area to a laboratory experiment. Granted, it didn't have the kind of measurable connections, but it was an approximation. This too contributed to the major formative aspects of my own development. Then I went back, got my degree in a very long period of time.

I might add, if you are asking how you explain what is sometimes called a critical approach, it's not only the formative experiences of the kind that I've mentioned, which were not necessarily unique to me, but even getting a degree, and I don't want to make this sound too personal—but I think it bears more than just an individual interpretation. I find myself saying that I feel I was fortunate that I never was what would be regarded as an ordinary graduate student as we understand a graduate student to be in present-day educational circumstances. I never had a very tightly organized curriculum; I wasn't under the sponsorship or under the tutelage of any preferred professors—I was all on my own. I was sort of a floating piece of flotsam in a huge institutional educational factory, left to my own resources. No one knew who I was. I was under no strict regime—not because that was a chosen educational policy but because the educational structure didn't give a damn, and I myself had at the time a family, young children. I was working, teaching in two different educational institutions, spending somewhere like twenty-three to twenty-five hours a week in the classroom, riding back and forth on the subway between these institutions. My only expectation was just to stay enrolled to be able to maintain my matriculation. If anything ever came out of it, it would be a miracle. That was the way I approached this.

Now I'm not saying that this is the way anybody should organize their graduate training, but the fact of the matter was that as a consequence of this very poorly structured and almost inadvertent getting of the degree, I never became part of that systematized structure of being led, being told, being influenced, being forced all the way along the line, even if one is not totally conscious of being put into a mold. So it's true, I was left to flounder. I certainly can't say I had a very profound education. I can't say that I got the kind of training that most of the people who now go through get. All of these could be regarded as serious deficiencies, but I think I got something that, though very intangible, was very important. I escaped this process of education, which, for the most part, may be far more successful in structuring the very nature of how people view processes and view the social order and their expectations. I think, as a result of my situation, I was able to avoid that. So I've never had that enormous regard, respect for the formal educational enterprise. I think that looking at it as honestly as I can, I escaped academic processing. Because of the extent that one is brought into that process, it's very difficult to see how your fundamental outlooks and approaches are shaped. And also, of course—and this is maybe the most important of all—one doesn't have the view that the academic enterprise is the "be-all" and "end-all" of life. Outside of the academic enterprise there is the work day, the life experiences and the day-in-day-out, you know, real tribulations and trials of people. Achievement is not just to get up and make a nice little presentation that's going to be very acceptable to a half dozen or two dozen types more or less who have gone through the same process that you're being forced to go through and that is edifying to them yet eludes popular understanding. To me these are very crucial matters. So that's the personal side of things. Now where do we want to go, John?

I find it interesting that you were with the military after the war but you went in a different direction than people like Daniel Lerner and others who were working in psychological warfare, etc.

Well, on this, of course, I guess I didn't cover all of the bases, but naturally, when I went into this job I didn't have any great illusions about political life. I did have by the time I went there in 1946—I had some sense of political organization and a certain amount of critical understanding about what kinds of policies were being imposed in Germany, whereas these other chaps that you're talking about were gung-ho and transferred their enthusiasms for waging World War II to pursuing and developing the cold war. My own experiences led in a different direction, as you indicate. I could see what was being done in Germany was the early stage of the cold war. I wouldn't date the cold war as it's dated in most of the commentaries that we read. We read that it began somewhere from 1948 on; to me the cold war was going on in 1944, 1945, 1946—in the creation of a Germany that would be regarded as a firm ally against the East. You're quite correct that these other individuals were, from the outset, accepting all of the goals and objectives of those who were really running the show and who were in positions of great power when World War II was over.

When you finished the degree, where did you start? At Illinois?

No, no, no. As I indicated earlier, I had been teaching in two schools in the New York City area while I was spending eight or nine years working and taking courses desultorily and eventually finding that I had finished all my requirements and, you know, I had to take the exams and had to knock out a thesis. I mean all of this was very ad hoc. During that time I was teaching both at City College in New York on a part-time basis and on a full-time basis at Pratt Institute, which was essentially an art and fine arts school in Brooklyn but which also had some social science.

When I finished my graduate work, I was still in both of these places, but then, of course, my stature was enhanced because I had the, *the credential.* I then became a much more respectable member of the academic community. Within a very short time after I got my degree, I left Brooklyn and Pratt Institute and City College and first spent a year visiting at the University of Illinois. I went back to Brooklyn for one more year at Pratt and then came back to Illinois on a permanent basis.

The first visit to Illinois was 1961–62 and then back to New York 1962–63, and then I moved permanently to Illinois in 1963–1964, and I stayed in Illinois from that date until 1970.

When you went to Illinois, Dallas Smythe and Tom Guback were there?

Dallas Smythe was there. Tom Guback, as I remember, was a graduate student of Dallas Smythe's. Now remember, when I moved to Illinois I was not in what is called communications. I didn't even know that there was such a field. I had heard of Dallas Smythe and, in fact, through other friends—I had never met him, but I had heard of him. I had heard of him, curiously enough—and I think this is amusing (I never even told this to Dallas)—through other friends and people Dallas knew. They had told me in a what they regarded as a friendly way—it was not hostile—that here was this, you know, basically very good, solid economist with a good point of view, getting off into this lunacy of communications. They thought he was a good man, you know, who somehow or other had lost his mooring. They didn't understand really what he was doing, but they thought, "Well, he's a very good guy anyway." That was what I first heard about Dallas. When I moved out there, as I say, as a visiting appointment in 1961–62, he was there and we saw each other a few times. He was, at the time, as I remember, the head of the graduate program in communications. He had done a great deal of work, but I wasn't in communications. When I moved out to Illinois I still regarded myself as an economist. Other economists were less generous in their estimate. But, to some at least, I was considered an academic economist, and that was what I was doing there. I had an appointment in the Bureau of Economics and Business Research, and I taught a course or two in the Department of Economics.

What gelled at Illinois that formulated your thinking as evidenced in *Mass Communication and American Empire,* among other writings?

Well, let's put it at two levels: the mechanics of making this professional transition and what were the more substantive conditions. The mechanics are easier to describe. Very shortly after I came back with a permanent arrangement in 1963–64, if I'm not mistaken, Dallas left, or certainly the year after. In any case, he left shortly after I came back the second time and returned to Canada and a job in

Saskatchewan, in Regina. That meant that the position that he had held in the Institute of Communications Research, and the courses that he initiated and had been the first really to present in American higher education—political economy of communication, political economy of international communication—these courses were unattended and the job was vacant. I had gotten to know him a little bit better and also met George Gerbner, who was in the Institute of Communications at the time. After Dallas left, I was asked whether I would be interested in taking a crack at the course he taught, and for reasons that I'll get into in a minute it sounded like quite an attractive idea. And that's exactly what happened. I remained in the Economics Bureau, but I was offered an adjunct arrangement in the communications college, the College of Journalism it was called in those days. I taught the "Political Economy of Communications," the graduate course. I can't tell you what year that began, but I have the feeling it was around 1966–67. Once I began, of course, it was all that was necessary to give momentum to other forces that were at work, that made me feel comfortable that I had made the right kind of shift and happy with the new direction of my work. From that time on, I considered myself in the field of communications. So, it's roughly twenty years [at the time of this 1986 interview]. That's the general "what happened at the specific job level."

In broader terms, as a political economist, which was what I was prior to becoming a political economist communications person, I had been very interested in the issues of economic development and, in particular, the juncture where politics and economics come together. I always felt that one of the real weaknesses, actually, total inadequacies, of formal economics was its total disregard of the political component and its effort to present everything in sealed, rigid economic categories, to say nothing of formulas, on development or what have you, leaving out this very crucial area. So that has been something I had thought about and I had considered for quite a bit of time.

Then in my own field, what I had been doing was more than just general development analysis. I had, as a result of courses I had taught, a fairly strong interest in economic geography and the disposition of not only where raw materials and resources were located physically but what economic use was made of them and the reasons that determined this use. For example, where would a steel complex be located? Not only because there was coal or iron but also water for transport, and where the steel was to be shipped. These were all questions that, having a certain kind of importance of their own, led me to certain types of thinking that became, for me at least, useful when I moved into the communications area. Because one of the areas that was—I guess you could say—at that point of transition, where I was asked to do a paper for a meeting of the Triple As in Montreal, right in this period—maybe it was 1966 or about that era—and in which I chose as my subject the radio spectrum as a natural resource. That was not an original idea, because, you know, the radio spectrum is regarded as a natural resource. It is a natural resource, but I tried to look at it as how that natural resource was being used or abused, and what were the institutional factors that led to the character of the utilization that was going on. That was the actual paper itself, and that course allowed me to get into this whole area of institutional structures in the field of communications. I think that probably is where this development question came into being, spanning from just strictly the political economic development into political communications development, and again that goes back just about twenty or so years.

I assume you must have been a very unpopular person in the 1960s, during the development decade, when people were pushing another type of communication.

No, you see, it's very curious, John, and I can't give you a completely satisfying explanation, but I think one of the factors that allowed me—well, there are several reasons that probably gave me a certain amount of space which I wouldn't have now, and I might not have had before that time. First of all, it was the 1960s—you can never forget that—and the 1960s, for a lot of reasons which we both know, allowed things to be a lot more fluid or open, if only temporarily, and so that was one consideration. A second factor was—again, this is on the personal side—I was totally unknown in the area of communications. I had never written anything in communications and therefore, for a while I was, you know, absolutely, I wouldn't even say ignored, I wasn't even regarded. You know, "Who is this guy?" So there was a period of a couple of years where I was just moving into this area and writing things and I guess I didn't get any attention whatsoever. Now, of course, you could say this was deliberate. That's also possible.

I remember being on a couple of panels with Daniel Lerner and Lerner acting as if, well, I was just young—I wasn't that young—and innocent. He too had had such a time when he had a more radical view of the world, but he had learned what reality was; I would eventually come to my senses. It was patronizing but almost benevolent. Wilbur Schramm, I had no contact with, whatsoever, although it was Schramm's work which I was probably coming most directly in collision with. But as could be expected, there was no reason for somebody who was a very established, highly regarded, prominent figure to take any note of some newcomer—even deign to consider the newcomer. That would be conferring legitimacy on the upstart. So I would say there was a period of, oh, quite a few years, when I was just writing stuff that eventually produced a body of material that finally could not be ignored. However in this time I don't think I ever was given any serious attention by the established people.

The graduate students in place after place got hold of it, though, or the young faculty got hold of it. That forced a certain amount of—I won't go as far as to say recognition—but at least a certain amount of visibility. Just to maintain the academic myth that there are open forums, I would sometimes be invited to speak, almost invariably at the insistence and under the auspices of graduate students and young faculty. It's a fact that over this entire time I had never been invited to any of our universities with an invitation coming from the senior faculty or from any of the significant leaders in the field.

Even today?

Even today. I don't mean to day that it is a flat and total condition. I mean, I'm sure there have been some instances—I can't remember too many—but there have been some occasions. Almost always, it comes as a result of graduate students or a couple of young faculty mavericks who say, "At least why don't you give this view a hearing?" That's how it comes about. But that's been the general run of things.

Then, of course—maybe we'll get into this if you want—by the time the decade had run its course, and a lot of the energies that had gone into the 1960s had begun to ebb, there was another source of energy, and that was the international movement toward what was at that time called the New International Information Order. So there was a whole new set of stimuli coming internationally, and it was that source that gave me a great deal of support and allowed me to be much more involved than I would be if I was waiting for the call from our, you know, highly regarded and most well-known academic communicology people. It goes without saying that the media has never been very . . .

Didn't you have something to do with the New International Information Order from its conception? Weren't you in Montreal at the 1969 meeting?

I wasn't there but my book [*Mass Communications and American Empire,* 1969] was there. The book had just come out. I remember I had gotten a call from one of the people who was there. Maybe it was Kaarle Nordenstreng, whom I had just had a passing acquaintance with, who had read the book and said, "Can you send fifty copies to the meeting?" I remember I did get copies, but whether or not they were distributed, I couldn't say. But from that time on, the momentum of the discussions from the Montreal meeting and meetings in many different parts of the Third World began to come with great regularity. I was involved in quite a few of those, and so there was this interaction. And, of course, the book which I wrote. I actually began writing it some time around 1966–67. It was published in 1969. That book was, I believe, an integral part of the whole developing issue. Many of the ideas in the book were tied very closely to, though without ever mentioning, a New International Information Order, because it hadn't yet been formulated in that specific language.

If I recall, that book came out in two different editions. Who published the first one?

Well, that story too, I think, is interesting in answer to some of your questions about the matter of recognition. The manuscript was made up of several individual chapters, essays really. Some of them had been published in places like *The Nation* magazine, *The Progressive* magazine, a few in the *Bulletin of the Atomic Scientist,* places like that. I put it all together and sent it—I can't remember exactly, but certainly to eight or nine or ten commercial publishers. Invariably, I'd get back a rejection with a very friendly note saying, "This is all very interesting, but we don't think that there's a market for this, and maybe you should take it somewhere else." All very cordial but all nonreceptive in that sense. I had more or less given up hope, really. I didn't have very many leads. As I told you before about my academic background, I didn't have a senior professor to whom I could say I have a manuscript, can you go through the channels? That was outside of my knowledge and situation. Now, people seem to think I have all of this background on how to do things. Yet for me, originally, it was a very difficult, tenuous, and, you know, constant trial-by-error business. I didn't have any of the customary academic channels to rely on.

In any event, I knew a fellow who was a reprint publisher, and his specialty of reprints was seventeenth-century economic tracts. You know, the early days of development of the economic profession. For example, Thomas Mun, way back before Ricardo. Adam Smith would have been a modern guy to my reprint publisher. He was concerned with people who were writing in 1650–70. He would get some tattered copy from some European library, then open it up, make a reproduction of the book, and sell maybe a hundred copies to various libraries. That was a very valuable kind of publishing, but certainly not what you would call a major commercial outlet. He wasn't part of a media conglomerate.

So I mentioned to this guy I had this manuscript. He said, "I'll publish it." So I said, "Well, it won't be more buried than the stuff that's coming out of the seventeenth century." So Augustus Kelley brought the book out. He did it all. In fact, the book was sort of a joke, in the sense of the way it was done. Again, it was very similar to my experiences as an academic. You know, we all know, that when you send in manuscripts generally, you get at least an edited copy. Sometimes the editors want you to do this and that and everything else. Many times you're not even very happy with all the things they're telling you to do, but you're certainly constantly being nudged and prodded and demanded and pulled to make their revisions. This guy took the stuff and just put it into type. Then he said, "I don't believe in interfering with the author in any way." I was sort of horrified that my book wasn't copy-edited in any way whatsoever. I think he did it this way because of his pinched economic condition. But he had a good rationale all the same. He said he wouldn't dream of interfering with what was the author's intention. So the book came out and it wasn't, as far as I could see, too egregious in its grammatical defects, because many of the pieces had appeared originally in articles. It came out in 1969.

When the book was published, no one knew who I was. They had never heard of Augustus Kelley either. It wasn't like being published by one of the big commercial houses. Given this treatment, the book might have been totally ignored, except for a few individuals who might have stumbled upon it. The publisher had no distribution channels, no circulation outlets, nothing. The book came out; that was it!

But a copy came to the attention of Bob Shayon, Robert Shayon, who at the time was the TV editor of the magazine that Norman Cousins edited, *Saturday Review.* He reviewed the book very favorably and said it was the first book that challenged the assumptions of the cold war era in communications. It was almost a full-page review in the *Saturday Review.* That was remarkable because, first of all, as you know, most book reviewing is tied to book publishers' advertising in general. There was no advertising for this book. Nobody knew the publisher, and he certainly did not give the media advertising revenue. I have always felt that Bob Shayon had a great role in getting this book to a national public. Once that review appeared, there was a certain amount of interest—not much reviewing in the major outlets, but at least in what you could call, not so much the "underground," but the more marginal and the countercultural and the independent press. They were all aware of the book. The next edition was a paperback edition that Beacon Press put out in 1971. If you look at most bibliographies—a sign possibly of some faulty scholarship—the citation is to 1971, Beacon Press, but that is not accurate. The book came out in 1969.

How has the field of communications changed in the last fifteen to twenty years?

Well, I think actually many of the things we've been talking about only began to get picked up, taken note of, and filter through the ordinary education channels several years later. For example, take my first book. It took four to five years for that book very gradually to begin to be given some kind of recognition. By recognition, I mean, you knew it was being read in some places and appearing in some footnotes and citations, or what have you. So even though there was this stimulation and all of this activity in the 1960s, the field of communications only begins to reflect this in the 1970s, in my estimation. There was a lag, which is paradoxical.

While the overall direction of American policy became increasingly conservative and increasingly controlled, communication research briefly became more questioning and critical, while this other larger trend is occurring in the economy. It was not until, I would say, the late 1970s, or maybe even early 1980s, that the general conservative trend began to overtake the field of communications.

In the 1970s, at least in my judgment, the field was in a stimulating era. Many began to regard communications as an area worthy of attention. Of course, that didn't come exclusively from the work that was being done in the field. It came primarily I'd say, because of the actual changing character of the productive system, the role of information. Changing information technology, and the new mix of production of goods and services in the United States. In other words, there were material changes occurring in the economy.

The 1970s, in my judgment, were a very prosperous time. (I mean in the sense, not of making money, but that communications enjoyed a certain vitality. I think many younger people came into the field and had an opportunity to encounter some of the newer work of the late 1960s, early 1970s.) It was a period of expansion. Many universities introduced it as a discipline, or if not a discipline, at least as an area of study. Some of the more established places, which had had communications programs, but in more restricted categories, such as speech and rhetoric or, as we know, journalism, felt obligated to open up a little bit and at least to include some representatives of this new field of institutional commentary, institutional analysis. So to me the 1970s were rather a favorable time, a very positive time of development.

Now, I would say, and this is more intuitive than empirically grounded, there's a certain slippage over the last five or six years [early to mid-1980s]. That, of course, I guess, is attributable to the general direction, tone, and political climate of the society at large, so I don't hold communications directly responsible. Some of the names, some of the thinking that had been practically, if I may say so, discredited, or certainly disregarded as not very useful in understanding the processes at work, some of that thinking has become, let's say, rehabilitated. It's almost like Mr. Nixon—ain't he rehabilitated? Similarly, some of the defunct economic theories are back, enjoying a certain amount of attention and support and prominence. So I think it's a very mixed time. A lot will depend on what happens to the economy and how our political situation evolves.

Picking up on that, I have had the same feeling that we're going back to the old development models, except now we're using satellites and computers, instead of radio and television, and technocrats are running the show, rather than social scientists. You said that perhaps that is because of the political climate in the United States. What else would that be attributable to?

Well, I'm glad you picked up on that, because I wouldn't want it to be left at that. That was only the first item that I mentioned. I would say it's far deeper than that and more troubling. It concerns the changed material underpinning of the society, now dependent on the new information technologies. These have been applied to the major power centers in the society, the government bureaucracies, and most importantly, the corporate giants, in particular, the companies operating on the international scale. Those with their disbursed plant locations who find communications absolutely indispensable to their activities. Therefore, communication today is not just a marginal sector. No longer is it just an area that some academics are fussing with and writing irrelevancies about. It's a field where the big boys are involved and concerned and in which, I would say, major decisions are being made.

In fact, I'm struck once again by how backward, how totally, let's say, behind the times the academic community is in conjunction with the real centers of decisionmaking, in terms of policymaking and interest. Whereas in the 1970s, communications analyses by some of us did seem to be ahead of things because there was this gap factor, now I think it's all been returned to where power actually is. That being the case, most of the stuff that's appearing on communications in the academic centers is just a pale reflection, if even a reflection, of what the reality happens to be. The reality today is information. Information technology now is regarded as the central bulwark of the advanced industrial system and as the basis of whatever power it possesses. It is hoped it would be maintained and expanded and for the whole system, corporate and military. This is reflected in the studies being made, or the studies that are not being made. I find it almost unbelievable that academic life ignores this.

Consider the issue of disinformation, for instance. I think it would be an interesting exercise to review the indices, the journals, what have you, and find how many papers, how many articles have appeared on the structural process of disinformation. Instead, we have to read the newspapers to find some, not much, material on this. Granted this kind of research wouldn't be very easy, but the fact that it hasn't even been attempted, that says a lot. Take the question of transborder data flows. Whatever has been done on these is only after the fact. The actual information, of course, is held in corporate hands. Most of it doesn't get published because it's regarded as proprietary information. But that would be a very useful study.

It's true, I guess, given my own inclination to look at the political economic aspect of things, and the larger macro-social relationship, I probably tend to underestimate the value of personal studies and that kind of research activity. I don't mean to argue that that type of work is of no consequence, but I would be very surprised if even that area can be studied productively without taking into account these larger macro forces. In short, I would say, we're in a period where there are very powerful forces that are hardly generous in supporting or wanting to see undertaken certain kinds of research. As we know, in the academic community it's not so much that scholars have to be openly censored, or that they have to be instructed in so many words. The academic mind—and that's what I was referring to at the very beginning of our talk in terms of what kind of an education you receive—is very finely tuned to what are the research possibilities and where are the funds and what kind of projects are safe. It's that academic mindset that makes the process seem to be unstructured or automatic decisionmaking without control. But that control is there except that it's pretty deeply structured and largely invisible.

You mentioned funding. Do you receive funding from agencies to do research?

I have never received any funding. I had one very small—by small I mean it was, I think, less than $3,000 from the University of Illinois Graduate Research Center—and that money went into a trip I made to Europe to do research on *Mass Communications and American Empire.* I did a little interviewing there. Since then, and that was a long time ago, I received about two months ago about $2,000 to hire a research assistant in a project I'm doing, again from the university research fund. I have never applied for and I have never received any kind of grant money. I'm not holding that up as some kind of a moral stand. My own work doesn't demand a huge amount of research monies. I don't have a big computer bill and any of these kinds of expenditures. I travel quite a bit. Most of the time, however, when I travel, I'm invited somewhere and the travel bill is met by whoever is inviting me. It's usually not—not usually, not—it is not a corporate enterprise. My needs are relatively modest. I can work within these limits. I'm not saying that this should be the standard for everyone else.

Of course, if you are a total purist—there are those kinds of people around—you could say that I am on the payroll of a major state university and what's the difference between conglomerate grants and a salary from that state university. But I think that gets a little unrealistic. At that point, I guess we'd all have to disengage from almost any activity, if you take it to that ultimate point. But I'm not working for Ogilvy and Mather or Exxon.

With the large corporations, the big boys, as you said, making a lot of decisions for us all, what is the status of critical studies in communications now, and what do you predict for the next few years? Are we going to retreat to a time when people shrugged off the types of things that critical scholars do? Will we be inundated by so much from those who are working for the multinational corporations that those people who are trying to do something different will not even be heard any longer?

I think it's perilous to give a prediction about this. I think there are at least two major forces going in different directions. I'll quickly sketch this out. You can take it from there.

On one side, I think there are forces that are trying to control and shape and lead and guide and basically defuse any kind of work that would tend toward both revelation and understanding. Those forces are no different from those that we've been familiar with in the past, except they may be a little bit more extensive, a little bit more powerful, and they certainly aren't relaxing their efforts. In fact, one could point to—and I won't do it here, I'll just mention it—the envelopment of the university itself by some of the tentacles of these forces. Certain areas of research, at least, are increasingly being sponsored by private corporations. It's true that it's not very evident, at this stage, in the social sciences. It's more microbiology and electronics and computer science and that sort of thing. But that type of intrusion into the university can't be sealed off on the premise that these areas benefit everyone. That is a very spurious kind of reasoning. If, for no other reason, those areas become the preferred research areas, other fields become the starved sectors.

There are many consequences. If this tendency goes unchecked and develops, we will see we'd get a great diminution of critical work, and diminution also of the numbers involved in critical work. There will be no market for critical research, and since everything is being put on a market basis, the activity will dry up. Even if you're trying to do the kind of work that we've been talking about, which doesn't require great funds, I could still see a time coming when just to get information, to be able to use the data bases in which all information increasingly is being stored, rather than hard copy—here I'm speaking of long-term trends—but if this were to occur, one no longer could say, "I don't have any special needs, I work on research which doesn't require expensive equipment." You would have to pay for these data. So there is a greater pressure. Looked at from this consideration, resources are going to be much tighter. In such a situation, the likelihood of a flowering of critical work would be very difficult to imagine.

But I don't think this is the only possibility. I think there's a counterbalancing trend. It's not a calculated one. It's not that on one side there is a force for control and on the other a force for liberation. I think we are now into a time when the dilemmas, the kinds of difficult and irremovable economic and political conditions, both inside the American economy and inside the world economy, are such that the capability to contain these enormous, fragile relationships gets more and more restricted. The ability to manage the many crisis points progressively lessens. The likelihood of breakdown, eruption, rupture, what have you, gets greater and greater.

For example, the most recent episodes—at this very time [1986]—the amount of money coming from arms sales to Iran being funneled to the Contras. Looking at this from a distanced view, it is quite indicative of the present general crisis in the United States. Why would the White House do such a thing? I am not talking about morality. Why would they get involved with something that had so many open ends to it, that would be at some time or another likely to be discovered and create great embarrassment, which is what happened? Could the explanation be (1) they're not all irrational people; (2) they're only adventurous idiots; or (3) they're only political fascists (all of which is true); or most importantly, (4) there are real problems? What do they do in the Middle East when there is an unsustainable policy? The policy is absolutely unsustainable! What do they do in Central America, where their policy also is unable to prevail over any long term? So they are driven, whoever they may be, into various kinds of actions, some more erratic, some more irrational, some more adventurous, some less so, and these things then lead to the kinds of breakdowns or fiascos of which we've seen so many in recent years. I think these crises tend to act as a counterforce. In the field of communications, this is an unusually opportune time for research. Tremendous social disparities are producing a wide variety of problems and circumstances demanding attention and seeking correction. I'm not saying communication students and researchers are going to supply the answers, but at least they can call attention to the problems and study them.

I would say there are these two large-scale influences at work. One is to reduce what we should regard as significant critical work, and the other is to promote it, to encourage it. I'm of the persuasion that the second is going to be more dominant in the years ahead. That is, I'm not saying this will be evident this year or next year, but over the next ten to fifteen years, I will be very surprised if the very nature of what's happening on the domestic scene and in the international order will not produce some very impressive work, some very thoughtful studies. I would look for this work (returning to the theme I have emphasized throughout) to be done not only in the strictly academic sphere. I could imagine it as independent work. I can imagine it coming, for example, from some of the more skilled and intrepid journalists. And from other sectors, too.

But not government reports? Do you think it might even come out in government reports?

No, I would say there it's a very chancy business. There are many more possibilities to control government reports. Still, I've seen some very interesting government reports that may not actually, you know, dot every "i," cross every "t." Yet the material in them makes it very clear what's going on. All the same, I wouldn't imagine that government reports will be the first place where new perspectives will be found. But maybe from the point of view that some of these problems demand some kind of attention, even at the control level, the government reports already do supply useful information—that's certainly true.

Do you believe in the concept that perhaps there are recurring themes, that we go through a period of some repression and then people revolt against that and out of that comes a new type of . . .

I don't want to endorse a cyclical theory: that is, now there is a downturn, but there will be an upturn coming. I wouldn't want to make it so pat, by any means. What I have been saying here is I see these two big forces promoting and discouraging changes. But the time dimension is another matter. There is a degree of exceptionality in the present period. Certain things could happen that could put a halt to the whole dynamic. There are some very dangerous currents active today. These may stymie the counterforces that I've referred to. So I don't believe in a predictable cyclical pattern.

I've heard some people say that you do not believe in a conspiratorial theory concerning what's happened with mass communications or mass communications studies. At other times, I've heard people credit you with a conspiratorial theory. Where do you stand on that?

Well, I'll tell you one thing. Whenever I hear somebody make that kind of a charge, my hair stands on end. I feel it's either uninformed—uninformed in the sense of not really trying to understand what it is that I have written or said—or just indicative of what I regard as a reflex ideological reaction.

I do obviously admit that I try to discover what I regard as the underlying forces, the underlying dynamics of social existence, where certain types of policies, programs, and actions can be examined. There are forces that produce social arrangements. These forces can have varying objectives, which themselves may have certain types of internal contradiction. But to attempt to give an institutional structural approach to what is going on, one has to look at the dynamics. Sometimes the approach is not as full and comprehensive or competent as it might be, but that's another story. That I can accept, of course.

The attempt to give some type of an underlying, institutional, analytical basis to whatever the subject happens to be, in my mind is not conspiratorial. And the use of the term "conspiracy" is an indication either of incomprehension of what's being attempted, or, more frequently, it is used to cut off discussion of this sort of an analysis. Therefore, I must say, it's not the kind of charge that makes me tingle with delight. I regard it as ideological in itself.

How are you accepted in San Diego? I've always thought of San Diego as a conservative community. How do you get along there?

Are we talking about San Diego at large?

Professionally.

Nobody knows I live there, you see. I live on a street, and I must say that I haven't had a large amount of interaction with my neighbors, not for any particular reasons, but I don't even think they know what I do. And that's all to the good. As for the academic community, I would say that, of course, there are a good number of individuals I enjoy meeting and talking with and with whom I have friendly social relations.

But if you're talking about my existence at the university, I'm a nonperson. I'm Ralph Ellison's "Invisible Man." You don't have to be a person of color to be treated to that type of invisibility. I serve on no committees by virtue of someone's decision that I shouldn't be on committees. Naturally, this isn't entirely negative. It relieves me of many onerous duties. On the other hand, one doesn't like to be regarded as a pariah. I guess I went through a period of about ten or twelve years without any kind of a wage increase or promotion. But these are small-scale matters. I mean, it's not as if I was in some, you know, really terrible coercive situation where my life—I don't want to jinx this now—I was physically threatened or had kinds of problems that people do in many, many other parts of the world. So I must keep everything in balance. But I can't really say that I get the feeling that I'm warmly regarded as part of the academic community, exclusive of the individual connections that I have with some people. This too is most understandable because I have a very different view of what the academic community and the university should be. The university is one of the structures that I'm analyzing critically, in terms of what kinds of information or messages we receive.

Do you feel that there are any groups or individuals who are misusing the types of things you've said over the years, and, if so, who are they?

I'd be interested if you could give some examples of that. I hadn't thought too much about it because it hasn't been something that I've had called to my attention—where somebody had taken my work and put it in a way that I would be unhappy with it. I think on a few occasions I've seen reviews of my work by, you know, conservatives or nonsupportive organizations in media, but it's not as if they're using my work in ways that I didn't like. They're just misrepresenting my work. For example, I remember reviews of, I think it was *Communication and Cultural Domination,* where I was writing about the need for societies to protect themselves and be conscious of what was happening in the informational, cultural sphere. The kinds of messages in film, TV, and books and magazines are no less powerful in affecting a country's development and the character of its development than are machinery, food, or whatever. I've seen that idea used to assert that I have the same views as the South African racists, that I want to keep out foreign influence. Or another time I'm linked with Idi Amin in Uganda. But I regard this as just what you could expect from those who don't like what you're saying and try to discredit, misrepresent, or distort it. That is one thing. But what you're asking is, I think a little bit different. I'm not sure that I've come across that. Maybe you've got something you could say.

I've heard media people say that you're a tool of the Soviet bloc, that your work has been used by the Soviets, that you're a cult hero in Cuba, and things of that sort.

Uh huh! That didn't occur to me. That shows why you have to mention it. It didn't even occur to me. Well, I couldn't actually say to what extent my work has been used here, there, anywhere else. I know most of the stuff I've done has been published in many, many places. I've got a shelf of my books in God knows how many languages. They're not only the languages that are used in Eastern Europe or the Soviet Union. Included also are Japanese, Spanish, Swedish, Korean, Portuguese, and a lot of others. So I think, in fact, it's just plain wrong to say that if one place uses my stuff it's exclusively in the interest of that one place.

I think the themes that I'm writing about are themes that are of great interest and concern to large numbers of nations and peoples. Some might agree; some might not agree. I would say there's a fair amount of unanimity that many of the things that I write and talk about are regarded as so sweepingly radical in the United States. The receptivity in many countries—which are not even so different in terms of their fundamental economic structures from the United States—is much greater. Certainly, Scandinavia is one region where my work is very well known. I can't speak about Cuba, where you say I'm a "cult hero." But I know in Scandinavia my work has brought me there many times. The Soviet Union has translated one of my books, but that's no big deal. Other countries have translated two and three books.

I'll give you one act that I don't think was done maliciously but is a good example of how sometimes these things work. I was asked and I agreed to have one of my articles reproduced in a book which was titled *Crisis in International News*—you must know that book—by Richstad and Anderson. They're nice people. Yet they were going to attribute the article which they were reprinting to a publication that came out of Czechoslovakia—*The Democratic Journalist,*[1] out of Prague. I had to tell them it did not appear in that magazine initially. It first appeared in *Le Monde Diplomatique,* and later in several other Western European outlets. Of course, it did appear in *The Democratic Journalist,* but only years after its first publication. I don't think this was done deliberately, but it may be where they saw it first. But for someone then to say that I am a tool of Prague or the German Democratic Republic would just not be correct. The article had appeared many, many places in Western Europe earlier.

You know yourself that when you write, you never know where your stuff is going to wind up. I'm not apologizing that it winds up in Cuba or the GDR or the Soviet Union by any means. I think any of us who are in the international sphere especially know how really controlled information about the world is in the United States, contrary to what most Americans think is the situation. Whereas most of us in this country believe that we have the widest range of information, we're really being short-changed, every day, up and down. When anybody calls attention to the fact that there may be another world out there, that's not the same as saying you're identifying with any one specific part of that world.

An area we touched on briefly that I would like to return to is development and communication. What trends have you seen in the studies of development and communications over the last ten years, and where does that field stand today in the United States?

Well, I think we've gone a little bit over the shift in the 1970s. I mean there was a question about the whole character, what kind of an economy one wanted to produce, what kind of society one wanted to produce. For example, go back and look at Schramm's book, *National Development and Communication.* In it you see implicit, maybe explicit, the assumption that a society should have a free enterprise structure. It should have advertising and the media should be supported by advertising. Those are very big assumptions. There could be many places that might not accept those assumptions and would have other ways of organizing their societies. Now I would say that these were the kinds of questions that were raised against the work of Schramm and others and the kinds of challenges made and given a certain amount of circulation and credibility in the 1970s. Many of these questions came up in the early discussions preceding what was eventually called the New International Information Order. For example, what kind of information would circulate? What should be the character of that information? Should it be commercial? Should it be noncommercial? Was a balance possible? All of those questions were widely discussed abroad. None of which, of course, got any serious attention in the United States.

Now, I would say—and by now, I mean the last several years—there has been a restoration, so to speak. The kinds of changes that have been occurring, that have been referred to earlier, are restoring respectability to development of the kind Schramm wrote about. Yet, it's being carried out under a different formula—high technology. In the late 1950s and the 1960s, UNESCO would publish statistics on how many cinema seats and how many radio sets and how many magazines or newspapers per hundred or thousand people, all part of the Daniel Lerner thesis. The idea that if there was a certain level of mass media, people would develop an outlook that would be empathetic to an entrepreneurial society, and all the rest of it. Everyone would live happily in a market-oriented world. That was the thesis in the late 1950s and 1960s.

Today, while nobody talks about cinema seats and how many people read newspapers—reading is more or less forgotten—today the emphasis is on high technology. If you don't acquire high tech—computers and satellites—you will miss the new age. You will be reduced to slavery. These are the assertions that are circulating in a great part of the world. Many leaders accept this kind of thinking and tell their people that they'll be able to escape from their current conditions of deprivation and achieve participation in the consumer world if they can only become "computer literate," whatever that means.

So economic development today is put in terms of transfer, adaptation, and utilization of high tech. That will lead to the preferred state of high consumption. All that's really changed in this is the addition of a new intermediate process, which is given a special capability to achieve social transformation. This being the case, we're revisiting the old way of thinking about development but appearing to be very modern. Yet if one goes just a little under the surface, you see the same old material dressed up in high-tech clothes.

You think you are going to see more and more of that, reflected in studies and journals?

I think you'll see more of it. But I think here, too, just as the other formula for development communications led nowhere, or led to great disappointment, shall we say, this, too—maybe even more rapidly—will be shown to be inadequate and totally misleading. If it goes down a path that it can't possibly do what it promises to do because it's not intended to do that. That's why some researchers, who may be very decent and honest and well-meaning individuals, to the extent that they participate in work emphasizing the great capabilities of, for example, rural radio, broadcast satellites, and telephone communications—all of which obviously are useful things—to achieve genuine social improvement without changing fundamental structures, are doing work which is, at best, I would say, misleading.

NOTES

1. Schiller's bibliography does not list *The Democratic Journalist* as the periodical that reprinted the article but does include *Soviet Russia* (October 17, 1975) as one that used it.

9

Herbert Schiller: Clarion Voice Against Cultural Hegemony

LAI-SI TSUI

Herbert Schiller has conducted research in topics as varied as TV and radio broadcasting, advertising, satellite communication, and the computer industry. His findings have become a base for research linking communication to political-economic structures (Becker, Hedebro, and Paldan 1986). He pioneered the study of the political-economic aspects of the transfer of media products of the West (especially the United States) to developing societies and the resultant economic and cultural degradation of national civilizations. His study enhanced the notion of cultural imperialism, and his findings have become a base for policy solutions calling for the NIIO (New International Information Order) (Katz and Wedell 1977). His longstanding interest in transnational corporations (TNCs) and their repercussions on developing societies has made his work particularly relevant in the last three decades.

Schiller also sets an example for critical scholarship by his insistence on analyzing and confronting the dominant power structure. It is this insistence that has earned him great respect as well as hostility throughout the worldwide communication science establishment. His writing, lecturing, and teaching have been an impetus for critical communication researchers all over the world.

Schiller's analyses are very controversial. His political-economic analysis is criticized as economic-deterministic and defeatist, and his attitude toward communication technologies is perceived as "technophobic" (Tehranian 1988). Careful and comprehensive reading of his works, however, reveals that he has responded

The author wishes to thank Bella Mody for her encouragement and guidance, Herbert Schiller for agreeing to be interviewed, and Closepet Ramesh for editing the chapter.

to critical commentaries and to global changes, and his analyses have become increasingly sophisticated over the years. An examination of his work is important because he is the exemplar of the political-economic perspective and a central figure in the history of communication research. In this chapter, I will review the major themes in his work and the changes he has made in them over the years. Such a review will provide a base for me to raise some issues central to debates in political-economy studies.

Major Themes in Schiller's Works

Mind Management and the Military-Industrial Complex

In his earlier studies, Schiller focuses on the political economy of the production of mass media. By tracing the history of the development of U.S. broadcasting, he shows how the communication structure has been shaped by the economic structure and how communication policy has been influenced by postwar U.S. foreign policy and the political ideology of the ruling elite.

The United States had attained economic and military dominance by the end of World War II. The ruling elite was worried that the Soviet Union and its Communist bloc would spread communism to newly independent nations. To protect its newly gained economic and political prizes from allies and adversaries and to counter the upcoming perceived threat of the Communist bloc, the U.S. military and corporations were eager to convert people all over the world to capitalism and to guard against the influence of communism.

Schiller points out that there is no explicit central direction from the government on the programming of the media. Nevertheless, the reliance on financial sponsorship of corporations conditions the content of media programs (at least by not antagonizing the patrons and not challenging the existing socioeconomic arrangement) and facilitates full-scale advertising. Moreover, the majority of media professionals do buy into the pro–status quo political ideology that serves to convert people to capitalism and guard against any search for alternatives.

People in capitalist societies such as the United States are exposed to messages that contend that people enjoy the freedom of choice among a variety of consumer goods, that the government, media, and the education system are neutral and are not biased toward any vested interests, that social pluralism exists and everyone's interest is represented, and that the existing socioeconomic arrangement is all right and there is no better alternative (certainly not the devil "communism"). The messages do not correspond to the social realities and serve to reinforce the existing myths of individual and personal choice, individual acquisition, competition, and mobility, the absence of social conflict and social inequality, the neutrality of government, education, and science, and media pluralism (Schiller 1973: 8–24).

Electronics and Economics for Crisis Management

Schiller (1984b) has focused on the political economy of the development and global transfer of new information technologies (ITs) in the United States since the 1980s. He points out that the new ITs in the United States were first developed to respond to the perceived Communist threat and subsequently to revitalize the declining economy, manifesting in crises such as inflation, plant closings, unemployment, and regional decay. New ITs, services, production, and know-how have become increasingly significant components of U.S. foreign trade and have supplied dynamism to the domestic economy.

Schiller demystifies the neutrality of new ITs. He claims (1976a, 1981) that technology is social construction; it is neither "neutral" nor "autonomous." Technologies have been conditioned and shaped to support the military-industrial complex. The U.S. government supported early research and subsequent development of information technologies and provided the initial market for these products. Once these products became viable and profitable, private corporations took over the operational facilities and techniques. Schiller also points out the significant participation of the scientific and academic communities in the design and development of ITs for military and commercial purposes.

Schiller considers TNCs to be the prime movers in IT development. ITs facilitate processing, storage, and transmission of information within and across national boundaries and thus make geographical distance obsolete. TNCs can set up offshore production plants in developing countries to exploit cheap labor and cut down on production costs.

ITs significantly change the means of production as they become commodities being bought and sold and as the possession of information represents means of profit making. In all arenas, functions that were rarely seen as revenue raising have been taken over and reorganized with the availability of new ITs and a new way of processing and disseminating information. In the United States, public informational and cultural institutions such as museums, public and university libraries, and art galleries have increasingly been subjected to the forces of commercialization and privatization. For example, a growing number of microelectronics and microbiology laboratories have been integrated, financially and structurally, with corporate conglomerates (Schiller 1989).

ITs and privatization have been promoted as a panacea for the economic crises striking all developed economies. European governments have been backing up the introduction of ITs, and they have started privatizing their telecommunications systems (PTTs) and public services.

Corporate Takeover of Cultural Expression

To counteract the growing dismissal of the cultural imperialism thesis, Schiller asserts its contemporary relevance in at least two of his latest publications, *Culture*

Inc.: The Corporate Enclosure of Public Expression (1989) and "Not Yet a Post-Imperialist Era" (1991). Schiller compares the corporate takeover of the sociocultural spheres of contemporary societies to Britain's Enclosure Movement in the early nineteenth century. He argues, "Enclosure is the appropriate description for what has been happening in the United States in the last twenty-five years, not to farmlands—most of that has long since been bought up by corporate agribusinesses—but to the sites and channels of public expression and creativity" (Schiller 1989: 89).

Schiller is concerned with the "commercialization and industrialization of the mind" of contemporary societies—that cultural production has become increasingly indistinguishable from industrial production. This is an inevitable result of capitalist development. With the advance in ITs, the nucleus of culture in a highly industrialized society—information itself—has become a commodity, an item for sale. The process of cultural production that generates information is subjected to commercialization and market principles and is made to be reliant on new ITs. "Thus, the cultures of the home, the factory, the office, the school, and the street, in their utilization of electronics, as it is currently embodied in the new technologies, are at the same time, adopting commercial modes and networks that integrate and 'rationalize' human consciousness, no less than industrial production" (Schiller 1984b: 78).

Schiller documents the corporations' takeover of cultural institutions. Museums, in his view, for example, are "becoming public relations agents for the interests of big business and its ideological allies" (Schiller 1989: 92).[1] Corporate sponsorship of museum exhibitions, as advertising-supported media, leads unavoidably to self-censorship. Shows that are based on centrist ideals and unquestioning subject matter, rather than those promoting critical awareness, can get sponsorship and thereby are being organized. Schiller quotes Brian Wallis: "Sponsorship of art exhibitions helps to conceal . . . the conflict between . . . humanitarian pretenses and the neo-imperialist expansion of multinational capitalism today by providing both the museum and the corporation with a tool for enriching individual lives while suppressing real cultural and political differences, for promoting art 'treasures' while masking private corporate interests" (Quoted in Schiller 1989: 94). In addition to museums, corporate sponsors have captured theaters, performing arts centers, public spaces (in which public events like street fairs, parades, and celebrations are held), and the airwaves (Schiller 1989).[2]

Cultural Imperialism: Transnationalization of the Total Information-Cultural Environment

In the 1960s and 1970s, Schiller consistently revealed the exports of Anglo-American media products, values, and practices to developing countries and the resultant standardization of life styles and consumption patterns and the domination of corporate culture around the world. Schiller defines cultural imperialism as "the sum of the processes by which a society is brought into the modern world system and how its dominating stratum is attracted, pressured, forced, and sometimes bribed into shaping social institutions to correspond to, or even promote, the values and structures of the dominating center of the system" (Schiller 1976a:9).

According to Schiller, the United States has consciously imposed its "politically correct" information policy on the world over the past few decades. The major principles and practices include (1) the free flow of information, (2) "objectivity" and "neutrality" of the informational apparatus, and (3) a rejection of international agreements that would endorse some degree of social accountability for the international system in general and journalists in particular.

The 1950s and early 1960s witnessed the free-flow doctrine implemented globally, with massive media flows from New York, Hollywood, and London around the world. Many developing countries realized the danger of informational-cultural penetration by developed countries as the entire character of development was defined by the media and governments of these countries. In a series of UNESCO meetings, developing countries collectively called for a NIIO (New International Information Order) to restrict the information flow from developed countries and to protect their national sovereignty.

Since the 1970s, the United States has taken the lead in counterattacking the NIIO by accusing such policy of depriving peoples of the developing world of access to "reliable" news and information and any government regulation of communication/media systems as violating the principles of "objectivity" and "neutrality." In the 1980s, during the Reagan era, the United States even initiated a cooptation policy by offering selective aid and collaboration to nonsocialist members of the NIIO coalition and promising to teach them the use of high tech to reduce the imbalance in the information flow. In addition, the U.S. government withdrew its membership from UNESCO in 1984, thus manifesting the U.S. government's advocacy of deregulation and privatization in the international arena and the developing countries. This move was a hard blow to UNESCO, and the effort to build a NIIO came to a standstill.

With the rapid introduction of new ITs since the 1980s, there was a transnationalization of a "near-total corporate information-cultural environment" (Schiller 1989: 128). The issues of concern today are not simply the one-way flow of media cultural products but the transmission of data and information. TNCs need information on developing societies so that they can target them as markets for consumer and high-tech products. To them, national control over the information system is an obstacle that must be removed. The United States has taken the lead to promote privatization and deregulation especially in the PTT in Europe and developing countries. Media TNCs can bypass national supervision by directly beaming programs to those audiences that can afford satellite communications. U.S. films, TV series, and even newscasts such as those of CNN, CBS, and ABC have been broadcast to Europe and many other countries.

Schiller documents the worldwide imitation of U.S. films, TV programs, music, news, entertainment, theme parks, and shopping malls. For example, Disneyland theme parks have been launched in Europe and Japan. The Brazilian media, as huge regional media and film exporting producers, make soap operas that copy Western values, norms, patterns of behavior, and models of social relations. Schiller also notices the former socialist countries' eagerness to adopt new ITs and Western managerial, business, and media outlook. Increasing numbers of countries accept Western–Japanese capital's advertising sponsorship in public events. The character of the developing economies is distorted to enable a privileged minority to enjoy Western consumption with diminishing basic need provision. National resources are being harnessed for consumption that leads to wastefulness and inequality. Schiller argues that cultural imperialism as such will result in increasing corporate control and decreasing cultural diversity and creativity.

Impacts of New ITs

Will New ITs Revitalize the Developed Economies? Schiller admits that there have been significant job increases mainly in the high-tech sector—computer manufacturing, telecommunications, data processing, information storage, retrieval, and dissemination, and automated equipment. But the benefits are enjoyed by technical and managerial professionals. New ITs have facilitated a tremendous shift in the balance of power between capital and labor, to the advantage of the former, as TNCs can organize the division of labor globally, play off labor at one locality against another, restore patterns of homework and piecework, force workers to accept wage cuts, and discourage unionization.

Schiller detects the self-destructiveness of capital: "Labor as an organized social force will largely disappear. Capital's dream may well turn out to be its nightmare" (Schiller 1984b: 105). He thinks that labor unions in developed market economies have actually served as a powerful economic and political stabilizer for the market system: "Capitalism without organized labor may become a capitalism of political gyrations and persistent and intense economic slump" (Schiller 1984b: 106). Capitalist production is sustained by consumption. New ITs that facilitate wage cuts, replacement of labor, and the resistance to unionization will lower consumers' purchasing power and thus reduce profit for capital.

Moreover, developed economies depend on developing countries as markets for their new ITs. Schiller doubts that developing countries, burdened by debt, will be able to provide a mass market so desperately required by the crisis-ridden Western economies.

The Weakening of the Democratic Order and the Withering of Radical Consciousness New ITs facilitate privatization of the public sector. People are getting less free access to services previously subsidized by governments and have to pay user charges. In a class-divided society, the societal knowledge gap will be enlarged with the introduction of new ITs.

With the service of new ITs and the prevalence of privatization, private corporations dominate all crucial sectors in market economies and penetrate both public and private space. The opportunity for independent, authentic expression is marginalized, diversity of opinion restricted, and democratic order weakened. Radical and egalitarian consciousness, as well as alternative conceptions of life, are unable to take root in developed market societies. People are unwilling to participate in activities that threaten the possession of, or the hope of acquiring, consumer goods.

The Endangering of the National and Economic Sovereignty of Developing Countries Schiller is concerned about the transborder data flow (transmission of computerized information or media messages across national boundaries). Once a developing country is linked to the data bases set up and administered by transnational corporations, it is easily subjected to information dependence and becomes vulnerable to external control. Transnational corporations can get access to a nation's data and utilize them to their own advantage. Furthermore, the content of most of the information transferred across national boundaries is beyond scrutiny by national governments.

Changes in Schiller's Analyses over the Years

Many of Schiller's critics tend to treat his works in a static fashion; they neglect the changes he has made over the years in responding to critical commentaries and the changes in the global capitalism.

Recognition of the Change in Global Capitalism

Over the past two decades, Schiller has recognized the decline in U.S. global economic influence and the rise of Japan and Western European countries. Nevertheless, he argues, the cultural domination of the transnational corporate system still bears a marked American imprint. It is on these grounds that Schiller still finds the critique of the American empire relevant. Schiller (1991) also points out that the victorious U.S. military deployment in Iraq, the accommodationist outlook of the then Soviet Union, and the subordination of the United Nations to the U.S. lead have consolidated the military complex of the United States, despite the decline of its industrial complex.

Schiller once echoed Cees Hamelink's strategy of dissociation that advised developing societies to delink from the political, economic, and cultural association of the world business system. Now he recognizes that at this juncture of history, with the absence of alternative development models, the failure of the socialist experiments, and the increasing dominance of transnational capitalism, it is very unlikely that developing countries would choose such a strategy, even though it would be wise and desirable (Tsui 1991).

Proactive Policy Suggestions

Schiller has focused on attacking the dominant power rather than proposing concrete actions to guide social actions. Many of his sympathetic colleagues, such as Nicholas Garnham and Majid Tehranian, have criticized his theory for its negativism and defeatism. They fear that in the Schillerian thesis the transnational power is so powerful and the ideological control so overwhelming that there is no space for change.

To counter the "defeatist" criticism, Schiller in his most recent book, *Culture Inc.: Corporate Enclosure of Public Expression* (1989), proposes not only a reactive policy but a proactive policy to change the information-cultural environment. First, privatization should be curbed and the public order restored. Second, the U.S. government should rejoin UNESCO and respect international efforts that seek cultural and informational sovereignty. Third, a new democratic interpretation of the "free-flow" doctrine should be made to reduce private monopoly power over media products, data processing, publishing, and advertising. Expanded public support and encouragement of noncommercial expression and creativity should be restored. This should be accompanied by managerial and administrative modes to insulate these activities from the direction of the state.

Is Schiller a technophobe? Such labeling is misleading and represents a caricaturing of his position (see Tehranian 1988). He does not deny the potential benefits of computerization, communication satellites, and cable transmission of messages (Schiller 1984a). He mentions the possibility of alternative use of communication technologies by social groups. However, his work is aimed mainly at advancing a political economy of communication, not at proposing strategies of technological intervention for communitarian movements. Therefore, he focuses primarily on the negative effects of technologies used by the social and political powers.

A Response to the "Active Audience" Thesis

Schiller has focused on the documentation and theoretical analysis of communication structures and policies and has seldom been involved in methodological debate. Nevertheless, he is apparently gradually becoming aware of the rising influence of the "active audience" thesis that is discrediting cultural imperialism, criticizing the former and reasserting the cultural imperialism thesis and his political-economy perspective (Schiller 1989).

The basic tenet of the "active audience" thesis is that an individual viewer constructs his/her own meaning of the images that the media disseminate and therefore is relatively autonomous from the influence of the message senders. Accordingly, audiences are not powerless and are not necessarily influenced by the media producer.

Schiller documents the research of "active audience" thesis advocates and counters it methodologically, theoretically, and empirically. Methodologically, he criticizes the thesis as reductionist because it refutes the cultural imperialism thesis based on the impacts on individuals of specific cultural products—a program, a TV series, a movie, or a genre of fiction. Schiller argues that individuals are influenced not only by a particular cultural product but by a combination of various cultural means in the existing totalizing information-cultural environment. Individuals, therefore, are unable to specify sources of an idea, value, perspective, or reaction. Schiller questions the "active audience" thesis advocates: If one does not find a direct impact of a cultural product on an audience, can one immediately argue that cultural imperialism does not exist?

Theoretically, Schiller criticizes this thesis on its dismissal of class, its overly optimistic attribution of social pluralism, and its excessive subjectivity. "Active audience" thesis advocates focus on the power shared by individuals, but they ignore the tremendous power in the hands of the corporate and ruling elite. Schiller does not object to the conception of heterogeneity in society. Nevertheless, he asserts that, however unique each individual is, he/she is subjected to the rule of market forces and the domination of capital over those market forces" (Schiller 1989: 53). The dismissal of class and the dominant power structure and the assumption of social pluralism are the biggest blindspots of their theory, Schiller says.

Empirically, Schiller documents evidence to support his argument. People are certainly not informational and cultural dupes. Nevertheless, they are simply not equipped to deal with a persuasive disinformation system and a totalizing cultural environment. A question he poses by way of example is that, in the face of several decades' disinformation on the socialist countries, their leaders, and their development records, "where, except for a saving few, has there been a public outcry against the enormous fabrication of fear (of socialism and communism) that has supported the edifice of the neutral security state for at least fifty years?" (Schiller 1989: 155).

A Commentary on Schiller's Perspective

The power of Schiller's perspective lies in its theoretical cogency, its broad coverage of various aspects of cultural life under capitalism, and its renewed relevance of explicating the socioeconomic control of TNCs. His political-economic framework is systemic in scope and essence. He focuses on analyzing the political and economic institutions—capital and the state and their policies in the service of the "world business system." Schiller not only explains the political economy of communication but also offers a theory to confront the power structure and to help advance social change (see Schiller 1976a, 1981, 1989). As Dallas Smythe and Tran Van Dinh rightly state, "Schiller's writings are in the methodological tradition of the classical economists and their predecessors in the 17th and 18th centuries." Like the latter, Schiller's works have an explicit ideological perspective and a coherent critical, institutional method. "Just as Smith and Ricardo inveighed against the policies and structures of their established order, so Schiller presents a case for economic and cultural autonomy for traditional and ex-colonial countries against the dominant pressure of monopoly capitalism (1983:35–36).

Schiller explicitly focuses on revealing the logic of capital accumulation, the capitalist relations of production, and the power center in global capitalism. He claims that TNCs are the "highest embodiment of the global capitalist system" (Tsui 1991:51). He explicitly argues for a class perspective (Schiller 1976a; Tsui 1991). He posits, "There has to be an understanding of how the social order evolved under capitalism for about 500 years. Such a perspective enables us to understand how the system developed, which classes, which particular strata received the greatest benefit. . . . Capitalist development is derived from the misery of a large number of people inside and outside the country" (Tsui 1991: 52).

Are Schiller's Analyses Still Relevant?

The world is experiencing an epochal political-economic transformation and technological change. Until the late 1980s, the global system could be seen as constituted by three major groups: the capitalist "First World," the socialist "Second World," and the peripheral capitalist "Third World." In the short span of a few years, Japan and Germany have experienced a rise as economic powers, and the United States has experienced a decline of its economic power, but a rise in its military hegemony, with its victorious military deployment in Iraq and the collapse of the Soviet Union. The Second World has all but disappeared. The Third World is increasingly differentiated. With the emergence of NICs (newly industrialized countries), many pro–status quo scholars proclaimed the demise of the concept of the Third World, or even the end of the Third World. They argue that economies that practice export-led growth economic strategies, free trade, and free flow of information will replicate the economic success of the NICs. Some recognize that certain developing countries (China, India, and Brazil) have more bargaining power vis-à-vis TNCs and can carve a share in the global market due to their abundant natural resources, domestic market, and technological capabilities. Many think that delinking from the global system is impossible.

As far as development communication is concerned, an increasing number of scholars question the thesis of media or cultural imperialism. They argue that several developing countries (e.g., Mexico, Brazil, Hong Kong, and Taiwan) have succeeded in producing media programs and films and in reducing their reliance on Western media programs. Technological changes have brought about cost reduction in video and audio technology, allowing for increased local and decentralized production. These enable more media production and social uses of media technologies in developing countries (Straubhaar 1991).

It is under these circumstances that many scholars question the validity of dependency theory (including cultural dependency and imperialism), on which Schiller's understanding of the global system is built. Many have modified their conception of power. The power of the TNCs and developed countries is not all-embracing and overwhelming. There is always space for developing countries to maneuver. Schiller's analyses are therefore questioned.

Schiller (1991) certainly recognizes these changes within the global system. Nevertheless, he argues that with the collapse of the Second World, the most powerful countries in the global system, namely, G-7, are less restrained in their cultural-ideological bombardment to countries on the "triumph of capitalism" through Western mainstream media.

Have the developing countries resisted cultural imperialism? Schiller's answer is no and is clearly illustrated in *Culture Inc.: The Corporate Enclosure of Public Expression* (1989) and "Not Yet a Post-Imperialist Era" (1991). Schiller uses Omar Souki Oliveira's (1990) research to counteract the argument of the developing countries' success in reducing cultural dependency: Brazilian programming is "the creolization of U.S. cultural products. It is the sliced up Third World copy of Western values, norms, patterns of behavior and models of social relations. . . . The overwhelming majority of Brazilian soaps have the same purpose as their U.S. counterparts, i.e., to sell products."

Schiller's analyses are empirically valid and currently relevant. The past decade's development experience provides support for Schiller's argument. The growing differentiation of Third World countries does not mean that there has been an end to the harsh realities faced by the Third World. Many Third World countries remain in similar development deadlock. Even the NICs are experiencing unfavorable global markets. The projection of the economic success of NICs as a result of economic liberalization and the practice of export-oriented industrialization is simplistic. External geopolitical factors, the timing of entry into the global system, and the internal structural conditions and history of those countries contributing to economic development are neglected.

Will the economic success of the NICs be repeated? The global economy has not been as favorable to newcomers as it was in the 1960s and early 1970s. Growth is slower, and protectionism in the G-7 countries is strong. There is an unemployment problem in these countries (except Japan). Technological innovation in some labor-intensive assembly processes will probably lead to a return of production to the G-7 countries.

In recent years, many Third World countries have been welcoming foreign investment by relaxing domestic ownership requirements, removing restrictions on foreign investments, liberalizing trade, privatizing state enterprises, and improving telecommunication technologies and services. So far, in most of these countries, such attempts to lure new foreign investments have not been successful.

The Third World has increasingly become a computer-import market. China, Thailand, Saudi Arabia, Brazil, Mexico, Venezuela, and Argentina have become large computer-import markets. The strong oligopoly in the production of computer equipment subjects the Third World to depending upon a very few giant

TNCs. Most Third World countries lack expertise in accessing computer technology and are often sold obsolete technologies.

It is argued that the Third World, through initial import, can equip itself with the capability to develop and export high tech and gain a market share in the global high-tech market. No doubt there has been an increase in the share of the Third World in this market in recent years. However, such participation in high-tech export has primarily been from a limited number of countries, with very narrow ranges of specialization in specific products. Such production is predominantly a result of foreign direct investment, not domestic investment. These countries are selected for their economic incentives, low-wage labor supply, tax privilege, and linguistic convenience (Hamelink 1986). The Philippines, Malaysia, Jamaica, and Mexico have become offshore data entry locations that offer cheap female labor for the production of fragmented parts of high-tech for TNCs (Hamelink 1986; Sussman and Lent 1991).

The NICs are no exception to the increasingly unfavorable global markets, the protectionism on manufacturers imposed by the G-7, the withdrawal of foreign direct investment, and the formation of trade blocs, in addition to domestic sociopolitical movements. Singapore experienced significant withdrawal of U.S. banking and finance in 1986, the removal of GSP in 1989, and the threat of automated manufacturing has forced the government to rethink its strategy of attracting foreign investment with low-cost electronic assembly resources. Korea is described as having fallen into an export-led trap.

The logic of the market, which is seen as the organizing principle of society, not only commands the process of economic development but also extends to the social and cultural life. Under this logic, not only trade but also the flow of information should be free. Most developing countries have given up fighting for a restriction of transborder data flow and a New International Information Order, which they supported in the late 1970s and early 1980s in UNESCO. Many countries have deregulated or even privatized their telecommunications and broadcasting sectors. Some of them are dominated by foreign capital (AT&T and GE in Asia, Cable and Wireless in the Caribbean, and IBM and Apple Computers in Latin America). Without adequate policy to restrict the transborder data flow, to regulate private sector participation, and to let private companies run these economically and culturally strategic sectors, these countries simply open themselves up to the bombardment of the liberal creed, business culture, and consumerist ideology through advertising and TV programming and thus to the corporate takeover of (popular) culture. The socialization process by which people learn what to want, which used to occur primarily in the home and school, is increasingly taking place through the media of the global communications industries.

Schiller's conceptual innovation of the near total information-cultural enviroment captures well the contemporary popular culture sphere. Schiller is right in criticizing "active audience thesis" advocates' argument as being reductionistic. Grounded in the uses and gratification tradition, they tend to overstate the power of the individual and understate political-economic power. While they do discuss class, they treat it as one of the descriptive categories along with gender, ethnicity, religion, and so forth. They may be well-intentioned scholars with the aim to empower audience, but their work may exhibit a sense of "inflated voluntarism."

Is Schiller's Political-Economic Analysis a Model of Economic Determinism?

Schiller's political-economic analysis is criticized for the fallacy of economic determinism because it argues that culture (as superstructure) is a reflection of the economic base and perceives that all aspects of life under capitalism are a mirror reflection of the systemic need of capitalism. Jennifer Slack (1984a, 1984b, 1989) describes Schiller's conception of the causal relationship between technologies and society as an "expressive approach," which characterizes every phenomenon as an expression and reflection of the totality that is imbued with an "essence." The way technologies are structured and used can be explained in terms of the essence. Slack (1984b) says that Schiller defines "essence" as the capitalist relations of production and says that technologies cannot have any impact other than enhancing the capitalist relations of production. Such an approach is reductionistic, says Slack.

No doubt there is a sense of determinacy in the political-economic theory of communication and culture. But does Schiller's model of determinism disregard history, changes and contradictions within capitalism, and is it therefore mechanistic and reductionistic? Does it commit the fallacy of functionalist tautology in various blends of orthodox structuralist Marxism? Or does it preserve space for the explanation of the existence of contingencies and contradictions?

In Schiller's view, the economic is determinant under capitalism, because capitalism is a social formation organized around an abstract system of exchange relations. This is why Schiller focuses on the systemic characteristics of capitalism—socioeconomic arrangements like property ownership, the market principle, the organization of production, the division of labor, and the distribution of income. Grounded in the historical materialist theoretical tradition, Schiller understands society and history in terms of the actual historical process, which itself concretely exhibits the play of class relations, power differentiation, and relations of domination and subordination. His analysis starts with the totality—the interaction of politics, economics, society, culture, and history.

Schiller's analysis, while focusing on the economic structure, does not exclude historical specificity or the interaction of various forces within each particular country (Schiller 1978b; Schiller and Nordenstreng 1979; Tsui 1991). Schiller (1979) agrees with Sunkel: "The analytical framework of classical political-economy, and particularly of Marxism, do at least go in the directions required to analyze development: globalism and wholism. But at the same time . . . they require historical specificity, that is, the analysis of the structural characteristics of a society at a particular time and place, since they are the determinants of the functioning and development of that society" (1976: 16–20).

For example, although he sees the state as the protector and promoter of capitalism, Schiller admits that if the workers' movement in a country is powerful, the state needs to constrain its intention to assist capital (Schiller 1986: 55): "A political-economy of culture and communication has to take into account that economy, history, and cultural difference, and attempt to explain how these work themselves out in specific state policies and practices" (Schiller 1984b: 88).

Schiller concedes that despite the systemic need of capitalism, "there is still considerable space remaining for the play of creative effort." He gives the example of alternative media efforts to push for authentic expression of culture. Another example is the push for a NIIO by the developing countries in the struggle against the cultural and economic domination of the West. However, empirical evidence, such as the difficulties of the alternative movements, the collapse of the Third World's collective effort to push for a NIIO, and the United States's withdrawal from UNESCO, compels Schiller to conclude that the economic structure of capitalism and the major political-economic institutions have been dominating.

Many scholars, including those influenced by the poststructuralist, cultural studies approach, tend to prefer to introduce a sense of indeterminacy in the logic of capitalism. The role of capitalist relations of production as the major determining force in the capitalist system, ideology, politics, and technologies is seen as an important force. This force does not totally reject any causality but prefers a position of causal pluralism.

What is problematic about such a position is that it fails to confront the power structure effectively. Advocates, while advancing a complicated picture of the interaction of forces in conditioning communication and culture, do not tell which is the major determining force and are therefore incapable of identifying the target of attack. One can get a picture that social structure is so fluid and social forces so different given a particular space and time that one cannot argue for any generality. If one were to ask what forces bring about what outcomes of technologies, the answer probably would be, "It depends." One wonders whether there is really no major contradiction within the social structure one can identify. What is the structure of domination that lies at the heart of the economic, social, and political power, if not class relations? What other social relations are at the foundation of social organization and global historical processes over the past few centuries, if not the capitalist relations of production and exploitation?

Does the Schillerian thesis commit the fallacy of functional Marxism, whose advocates explain every social phenomenon in terms of the functions of the capitalist system? Schiller does convey such an impression at times. For example, he explains mind management in terms of the "systemic need" or the "systemic characteristics" of capitalist system. But through a thorough reading of his works one can see that the analyses he has done are causal but not functional. He does assume capitalism as a ubiquitous system, but he does not see it as static and argues that every social phenomenon functions to serve the system, as functional Marxists do. To him, capitalism is full of contradictions and is a constellation of various forces given a particular time and space. Social development is determined not totally by the capitalist economic arrangement but also by a series of shifting relationships between economic and other forces, each interacting with the others in a process of uneven and contradictory development. The social totality at any historical moment is expressive only of the actual state of those shifting interrelationships, not of any abstract systemic need of capitalism regarding time and space. Such an expressive approach is not deterministic and mechanistic but relational. Schiller uses historical and institutional analysis to trace the causal connection between the decisions and policies of major political and economic institutions and the communication structure, policy, and content. He does not apply functional analysis to his works.

Overall Appraisal

The power of Schiller's writing lies in the fact that it is not heavily theory-laden but empirically informed and passionate. Schiller's framework is built on the Marxist and classical political economic traditions. Nevertheless, he starts not with theory but with empirical phenomena and history. He begins with a documentation of policy materials from the boardrooms of capitalists and the state rooms of governments as well as with his observations of social phenomena. His theoretical arguments and central tenets reflect the influence of various intellectual traditions. Therefore, his writings can be appreciated by readers both with and without theoretical training.

Some mainstream academicians, such as the late Ithiel Pool, criticized Schiller's works as polemical, ideological, and poor in substance. Behind Pool's argument is the tenet of positivism, supporting value neutrality for scientific research and theory construction and the testability of hypothesis.

Schiller is certainly ideological, as are Ithiel Pool and others. Schiller's ideological orientation compels him to detect the structural inequality along class lines and to confront the power structure in global capitalism.

Schiller's writing is certainly passionate as well. His refusal to use quantitative research techniques to arrive at statistically sophisticated (but mostly trivial) findings does not lead him to unsubstantiated theoretical formulation or to empty polemic. He does not hide his value judgments or his passion in his writings. He is concerned with human well-being. He is dissatisfied with the sociocultural degradation in contemporary societies in that individual acquisition, competition, fame, and money overwhelm community solidarity, care, and collective welfare. He urges readers to reflect upon what kind of society we are living in and what kind of society we wish to be in. His work aims not only to expose the political-economic arrangements and structural inequality but also to heighten our awareness to seek change. He strongly condemns the unjust system. It is this passion that makes his works powerful. More importantly, passion has not replaced substance. His works are based upon his reading of history and contemporary world development, as well as his historical documentary research.

NOTES

1. For example, the Metropolitan Museum of Art in New York City began the practice of putting up temporary exhibitions with huge banners showing the corporate sponsorship. Schiller documents the corporate sponsorship of exhibitions at various museums by Mobil Oil Corporation, Chase Manhattan Bank, AT&T, and Tiffany. Tiffany took over the fiftieth anniversary of the Metropolitan Museum of Art and used it at the same time for an exhibition on its company history, "Triumph in American Silver-Making: Tiffany & Co. 1860–1900" (Schiller 1989:94).

2. Public TV has been given the less preferred part of the frequency spectrum—the UHF band. Nevertheless, public TV did succeed in getting a small stratum of viewers composed of affluent and influential intellectuals and professionals. This higher income group has become a target of big luxury goods advertisers. Discreet announcements at the beginning and end of programs are in place to remind the audience that the programs are being made available by the funding of "public-spirited" corporations. The erosion of the noncommercial broadcast principle has thus increased.

REFERENCES

Becker, J., G. Hedebro, and L. Paldan. (1986). *Communication and Domination: Essays to Honor Herbert I. Schiller.* Norwood, NJ: Ablex.

Bolton, R. (1989). Communication in the age of the Fortune 500: An interview with Herbert Schiller. *Afterimage* (November):14–18.

Dagnino, E. (1973). Cultural and ideological dependence: Building a framework. In *Struggles of Dependency,* edited by F. Bonilla and G. Robert. Stanford, CA: Nairobi Bookstore.

Hamelink, C. (1986). Information technology and the Third World. *Communicator* (July–October):10–16.

Jayaweera, N. (1984). Communication satellites: A Third World perspective. In *Information Technology and a New International Order,* edited by J. Becker. Stockholm: Studentlitteraur.

Katz, E., and G. Wedell. (1977). *Broadcasting in the Third World.* Cambridge: Harvard University Press.

Kumar, K. J. (1988–89). Communication and development. *Communication Research Trends,* 9(3):1–16.

Oliveira, O. S. (1990). On Brazilian soaps outside Hollywood: Is cultural imperialism fading out? Deutsche Gesellschaft für Semotik, Internationaler Kongress, Universität Passau, October 8–10.

Pool, I. De Sola, and H. I. Schiller. (1981). Perspectives on communication research: An exchange. *Journal of Communication,* 31(3):15–23.

Schiller, H. I. (1969). *Mass Communications and American Empire.* New York: Augustus M. Kelley.

———.(1973). *The Mind Managers.* Boston: Beacon Press.

———. (1975a). The appearance of national communications policies: A new arena for social struggle. *Gazette,* 21(2):82–94.

———. (1975b). The balance of power and the ecology of ideas. Society for General Systems Research, AAAS meetings, Denver, Colorado, February.

———. (1975c). The material side of consciousness. *Democratic Journalist* (June):6–10.

———. (1976a). *Communications and Cultural Domination.* New York: International Arts and Sciences Press.

———. (1976b). Fabricated culture. *Lier en boog,* 4:153–63.

———. (1976c). Transnational media and national development. In *Fair Communication Policy Conference,* edited by J. Richstad, pp. 21–31. Honolulu: East-West Center.

———. (1978a). Computer communications for whom and for what? *Journal of Communication,* 28(4):184–93.

———. (1978b). Decolonization of information: Efforts toward a New World Information Order. *Latin American Perspectives,* 16(5):35–48.

———. (1980a). Electronic utopias and structural realities. In *A Reader on the McBride Report,* edited by C. Hamelink, pp. 53–61. Rome: IDOC.

———. (1980b). Transnational communication and national self-reliance. *Third World,* 6:64–66.

———. (1981). *Who Knows: Information in the Age of the Fortune 500.* Norwood, NJ: Ablex.

———. (1983a). The communication revolution: Who benefits? *Media Development,* 30:18–21.

———. (1983b). Critical research in the information age. *Journal of Communication,* 33(3):249–57.

———. (1984a). Informatics and information flows: The underpinnings of transnational capitalism. In *Critical Communication Review,* edited by V. Mosco and J. Wasko, pp. 3–31. Norwood, NJ: Ablex.

———. (1984b). *Information and the Crisis Economy.* Norwood, NJ: Ablex.

———. (1984c). Remote sensing by satellite: Global hegemony or social utility. In *World Communications: A Handbook,* edited by G. Gerbner and M. Seifert, pp. 236–45. New York: Longman.

———. (1986). The erosion of national sovereignty by the world business system. In *The Myth of Information Revolution,* edited by M. Traber, pp. 21–34. London: Sage.

———. (1989). *Culture Inc.: The Corporate Enclosure of Public Expression.* New York: Oxford University Press.

———. (1991). Not yet a post-imperialist era. *Critical Studies in Mass Communication,* 8:13–28.

Schiller, H. I., and K. Nordenstreng. (1979). *National Sovereignty and International Communication.* Norwood, NJ: Ablex.

Slack, J. D. (1984a). *Communication Technologies and Society: Conceptions of Causality and the Politics of Intervention.* Norwood, NJ: Ablex.

———. (1984b). Survey of the impacts of communication technologies. In *Progress in Communication Sciences, 4,* edited by B. Dervin and M. J. Voight, pp. 73–109. Norwood, NJ: Ablex.

———. (1989). Contextualizing technology. In *Rethinking Communication,* vol. 2, edited by B. Dervin, L. P. Grossberg, B. J. O'Keefe, and E. Wartella, pp. 329–45. Newbury Park, CA: Sage.

Smythe, D. W., and T. Van Dinh. (1983). On critical theory and the political economy of communication. Unpublished paper.

Straubhaar, J. D. (1991). Media: From imperialism to asymmetrical interdependence and cultural proximity. *Critical Studies in Mass Communication,* 8:1–12.

Sunkel, D. (1976). *The Development of Development Thinking.* Sussex: University of Sussex, Institute of Development Studies.

Sussman, G. (1982). Telecommunication technology: Transnationalizing the New Philippine Information Order. *Media, Culture and Society,* 4:377–90.

Sussman, G., and J. A. Lent, eds. (1991). *Transnationaal Communications: Rewiring the Third World.* Newbury Park, CA: Sage.

Tehranian, M. (1986). Totem and technologies. *Intermedia,* 14(3):20–28.

———. (1988). Information technologies and world development. *Intermedia,* 16(3):30–38.

———. (1990). *Technologies of Power.* Norwood, NJ: Ablex.

Tsui, L. S. (1991). An interview with Herbert Schiller. *Media Development,* 1:50–52.

Williams, R. (1973). Base and superstructure in Marxist cultural theory. *New Left Review,* 83:3–16.

Wood, E. M. (1986). *The Retreat from Class.* London: Verso.

10

Continuity and Change in Critical Communication: A Generational Analysis

VINCENT MOSCO

Questions 1 and 2

How has critical research in communication changed since it was conceived about a generation ago?
Do you believe that critical research in communication has advanced during the past generation?

The past generation has brought both continuity and change in critical communication. It has also been a time of considerable advancement. Since these developments are closely connected, this chapter provides a response to both the first and second questions.

In order to understand some of the changes in critical communication research, it is useful to start with a general sense of its meaning and scope. Critical research challenges mainstream perspectives in communication research, which have traditionally supported established systems of power. In doing this, critical communication makes use of a wide range of historical, social, and moral philosophical perspectives.

There is no formula for critical communication research, and any attempt to devise one or more risks mechanizing what is a rich and variegated tradition. However, in general, critical research starts from the view that most established systems of power restrict the ability of people to free themselves for self-determination. Critical research examines the historical forces that bring about and change systems of communication power. It is continuously sensitive to the need to connect communication problems to the wider institutional system of power and resistance. With this said, critical research most clearly distinguishes itself by its focus on the moral philosophical dimension. In essence, the point of explaining the world is to change it. Specifically, critical researchers have been most interested in advancing what Bernard Barber has called "strong democracy," or the fullest possible public participation in the decisions that affect our lives. This involves research that advances equality and the expansion of public space in all institutional forms, including the mass media and other systems of communication.

Although there have been changes in critical communication over the generation, the fundamentals have remained the same. In spite of the many changes that have shaped the past generation, most recently the end of communism in parts of Europe, the problems that gave rise to this approach remain. These include the growth of transnational business, including the globalization of the communication and information industries, the concomitant spread of mass consumption and consumerist values, and the growth of the state, particularly its own mass media, public relations, and information apparatus. Indeed, one of the chief sources for the growth of critical research is the increasingly dismal economic record in both the highly developed and lesser developed regions of the world. Particularly in the last decade, economic growth worldwide has slackened or reversed, and divisions between rich and poor have grown. All of this is fertile ground for a critical perspective.

Critical communication research began as an effort to document, explain, and challenge these developments because they restrict our capacity for full democracy. Contemporary critical research continues to be bound up with these central problems. Moreover, critical research began as an effort to document and advance social movements that mounted challenges to these dominant tendencies. Movements for liberation organized around class, gender, race, and nation built what Raymond Williams called oppositional and alternative cultures, fundamentally alternative ways of being and seeing. These movements have also developed and changed, but the basic forms of resistance and social transformation continue to provide a significant grounding for critical communication research.

If one or two generations have not changed the fundamentals, what has changed? To begin with, there are more of us. Critical communication, particularly in North America, developed for quite some time in the work of a handful of scholars working alone in scattered universities. Although these scholars might find themselves in the same location for a period of time (e.g., Dallas Smythe, George Gerbner, and Herbert Schiller at the University of Illinois), the time was brief and the standard work mode was the individual scholar working alone. Over the past generation, the number of critical communication scholars has grown. Most of the world's university communication programs house one or two critical academics. This has brought about more collaborative work, including informal systems of mutual criticism, joint research projects, jointly edited books and series, and collaborative alternative media activity and political/policy activism.

This has achieved some greater degree of formalization in organizations such as the Union for Democratic Communication and the International Association for Mass Communication Research and in journals such as *Media, Culture and Society* and *Critical Studies in Mass Communication Research.*

This growing number of critical scholars has deepened and extended the scope of critical research. Most of the earliest communication scholars were men, and although concerns about patriarchy and feminism were raised from time to time, gender was hardly a central consideration. However, with the support of an earlier generation of critical scholars, the number of women in critical scholarship and activism has grown, as has the presence of feminism in both theory and method. Of course, this is a recent development, and "backlash" inspired by such pseudo-issues as political correctness is a persistent problem. Nevertheless, one can observe efforts to comprehend systems of communication power as patriarchal, as well as capitalist, *and* to support forms of resistance organized around the struggles of women.

Critical communication has maintained a strong base in materialist traditions of political, economic, and sociological research. Contemporary research has taken several directions. Two are particularly notable. First, it has recognized that traditional definitions of the mass media have lost much of their usefulness. "Broadcasting," "telecommunications," "data processing," "film," "video," "publishing," and so on, are terms that capture pieces of a rapidly integrating and expanding electronic information industry. This development is propelled by companies that would not occupy a traditional political economy or sociology of the mass media. As a result, critical communication scholars have found it necessary to expand their reach. This is both exciting and challenging: exciting because critical communication increasingly takes up problems that are central to both public debate—the nature of the information society—and to a general political economy or sociology; challenging because it means working well beyond secure and comfortable disciplinary borders.

In addition to this expansion of reach, researchers in the political economy and sociology of communication have made their analyses deeper and more fine-grained by spending more time on the wide range of processes at work in the social construction of communicative hegemony. Concretely, this means examining the specific processes at work in different media industries, which are distinctly shaped by particular constellations of capital accumulation patterns, industry structure, production processes, technologies, forms of regulation, and relationships to consumers. Such richly textured analyses suggest the many ways that different media of communication are shaped by patterns both common to capitalism and unique to the specific ensemble of productive and social processes bound up with the pattern of development and structure of a particular medium.

Critical communication scholars have also built on the work of those, like T. W. Adorno, Max Horkheimer, and R. Williams, who pioneered the development of a critical cultural studies. This set of approaches challenged elite definitions of culture by recovering culture as a significant form of social self-definition, albeit within the constraints of hegemonic relations. It also has examined the concrete ways culture provides a site for opposition, resistance, and the construction, of alternative ways of communicating for people whose race, gender, class, and other forms of social identity have been marks of oppression.

Question 3

What are the impediments to carrying out critical research in communication?

The answer to questions one and two showed how critical communication has advanced during the past generation. It also suggested some of the conceptual, institutional, and political contributions to this advance. Nevertheless, critical communication cannot be entirely satisfied with the progress. There remain numerous impediments to carrying out critical research. Although there are more critical scholars, the critical approach is very much a marginal perspective within communication research and across the university. As a result, critical scholars, particularly junior ones, continue to experience problems in teaching their specialty, in receiving research support, and in tenure and promotion consideration. External sources of research funding tend to ignore critical research or, at best, marginalize it. Critical researchers therefore tend to face two major challenges in the university and in other institutional settings. In order to overcome the presumption of otherness, or alien status within institutions, critical scholars have to work harder than their mainstream counterparts. They have to do more and better research, teaching, advising, and so forth. Secondly, critical researchers face the daily tactical problem of determining how far one can go in advancing a critical perspective. This extends to the substance and the tone of lectures, writing, and social interaction. In essence, we work in a world where common sense, the taken-for-granted reality, tends not to be receptive.

This makes it all the more important to maintain outlets for our work. One of the most important lessons provided by the founding figures of critical communication is that one can accomplish a great deal with a good library and the drive to write—provided one can find a reasonable publishing vehicle.

In the early 1980s, critical communication was able to expand in part because two publishing sources were particularly supportive: Ablex Publishing and the *Journal of Communication.* The complex stories that explain the support are best told at another time and by other people. Suffice it to say that both sources were caught up in the same struggles that confront low-budget operations and critical scholars everywhere. Nevertheless, to their credit, Ablex and the *Journal* provided significant outlets for a new generation of critical scholars and helped make critical communication a perspective to contend with in the discipline.

Ablex has substantially cut back its communication studies list, and the *Journal* has returned to the International Communication Association under new editorship. Although Sage Publishers and Westview Press have expanded their critical communication work, it is uncertain whether they will be able to offer the same sort of home (keeping in mind that homes are places of contention and dissatisfaction as well as cooperation and pleasure) that Ablex provided. It is difficult for mainstream professional associations, particularly those based in the United States, to do more than provide a vehicle for the range of work in the field. Given that critical work is marginal to the field, it will require a substantial effort for the new *Journal* to give critical research a major presence. For these reasons and in spite of its title, it will be difficult for *Critical Studies in Mass Communication,* an official journal of the Speech Communication Association, to reflect with some consistency the concerns of critical scholars.

It is important to conclude this answer by pointing out that the response to critical research tends to vary according to a range of institutional and cultural factors. My experience in Canada is illustrative. Although there are many similarities between the Canadian and U.S. experience, the former has a strong social democratic tradition that makes it more receptive to critical research. Canadian social democracy is limited and constantly under attack from forces very familiar to Americans, but it has built a stronger public infrastructure in health care, education, the mass media, and social services. Canada also has a more potent trade union movement. As a result, the Canadian system is open to critical perspectives built on democratic communication.

For example, Canadian scholars working chiefly for trade unions have received substantial research funding to study the impact of new technologies, including computer communication systems, on working people. This has also been the case for Canadian academics who study the cultural industries and telecommunications policy. Let me hasten to point out that the struggle to bring about democratic change based on what research documents is not much less difficult in Canada. However, the community of feminist, trade union, and other movement organizations, linked to federal and provincial social democratic parties (which, in 1992, ran three provinces with 52 percent of Canada's population), offers considerably wider scope than exists in most parts of the United States.

Question 4

Where is critical research in communication heading?

A very important challenge for critical communication research is to comprehend both the continuities and the changes taking place in the world. The continuities include the globalization of business, the formation of continental and global state and statelike institutions, the accelerating and diverse spread of commercialization, and the social movements that arise to defend the public sphere and civil society from the reduction of social relations to commodity relations.

Related to these continuities are a number of developments that continue to rock the global political economy and threaten the relative stability of the post–World War II era. These include the end of communism as a political force, with the not insignificant exception of China; the persistent economic crisis, mainly a crisis of accumulation, in global capitalism; and, in what might be called a crisis of overaccumulation, the devastation of the natural environment.

These developments give critical communication scholars an enormous research agenda. Media businesses and, increasingly, integrated companies that include media subsidiaries are among the companies propelling the global economy. These companies, along with numerous firms that constitute the amorphous, although identifiable, information sector, are looked on as the next generation's engines of accumulation and one of the few hopes for sustainable development. Governments have developed media, public relations, and information divisions that rival those in the corporate world. These developments are taking place in a world of diminishing public ownership, control, and public interest regulation and oversight. More than ever, critical scholars need to examine these developments, map the changing contours of the world communication and information order, and assess the consequences of a system built on state-supported market principles. Absent corrective action, complete control of the world media and information system will fall into the hands of increasingly concentrated corporate capital, the ranks of the information poor will swell, and we will accelerate the establishment of a surveillance society.

In addition to having the moral conviction necessary to address these issues, critical communication research is well positioned to examine them because its interest in the social totality leads critical scholars to think about the relationship of the material to the ideological, of political economy to culture. Unfortunately but understandably, a gap appears to have grown between these two modes of analysis. James Curran speaks of a "new revisionism," but to the extent that this exists, it smacks more of the latest cycle in revisiting the mainstream than it does of a rapprochement between critical political economists and cultural analysts. A major challenge for critical analysts is to forge the necessary strong ties between the approaches *and* sustain the principles of a critical view. Such a development is doubly important because the division in approaches contributes to a gender division in critical work. There are numerous notable exceptions, but political economy tends to be male, cultural studies female. Overcoming the analytical divide is one step to overcoming the gender divide in critical studies.

Critical communication studies face a challenge that the entire discipline is confronting—its relationship to other disciplines that have taken a stronger interest in communication studies. For example, historians are interested in how the development of communication influenced the growth of business and mass consumption, political scientists in communication policy, economists in the structure and performance of the communication industry, and sociologists in the organization of media production and the social construction of hegemony.

This interest has always existed but has accelerated recently because the media business has grown, diversified (the boundaries separating mass media, telecommunications, and computers are fading), and taken on a more central, active role in society. For the discipline of communication studies, this development strengthens identity problems: Is communication a discipline or merely a site for interdisciplinary work? For critical communication scholars, the wider interest in our field offers real opportunities to expand the perspective.

Most academic disciplines have established progressive networks, caucuses, journals, newsletters, electronic bulletin boards, and the like. These include the well-known Union for Radical Political Economists, the Radical Historians Association, and Computer Professionals for Social Responsibility. These and other similar organizations have taken a growing interest in communication studies and thereby provide substantial grounds for expanding critical communication. In order to do this, it would be useful for critical scholars to look beyond the bounds of the communication discipline and the energy-sapping turf wars that occupy so much of academics' time. Those that are looking beyond are finding a wider community of critical scholars with substantial opportunities for joint scholarly and political work.

Question 5

How and why did you decide to take the route of critical researcher in communication?

There are numerous personal and professional influences that led me to become a critical scholar and to concentrate on communications studies.

My class background has had a substantial impact on my perspective. I grew up in a second-generation immigrant family in a working-class ghetto on Manhattan's Lower East Side. At the risk of telling another of what my students and children like to call "my poor stories," the "ghetto" designation seems appropriate to my poor tenement neighborhood. Our place was a three-room apartment for six with no bath or shower, although we were considered fortunate because most buildings had shared toilets. The first eighteen years of my life were spent in a place that resonated with the tension between where we were and where the society, particularly its media, told us we should be. Notwithstanding the simple pleasures we all carved out of this very unforgiving place, I knew my class and for as long as I can remember hated the consequences for the people in my life.

Among those people, my father, a semi-skilled worker in the lithography trade, had a substantial influence on my critical sensibility. From my childhood, he was always active in the community and in his union. He had been a marine in World War II who came back from China with admiring stories about the country and Mao. He and the missionary nuns who taught in our parish school (to train them for what would be the practice of liberation theology in Latin America) gave me a clear sense that there was a lot of work to be done. I learned discipline from Jesuits in high school and university. One of my high school disappointments was a veto from my parents, who feared for my safety when I was asked to join a group in a nearby community going down to Mississippi to register black voters. Three young people from the Lower East Side had been murdered.

The protest movement of the 1960s and early 1970s gave me enough opportunities to demonstrate and sharpened my critical thinking. I arrived at university in Washington, D.C., in 1966, worked in antipoverty programs there and during the summer in New York City, marched in most of the demonstrations, joined with other Georgetown students in closing down the university after the Kent State murders, and graduated without knowing whether I would enter Harvard's doctoral program, earn conscientious objector status, go to jail for resisting the draft, or leave the country. It was not just the public movement to end the war that marked my generation. So too did the deeply personal, often complex, seemingly daily confrontations over deciding how to do the right thing.

My graduate education at Harvard included studying with several very bright people who convinced me that I needed to concentrate on the analysis of communication and information. I also participated in what amounted to an alternative university of informal, student-run courses and attempts to organize a union of teaching fellows that did succeed in shutting down the university in a one-day walkout that convinced the administration that it needed our underpaid labor.

As a high school and university student, I was deeply impressed with the work of black writers, particularly *The Autobiography of Malcolm X, Manchild in the Promised Land,* and *Invisible Man;* with critical social historians who helped me to understand my class and ethnic experience, and the roots of the Indochina War; and with the work of Marx, particularly *The German Ideology* and *The Economic and Philosophical Manuscripts.* In graduate school, chiefly under Daniel Bell's supervision, I read the work on the information society debate and from there moved into the study of new communication and information technology. With the guidance of fellow doctoral students and colleagues in sociology at the University of Lowell, my first academic job, I read through the literature in radical social science, particularly theorists of the state and power, like Nicos Poulantzas, G. William Domhoff, Immanuel Wallerstein, P. A. Baran and P. M. Sweezy, and Harry Braverman. One of my first teaching assignments was a course on the sociology of sex roles, which took me into the academic and political literature of the feminist movement.

It was not until about 1977, and my second academic job at Georgetown University, that I decided that there was a real need to bring together radical social science and the then sparse but growing literature in critical communication. Along with my student Andrew Herman, I spent a considerable time mastering the work of Armand Mattelart, Herbert Schiller, Dallas Smythe, Thomas Guback, Graham Murdock, and others in the critical media field. This search put me in touch with new doctoral recipients in critical communication, people like Janet Wasko, Dan Schiller, Eileen Meehan, Tim Haight, Oscar Gandy, Jennifer Slack, and Fred Fejes. Their work promised a significant surge in critical communication research, and I decided to contribute to it in research and through the founding of the Union for Democratic Communication.

Conclusion

I conclude this admittedly sketchy response with three points that matter a great deal in my thinking about critical communication today.

First, our work must extend beyond university life. For me, this has meant numerous associations with activist organizations and policymaking bodies that require our research skills and our commitment to democracy. These organizations have a lot to teach, not the least of which is the value of clear writing. For any ability I have in this area, I owe an enormous debt to my editors, but particularly to Anthony Oettinger of Harvard and my colleague and spouse, Catherine McKercher.

Second, good critical scholarship requires that we move beyond the bounds of our chosen or working discipline. Currently, this means examining critically the development of political economy and addressing its importance in research on communication and culture. Such an approach takes me into economics, political science, sociology, history, policy studies, and cultural studies. It does leave one with the occasional feeling of drifting, but this is almost a necessary prelude to doing serious critical work.

Finally, listening to one's students is essential to maintaining a critical edge. They are most supportive when they challenge you to live up to your critical aspirations. We are remiss in our teaching when they stop providing us with this vital service.

PART FOUR

JAMES D. HALLORAN

Photo courtesy of James D. Halloran

James D. Halloran

Born:	April 30, 1927, Birstall, Yorkshire, England
Education:	B.Sc. Honors (Economics), Hull University College, 1952; (postgraduate) Certificate in Education, Hull University College, 1953; (postgraduate) Diploma in Education, London University, 1955; (postgraduate) Diploma in Educational Administration, Leeds University, 1955

Employment:

1991–	Professor, Centre for Mass Communication Research, University of Leicester.
1966–91	Professor and Director, Centre for Mass Communication Research, University of Leicester
1959–66	Lecturer and Senior Lecturer, Department of Adult Education, University of Leicester
1956–58	Further Education Officer, Rochdale, Lancashire
1953–56	Secondary school teacher, Leeds Education Authority
1954–56	Lecturer, Workers' Educational Association, Leeds
1954–56	Tutor, Askham Grange Prison for Women, Yorkshire

Other Service:

President, International Association for Mass Communication Research, 1972–90; member, East Midlands Regional Board of Central Independent Television, since 1982; International Advisory Board, Prix Jeunesse International, Munich, 1966–; Chairman, Prix Jeunesse International Research Group, Munich; Council member, Media Society of the Institute of Journalists; research consultant to UNESCO, MacBride Commission of UNESCO, Council of Europe, Danmarks Radio, Asia-Pacific Institute for Broadcasting Development, Ford Foundation, Committee on the Future of Broadcasting (Annan Committee); member, U.K. National Commission for UNESCO, serving on its Communication Advisory Committee; member, Board of Consultors, Centre for the Study of Communication and Culture, London; consultant, Centro Internazionale Studi Famiglia, Milan; Governor, British Institute of Human Rights; member, BBC Advisory Council (Midlands Region); Secretary, Home Office Television Research Committee (British government), 1963–68; external examiner at many universities throughout the world

Editing, Publishing:

Former editor, IAMCR newsletter; editorial advisory boards of journals, including *Journal of Communication* and *Media Asia.*

Research:

For more than twenty years, designed, organized, carried out, and reported on a wide range of research projects on the media and all aspects of the communication process. Some included an international dimension; others, including a longitudinal study of the new implications of new communication technology, have called for close working relationships with media institutions.

Awards and Honors:

McLuhan Teleglobe Canada Award, most prestigious prize in international communication studies, 1991; D.Sc., University of Tampere, Finland, 1975, for "The great scientific merit of his work in mass communication research and his contribution to international understanding"; Doctor Philosophiae Honoris Causa, University of Bergen, 1990; Yugoslav Flag with Golden Star, highest honor conferred by Yugoslavia on foreign nationals, for his "development of communication science and contribution to international scientific cooperation"

11

Interview with James D. Halloran

CONDUCTED BY JOHN A. LENT
LAKE BLED, YUGOSLAVIA,
AUGUST 30, 1990

What in your background influenced you to become a critical scholar?

I was born and brought up in a working-class family in a working-class area, so I presume, although I have never tried to rationalize my position in these terms, that it was undoubtedly an important influence in my becoming a *critical* scholar and adopting a radical approach.

My father was a trades union official, and all my relatives worked in factories, mines, or shops (when they were not unemployed) and supported the Labour party. Many of my school friends were very poor in those days—recession of the 1930s—I remember the conditions to this day. All these factors were clearly not without influence, but again I have never really consciously thought about my work in communications in such causal terms.

Later I was president of the Students Union at the university, and two of my professors, whom I admired and who helped and influenced me, were both left of center—caring, considerate social reformers, seeking change from a conservative, class-ridden, self-seeking society. Later still, I taught in working-class schools (poverty was still in evidence even in post–World War II years), where I lectured for the Workers Educational Association and worked in prisons—all undoubtedly formative in some way or other but, in my own case, more socially practical than ideological—more Fabian and Christian Socialist (I was brought up in a strict Catholic environment) than Marxist.

You ask how I became a critical scholar in communications. The simple answer (too simple, I appreciate) was by chance. Incidentally, although I had been teaching sociology (mainly with regard to social problems) for some years, I did not become interested in communications until the early 1960s—my first article in the field was in 1961, when I was thirty-four years old, and my first book two years later.

In my job as a tutor in the University Adult Education Department, I taught extramural classes to mixed groups in the evenings. I taught one of these groups in a small town some fourteen miles outside Leicester every Monday evening for twenty weeks in the autumn and winter terms. After two years I thought I had exhausted all I knew, but the class persuaded me to come back for a third year to give a course on the sociology of mass communications. I knew little about this subject at the time and had to work hard to prepare the course. The editor of a radical Catholic journal, *Doctrine and Life,* published in Dublin, whom I met by chance, persuaded me to write up my lecture notes in article form; he published seven or eight articles. A publisher in England (again left-wing and radical), who had published an earlier book of mine opposing capital punishment, saw the articles and published them in book form (*Control or Consent: A Study of the Challenge of Mass Communications*) in 1963.

If I may say so without undue immodesty, this critical book (the first of its kind; in fact, the first general book about the mass media in England) was very favorably reviewed. It came to the notice of the newly appointed vice chancellor (top man) at Leicester University, who had also been appointed as chairman of a government committee to study the influence of the media on children and young people. A senior civil servant would normally service such a committee as secretary, but apparently there was no one in the British Civil Service who knew anything about communications (arguably this is still the case), so the vice chancellor asked/told me to be secretary, and I remained secretary throughout its work. This is what I mean by chance.

Which years did this committee function?

The committee was established in 1963 and produced its final report some four or five years later. In the intervening years, I produced several working papers, monographs, research reports, and a book, all of which were published, and this is essentially how I became known to a wider public. These publications were very well received—they came at an opportune moment—increasing interest in the field (particularly relative to social and political concern). Very few people were writing in this area in England.

In 1964, you visited mass communication programs in the United States. What impact did that trip have on your position regarding the field?

Of course, this was not the case in the United States, where there were numerous publications in the field. Obviously, I had to make myself familiar with this literature, and I was also sent by the committee to make a tour of prominent people and institutions in the United States in 1964.

My tour was arranged by Joe Klapper from CBS, and among those I met were Leo Bogart, Wilbur Schramm, Jack Lyle, Nathan and Eleanor Maccoby, John and Matilda Riley, Charles Wright, Bernard Berelson, Alex Edelstein, Peter Clarke,

Percy Tannenbaum, Len Berkowitz, Al Bandura, George Gerbner, and Leon Festinger.

I found these visits and meetings extremely useful, albeit in a somewhat strange and negative manner. This led me to report back to the committee on my return to England that, although I did not know precisely what to do in research, I had a pretty idea what *not* to do, namely, what, on the whole, was being done in the United States. Perhaps I should add at this stage that the Television Research Committee, of which I was secretary, was charged with formulating a research program in mass communications primarily in relation to children and young people. It had a quarter of a million pounds available for this purpose—a considerable amount in those days.

Not all my learning from the States was on the negative side of the ledger, so to speak. My contact with John and Matilda Riley, Charles Wright, and, to a lesser degree, George Gerbner and Joe Klapper, had served, *inter alia,* to reinforce my belief that (to oversimplify) the way ahead should be sociological rather than psychological. I took this line fully aware that some of those whose names I have just mentioned were functionalist (just as functionalist as some of the psychologists) rather than critical. (In fact, in our field, there was little critical scholarship, as we now know it, in the States at that time.)

At the risk of convenient, *post hoc* rationalization, I would say that I reached the tentative conclusion that the *sine qua non* of progress in the field was the adoption of a sociological perspective. I realized that this begged many questions, but at that stage it was the only holistic framework I could identify that would enable me to adequately study the communication process and media institutions and to develop the critical/social reform approach that I had set out a few years before in *Control or Consent.* This was not critical with a capital "C" or "K," and it was not the product of a clear ideological stance on my part.

Parallel to—in fact part and parcel of— this general approach was the rejection of the sterile, positivistic, behavioristic, causal, psychologistic, media-centered, pseudo-scientific, essentially conservative, unquestioning, status quo maintenance work that permeated the U.S. research journals at the time.

Perhaps this approach (acceptance and rejection) can be best illustrated in terms of output and outcomes in the recommendations of my committee (and in my work since) in the area of the alleged relationship between the media and violence. Briefly put, the line adopted was that what really mattered was violence in society, not so much violence on the screen (although no attempt was made to excuse those who favored the gratuitous insertion of violence for whatever reason). It could be, for example, that violent behavior might result more from the frustration stemming from the viewing of affluent life styles by deprived people, and the creation of unrealistic expectations, than by the direct viewing of violent incidents on the screen.

Violence was central to the initial remit given to the Television Research Committee by the government, but the committee, advised by me, refused to be confined in this way and produced a research strategy and program that went well beyond the "effects of television" approach and called for a comprehensive approach to all aspects of the communication process and the operations of media institutions.

This is the base on which the center was established as a research and postgraduate training body within Leicester University in 1966 (not without controversy), and this, with some modifications, is the overall framework within which we have worked ever since.

The Leicester center was certainly the first of its kind in England, although there was a research unit focusing on media and elections at Leeds (Jay Blumler), and around that time Richard Hoggart and Stuart Hall established a center at Birmingham in contemporary cultural studies.. The BBC had its audience research department, and a few individuals such as Hilde Himmelweit had carried out relevant research, but on the whole it was very thin on the ground.

You must have been one of the few criticizing U.S. positivistic research at that time?

I presume I was, at least within the specific field of mass communication research, but, of course, there were other nonpositivistic approaches, mainly European, in the wider field of sociology and the social sciences more generally, and some of this work indirectly dealt with media and communications. More directly, there were people like Kaarle Nordenstreng from Finland, Himmelstrand from Sweden, and Martin Brouwer from the Netherlands, who certainly wouldn't like to be thought of as positivists. Additionally, in France the journal *Communication* became a vehicle for the semiologists associated with Roland Barthes.

Was George Gerbner among the critics of the positivistic approach?

I first met him in 1964. He was, and still is, difficult to categorize. He has never been directly associated with critical scholarship (again, not even today), yet he cannot easily be placed alongside the practitioners in mainstream communication studies in the States. Some of his work has been conventional; on the other hand, some of it has contained interesting sociological insights, and in some ways he was a pioneer.

What premises were behind critical studies as you saw them in 1963–64?

I think these are best identified in the book *Control or Consent* I mentioned earlier. A quarter of a century on, I could give them a more intellectual gloss, but at the time the main thrust had to do with social political reform—a realization that the media (even in England) were not primarily concerned with the public good, meeting basic social needs, but essentially, BBC excepted, with making profits for the few.

When my sociological training is added to my social upbringing, the concern becomes holistic and processual, rather than psychological and individual. Crudely put, reform called for the changing of systems, structures, institutions, and organizations—not just individuals. The heavy focus on the individual (psychology) was essentially conservative. I did write at the time that I was not simply concerned in communication research with "How to get the message across?" but "Was the message worth getting across?" "Who wanted to get it across and why?" and "Who benefited from it?"

What were the drawbacks, the disadvantages of this approach?

In the first instance, there was not much *public* opposition because we were not considered important. The first opposition we encountered was from the press, particularly the right-wing press, when we redefined the terms of reference of the Television Research Committee looking for the causes of violence in the wider social system and not simply on the screen. Pressure groups of the grass-roots moralist variety, who knew how evil TV was, also did not take kindly to this view.

Most broadcasters ignored us at the start (in their arrogance, they considered that any worthwhile academic research would automatically favor them), but later they became hostile (particularly in news and current affairs) when we began to argue that there was no such thing as objectivity, introduced "news values," and called for a thoroughgoing investigation into all the forces (economic, political, professional, technological, etc.) that impinged on the production process. Our book, *Demonstrations and Communication* (now regarded as a classic), reporting on the media coverage of a demonstration in London against U.S. involvement in Vietnam, brought this to a head. Even radical or left-wing journalists were outraged that the values and operation of journalists and journalism had been exposed for what they really were.

The book was universally condemned by the press and universally acclaimed by academics, including those academics with a literary, critical, or cultural studies background who did not always see eye to eye with us on the relative merits of our different approaches to the media and communications—but both schools shared the same concerns.

In the British academic world generally at that time, interest in the subject was low. To some elitists, television, or even the media generally, was not a proper subject for university study. There were no schools of journalism or communication in the U.K. Sociologists and psychologists seemed more intent (certainly in my university) on asserting their own academic purity and separateness than in dealing with the social issues of the time. We were regarded as philistines, prostitutes on the fringes of, or even beyond, real academic life.

All these "distant" attitudes from both media and academics at the outset served us well (I now see in retrospect). To be brief, it enabled us to become established without too much interference (this was particularly so in the university, where to set up a new department required a revolution), and by the time our true role and function (at least the one we had adopted) had been recognized, it was too late; we were too well known. Even the university began to benefit from our work. Of course, this should all be seen at a time of increasing interest in the media—mid-1960s to mid-1970s.

You must have had a sympathetic vice chancellor or administration in Leicester.

We certainly had a most helpful and cooperative vice chancellor, who was really our mother and father, and in those days, the vice chancellor virtually controlled the administration. You will remember that the vice chancellor was chairman of the Television Research Committee (TVRC), of which I was secretary (he appointed me), and the initial funding for our research came from this committee for our first six years. The university, of course, provided all overheads, premises, etc. free, thanks to the vice chancellor.

Of course, he had to have the full support of the TVRC in allocating such a large proportion of the available funds to establish a center in Leicester. He obtained this without difficulty, due to another principle, so to speak. The committee members were convinced that the best way they could use the funds at their disposal was to set up a center or institute with some degree of permanence, rather than dissipate their funds on several applicants. This didn't please everyone outside the committee, particularly the potential applicants.

The center was established in 1966, and I was appointed director at the outset, this mainly because of what I had written in the first half of the 1960s. By that time, I had probably written as much on mass communication research as all the other British social scientists taken together—but to be fair, there was not much opposition at the time.

When the initial funds from the TVRC ran out in 1972, the university took over the total responsibility for running the center, just like any other university department. Again, the vice chancellor was instrumental, but by that time we were (somewhat reluctantly at first) considered to be one of the university's main assets, particularly in view of our international standing. The university, on the whole, was pleased to take us over, as it had been to grant a full professorship—in fact a personal chair some two years earlier. The vice chancellor, Sir Fraser Noble, therefore was a great help throughout, but, as a canny Scot, he expected good returns for his support and investment. I think he feels he got these; he still keeps in touch with our work in his retirement.

Because of your critical writings and speeches, you have been characterized as anti-U.S., as angry and anti–mass media. How do you respond to those charges?

No, not really, certainly not anti-U.S.; just opposed to the mainstream of conventional U.S. communication research for the reasons already given and also—perhaps above all—for its implications and applications, particularly in the field that you are so familiar with, media and development and international communications.

What does annoy me at times, however, are the writings and stances of those (and there are still plenty of them) who regard critical research as being politicized and their own conventional, positivistic, "value-free" work as truly scientific. They either refuse or are unable to recognize the value loading of their own work, which is essentially conservative, establishment oriented, and geared to the maintenance of the status quo, and, I should add, although the conventional researchers are still in the majority in the United States, recent years have seen an increasing number of critical researchers.

What have been the main changes in communications studies over the past twenty years?

At the risk of oversimplification—and I repeat—the change has been from a predominantly positivistic, behavioristic, "value-free," psychologistic, individualistic, disembodied, fragmented, conservative, status quo maintenance type of research to a sociological, holistic, processual, critical, autonomous approach that seeks to challenge and question the system and all its parts rather than to blindly serve it. But this should not be seen as a *change* or takeover from one to the other. The conventionalists are still in the majority (look at the journals), but the other critical stream (with its several tributaries) has emerged and started to flow quite strongly over the period in question.

It is easy to go too far in creating simple dichotomies such as critical versus conventional, and the shorthand presentation I have just given could lead to this. There are scholars, perhaps Gerbner and Denis McQuail, for example, who may fall between the two schools, and, as already indicated, there are several tributaries to the critical stream—even all positivists are not the same.

As I see it, one of the main faults in analyzing developments over twenty years is to assume that all critical scholarship is essentially Marxist oriented. This is not the case, although Marxist thinking, in its several forms, has undoubtedly contributed much to our work over the past quarter of a century. Incidentally, its contentious presentation has often led to research results being taken less seriously than they might have been. And, of course, even Marxism (let alone critical research) is not a homogenous entity. For example, in England there have been (and still are) clear distinctions between the cultural approach of Stuart Hall and the political economy of Murdock and Peter Golding, both of whom I appointed to the center and employed for twenty years.

Not that a Marxist political approach dominated the work at the center over this period. A uniform center policy was more apparent to those outside the center than to those inside—universally critical, yes; ideologically at one, certainly not. In more recent years, I developed an outlook at the center that is best described as *critical eclecticism.* The complexity of the situation, processes, and relationships we study demands the application of complementary perspectives; there is no room for dogmatic and doctrinaire positions. After all, ideology already "knows" all the answers to the questions that social science, of necessity, must pose.

The cultural studies approach has been very influential in Britain in the last decade or so, as communication or media studies courses (many of dubious value) have proliferated in colleges and polytechnics. Some of these have gone to the opposite extreme from the conventional positivists, eschewing any discipline or systematic inquiry, and never allowing an inconvenient fact to disturb a firmly held, unsubstantiated opinion.

Another crude interpretation in terms of three stages of the development of mass communication research in Great Britain would be (1) bad or nonexistent, (2) improving (mid-1960s to mid-1970s), and (3) deteriorating.

The deterioration may be identified at several levels, one of these just mentioned being certain aspects of the proliferation of media studies. The second has to do with the reluctance of broadcasters to cooperate with researchers who (so experience suggests) might produce results that do not support media mythologies and conventional communication wisdom. A third related reason stems from the increasing competitive atmosphere in British broadcasting, where what research is carried out by media institutions tends to be very narrow, policy oriented, in-house, and confidential. Finally, government policy toward higher education, both to research (and research funding) and the finance of universities generally, has commercialized the universities, with cost and profit considerations taking over from creative thinking and critical inquiry.

Of course, one can be critical from one's desk. Large-scale funding is not vital to all critical thought, but it is vital to inquiries that explore both organizations and audiences—inquiries that are essential if one is to maintain and *substantiate* the critical thrust. Funds for large-scale, critical work are in very short supply. It was much easier to obtain funds for independent, autonomous research fifteen years ago than it is today. Policy research, not policy-oriented research, is the order of the day.

In the United States, we have the Union for Democratic Communication. What is your impression of UDC as an alternative in these financially strapped times?

This, nor anything like it, was not in existence when I first visited the United States in 1964. To me, it is an encouraging development, and they seem to be quite active. What influence they have outside their own groups and certain segments of academia, I just do not know. Talking quite recently to some active members of the Union for Democratic Communication, I noticed a tendency for them to cooperate with media industries and the large communication corporations. Their argument was that this was the only way they could obtain the necessary information.

In this way, I presume that they are experiencing the same problems as we have experienced in England. We cooperate, for the same reasons. How honest we all are in this, it is hard to say. At one level, it may pay to sup with the devil, but at another level, you may be contaminated, or even join him in the inferno. There is no doubt that because of prevailing policies in both countries we have been forced into this position. I know that, in recent years, I have taken on projects that I would not have touched with a barge pole twenty years ago. I do this—I hope without loss of integrity and still with some critical benefit—to keep colleagues employed, in an attempt to keep the department's research standing at an acceptable level in the university, and sometimes simply to meet the university's financial requirements. I have attempted to rationalize my policy by adopting a two-tiered approach, which I refer to as using internal and external criteria in our research. This means that I will attempt to evaluate the media organization's policy and practice on their declared terms (internal), providing I can also evaluate by using my own (external), what I hope are more critical criteria. History will tell what we should have done, but right now the environment is certainly not conducive to the pursuit of critical inquiry.

What about the Third World? How much critical communication research is being done in Africa, Asia, or Latin America?

This is a difficult one, particularly as far as research is concerned. I think we have had some impact here and can hope for more through the influence of our many postgraduate students from overseas.

With research, the reasons already given relative to the U.K. and the States apply *mutatis mutandis* in most Third World countries. Where research is allowed, it is likely to be geared to policy. We have carried out research with critical components in India, Malaysia, Nigeria, and the Philippines; have cooperated and coordinated several international comparative research exercises involving many countries; and have guided the research of our students, again in many Third World countries. What impact all this has it is impossible to say; perhaps the greatest hope lies with the students.

Two points need to be made in this general connection. The first has to do with the understandable wish that research in Third World countries should be carried out by Third World scholars from Third World institutions, rather than by "safari" researchers from abroad. A laudable objective up to a point, but what if most of these scholars have been trained in the conventional traditions in the United States, as most of them have?

A more fundamental issue relates to the very nature of a social science in which theories, models, concepts, and methods have been derived from, and developed in, Western industrial societies. How relevant and applicable are these in Third World situations?

An encouraging sign over the last decade or so has been the increasing indigenization of research—from the bottom upward—in Latin America, where scholars appear to share many of our critical views and seem capable of applying them in their home circumstances. But again, not without opposition.

How has the staff at the Leicester center changed over the years?

Some colleagues have been with me from the outset. I appointed P. Elliott, Golding, Murdock, and Paul Hartmann in the first few years. Elliott died some years ago; Hartmann has retired, and the other two moved on promotion to another university.

I am often asked not why they left but why they stayed so long—twenty-two years. I think the answer is quite simple. For the first decade there was little, if any, teaching; we were essentially a research department. So these people had an opportunity second to none—virtually unparalleled—to spend all their time doing their own research and making an international reputation for themselves. This they undoubtedly did, and must receive due credit, but if they couldn't flourish in this environment at that time, they would never have flourished anywhere.

But times change. The political-economic circumstances already mentioned play an important part—quite simply, more teaching—much more teaching—less money for everything, fewer research opportunities, and few chances for promotion in Thatcher's universities.

We have replaced these old stalwarts with new, younger staff, some of excellent caliber and high potential. But their workload and the overall environment in which they will have to operate will be radically different from the one that prevailed in the 1960s and 1970s. They may do well; the center may continue to do well. I certainly hope so. But they will never have the opportunity, freedom, abundant resources, and good fortune of Murdock, Golding, Hartmann, and the others who were with us in the early days.

I ought to add a little to the above because, all pressures and problems apart, it would have been unrealistic and, I believe, irresponsible to remain altogether outside teaching. As we became internationally famous, we were reminded by several bodies, including UNESCO, that we had a responsibility to pass on our research expertise to others, particularly from the Third World. I readily accepted this, and that is why we changed after the first decade from a pure research institution to a research and postgraduate teaching center. No one with my concerns and interests can regret this necessary development, although one may argue that today, under financial pressure, the pendulum has swung too far, and the necessary resources to cater to an ever increasing number of students have not been made available.

Teaching is at its best when it is closely related to and reflects the research and interests of the individual teacher. But what if a commercially driven situation develops where there is so much teaching that there is no time for research? Some would argue that such a situation is not far away.

You are about to retire. What are your plans?

I shall retire as director of the center formally in September 1991, but I shall continue as research professor—do my own research, teach a little, and supervise some Ph.D. students. The important thing—and I look forward to this—is that I shall be free from administration and committee work—80 percent of my time in recent years, with 20 percent for "real work," a complete reversal of the proportions when I first established the center.

How did you get involved in the International Association for Mass Communication Research?

I joined IAMCR more or less by chance around 1965–66, but took little interest in it at first. I attended my first meeting in 1970 in Constanz, West Germany, when I was asked to stand for president. I refused because of my lack of experience and familiarity with the set-up, but I agreed to be a candidate for a vice presidency, was elected, and there began a long history of association that is not yet at an end, although, as you know, I have now retired from the presidency after eighteen years in office. I was elected president in Buenos Aires in 1972.

At the Constanz meeting in 1970, and immediately thereafter, there was a move by some of the younger and newer (not the same thing) members of the association to change and enliven what they saw, rightly or wrongly, as a somewhat sleepy, moribund body run mainly for the benefit of "old conservatives" from both sides of the Iron Curtain. There was at least an element of truth in this, because as I quickly learned on taking over, there was no real program; UNESCO had ceased to support it some years previously because it was not fulfilling its own declared remit, and there were very few paid up members and no up-to-date records.

I brought the headquarters from Lausanne to Leicester in 1972, determined to make a go of it (I find it difficult to be closely associated with something that isn't a success). Things went well, and you know the story from that point on. So today, we have some two thousand members from over seventy different countries, and over the years we have become famous for the high quality—intellectually and socially—of our genuine international conferences. We can rightly claim to be the only genuine international association in our field.

This quite outstanding development over a period of eighteen years was not achieved without a great deal of work and the assistance of quite a number of people both at the Leicester center and elsewhere. In the early days, Kaarle Nordenstreng was a great help, and in more recent years, I have benefited tremendously from the support and friendship of Cees Hamelink, Tamás Szecskö, and Olof Hulten. Peggy Gray has ensured the success of all of our conferences.

IAMCR has been contrasted and compared with ICA, particularly by Ev Rogers, who falls into the trap of drawing the too simple dichotomy that I mentioned earlier, i.e., positivist, empirical, conventional versus critical, sociological, "political." Yes, IAMCR has certainly a more critical orientation that the multifaceted ICA—with me as president and given our more focused structure this was well nigh inevitable. But—and this is a good thing—there is no homogeneity about IAMCR (in fact there is a considerable overlap in membership between IAMCR and ICA), unless it is in a concern for better communications, communication systems tuned to meeting the needs of people throughout the world, and this is sought by a multidisciplinary approach that, if not always coordinated, at least shows a recognition of what our different disciplines may contribute to the association's overall aims and objectives.

You ask about the future. I am not really in a position to comment because so much will depend on what administrative and financial structure and arrangements will be made when the headquarters leaves Leicester.

There is no doubt that Leicester has enjoyed many intangible benefits from being the headquarters of IAMCR, but more to the point, IAMCR has been very heavily subsidized by Leicester at many levels, direct and indirect. Some other institution will have to take on this responsibility now, or, failing that, the whole financial structure of the association will have to be reviewed and more income sought. It will be interesting to see what the future holds.

12

James D. Halloran: A Multi-Perspective Presentation

TAMÁS SZECSKÖ

"In mass communication research we need not apologize for adopting a 'multi-perspective diagnosis.' We should seek to promote eclecticism rather than try to make excuses for it."

This advice of James D. Halloran is so suggestive, useful, and applicable—especially if one realizes that it is a "critical eclecticism" that is advocated (Halloran 1983)—that one easily becomes tempted to translate its message into a working method for presenting Halloran's oeuvre within the narrow compass of a short essay. The author of this chapter did not resist this temptation and tried to act accordingly in what follows. So our password is "eclecticism"!

In our case, it means concretely that (1) we do not refer to all the works of J. D. Halloran but only to those that seem to us most significant in determining his intellectual development and, hence, its impact on communication research as a worldwide discipline, (2) the sequence of ideas, concepts, and statements to be highlighted below follows not a simple chronology but rather the logic of a "multi-perspective" presentation, and (3) with an ample selection of quotations from Halloran's writings, we wish not simply to let the texts speak for themselves but also to reflect the multicolored aura of Halloran's thinking.

However, this chapter does not intend to become "H's Breviary," not only because of its excessive brevity, but primarily because the author of the text-mosaics to be cited in what follows has been rejecting any kind of dogmatism and doctrinaire behavior for his whole professional career.

Violence and Communication

In one of his lectures in the early 1970s, Halloran, looking back to the then short history of the Leicester center, stated that "after all, in a manner of speaking we had our origins in sex and violence" (Halloran 1974:5). Beyond this eye-grabbing, pointed formulation, one may discover the undeniable historical fact that a growing social uneasiness about juvenile delinquency and crime in the 1960s gave a new impetus to mass communication research in several Western countries, notably the United Kingdom and the United States.

Studies, some reassessing earlier research findings and some presenting the results of new scholarly ventures, were much in evidence. The results of these considerable intellectual and financial inputs, however, proved to be rather disparate. Some reinforced old simplistic ways of public thinking, which led to making the media in general, and television in particular, the scapegoat for the deviant behavior of certain social groups. Others, although more sophisticated in their scholarly approach (even introducing some innovations in methodology), were unable, or unwilling, to escape the confines of structural functionalism predominant at that time in social science in the Anglo-Saxon world.

It is to the credit of Halloran, a critical sociologist from the beginning, that he recognized that the time had come to recruit some intellectual allies, whether in the government's research committee, UNESCO, or the newly established CMCR of Leicester, who could share his scholarly convictions about this issue. Halloran believed that what society really needed was a thoroughgoing, deep, multi-perspective, critical examination of violence as a complex social phenomenon. In such a schema, TV violence was but one component and could not be understood in isolation from the intricate web of social relations of which it was a part. So, Halloran argued, instead of unwillingly assisting a scapegoating process with pseudo-scientific findings, social research should explore the alleged TV–violence relationship in this much wider sociological context.

Surpassing Conventional Research

Those were the years, in the late 1960s, when Halloran, experiencing the sympathy of a broadening segment of the international research community and finding more and more platforms for expressing his views on research methodology and strategies, launched a full-fledged crusade against conventional research and its fundamental deficiencies. He explained, "By 'conventional research' I mean that with a mainly value free, positivistic, empiricist, behavioristic, psychological emphasis" (Halloran 1981:165). Even years later, dealing retrospectively with the achievements of the British government's research committee (which he served as a secretary), he found it necessary to stress, "Fortunately, it was not shackled by the historical, political, commercial and institutional impediments of American communication research. In fact, its aim and hopefully its achievement was to break (although not by any means completely) and reject the North American connection" (Halloran 1978:122).

Halloran emphasized that he was not rejecting North American research *in toto,* that it was the "contamination by the disease of hyperscience" (Halloran, Elliott, and Murdock 1970:19). that communication research was to avoid. He comes back several times to the roots and symptoms of this disease. At one place, he contrasts reliability to validity: "*Reliability* has often been achieved at the cost of *validity,* and statistically definitive 'scientifically acceptable' statements about the trivial, the inconsequential and the erroneous abound. Statements of high probability about matters that are not central are not as useful as statements of somewhat lower probability about matters that are central" (Halloran 1991:2).

One of the origins of the erroneous route that many researchers followed was their failure to formulate the basic questions of the research project in an appropriate way; they did not ask the right question. Halloran is quick to play with a mock-description of this situation: "Conceptualize the problem inadequately, ask the wrong questions, get your directions and priorities wrong—and no matter how sophisticated your methods, no matter how much effort you expend, what facilities are available, what cooperation you obtain, you will still do little or nothing to increase knowledge, to further understanding, or to be of practical assistance to those working in the media" (Halloran 1978:121).

The apparently banal but difficult to follow methodological advice of "asking the right question" can be traced right through Halloran's writings and speeches. Considering also that the appropriate formulation of basic questions necessitates a good theory, and being a skillful tactician himself, he returns frequently to the accusations practical-minded communicators level against researchers for being too abstract and remote. "When academic researchers refer to 'theory,' broadcasters tend to reach for their guns, fearing yet 'another escape to the obscure heights and remoteness of the ivory tower'" (Halloran 1990b:16). His pet answer to this problem tries to cater to the practicality of communicators' thinking: "Theory is a practical necessity; in fact, it is the most practical thing we have. It should prevent us from attempting to reinvent the wheel every time we go into the field" (Halloran 1991:1).

Researchers and Communicators

Of course, the relationship between researchers and every kind of communicator (from journalist to policymaker) is much more complex than a few aphoristic statements can illustrate. This is why Halloran turns toward this field of consideration several times, in a more analytical way. He is far from being hostile toward communicators in general, but he reminds researchers not to accept information about communication institutions at face value. Notwithstanding subjective bias and distortion, communication research needs this type of information, too, but in a broader frame of institutional research. This approach, borrowed from organizational sociology, he outlines as follows:

> We might seek information about what the institution is legally or formally charged to do; what it officially and formally states as its aims and objectives and what it claims with regard to the achievement of these (studying annual reports, etc.); what those who work in the institution, at different levels, claim to be doing; what is actually being done, say, through participant observation, and what has really been achieved; and possibly how others external to the operation, evaluate all this. (Halloran 1983:128)

In studying fields of social activity other than mass communication, this approach is considered less of a novelty, but it seemed an innovation for mass media in the 1960s, partly because "journalists claim the right to probe into all areas of society, but they are not very keen to submit their own operations to scrutiny" (Halloran 1974:10). Moreover, we have not yet mentioned the opposition of media operators and policymakers, among others, which would hinder, even more massively, the scholarly progress in this field. Without accepting it, one can understand it, because "for many people, particularly those with vested interests and something to lose, ignorance could be functional, and new factual information could often be a source of embarrassment" (Halloran 1990a:5).

Of Critical Research

The encounters between researchers and communicators gave rise to a more promising set of ideas in the professional debates of the 1970s that distinguished policy research from critical research. While stressing that good research should be neither a kind of apology for the existing state of affairs nor irrelevant to the major information needs of the society, Halloran makes the distinction between policy-oriented research and policy research:

> The latter is frequently of the variety which seeks to bring about the efficient execution of policy and thereby make the existing system more efficient. On the whole, it is not concerned to ask questions about the validity of the system or to challenge predominant values or suggest alternatives. Policy-oriented research, on the other hand, ideally addresses itself to the major issues of our time, and is concerned, amongst other things, with questioning the values and claims of the system, applying independent criteria, suggesting alternatives with regard to both means and ends, exploring the possibility of new forms and structures, and so on. (Halloran 1981:168–69)

It is not difficult to see that, in Halloran's terminology, "policy-oriented research" is the type of critical research that has no inclination to retire to the ivory tower or pure theorizing: "Critical research does not ignore problems central to the media, but ideally it never takes these problems as defined by media practitioners or politicians. Its starting points are the major social issues of our time, not necessarily the major media issues as narrowly defined by the professionals, owners or controllers" (Halloran 1981:170).

Be it called policy-oriented or critical research, it has three dominant characteristics: it treats communication as a social process; it scrutinizes media institutions within wider social contexts, both nationally and internationally, and not in isolation; and it conceptualizes research in terms of structure, organization, professionalization, socialization, participation, and so forth.

All these exigencies define not only the social function of good research but also the role of the researcher, which is akin to that of "scholarly warrior" and therefore not easy to perform. Halloran does not seek to cover up the difficulties:

> Once the critical stance is adopted and responsibilities as independent researchers, scholars and intellectuals accepted, the researchers almost inevitably find themselves in conflict with extremely powerful national and international forces who are convinced that they (and the world at large) have nothing whatsoever to gain from critical investigations. . . . Alternative forms of thinking are not welcome because they might lead to alternative systems. What is more, they are most favourably placed to defend their position, because they set the agenda and control the discourse. (Halloran 1981:172–73)

The "warrior" is not alone in his fights, however. As early as 1970, Halloran could already circumscribe the two groups of professionals where the critical researcher's potential allies are to be found (Halloran 1970:12): those critics who claim that the elitism and/or commercialism of media institutions and the structure of their ownership are antagonistic to the values of a democratic society; and those creative people inside the media organizations who deplore the policies and development strategies of those same organizations. The developments of later years, such as the aspirations for "access and participation," the multifold contributions to the work of the MacBride Commission, the international debates around the concept of the New International Information and Communication Order, and, much later, the birth of the Cultural Environment Movement, showed that Halloran was right in his early guess: The researcher is not alone.

Strategic Proposals

In a world where the internationalization of several scientific disciplines—communication research among them—has been rapidly progressing for the last decades, it is not difficult to understand that an intellect of Halloran's magnitude could produce an impact on the development of a discipline most efficiently on the international level. Having had the privilege of participating in different co-operative research ventures and being involved in the transactions of more than one international scholarly body and forum together with Halloran (consequently sensing the pervasiveness of this impact at first hand), I would even state that the most important component of Halloran's work is his lion's share in remodeling mass communication research at the international level.

Perhaps the main instrument by which he did this was a set of research proposals that he elaborated in the late 1960s. These proposals, which at the time were thoroughly discussed and widely accepted under the aegis of UNESCO, proved to be so farsighted that even now, more than two decades later, they have not lost their topicality. As Halloran said, "[They] stressed the urgent need for concentrated and coordinated research into the mass media and the functions of the media in society, the aim being to fully understand the communication process, its relationship to economic, social and cultural developments, and in doing this provide a base for the establishment of national and international policies and strategies" (Halloran 1990a:2).

This set of priorities—what was later called, by both friends and foes, a "watershed" in UNESCO-related communication research—became a sort of "Fifteen Commandments" for critical researchers of mass communication and was reproduced under different headings so many times that rather than risk here any apocryphal text, I will quote the latest and truly genuine text from Halloran's keynote speech delivered to the Seventeenth IAMCR General Conference at Bled in 1990 (Participants could not only note the topicality of the proposals but also realize that developments in research had been rather uneven across various lines of inquiry that Halloran had proposed some twenty years earlier).

1. In what way, to what extent, and over what time period will new developments render existing communications technology obsolete?
2. Does the "communication revolution" represent an entirely new factor in the socialization process, and, if so, how?
3. Does the new technology demand an entirely new institutional and organizational structure, or can existing structures be suitably adapted?
4. How should one decide between:
   a. private interests and public control;
   b. public accountability and freedom of speech?
5. Many decisions in media policy formulation are made in the name of "the public good" and the "national interest." But what do these terms really mean, and who decides what is good, etc.?
6. Granted existing structures of news gathering, selection, presentation, etc., is it not inevitable that the "free flow of information" will work to the advantage of those who possess the information and the means to disseminate it?

7. Is it not time that the media were demystified, and that we began to question the restrictions and the possible tyranny of professionalism?
8. Will the multiplicity of channels made possible by the new technology lead to cultural diversity and better opportunities for minority interests?
9. Is public monopoly the only real guarantee of diversity?
10. Granted existing systems of ownership and control, are the media ever likely to provide the amount and quality of information necessary for people to act intelligently in the participatory democracy?
11. Is there not a grave risk that we shall become paralyzed by an overload of information? How much can we tolerate? How much can we understand?
12. Internationally, will the "communication revolution" lead to an increase or decrease in the gap between the haves and the have-nots?
13. As far as the developing countries are concerned, is not the main, perhaps even the sole, concern—how to use the media in the interest of national identity and development? How can one harness the new technology to national as distinct from sectional objectives?
14. How can we guard against the possible homogenizing influence of the new technology as traditional cultures may become swamped by the commercial off-loading of cheap alien material?
15. What do we know about the processes of media influence? (Halloran 1990a:4–5)

One needn't do a thorough content analysis of the text of the proposals to perceive that their meta-text radiates some of the best humanistic and democratic values of European social sciences. It is easy to understand why, at the time of its original publication, it scandalized some policymakers sticking to their customary economic and/or political monopolistic situations. But after all, as I suggested earlier, the critical researcher is usually a kind of warrior!

Old Concepts in a New Light

With the internationalization of social research, cross-cultural empirical studies proliferated spectacularly. Raymond Aron gave an early warning at the World Congress of Sociology in Evian in the 1960s when he spoke disparagingly of "safari research," surveys for which the researcher does not possess any deep understanding of the alien cultural context on which he/she imposes a set of prefabricated, ahistorical variables, deducing false generalizations and joggling the information acquired safari-style.

In his "state of the art" overview of communication studies prepared for the MacBride Commission, Halloran also cautions us against this pitfall, emphasizing that "we not infrequently encounter universal generalizations and cross cultural applications which are just not valid" (Halloran 1981:164). He rejects the "carbon-copy approach" that applies exactly the same data-collecting instruments to the multifarious conditions of different societies. In reference to his positive experiences with the multinational studies of the Prix Jeunesse research team, he notes "a shift from 'comparative' research to 'comparable' research. In the latter, as distinct from the carbon-copy approach, there were points in the research which intersected, and points that were particular to each country" (Halloran 1990b:5). (This "shift" was mostly due to the tactful obstinacy of J. D. Halloran, at the helm of the team, in finding those intersections.)

In a peppery book review, Halloran repudiates Elihu Katz and Denis McQuail's opinion, according to which the "1960s revival" in communication research could be best characterized with a return to the concept of the powerful media. Instead, he asserts what is really important, that is, "the development of a sociological perspective, hitherto lacking, which *inter alia,* set out to examine the total communication process and looked at the concept of influence in ways other than those that depended on such processes as imitation and attitude change" (Halloran 1978:125). Halloran's entire work has been a complex reflection of this transformation, which he himself helped to bring about and which he promoted with all his intellectual capacity.

It is only too obvious that in this radical transformation of mass communication research, not only do the new concepts have to be elaborated but some cornerstones of the conventional research traditions must also be reassessed in order "to ask the right questions." For instance, there is the question about the concept of gatekeeper, where the conventional approach was for the most part psychologically oriented. This is why Halloran urges us "to study the mass communicator as a member of an occupational group or profession . . . who occupies a sensitive central position in a social network, rejecting and selecting information in response to a variety of pressures" (Halloran, Elliott, and Murdock 1970:17–18).

The news value and the entertainment value, the two fundamental criteria for elaborating any kind of programming or editorial policy (albeit never treated by research conjointly), must also be put into a sociological perspective, with special attention to the "dangers, nationally and internationally, of increasing the gap between the information rich and information poor, and the leisure rich and the leisure poor" (Halloran 1983:276). From another aspect, that of the policymakers: "A knowledge of what television and the other media have to say in both fictional and non-fictional output about a selected topic should be a vital component in the formulation of any communication strategy or programme" (Halloran 1990b:26).

Agenda setting is another of a group of traditional concepts that need a new light shed on them, primarily because an analytical knowledge of its functioning could greatly help both researchers and policymakers understand the entire mechanism of the media system: "This agenda-setting function is probably the most important function that television and other media can perform, and research indicates that the overall implications of this—no matter how certain people may complain about the radical nature of programmes—is to legitimate and reinforce the status quo" (Halloran 1990b:25).

Information needs is another similar concept that did not receive more than lip service from the conventional researcher, yet it too is a key that may unlock the mass communication system. This is why Halloran and most critical researchers pay specific attention to its elaboration in a way that gives precedence to sociological as distinct from psychological elements. Moreover, one should also draw attention to the "historical connection," because communication research need not be ahistorical by definition. Fortunately, Halloran proved to be artful enough to smuggle an historical insight into it.

Onward to Néo-Studies

French sociologists ever eager to give *frappant* names to phenomena observed assert that from the age of *paléo-television,* we have now arrived at the stage of *néo-television.* Halloran, who also used the term "new television," has become a historical personality of this transitory period, having done everything to move communication research from the stage of paléo-investigation to that of néo-studies.

To demonstrate this, I have lined up and elaborated a limited number of his ideas, statements, and proposals. Of course, I could cover only partially even the outlines of the intellectual construction he has been building for the past three decades and have had to exclude his work as a teacher and science organizer. Thus, two institutions closest to his heart, his institute at the University of Leicester and the International Association for Mass Communication Research, have received no more than sporadic mentions. Also omitted are the controversies around Halloran's professional activities, the fierce attacks blaming him for being too radical, on the one hand, and, on the other, the public appreciation of his work, as evidenced by his honorary doctorates and professorships from foreign universities, climaxing in the McLuhan Prize.

This chapter's "eclectic" approach allowed me to use fragments of Halloran's text as fully as possible but also relegated my role to that of (scholarly) disk jockey, announcing and linking pieces together. (Not that concepts of mass culture are alien to Halloran's thinking.)

In conclusion, let the disk jockey put one last record on the turntable. Originally composed for an information booklet on Halloran's institute in Leicester (Centre for Mass Communication Research 1991:3–4), it summarizes adequately all that this chapter set out to show and what—excuse me—our "pop star" has elaborated many times in formulating research policy:

1. The adoption of a *multi-disciplinary approach* and the acceptance that mass communication is a field of study rather than a single discipline.
2. A concern with the *entire communication process.* Media content, and all the factors that impinge on the production and presentation of that con-

tent, as well as those that impinge on its reception and use and influence the ultimate consequences of that use, are all studies.

3. Studying the media and the communication process not in isolation but in relation to other institutions and processes in the wider social context: *the approach is essentially holistic.*
4. A recognition of the need to explore not just how the media currently operate but how they might possibly operate and *how they might be used to achieve given objectives.*
5. A concern with *basic "social needs" and "communication needs,"* which may or may not coincide with the needs and wants defined by media practitioners and policymakers.
6. *The development of a problem and policy orientation in research* so as to increase understanding of the role of the media in society and to supply the information that is the *sine qua non* of intelligent decisionmaking and policy formulation.
7. *A willingness to cooperate with broadcasters, other media practitioners, policymakers, the professions, business, and industry,* to serve their needs without compromising the independence or critical thrust of research.

REFERENCES

Centre for Mass Communication Research. (1991). *Research Programme.* Postgraduate Studies and Publications. Leicester: University of Leicester (March).

Halloran, J. D. (1970). *The Effects of Television.* London: Panther Books.

———. (1974). *Mass Media and Society: The Challenge of Research.* Leicester: Leicester University Press.

———. (1978). Further development—or turning the clock back? *Journal of Communication,* 28:2 (Spring):120–32.

———. (1981). *The Context of Mass Communication Research.* Occasional Paper No. 13. Singapore: Asian Mass Communication Research and Information Centre.

———. (1983). Warring schools or complementary perspectives? A case for critical eclecticism. *Journal of Communication,* 33:3 (Summer):270–78.

———. (1990a). Developments in communications and democracy: The contribution of research. Keynote presentation, International Association for Mass Communication Research, Bled, Yugoslavia, August.

———. (1990b). *A Quarter of a Century of Prix Jeunesse Research.* Munich: Prix Jeunesse International.

———. (1991). What can be learned from the evaluation of health education campaigns and programmes, and from the general field of mass communication research. Second International Workshop on Preventing the Sexual Transmission of HIV and Other STDs, Cambridge, England, March.

Halloran, J. D., P. Elliott, and G. Murdock. (1970). *Demonstrations and Communication: A Case Study.* Harmondsworth: Penguin.

13

Who Is (Not) "Critical" Now? On Engendering "Critical Scholarship" in International Communication

ANNABELLE SREBERNY-MOHAMMADI

Echoing William B. Yeats and Chinua Achebe, in an epoch when things have fallen apart and the center does not hold, there is uncertainty as the old verities of critical scholarship come under attack. Indeed, it is no longer clear what constitutes "critical" scholarship or what we are, or should be, "critical" about. Any putative theoretical coherence lies in tatters, a kind of truth in that lying. A vein of neo-Marxist teleology that always presaged a better future is challenged, but perhaps even more important, the "old" epistemologies and discourses no longer hang together. Language, our most flexible friend, is strained in the process. but perhaps there are also new possibilities—both conceptual and actual—to reconstitute a progressive research agenda.

I intend to focus here on the subfield of international communications, an area where all the central protagonists of this book have made a contribution, particularly in the context of demands for a New International Information Order (NIIO), where a number of real-world changes challenge the shaky epistemologies of our accepted models, the increasing impossibility of thinking in certain ways. My "we" is the community of media scholars, broadly conceived, who have been concerned about Western hegemony over the developing world and have worked within and promoted an NIIO paradigm since the 1970s. In the true spirit of an essay—foraying out, testing ideas, an incomplete project—my focus will be

---

I would like to acknowledge the useful, very critical comments of a draft of this chapter by Olga Linne, Keith Negus, and Karen Ross, who bear no responsibility for the final version.

a critique of some problematics facing international communication in the 1990s. These include the issue of spatial metaphors and levels of analysis, the gender problem, the reflexivity of the scholarly community and our intellectual/political commitments, and a future for international communications research.

Defining "Critical" Scholarship

I do not intend to define "critical approaches" in a very specific manner. I would suggest that in the most exciting current theorizing, orientations derived from neo-Marxism and political economy are interrogated through the broad perspectives of cultural studies, postmodernism, feminism, postcolonial, and subaltern studies. All these are in their various ways, "critical," if that is taken to mean questioning the status quo, attempting to conceptualize inadequately understood areas of social life and cultural formations, refusing to accept older frameworks as sufficient for understanding contemporary social, political, and cultural formations.

If "critical" also means possessing a social "project," then that too has to be rearticulated, developed afresh amid the ruins of the practice of the old socialist project and in combination with other visions. At a moment of increasing interest in ethics and values, we seem to need a renegotiation of "positive" social values that should/could be the basis for a tolerant, equitable world, a return to the discussion of some fundamental principles without retreating into fundamentalism or the reconstruction of new dominant authorities. We seem to be living through a new world disorder, but by reversing the word order, I think we arrive at a much more interesting problematic, which is truly how to *order a new world?* "Order" here as in "summon up," "command into being," "envisage" an alternative global system. As identity politics come to dominate both political discourse and political conflict, it might be an appropriate moment not to celebrate but to refuse what we are, the new identities we seem to be hailed by and the new world order we are being offered.

Real-world changes demand a rethinking and historical critique of the old conceptual categories of international communication. The "Third World" was the first to be numbered, but always as a residual category, collecting under one heading all those countries which did not fit the model or sphere of influence of capitalist industrialization or of state socialist development. It was always a slippery and disputatious concept (Worsely 1984; Ahmad 1992) and today has disintegrated both conceptually and empirically. It is challenged by the demise of the "Second World" of state socialism in 1989, one of the politically constituted "others" against which the Third World was named. It is challenged by the rapid development of certain economies such as Brazil and Mexico in Latin America, the little dragons of rapid development in Southeast Asia, and the oil wealth of many OPEC states. On the other hand, there is unrelenting poverty and economic stagnation in other parts of the South, sometimes actively worsened by interventionist global institutions and structural adjustment programs, which make any continued economic categorization of all these nations together a ludicrous proposition.

The notion of a "Third World" is also challenged culturally by the claims by indigenous peoples such as native Americans to inhabit "fourth worlds." The simple spatial geography of three worlds has also been challenged by large and growing gaps of wealth and poverty *within* industrial economies (including both rural and inner city poverty) so that not only can a "First World" lifestyle be found among the cosmopolitan elites inside the Third World, but increasingly the "Third World" is to be found inside the First (Minh Ha 1987). Can we rescue the old project? Can we resurrect "positively" the Third World as an "imaginative geography," not any longer (if ever) a clearly demarcated territorial location, but now a cultural space of signifiers and strains of music, of diverse tongues, of a real multiculturalism along the lines of "third cultures" and "third texts"? The putative triangulation is tempting, but its individual elements are confused. So we suffer a categorical and cartographic collapse, which although evident for some time now, has hardly been seriously addressed by "critical" international communications scholarship.

What about the suitability of other terms? "Postcolonial," which emerged in the attempt to demarcate especially a kind of literary production as well as a centered position from which to read and produce texts (Spivak 1990), and was thus the chosen term of a progressive and critical project, has itself been roundly critiqued (McLintock 1992; Shohat 1992). Like other "post" terms enjoying a current vogue (poststructralism, postmodernism), it suggests the complete passage of a historical moment, that colonialism is indeed over and postindependence nation-states are "free" to develop as they please. Appiah (1991) has appositely asked "if the post in post-colonialism is the same as the post in post-modernism," and a satirical postcard declares, "I will be proud to be called a post-feminist in a post-patriarchy." Thus, although the notion of a "Third World" proffered both a sense of solidarity in a shared structured experience vis-à-vis imperial power as well as a progressive politics engaged with global inequalities of power and resources, "postcoloniality" serves to reposition the nations of the South vis-à-vis their particular imperial "mothers," all the while suggesting that the impact of such colonialism has been attenuated.

The much-used alternative term, the "South," is clumsy in its neatness, drawing a line across the globe, in sand and sod and water, that does not begin to address the diversity of economic and political formations or levels of economic development among the nations so designated. Indeed, the use of the new cartography of Peter's Projection, adopted by the UN system and development-oriented nongovernment organizations (NGOs), helps us to see the world in a more accurate spatial representation than Mercator's, with the equator clearly centered, and to note that the "South" is no self-evident geographic location since much of the "South" is indeed north of the equator. Thus, the term "South" functions much like "Third World" as a categorical other, only gaining its meaning in a relational opposition to some putative "North." These conceptual difficulties evidenced in our language will quickly become apparent here, as the remit of this chapter requires some wave toward broad clusters of countries that I can find no preferrable label for than "Southern."

Can the newer language of globalization and the dialectic between the "global and the local" take on the burden of older failed vocabularies? It is perhaps a sign of our categorical confusions that, at a time when meta-narratives are challenged, we are invited to live within the conceptual space of what appears to be the most totalizing paradigm of all, globalization. Developing first as the strategic language of marketing, it has slowly inched its way into theoretical prominence, providing quite a boon to the post-post-modern publishing industry.

Globalization is theoretically significant, in Giddens's formulation (1990), for identifying four skeins of global relations, rather than just the traditional lone political-economic world system: a global system of nation-states; the development of a global market; global military alliances; and the spread of global networks of communication and information. In its fourfold logic, it avoids an economistic reductionism, for too long the basis for much critical communications scholarship in the 1970s and 1980s. It puts communication and information channels into prominence as major infrastructural elements of globalization; and from this, there seems an easy move to recognizing the significance of culture (ideology?) within these relations. It recognizes the challenge of trying to conceptualize the "world as a whole" (King 1991: ix), although the very concern with completeness may be part of our problem.

If the logic of this model of globalization is that all parts of the world are somehow affected by these structures, then the interesting empirical focus is to explore exactly how and in what manner different locales are implicated in the processes of globalization. One of the most important strands of globalization theorizing is the recognition of the opposite tendency, toward localism, toward "difference and disjuncture," as Appadurai (1990) describes these complex patterns of interaction. Currently, the dynamics of localism appear to be as powerful as those of globalization. Yet, in developing more complex models of global connectivity, using Gidden's four strands of globalization or Appadurai's five "scapes" of interaction, we lose any notion of any single determining element, any generally privileged set of relations. A danger is that the global–local construct seems to contain everything, is everywhere and thus nowhere, taking on a mythical—even ideological—tenor as it reveals less and less. Hence, we seem to need more than ever detailed case study analyses of particular global–local dynamics. But in the shifting focus toward the local/the micro, the endless description of the small-scale, we face obliterating a center or assuming there is none to examine. No doubt the centers are more diffused, more complex and contradictory than once was the case, but that is no argument for abandoning the search for the center around which much of global economic and political life still turn.

Despite the emergence of both globalizing social movements as well as fragmenting and localizing forces of ethnicity, a significant level of analysis that gets obliterated in the "global–local" focus, but remains central to the project of "international communication," is the level of nation-state policymaking and interactions with other nation-states. The whole nation-state system depends on mutual, widespread acceptance and the desire of other groupings and nations who wish to join the global state system. Thus, the nation and the state are indeed each other's projects (Appadurai 1990), and much ethnic conflict, especially in 1994 in the Balkans, is precisely about the struggle to become and define the state boundaries—territorial and cultural—of emerging nations. So the nation remains as central as ever, even at the moment of its apparent fragmentation.

The nation-state also remains a potential bulwark against the economic and cultural penetration of multinational corporations, as the locus of governmental policymaking and monitoring of international regulation. However, while defensive of cultural identity vis-à-vis external pressures, states can also be internally repressive of cultural diversity, enforcing ethnic and linguistic dominance or a religious or moralistic cultural hegemony rather than tolerance and multiplicity. Given the varied movements of people that make up the global "ethnoscape"—whether as refugees or migrant workers, students or businesspeople—nations have increasingly diverse populaces, so that the "foreign" is no longer simply outside the nation but actually next door. This has major implications for the way we study "flows" and what is defined as "international." In 1994, international communication is everywhere and nowhere and needs to be disaggregated into new and clearer problematics, as does the concept of the New International Information Order. Although the demand for an NIIO was a progressive slogan in the 1970s, developed as it was by Third World communications policymakers together with Western critical intellectuals, it is perhaps time to interrogate some of its assumptions and dynamics as a different world (dis)order becomes manifest.

Some Limits and Lacunae in the NIIO Debate

The NIIO debate is too well known and documented to need much recapitulation here. It arose out of concern for global imbalances that had become evident with the expansion of Western media and culture industries. The arguments about "cultural imperialism" and "media imperialism" usefully generated an avalanche of empirical work in the 1970s that tested their hypotheses. Imbalance in flows of news, film, television programming, the export of professional practices, and media structures have all been researched and debated, loudly by some of the "critical founding fathers" of the field, such as Herbert Schiller, Kaarle Nordenstreng, Cees Hamelink, George Gerbner, Dallas Smythe, and James Halloran. Yet, while admirably launching a new approach in the 1970s, many appear locked into that same vision even in the 1990s and have not generated any new avenues of investigation. Thus, we do seem currently somewhat tongue-tied, lacking adequate and useful categorizations of groups or nations that cluster them in meaningful ways and allow us to make appropriate comparisons between them. However, at least we have started to dismantle some of the conceptual superstructures that have determined thinking for a long time and are beginning to ask some novel questions.

For example, rarely has the complete cultural environment or media ecology of a country been analyzed, to see how imported Western television programming sets up contradictions or resonances with traditional, preexisting cultural forms, such as dramatic performance or oral poetry, or with images in the cinema that arrived before television. Analysts have tended to focus on single medium diffusion and single medium impact, whereas a range of indigenous and exogenous expressive forms and of old and new media (oral, written, broadcast, and electronic) constitute the cultural ecology almost everywhere.

There has also been insufficient recognition of the time factor, the comparative youth of many Southern "culture industries," which are still establishing their own systems of production, educating and training personnel, developing their genres. A brief look at two media forms, film and the novel, provides a point of contrast and indicates what has been missing in international communications analysis. Filmmaking, which developed in the West but whose global diffusion is decades longer than the diffusion of television, has now clearly evolved into numerous well-known national film industries, some acknowledged for their dynamic production schedules (India, Egypt), their recognizable national film identities (the "Indianness of the Indian cinema" *pace* Binod Agrawal), their hybrid genres (spaghetti westerns to curry easterns), their exciting film festivals (Carthage, Ougadougou), and innovative thematic, aesthetic, and political concerns (China, Iran, Senegal, Algeria, Nicaragua, and so on) (Diawara 1994). As a medium, film has often encountered political and social resistance, and still does—and nowhere more vocally than in the West—but through economic and political struggle, with ingenuity and vision, the medium has been worked and reworked to suit, to represent, the political and cultural environments of different places, of difference. Indeed, film is a prime medium for the development of an alternative media practice, a counter-practice that can not only subvert the often racist stereotypes of many "others" carried in the cultural products of the developed world but also provide a guerrilla response vis-à-vis national hegemony and may find an international showcase. Thus, a film about an Indian female Robin Hood directed by an Indian feminist filmmaker was banned in India but was shown on British Channel 4 during the autumn of 1994.

The novel, *the* challenging prose form of the Western social transition to modernity, has been transposed to non-Western cultures, again frequently encountering resistance to its linguistic style, its open form, and its challenge to older modes of writing. Now it returns to the West in manifold ways, sometimes as Latin American or African magic realism, novel plays with form, and in fictional exploration of colonial and postcolonial dynamics both here in the hearts of empire and there in the new/old nations of the South, novel plays with identity.

In both cinema studies and literary theory, there are rich debates, serious analyses of emerging and changing forms, arguments about hybridity and genre boundaries, questioning of the role of critics and intellectuals and their positioning, their vantage points (Sreberny-Mohammadi 1994). Such trends have never been addressed in the field of international communications, even by the "critical" protagonists, perhaps because they challenge the neat simplicity of the hypothesis of "cultural imperialism." Even now, where is the debate about Southern broadcast texts? One of the few content areas (apart from popular/world music, analysis of which develops to its own rhythm) that has provoked considerable debate is Brazilian *telenovelas*—whether they constitute an "indigenous" genre or merely mimic a soap opera format developed elsewhere, and whether they embody development-oriented messages or celebrate commercialism. Is there nowhere else in the South where there are emergent televisual forms worthy of analysis, or does this lacuna merely reflect the narrow purview of traditional scholarship in international communications? In the mid-1990s, we need to pay much closer attention to the actual media products of the Third World. Potentially we have a lot to learn in this regard from other forms of critical cultural studies.

It is also only recently, surprisingly enough, that we have seen the beginnings of audience-centered research in the South, studies that examine the patterns of use and interactions with the media that occur, using focus group and ethnographic methods (Lull 1988). Also belatedly, anthropologists are beginning to pay attention to media and examine how electronic public culture interacts with different modes of traditional cultural practices (Kottak 1990; Davis 1989; Abu-Lughod 1989). The upshot of such work is to paint a far more complex picture of what "media" means in the Southern world, what counts as "foreign" and how Western/foreign content is or is not appropriated. For example, gender is one key factor that emerges in the negotiation of private and public worlds; video, for example, providing many sequestered Middle Eastern women with glimpses of other worlds that they have little chance of experiencing. Does imported media content help to upset the gender balance? Perhaps it does, and perhaps that is not a bad thing. The logic of some Western argumentation, and reverberating through NIIO literature, is a concern about the loss of "tradition." Yet for many in the Third World, certain elements of received tradition may well be authoritarian/patriarchal practice, part of an oppressive structure that they wish to resist. Gender representation, particularly the export of Western, glamorized, images of female sexuality, to the South is thus a particularly complex area of analysis, producing mixed and contradictory reactions in receiving populations, effects that cannot be assumed and should not be ignored.

The political economy of global media structures that has dominated—and continues to dominate—work in international communication, has provided thin analysis (not thick description), which cannot begin to address, let alone answer, many crucial issues about the actual circulation of texts in a society or changes in a culture as a consequence of media development. I am not arguing against the useful analysis of the structural features of global tele/communications realities, which such an approach has highlighted. Rather, as already suggested, sometimes political economy has been overworked at the expense of other forms of analysis, and sometimes it has not been taken far enough, so that we still know comparatively little about the precise value generated by cultural production, particularly the export dollars earned through sales, for example, of *telenovelas* and film by Third World producers. National encouragement of and provision of resources for media production in the South might be generated if research could clearly show the major financial contribution that cultural production could make to Southern national balance of payments. Detailed analysis of the contributions of telecommunications to development, both in terms of satisfying social needs as well as of providing economic benefits, is slowly being applied to a broader media picture, as in recent work by Meheroo Jussawalla, Jill Hills, and Sandra Braman.

A major shortcoming of NIIO rhetoric has been the apparently stronger concern for the protection of indigenous culture and the limitation of Western cultural products over concern for democratization, human rights, and access. Within social theory, there has been over the last decade increasing interest in the functioning of the "public sphere," a Habermasian conceptual legacy, particularly in the context of burgeoning civil societies in the former Soviet Union. No longer merely dismissed as a smokescreen for bourgeois ideology, there is renewed interest in rethinking democracy, including how well democratic practices allow for multiple modes of political action, the development of social movements such as feminism and ecology, and the mechanisms for the adjudication of competing claims in a pluralist society.

But what about the South? What can the role of media be if there is no civil society, no public sphere? Can media be the prefiguring of these? Yet how can there be development planning and national policymaking without a stable state? Part of the tragedy of the NIIO is that it has been too soft on hard states; some of its strongest voices have also been the most authoritarian, and the stress on national cohesion has far outweighed the concern for democratization. Although too mechanistically conceptualized, Frankfurt School interest in the social psychology of the "authoritarian personality" and repression—political as well as sexual—remain useful approaches to analyzing the enduring power of one-party systems, state censorship, and the general fragility of democracy in the Third World (and indeed, in the First World). Here, human rights monitoring organizations can sometimes mobilize an embryonic "international public opinion" in condemnation of the worst abuses; Southern journalists themselves mobilize to defend free speech, and even "critical scholars" in the West note that such a modern, bourgeois value can be of enormous significance in the development of the South. Many women's groups, ethnic and other minority movements that may base their mobilization on indigenous cultural practices and genres are not solely "cultural" but often defiantly "political" movements in the face of state autocracy. The jargon of authenticity can be a smokescreen for control, as well as a (n)atavistic regression, ending up as a superficially defiant anti-Westernism with internally repressive consequences. Regime policies toward DBS (Direct Broadcasting System) from Malaysia and Singapore to Iran can be seen as embodying the contemporary dilemmas of cultural development in the tension between religiously inflected cultural habits and the worldly, commercial attractions of programming satellite broadcasting. However, such simple attempts to ban popular cultural encounters with the West are hard to justify in theory and clearly impossible to enforce in practice.

It seems far more useful to take a longer historical view and recognize and analyze the manner in which Western culture has had and continues to have cultural impact, well before and beyond the influx of media, through religion, education, language use, administrative practices, professional training, and so on (Bitterli 1992; Said 1993; Sreberny-Mohammadi, forthcoming) as well as the complex sociopsychological reflexes and reactions that imperialism and its neo-variants have engendered in the South. Indeed, in works such as Memmi's *Dependence* to material on *codependency* in addictive relations in the West, there is renewed interest in the social psychology of unequal, dependent relations. Giddens's turn to the self in modernity (1991) is curiously reminiscent of certain concerns of the once much discredited modernization literature and could be profitably read against the concerns of 1960s' theorists such as Daniel Lerner and Alex Inkeles. The NIIO argument disallows resistance or critical engagement and assumes assimilation, or at least abandons any nuanced class- and gender-based analysis for general concern about cultural loss.

Engendering Research

Gender presents itself as a pivotal issue. Both the Third World and women sometimes function as the West's "others," and the questions around social/sexual repression and the position of women are stubborn keys to unlocking Third World development, as the muted rhetoric of the Cairo Population Summit in September 1994 finally recognized. Indeed, we know that in many parts of the

Third World the position of rural women may actually decline as they become assimilated into the global market economy and that Western-style "development" can actually reduce the economic and political status of women. Thus, it is not that women are omitted from the processes of modernization and development but rather that these processes can have even more deleterious impacts on women than on men. Many concepts long considered central to models of international relations, such as rationality, security, and power, are now seen as gendered, not neutral, concepts, whereas the gendered dynamics of international relations, from the sex economies around military bases to the private socializing that underpins public diplomacy, can no longer be ignored (Tickner 1991). Gender is implicated at every level of analysis: global, regional, national, and local.

If women are on the fringe of the periphery, less involved in hegemonic structures of power but more involved with alternative social movements concerned with peace, ecology, and economic justice, then it stands to reason that feminist thinking and women's actions can also contribute greatly to the formation of counter-hegemonic perspectives and alternative modes of social organization (Barrett and Phillips 1992; Benhabib 1992). Given contemporary concern about human agency and the conceptualization of historical subjects as subjects of their own lives, the silence about gender in the NIIO debate and its policy formulations echoes.

Yet, when gender does creep into international communications rhetoric, it appears as a discrete problem that belongs to somebody else. The final statement of the MacBride Roundtable, held in Honolulu in January 1994, speaks of the need for the "empowerment of women" and "indigenous minorities." Who is speaking here, and what does their speaking actually add to the difficult processes involved in women's empowerment? Are not women already empowering themselves? A recent overview of women's global media activities, while still gloomy vis-à-vis mainstream media's range of female representations and the lack of women at upper levels of media production and management, nonetheless found considerable evidence of alternative, grass-roots, women-run media activities using all possible forms of media (Sreberny-Mohammadi 1994). Do women need to be told that they need empowerment? At the same time as the MacBride report mentions the "need for women's empowerment," it omits any mention of policies or resources that could support such empowerment. Most importantly, it now carries almost no critique of the processes of media conglomeratization and privatization occurring in the industrialized world and elsewhere and makes no mention of the need for public political debates and strategies of action in the North about media inequality and public access. In what I would term a politics of displacement, the South—especially women and indigenous peoples—now becomes the locus of false expectations regarding sociocultural change that seem to suggest either that these issues have all been solved in the North or that nothing can be done there. We need a richer political vision, one that does not exhort others without taking on any personal responsibility for change, one that does not displace the burden of change onto others. In "Are My Hands Clean"? the a capella singing group Sweet Honey in the Rock laments the global journey of a blouse. Labor exploitation, ecological damage, and gender inequalities are all implicated in the detailed story of the processes involved in the production of a polyester blouse that ends up on sale in a popular U.S. department store. Are our hands clean? Such a question presses the issue of personal commitment, yet the very notion stems from a religious sensibility of purity and uncontamination, tropes much used in political discourse in Iran before and after the Iranian revolution (see Sreberny-Mohammadi and Mohammadi 1994). The real world offers far murkier realities, as with the controversy surrounding the "ethical trading practices" of the Body Shop, which is thus revealed as both clean (or at least selling cleanliness) *and* dirty. Yet to ask questions about our own positions and commitments seems justified in a field that has adopted a highly moralistic tone in its global analyses.

The project of international communication of the "founding fathers" remains resolutely masculist with little evidence of attempts to include gender analysis. One example, a recent volume about the Gulf War, *Triumph of the Image,* edited by Hamid Mowlana and two of this volume's gurus, George Gerbner and Herbert Schiller, includes no pieces by women out of thirty-four contributors nor any analysis of the gender dynamics and implications of this war. This is all the more puzzling for considerable evidence suggests that a far larger percentage of women than men in the United States (and elsewhere?) were opposed to the Gulf War, women were involved in the armed forces of both sides, and women were not only victims of military and political activities but, as migrant workers, suffered the economic dislocations the war brought to the region. In the United States alone, many women spoke out against the war and offered critical analyses of media coverage (Elayne Rapping, Nawab El Saadawi, Ella Shohat, Barbara Bowen, myself, to name but a few), and there is a substantial literature by women not just on peace but also on the connections between war, weaponry, and sexuality (Helen Caldicott, Cynthia Enloe, and Evelyn Accad, to mention just three diverse writers). Gendered analysis questions the relationship between production and reproduction, between the public and private spheres, between modes of political representation and forms of mediated representation. There is a growing number of women academics whose work has and does directly impinge on NIIO issues (M. Gallagher, M. Jussawalla, J. Hills, R. Mansell, S. Braman, B. Dervin, R. Rush, C. Ogan, C. Roach, T. Leibes, I. Ang, for starters), and yet unlike the broader field of cultural studies, questions about gender, gender power imbalances, gender representation still do not resonate as significant issues among the "critical scholars" in international communication.

Thus, in a critical spirit, I am bound to engage with the organizing notion of this very volume, which seems to reinforce a questionable "great men of history" position. Apart from the obvious feminist saw, another strand of argument would want to situate these "great men" within their broader social and political contexts, their moments of history, which both constrained and enabled their research, and thus to also appreciate the institutional, organizational, and financial structures that supported them, colleagues who worked with them, and structures in which they operated. It is not a matter of quibbling over the inclusion or exclusion of any one person but to suggest that the very premise of such an individualistic focus is itself open to question.

Theory and Research Difficulties

Clearly some of the difficulties experienced in theorizing and researching issues in international communication have been particularly affected by real global events, particularly the U.S.-prompted demise of UNESCO as a global forum for assembly, debate, and financial support for studies in the field. Partly we have been condemned to endless essay writing because of the lack of monies and vision to support empirical research programs, particularly large-scale and comparative projects that are needed at least periodically in this field. If one were to sketch a review of new research in international communication over the last decade, it would be very thin indeed. Yet, as already mentioned, perhaps one implication of the global–local model is to push us in the direction of small-scale but conceptually broader projects using a variety of methods, mapping out the complex cultural environments that peoples of the South inhabit.

Yet there is no longer any simple politics of location—the South. There are numerous Arab broadcasters operating from London, for example, broadcasting to Arab-speaking communities across Europe as well as to the Middle East, language binding peoples across tense national divides. Many nationalities of exiles are writing or transmitting to their various "homes." Meanwhile, the typically family-oriented media practices are eliminated for First World homeless. Nor is there any simple politics of identity: Women have long recognized the impossibility of speaking for all, and there are many feminisms; any category seems to contain as much diversity as it keeps out. Thus, notions of "indigenous culture," "authentic expression," and "primordial identities," which have lurked in NIIO arguments, seem to presage simple returns to uncontaminated pasts, a naive view of real human history, which is full of cultural contacts, conquests, contaminations (Sreberny-Mohammadi, forthcoming). Sometimes the invitations seem to be to reconstruct atavistic formations that presage not a peaceful and tolerant but a violent and prejudicial future.

Indeed, the current situation embodied in continuing demands for an NIIO seems to be characterized more by Western liberal nostalgia for a past that was never ours, a romanticism about the Third World not shared by many of its inhabitants, than by Third World concerns. This is the opposite of the phenomenon that Appadurai (1990) poignantly describes, whereby much of the Third World appears nostalgic for the past of Western popular culture that they never had, enjoying bad 1940s popular hits and other passé pop styles of the West. Thus, in 1994, it is important to ask for whom is the project of "national identity" or "cultural authenticity" an issue (see Parker et al. 1992)? For whom is the NIIO a significant demand? Who is articulating it?

One of the most progressive changes to have emerged from the period of comparative stasis over the last decade in Western theoretical and empirical work in international communication is the emergence of strong scholarship, empirical and theoretical, from the South, including by and about women; for example, the work of Souki Oliveira, Fox Cardona, and Martin Barbero in Latin America, Abu Lughod and others in the Middle East and Asia. Some of the most interesting descriptions of innovative media use come not from the academic scholars of international communication but from travel writers, assorted "intellectuals" such as Pico Iyer and Gunter Grass. We run the risk of neither conducting good critical research nor popularizing our discourse into the wider public culture, so that it barely ripples beyond our own journals and conferences. Other kinds of writers seem to do that far better. Russel Jaccoby (1987) and Douglas Kellner (1990) have raised serious questions about the kinds of communicative practices used by "Western intellectuals," including a delight in abstruse prosody and a disdain for electronic media, somewhat bizarre choices for "communicators."

In the 1990s, we are forced to ask from where do we speak, to analyze who we are and of what are we critical? Indeed, what can our criticism achieve? We need far more nuanced concepts, for example, to acknowledge a difference, as Kellner (1989) suggests, between consumption and consumerism, between a life-enhancing use and enjoyment of material and cultural products and a way of life dedicated primarily toward the possession and use of commodities. Although it may be true that the central ideology of capitalist production is a consumerist ideology, that does not mean that every hamburger eaten in the Third World is a celebration of that ideology. There is an awful hubris involved in sitting in centrally heated houses with electricity, running hot water, and telephone as the basic infrastructure of one's personal life, surrounded by a panoply of cultural consumption, and pontificating about consumerism coming to the Third World.

In many ways, the field of international communications is remarkable for its lack of self-reflexivity. Although other areas of social inquiry slowly resound with interrogations of identity, definitions of the self, and debates about the positioned nature of knowledge, it is almost impossible to discover a parallel literature in our field, even though it is one of the areas in which such auto-critique is vitally necessary. Many of us critiqued the rush to "developmentalism" of the South, but we have enjoyed running hot and cold water, twenty-four-hour electricity, well-stocked supermarkets, and a wide range of cultural products in a relatively unfettered environment. We have written and analyzed the imbalances in flows of cultural products, the export of educational practices and professional orientations, and research imperialism, but we remain in the main based in the North, offering just such programs to students and others from the South, eager to take their foreign exchange in return for our expertise. We are, and have been, part of the conditions we study. My point is not merely to condemn such activities—in which I am a participant—but to raise as a complex of issues the interesting fact that rarely do our own politics, our own involvements in teaching, training, and research, come under any scrutiny. Nor does our ability to talk with a forked tongue, from positions of great safety and comfort, critiquing the choices of the South while enjoying many of those very basic things they have come to want.

There is still little recognition of gendered vantage points (although such arguments are loud in other disciplines), and even "critical" essays on ethnicity and national culture are often written as though the author occupied no ethnic or raced position, being privy to some transcendent perspective from which to look down on the messy reality of global political and social life. Neither the positivist, developmentalist models of "communication and development" nor the so-called critical models of cultural imperialism and dependency have seen anything out of order in the fact that both were essentially articulated by white Western males telling the Third World what to do. Many of our arguments have supported concepts of "national identity," and then we rail against ethnic cleansing; we've supported national policymaking and then are confronted by despotic and intolerant regimes. Much of our discussion takes place at such a level of generality that it absents the real politics of place, ours and those with whom we claim solidarity, and even those whom we oppose. Our own complicity has rarely been challenged; we have been remarkably long in rhetoric and short in our own politics, even in matters that directly pertain to our academic concerns. Where is the academic community's public support for a Freedom of Information Act in Britain? Who has organized a U.S.-based movement to pressure Clinton to rejoin UNESCO? Finally, after years of generalized rhetoric in support of human rights, particularly the "right to communicate," the International Association for Mass Communication Research, at its Nineteenth General Assembly in July 1994, took up a critical stance against the now five-year-old *fatwa* against the British writer Salman Rushdie and the more recent one against the Bangladeshi feminist writer Taslima Nasreen.

The lack of self-critique of the implications of our own practice in the new global system makes a mockery of our highly ethicized, normative analyses of this system. In many other areas of current social inquiry, the moral and ethical role of the critic has been engaged (Wolfe 1989; Merod 1987). Media studies displace ethical inquiry onto journalistic practices, allowing academics to keep it distant from our own work and the implications of our own work for theory building and policymaking. Similarly, work that interrogates the actual or possible role of intellectuals within the processes we describe is barely posed, despite a voluminous literature that suggests a deep historical shift in the roles of intellectuals from legislation to interpretation and a consequent loss of authority (Baumann 1987) or the possible global middle-class camaraderie of intellectuals (Gouldner 1979) that has implications for the constituencies we might influence. Although other disciplines have begun to interrogate the seeing eye/writing I of academic discourse, particularly in anthropology and women's studies and ethnographic work in media/cultural studies, that has hardly spread through the discipline at large. I think it is salutary to stop and inquire whose project an NIIO really is now, how critical our "critical scholarship" has been and is now. Essentially, the field of international communication is suffering from an inadequate engagement with a range of new theoretical positions that have emerged over the last decade and from a narrowness of focus that has not probed many unarticulated areas of assumed consequences and unclear relations that need to be critically engaged and understood.

In the end, it seems to me that the very singularity of the notion "*a* new international information order" requires that we ask whose order that would be. It is an argument that increasingly requires reconsideration. With our recognition of multiple identities and varied life-worlds, surely a multiplicity of (dis)orders, a harmony or antiphony of voices is what we want, not a singular alternative to that which exists. In international communications we have been too locked in a moralizing binary logic, a bad Western capitalism and a good Southern authenticity, a far too simple "orientalism" that was never accurate and that the hybrid cultural conditions of the 1990s can no longer support. Alternative, resistive, counter-hegemonic voices in "both" poles are already functioning and being examined and refined in many locales. Thus, it is not that something completely new needs to be done, or even that all this activity needs coordination. Perhaps we should simply be more wary of our own desires to totalize and control.

It is a time of some considerable crisis in the West and in capitalism, despite the triumphalist rhetoric. Economic problems include mass unemployment, recession, export of capital, labor migration, and rising racist/fascist sentiments. The social sphere sees debates about the collapse of the family, the lack of moral socialization leading to violence, substance abuse, and alienation, while in the political sphere there is increasing withdrawal from the political system, evidenced by falling voting rates even for major elections, growth of right-wing racist parties, relying on fear of the "other" to mobilize sentiment, and an apparent collapse of "vision" on the left. I think the NIIO needs to be re-turned to include the so-called developed world, where most of its concerns apply and where increasing media conglomeratization, spreading knowledge gaps, and rising illiteracy require real political debate and policy formulations. There are many local practices, local solidarities, and local solutions already—perhaps we can act as facilitators, translating them from place to place, culture to culture. It is an odd moment in our collective conversations, when determining structural analysis is being challenged by voluntaristic, participatory models. Giddens's structuration theory proposes that structures are both constraining as well as enabling, and so are media technologies. Although I am wary of falling into optimistic naiveté, the current global confusion is also a moment of possibility, openness, and intellectual debate. We should not pass it by.

Of the Future and, Therefore, Unimaginable

Perhaps we need more of the imagination and writing about the future that critical theorists have always abjured. When we bracket our own visions, it is hard to complain when this aporia is filled with consumer fantasies and Hollywood glamour. The need for utopian thinking seems to be enjoying a vogue. Anthony Giddens suggests that "we require a *new* injection of utopianism if we are, as collective humanity, somehow to emerge unscathed from the turbulent and risky world into which modernity has launched us . . . utopianism . . . has to envisage futures whose achievement is both contingent and highly risky. I call the conjunction of these characteristics *utopian realism*" (1990). The human problem is that we can only look in one direction at a time. Walter Benjamin describes the tragedy of human progress through the metaphor of angel of history being propelled into the future, to which his back is turned as he looks out on the wreckage and suffering of past history that is irredeemable. It is anamnestic solidarity that often binds us, perhaps even more than contemporary ties of community. Marshall McLuhan employs the image of the rearview mirror: We drive into the future while our concentration is on what has gone before or what is coming up from behind. Harold Innis, however, suggests that "most forward-looking people have their heads turned sideways" (cited in Maxwell 1993), presumably to see what is happening around them. These are powerful images, about the limits on vision, about the human difficulty of looking in many directions at once and, hence, the dilemma of looking forward with eyes open to the future without forgetting what lies "behind" in the past and the contradictions of the present. It is time not only to re-explore the moral groundings for a secular communitarian society but for a global civil society, using current theorizing about the reinvention of solidarity, female ethics of caring, and new forms of community. This can help to redeem modernity as an unfinished and undervisioned project and protect it from the atavistic reconstruction of putative primordial identities.

We are at, or are fast approaching, a time-space edge. We are at the cusp of the twentieth century, the third millenium (at least in the globally dominant Christian calendar). If the centers are not holding, the margins too are shifting. There are new boundaries and demarcations, new inclusions and exclusions, new vantage points for argument on those margins. We need to tolerate ambiguity, disjuncture, diversity. No single model can contain all this. Edges are such boundaries. If too blurred or too sharp, edges can be frightening, but they also offer opportunity and lead to something new. Risk, too, can be exciting.

Apollinaire said

"come to the edge"
but they said "we're too frightened, we might fall."
Apollinaire said "come to the edge."
So they did
and he pushed
and they flew.

I think what we need is a new word order: Order a New World. Now.

REFERENCES

Abu Lughod, L. (1989). Bedouins, cassettes and technologies of public culture. *Middle East Report,* 159 (July–August):7–12.

———. (1993). Screening politics in a world of nations. *Public Culture,* 5:3.

Ahmad, A. (1992). *In Theory.* London: Verso.

Appadurai, A. (1990). Disjuncture and difference in the global cultural economy. *Public Culture,* 2:2.

Appiah, K. A. (1991). Is the post in post-modernism the same as the post in post-colonialism? *Critical Inquiry* (Winter):17.

Barrett, M., and A. Phillips. (1992). *Destabilizing Theory: Contemporary Feminist Debates.* Cambridge: Polity.

Baumann, Z. (1987). *Legislators and Interpreters.* Cambridge: Polity.

Benhabib, S. (1992). *Situating the Self: Gender, Community and Postmodernism in Contemporary Ethics.* Cambridge: Polity.

Benjamin, W. (1970). *Illuminations.* London: Fontana.

Bitterli, U. (1992). *Cultures in Conflict: Encounters Between European and Non-European Cultures 1492–1800.* Cambridge: Polity.

Davis, H. (1989). American magic in a Moroccan town. *Middle East Report,* 159:12–18.

Diawara, M. (1994). On tracking world cinema: African cinema at film festivals. *Public Culture,* 6:2.

Giddens, A. (1990). Modernity and utopia. *New Statesman and Society* (November 2).

———. (1991). *Modernity and Self-Identity.* Cambridge: Polity.

Gouldner, A. (1979). *The Future of Intellectuals and the Rise of the New Class.* New York: Macmillan.

Jaccoby, R. (1987). *The Last Intellectuals: American Culture in the Age of Academe.* New York: Noonday.

Kellner, D. (1989). *Critical Theory, Marxism and Modernity.* Baltimore: Johns Hopkins University Press.

———. (1990). *Television and the Crisis of Democracy.* Boulder: Westview.
King, A. D., ed. (1991). *Culture, Globalization and the World-System.* London: Macmillan.
Kottak, C. (1990). *Prime-Time Society.* Belmont, CA: Wadsworth.
Lull, J., ed. (1988). *World Families Watch Television.* Newbury Park, CA: Sage.
Maxwell, R. (1993). Caught in the maelstrom: Globalization and social immobility. *Directions,* 7:1–2.
McLintock, A. (1992). The angel of progress: Pitfalls of the term "post-colonialism." *Social Text,* 31–32.
Merod, J. (1987). *The Political Responsibility of the Critic.* Ithaca: Cornell University Press.
Minh Ha, T. (1987). Of other peoples: Beyond the "salvage" paradigm. In *Discussions in Contemporary Culture-Number One,* edited by H. Foster. Seattle: Bay.
Parker, A., et al. (1992). *Nationalisms and Sexualities.* New York: Routledge.
Said, E. (1993). *Culture and Imperialism.* London: Chatto and Windus.
Shohat, E. (1992). Notes on the post-colonial. *Social Text,* 31–32.
Spivak, G. (1990). *The Post-Colonial Critic.* New York: Routledge.
Sreberny-Mohammadi, A. (1994). The cultural politics of the possible. *Journal of Communication,* 44:2.
———. (Forthcoming). The many cultural faces of imperialism. In *Beyond the NIIO,* edited by P. Golding and P. Harris. Newbury Park, CA: Sage.
Sreberny-Mohammadi, A., and A. Mohammadi. (1994). *Small Media, Big Revolution: Communications, Culture and the Iranian Revolution.* Minneapolis: University of Minnesota Press.
Tickner, J. A. (1991). On the fringes of the world economy: A feminist perspective. In *The New International Political Economy,* edited by C. N. Murphy and R. Tooz. Boulder: Lynne Rienner.
Wolfe, A. (1989). *Whose Keeper? Social Science and Moral Obligation.* Berkeley: University of California Press.
Worsely, P. (1984). *The Three Worlds: Culture and World Development.* Chicago: University of Chicago Press.

PART FIVE

KAARLE NORDENSTRENG

Kaarle Nordenstreng, Lake Bled, Yugoslavia, 1990 (Photo by John A. Lent)

Kaarle Tapani Nordenstreng

Born:	June 9, 1941, Helsinki, Finland
Education:	Studies after high school matriculation (1960) at the University of Helsinki in psychology (major) and phonetics/general linguistics (minor); B.A., 1963; M.A., 1965; Ph.Lic., 1966; Ph.D., 1969

Employment:

1971–	Professor of Journalism and Mass Communication, University of Tampere, Finland
1991 (Spring)	Visiting Professor, University of Maryland, College Park
1987	Research Fellow, International Journalism Institute, Prague
1982 (Winter)	Visiting Professor, Southern Illinois University, Carbondale
1981	UNESCO consultant on international communication, Dar es Salaam, Tanzania
1977 (Spring)	Visiting Professor, University of California, San Diego
1975 (Spring)	Visiting Professor, Simon Fraser University, Burnaby, Canada
1972 (Winter)	UNESCO consultant on audience research, Kuala Lumpur, Malaysia
1967–71	Head of Research and member of long-range planning group, Finnish Broadcasting Company
1966 (Fall)	Postgraduate Fellow, Southern Illinois University, Carbondale
1965–66	Instructor of Journalism and Mass Communication, University of Tampere
1962–63	Editor, Youth Programs, Finnish Broadcasting Company

Other Service:

Member, International Council, 1970–, Vice President, 1972–88, President of Professional Education Section, 1988–, International Association for Mass Communication Research; President, International Organization of Journalists, 1976–90; founding member since 1974, President, 1983–84, Finnish Association for Mass Communication Research; National Committee for the Conference on

Security and Co-operation in Europe, 1974–84; board member, Finnish Institute of International Affairs, 1973–87; Chairman, National Committee on Journalism Education, 1973; Vice Chairman, National Committee on Communication Policy, 1972–74; board member, Nordic Documentation Centre for Mass Communication Research, 1972–76; member, National Committee on Freedom of Information, 1971–72; Chairman, UNESCO Meeting of Experts on Communication Policies and Planning, Paris, 1972; member, UNESCO Panel of Consultants on Communication Research, Paris, 1971–76; participant, UNESCO Meeting of Experts on Communication and Society, Montreal, 1969; member, 1969–77, Chairman of Communications Division, 1975–77, Finnish National Commission for UNESCO; freelance journalist with various Finnish newspapers and magazines (columnist, *Uusi Suomi*), 1957–65; freelance journalist, Finnish Broadcasting Company's radio youth programs, 1956–62, reportage and actualities programs, 1958–65, television documentaries, 1958–65

Editing, Publishing:

Editor, *Sosiologia,* journal of Finnish association of sociologists, Westermarck Society; member editorial advisory boards, including *Journal of Communication*

14

Interview with Kaarle Nordenstreng

CONDUCTED BY JOHN A. LENT
BLED, YUGOSLAVIA, AUGUST 30, 1990

What in your early background moved you into the critical perspective?

It is a combination of accidents in my life and certain objective factors which had to do with my home background and my class position.

First of all, the background. I come from an upper-middle class, or almost upper class, family. My father was an officer in the Finnish army, and after the war went to a civil servant occupation. My mother came from a small businessman family, but my home political environment was right-wing, with almost fascist tendencies. In my school years, I was either apolitical or inclined to follow the right-wing way of thinking.

But I was never very active in the school fraternity circles or any social or political movements in my youth. I rather was a man of action in many hobbies, and I had amateur radio-type activities as my prime hobby. I was supposed to become an engineer.

I was a typical, apolitical technocrat by my orientation, with an upper-class family bias, and I chose to study psychology, philosophy, linguistics, and economics at the University of Helsinki. This was after abandoning engineering as a main type of occupation. I suddenly became interested in myself and turned into an introvert. Often, when people have character problems with themselves, they become humanistically oriented and psychology fans like I did.

That led me to the College of Philosophy in Helsinki University. At that time, I was very apolitical with a devotion to psychology, including psychoanalysis. I became interested in Carl Gustav Jung, and I was the last one to interview him before he died in 1961. That interview I still have on tape. This interview brings me to my other part of—sort of—youth development, namely, journalism.

I became active in radio journalism at the age of fifteen when the Finnish Broadcasting Company started to recruit young persons to produce programs for other young people. I was at the time the youngest radio reporter in Finland. I did it while I was in high school.

I had very great devotion and it was active work. But again, that was not scientific and even less critical. I was very naive, with a typical boy scout mentality of journalism. That continued to some extent during the study years, with such exceptional programs like this interview with C. G. Jung. The third year of my studies I did while working full time as editor responsible for youth programs.

My first attachment to communication and journalism research and a scientific approach of any kind in our field was during that year when I happened to be recruited on behalf of my employer, the Finnish Broadcasting Company, to the Salzburg seminar in American Studies for a course devoted to mass media. In that course there were mainly practically oriented journalism teachers. Among them, by the way, was a freelance magazine journalist, not so well known at the time—Alvin Toffler.

During that semester, I was introduced to several books dealing with radio research or communication theories and so on. It suddenly appeared to me that my hobby, journalism, and this psychological or scientific career could meet each other in a point called communication research.

It was completely new to me. I never knew that it existed and I never considered studying journalism in Finland, even though it was possible because we have the oldest program in the Nordic countries. Since 1925, Finland has had a journalism program at the college level—later University of Tampere—but I was never interested in that. Only after this triggering effect of the Salzburg seminar was my attention brought to this particular topic. But that was not yet critical at all. It was only of a general academic interest and clearly in line with a positivistic orientation.

I continued then to combine my psychology and linguistic studies with an interest in the media, and then I was recruited as in instructor in journalism and mass communication after my M.A. degree in the mid-1960s. Soon after that, 1966, I got my second degree, *licentiate,* which corresponds to the American Ph.D. After that, I immediately went to the United States and to Southern Illinois University to spend a semester as a visiting fellow in exchange with Kenneth Starck, who came to take my position in Finland. At that time, I was still a rather conventional, positivistically (to use this misleading slogan) oriented young communicologist who really did not have a critical approach.

Well, partly, my critical turn was influenced by the crazy years of the late 1960s, which somehow became tangible to me already while I was staying at Carbondale, Illinois. That was the time when Vietnam and all this turmoil was very much felt in the States, as well as increasingly in Europe, and although I was like a naive, untouched person, my world outlook was somehow influenced, or I could not go on without noticing that there was something in the world that was not proper, and I started to see social injustice and so on.

I also became engaged and later married a girl who was a little bit radical, and she influenced me in that direction. Then I got to know some Finnish social scientists in a circle which is called Nordic Summer Academy, which is a voluntary organization meeting every summer from country to country. Johann Galtung, by the way, started his peace research activities there in the early 1960s. Many other critical social scientists in Scandinavia have gone through this summer academy. I was introduced to it by accident through family friends. That pattern influenced me towards the critical direction, but that critical study was very mild. It was sort of bourgeois liberalism; the pluralistic critical approach rather than a fundamental Marxist type of approach. Still, little by little, my worldview changed. But what is important, it was not a systematic change by means of reading the big classics of critical thinking. It was rather the circumstances. It was the environment, the general tide of the day, as well as certain personal experiences.

It was liberal when pitted against the uniform, almost totalitarian bourgeois mentality that used to dominate our scientific environment. So I was influenced by those factors a little bit. But then the decisive push for me came through the Finnish Broadcasting Company. As I said before, I used to work there as a journalist, but in 1967, immediately after my U.S. year, I returned to the company as head of audience research and a member of the long-range planning group. I was recruited to that post because I was considered to be an effective and useful character to launch such a service in a company that was in a dynamic state of reform—from a passive institution reflecting the establishment voice of society into an active facilitator and stimulator of the social and cultural sphere of the country. This dynamo type of function that broadcasting assumed was very close to me because I was employed in management and I was in the policy planning group next to the director-general, who was a sort of cultural liberal and, later, radical in Finland.

These personal influences then brought me very quickly more and more to the left. The year 1968 came: I was employed there, and I became more and more polarized—along with my working environment and the general environment in Finland—to the critical thinking. I kept in that line while finishing my Ph.D., which, in Finland, is a major degree, with a published work, and so forth. My doctoral work was far from normal communication research and even further from critical theory. It was on the semantic differential technique and included quite sophisticated statistical methodologies.

But while I did that I became more and more radicalized in my broader and social and communication outlooks. I cannot identify certain, for instance, books or scholars in the outer world who influenced me apart from a Finnish philosopher who was my colleague at the Finnish Broadcasting Company, Yrjo Ahmavaara. There is more on this aspect of the Finnish communication research in a 1990 issue of the *European Journal of Communication,* where I have written with my colleagues a history of our paradigm developments.

Anyhow, it was mainly again sort of atmospheric influences. If I critically reflect backwards and look at myself, I have been a typical, relatively unindependent person who has had a sort of black-box mind, open for influences, and those influences have been a direct function of my environment. When I happened to be in a conservative home environment, that was it. Then, when I was living thought those years of turmoil in the late 1960s, I became directly involved in an institution that was in the center of those changes in Finnish society, an institution that became more and more radical to the point that it was considered to be one of the biggest points of controversy in Finnish politics. The director-general, my boss, was kicked out in 1970.

Through that personal experience, through living, rather than thinking or reading, I was brought into this polarization that made me choose my side. But I was not with poor masses and not going through any personal hardships, that it would have been a revenge in life to become radical. It was simply that I held a good position in a well-to-do institution that just happened to be on its way to the left.

I first became introduced to Herbert Schiller and George Gerbner at the time when I came to the United States in 1966. I met them for the first time in the International Association for Mass Communication Research (IAMCR) conference in Herzeg, Yugoslavia, on November 1. Jim Halloran I got to know two years later. Dallas Smythe I didn't get to know at that time but learned to know him a couple of years later, first at an IAMCR conference in Ljubljana in 1968, and one year later at the UNESCO meeting of experts on communication and society in Montreal. In 1969, Herb's book, *American Empire,* was published. I got hold of it from Dallas, who sent it to me right away. I remember very well reading *American Empire.* It was in Rome. I was in a hotel close by the Vatican, spending a couple of days after my meeting with the International Broadcast Institute—the predecessor of the International Institute of Communication—which was held somewhere in Italy. I had a couple of days in Rome, reading this book, and I was soon impressed by both Dallas's foreword and Herb's whole message. This is one of the experiences that I can identify where some message really touched me and had in impact on me. But yet, I would say it did not do much more than just articulate or confirm what already was there, and what was there was an orientation created by these various personal experiences, institutional environments, atmospheric things, and so on.

Incidentally, in these years prior to 1970, when I read *American Empire,* my contacts with IAMCR did not much encourage critical thinking. They only encouraged my conviction that the field of communication research is something that is very relevant to me and felt whole, increasingly, in this particular era.

In 1970, I invited Dallas to a roundtable seminar that I organized under the auspices of the Finnish National Commission of UNESCO. Dallas had a strong impact on our community of colleagues and also on me personally.

Roughly at that time I realized that there really is a sort of difference between schools, and I increasingly found myself at home, and wanted to work, with this critical school. Maybe it was a bit earlier because, after all, it was 1968 when I wrote the piece in *Gazette* about communication research in the United States, which was a critical assessment of the lack of thinking or doing that I found in the States during my stay.

Actually, if I look back on those years, I may say that my stay in the United States had an impact on me. First, it was the polarization and politicalization of the whole society, and second it was my observations and conclusions of the communications research area where I was impressed by the abundance of what some people call positivistic crap against the relative lack of critical thinking.

But again, it was not based on systematic reading and analytical assessments of research trends. I hardly knew that such persons like T. W. Adorno and Hork ever existed. I had of course known by that time that [Herbert] Marcuse was there, but I knew about him only superficially. I never read his works. I only read Marcuse's book in 1969, when it was translated into Finnish. So my shift to the critical side was not based on systematic reading but rather a sort of gliding with the time. Well, this I've now said so many times.

So, what else? I think 1971 . . . well, there was a new professorship established for electronic journalism and mass communication at the University of Tampere for which I, again by more or less good luck, happened to get as the first nomination. I was only thirty at that time, and I left broadcasting. I just barely reached minimum level of formal qualification with my Ph.D. and some publications in the area, but very little of that publication activity can now be classified as critical. Most of it was conventional, positivistic stuff. There was one little piece that had elements of critical thinking and that was about to become a casualty for me because, of course, Finnish universities were predominantly conservative. Some of the professors who were in the decisionmaking body paid attention to this unscientific, political tendency in my writings.

Students were really very much behind me. It was the time of student radicalism. I became the candidate of the young, rebellious students. They wanted me as a young person. It's an irony that my scientific contribution was quite conventional. When I was appointed, it came at a time when in my own personal development I had become absolutely convinced of the superiority of critical thinking. On the other hand, also the environment in society was very much polarized and politicized. Moreover, when I got such a fantastic tenured position, I had no inhibitions to go full steam into this line.

In my inaugural address when I was installed, I outlined a program in communication research and theory that was pretty radical at the time. But still, in today's perspective, it can be said that it was only superficially radical.

Anyhow, since that year, 1971, I continued to achieve in promoting, both in the scientific as well as in communication policy and other circles, the radical or progressive or leftist view. In that pursuit, I had a lot of contacts with Herb Schiller, Dallas Smythe, and Jim Halloran. Dallas visited us just after his first trip to China.

Herb also visited us. I organized this famous symposium in 1973, on the flow of television programs, after completing, with my student and colleague, Tapio Varis, a study on the matter. I wrote, together with the former director-general of Finnish Broadcasting Company, Mr. [Eino S.] Repo, this boss who was ousted due to his radical views but who continued to be a close friend of our president. I wrote a speech for Finnish President Kekkonen which became a classic. Herb was there in Finland for that symposium. On the eve of the symposium, I was in contact with Herb, who helped me formulate some passages of that speech. For instance, Herb was the one who passed to me the quotes from the Hutchins Commission that you will find in that speech. So even Herb had his fingerprints on that speech.

But anyhow, the times in the 1970s in Finland, as well as elsewhere, were rather wild. I got to know further critical colleagues in Sweden, Robin Cheeseman, for instance. In England, Nicholas Garnham. All of us, we were very much convinced that you can change the world through institutions, through political activity, and that you should be action-oriented and yet critical. I never got so politicized that I would have entered any party. I always remained independent from party politics. Still, I sympathized with the left-wing Socialists and Communists.

In the 1970s I have to say that I was so active in domestic and international communication policy that I did not have enough time to read, including classics from Hegel to the Frankfurt School. I found that there was such fantastic drives going on towards progressive ideas, and, in a way, I could sell my product without too much in-depth studying. Later on, I have regretted a bit that I became, in a way, a victim of an instant leftism, rather than getting into these matters through a systematic study.

But there simply was no time, because I had become involved in a lot of circles —from Finnish foreign policy to UNESCO matters and, naturally, journalism education and communication policy. I was involved in a number of national commissions and committees, and all the time I had my chair at the university with teaching and administrative tasks. The international component, to summarize that aspect, started actually in that article of mine published in *Gazette,* in 1968, criticizing U.S. communication research.

After that, my next critical input was during my time at the broadcasting company in a symposium organized by Jim Halloran in Leicester concerning broadcaster–researcher cooperation. I was always advocating very much the political research, and I did it—continued the same line also in this UNESCO conference in Montreal. By the way, I went back to this Montreal meeting and UNESCO involvement in communication research thereafter until 1975, in preparing my chapter to Jim's *Festschrift,* which was handed over to him today. It was a fascinating task. I did it in the last few weeks only.

I am grateful that Cees Hamelink pushed me to that (the contribution to Halloran's *Festschrift*) because that brought me back to reflect also my personal history of ideas and activities in this time. I was sort of an emerging critical scholar in 1968, when this article in *Gazette* appeared, and in 1969, when the Montreal meeting was held.

In 1975, when the UNESCO panel of experts practically was dissolved, I was at the peak of the critical period. Reviewing that time against the present of the UNESCO panel was very illuminating. It shows how much we people affect. I've had faith in institutions such as UNESCO, to be able to influence through them and to think that the world can be changed through them, and how research can be an independent force to push humanity—or to be more modest—the media world on a better and more just and human track.

All that we believe very firmly and yet, now, in the present assessment, it turned out to be largely a great illusion. The kind of critical thinking we pursued at that time was largely superficial, and partly we can even say that it may have served the system and establishment more than it was the reflection of reality because we got too directly involved with being partners in the system and its change.

That can also be said of my personal experiences in the Finnish Broadcasting Company, which was the crucial factor changing me in the domestic environment. It was a personal activism that made me radical by heart and perhaps also radical by brain. But the fruits of radicalism are not that convincing. I don't suggest to question and completely challenge the past and would not like to undermine the critical orientation and its value. It was obviously necessary at its time. But somehow, perhaps I, as well as many others, invested too much hope and belief in such an orientation and its power to change the world.

You mentioned earlier that when you accepted your professorship there was some concern at the university, and the students rallied for you. Have there been other occasions when you paid a price for being radical or progressive?

Yes, there have been times after the mid-1970s. Until the mid-1970s, I was privileged in being radical in an environment where the social forces were rather much in balance. Roughly half of the political-parliamentary spectrum was more or less on the left in Finland. Therefore, I could feel that I am not alone and marginalized but rather representing a significant social constituency. That is quite different from in the United States. We have, after all, significant parties on the left. We have included Communists, and we have a party press, and media have been organized in a fairly pluralistic manner. I did not need to pay a price for my radical or progressive ideas in a notable degree until the mid-1970s. But then, when I accepted in 1976 to become president of the IOJ [International Organization of Journalists], that led me to a situation where I had to pay a price in the form of being a stigmatized or labeled person who could not be taken as uncontroversial or neutral, not to the extent of before.

Perhaps I should qualify that. It was not too harsh a statement earlier when I said that I was not compromised before the mid-1970s. There was a polarization of the Finnish media world and the media owners, the capitalists of the press, who, associating themselves with the Finnish right wing, had, in a way, stigmatized me already as a hostile force. They used these normal phrases of somebody being against freedom of speech and for government control, and so forth, to describe me. It was a domestic version of the later UNESCO debates. There was such a thing, and I suffered somewhat. I became a little bit controversial. At the same time, I was sort of a juicy item in the Finnish cultural, political arena, which had a certain value as a controversial figure.

But that was not a big burden. My burden became much bigger, to the degree of a stigma or labeling for a leftist associated with a Soviet or East [European] interest, when I accepted to become president of the IOJ. That period has lasted practically until these years. [Nordenstreng was president of IOJ from 1976 until 1990.]

Now, the situation is a bit different in the Soviet Union, and the East is rapidly changing, of course, and I am in the process of leaving the IOJ. Not because of this change, but because of the simple fact that I have been there so long, that due to any normal rotation, one should leave an organization. But this has certainly become a sort of burden, not so much internationally, but more nationally in Finland, perhaps because of the fact that the Finnish national political spectrum has been turning more and more to the right, and the constituency on the left has become more and more limited. The space on the left has become more and more limited. Therefore I have found myself, in several instances, not being legitimate enough for this or that function. But it doesn't mean that I would have become an outcast.

In some respects, I have even won prestige due to this position [president of IOJ]. I don't view my decision to accept that position to be any major setback in my life. On the contrary, it has even given me a unique platform for observing developments in the East and the Third World. But as far as critical thinking is concerned, these professional organizations have been more covertly political and not always political in the red color or Marxist orientation. But, still, it has been raw politics rather than the kind of intellectual exercise that I personally find to be a most important element in critical thinking. Therefore I have found it continually important to be in close contact with colleagues such as Herb and Dallas and George and others, because that's where you get your real critical bread and butter, rather than from the hardcore political institutions and forces.

So I think that there has been a development of my critical thinking which has gone through a very active, almost overactive, participation period into a state where I find nowadays it is more and more important to emphasize detachment and critical reflection as a value in itself, instead of being involved with progressive activism as such.

This doesn't mean that I would advocate refraining from activism. Ideas and their continuous creative renewal depend on a dialectic relationship with real life. But since the late 1960s, my generation has been too much impressed by activism and personal involvement in various progressive movements. That has not always brought such good and effective outcomes as we thought.

Maybe a better outcome is provided by critical thinking remaining in a kind of ghetto, where it can be cultivated in a systematic manner—the kind of Frankfurt School approach, which then radiates in its own society, in its own time, and even beyond into general society through indirect channels. This is something which I have learned to realize or appreciate only recently, whereas I was almost totally against such an attitude—ivory towerism as I saw it at that time.

But now, I think it is better perhaps to see that there is a kind of division of labor, whereby critical scholarship remains as a kind of relatively autonomous island and thus protects itself from the hard and dirty hits of the real institutional environment. If you are within the system, you get too easily prostituted or castrated from exercising effectively your critical thinking. This is a rather general, abstract statement, but perhaps it can be understood in this context.

What do you think your contributions have been to the world of scholarship? What do you think your contributions have changed in the world of scholarship?

I think my contributions are very limited indeed, and if they are anything, they have been caused by good luck and chance. Again, I mean chance in the sense of accidental. I have happened to be pursuing matters which were needed by the situation in the mental environment, and I have just been very lucky in a way, to be living at a time and appearing at proper moments in proper places.

For example, let's take this UNESCO flow study and the symposium to assess it, which became a kind of classic in this new information order debate. It was more or less by chance that we got to carry out that study. Of course, I had some intuition that now it is time to document statistically how things are. Incidentally, at the same time, I did a similar thing about the distribution of financial resources in Finnish media and the relative share of private sector versus governmental and organizational-political sector in media financing—their income, their turnover, and so on. Who controls what in the country? I produced simple statistics which became very influential in determining the terms of debate in Finland about communication policies. The same was true with this simple data about TV flow, the dominance of American exports to the rest of the world, which was then graphically illustrated in the UNESCO report.

Then it was even highlighted by this symposium where both Herb Schiller and Dallas Smythe attended, along with Jim Halloran's assistant, Peter Golding, Robin Cheeseman, and others. And when all of this was put into a nice and prestigious package of a UNESCO report, *Television Traffic—A One-Way Street?,* it was such a blow which came just at the proper time. *If* I were a religious person, I would say God put me in a position to do it.

Maybe there was some benefit in having a sensitivity to see that it's now time to do it, and maybe there was a skill and an organizational ability to maneuver things so that it was done. But if the environmental factors, again the atmospheric situation, would not have been such that it was needed—to become a point of reflection in a wider sense—then nothing would have helped.

But I would say that it was intellectually, and in an academic sense, a very limited contribution after all. Yet it became a very big thing. Similarly, my later contributions . . . I would rather like to see myself as a fish swimming in a big stream which is going somewhere, rather than a strong independent camel moving alone in a desert and making history.

Rather, I have been privileged to be swimming in a stream which was making history. Therefore, I feel a little bit embarrassed that you have placed me in such company. Especially Dallas Smythe, a person who deserves to be taken as an independent mind far from myself. Jim Halloran is perhaps more like myself, who has been in a way fortunate to appear and perform at the right time—when his words happened to have echo and a progressive and political echo.

Jim Halloran said something along the same lines when I interviewed him this morning—that it was by chance that he had entered communications.

Indeed, chance plays a fantastic role. I find it contradictory because, at the same time, I still have a very firm belief as a critical, Marxist-oriented scholar that history is not just a chain of chances but a broadly determined process. Yet I can't help admitting that there is a big scope left for pure chance to determine.

For instance, if I had not attended the Salzburg seminar in American studies, maybe I would never have been interested in communication research. If I had not been recruited, more or less by chance, to become instructor of journalism and mass communication in the mid-1960s, I may not have been sent to the United States by my professor. And if I had not gone to the United States, I may not have gotten that germ of critical thinking. It's a paradox that in the United States these children get radicalized. Of course, there are others who are influenced by hard, systematic studies—reading, thinking, and so on. But that definitely was not my case.

During the time that you were IOJ president, you also maintained your professorship at Tampere?

Well, it's true that I have, out of these fourteen years when I was IOJ president, maybe one year altogether in leaves of absence in bits and pieces for the IOJ or for projects related to IOJ. But most of the time I have been doing IOJ work over and above my normal duties. It has been very hard. That's why I am a bit overworked and stressed, and that has diminished my scientific productivity. I have not been able to publish so much as I might have done otherwise.

You will be increasing your productivity now that you are stepping down as IOJ president?

I don't know.

Do you have some projects in mind?

Well, I have a lot of projects in mind, yes. But you never know how you are able to perform. Writing has always been very difficult for me. I am a slow writer, and it's not so easy. But anyhow, I do want to continue in the field, and of course, all of these changes in our arena, especially in the field of international communication is quite challenging. This passing gradually beyond the cold war is all very interesting. I think that our scholarship and understanding of the issues of cultural and communication matters have advanced a lot internationally.

Perhaps the scholarship has been in its childhood until these years, and now there is a time of maturity on the horizon and it's, on the one hand, more demanding but, on the other hand, more challenging to be in the field. Critical thinking now, I would say, has become practically a mainstream thinking because, in general, it has proved vital in a free and open competition of intellectual power.

There are different forms. Some lead to creative ideas. Some just remain uninteresting. But I think that, for example, the tradition which Dallas started has been very influential and remains important even now in this increasingly international world, where also the Third World is establishing its own scholarship.

How do you think communication studies are being conducted in the Third World? Do you think the critical approach is moving into the Third World very effectively?

It's a mixed picture, of course. It is being continuously needed and wanted there. There is a great demand for that, and, of course, against it comes the huge institutional and administrative support of the more conservative research branches, which are supporting modernization and uncritical relations to technology and so on. But I think there is great potential.

What has been your leadership role in IAMCR?

I have now a low profile, as you understand. I dropped my activity in the IAMCR after becoming IOJ president, but I remained in IAMCR as vice president until the 1988 Barcelona assembly. It was a little bit delicate, and it was not so obvious. I wanted to step down from IAMCR earlier, but some other colleagues, including George Gerbner, said, "No, you should not." I became active, and I was one of the instigators, together with George, of the overthrow of Jim Halloran.

I'm also the one who got this idea of splitting the four-year term into two—to cut it short—so that he would be stepping down already, because we became increasingly disillusioned about his way of running the organization. I could sense through my contacts with the younger generation how the distance between his regime and grass-roots sentiments was growing. I did this after being the person who, in the first place, introduced Jim to IAMCR. So I have played a role, but not so much in the public profile. Behind the scenes. But, you see, until about 1976, I was Jim's closest sort of associate. Then it was natural that the distance grew between us, because I became so actively involved in IOJ, and Cees Hamelink took my place as Jim's associate. [Dutch scholar Hamelink succeeded Halloran as IAMCR head.]

I would say that my role, at least—maybe even all of these five [featured in this book]—has been as spokesperson for certain fundamental tendencies in the whole mental superstructure and the intellectual environment, or history of ideas, that was going on. But it would have been coming anyhow. These ideas would have gotten attention anyhow, regardless of this or that person. It was much less a situation pursued by us than it was a sort of reflection of the objective reality of those times and of the media world.

I think that, in a way, more essential than such individuals, such gurus, is the whole rapid mushrooming of people—both senior people, yourself as a typical example, and young, new people coming to the field and advocating these ideas. It's the same in sociology, political science, or critical theory. I think it goes though the whole humanistic, social science area in the same way.

15

Justice, Equality, and Professional Ethics in Journalism: Kaarle Nordenstreng's Actions and Reflections

WOLFGANG KLEINWÄCHTER

Kaarle Nordenstreng's profile as a researcher in the field of international communication is determined not only by his theoretical reflections but also by his practical actions. Unique in his career is the fact that he combines theory and practice in international communication policy. The result has not always been to his satisfaction, as he has seen his idealistic dreams of a new, more just, and more equal world information and communication order and the practical realities of the international communication flow move in different directions and his own career embodied with many contradictions.

Nevertheless, many of his scientific and practical activities were very successful. His numerous published works in many languages determined the way of thinking of perhaps thousands of communication scholars. His arguments in favor of a free and balanced flow of information were quoted in hundreds of theses and monographs, and his ideas of a free and responsible journalism were reflected in many international instruments and adopted by various bodies at the governmental and nongovernmental levels, including the United Nations, UNESCO, and the Non-Aligned Movement. He is also the father of many international projects known worldwide: from textbooks on communication theories for Third World students to the MacBride Round Table on Communication.

However, Nordenstreng's ideas were very often disputable and he was not free from errors. His articles and speeches provoked strong criticism, mainly by the established Western media. The World Press Freedom Committee saw, in particular, his engagement for a New International Information Order (NIIO) as a "threat" to the freedom of the press; they blocked a number of Nordenstreng initiatives, such as the planned symposium on the evaluation of the implementation of UNESCO's Mass Media Declaration. His ambitions to strengthen the "information sovereignty" of small nations and to help underprivileged media in developing countries made him partly blind to deficiencies in the media policy of a number of Eastern and Southern countries, and his relevant initiatives were also misused by certain regimes to justify restrictive measures against independent media. He also failed to reach one of his basic practical and political aims: to unite the international professional community of working journalists under the umbrella of a common "World Union of Professional Journalists."

Regardless of the use or misuse of his ideas, however, and irrespective of misunderstandings, dilemmas, and counterproductive reactions, all dimensions of Nordenstreng's international activities stand in a clear continuity for two fundamental democratic principles: justice and equality between the strong and the weak participants in national and international communication processes; and professional ethics in journalism. These principles have determined both his theoretical reflections and his practical actions.

Theoretical Foundation, Practical Actions, and Historical Description

Nordenstreng's involvement in international communication theory and practice can be subdivided into three general parts: first, the theoretical foundation of the need for an establishment of a new, more just, and more equal world information and communication order, for a balanced flow of information and a free and responsible journalism; second, efforts to implement these ideas by practical actions on different levels, such as in the system of the United Nations or in the professional organizations of working journalists; and third, a detailed scientific, historical description of the processes of multilateral negotiations on international communications, in both the governmental and nongovernmental spheres. Maybe a fourth part will be added in the years to come: the redefinition of the theoretical framework.

In the first period, the 1970s, Nordenstreng developed his own theoretical framework for a scientific analysis of the international system of information and communication. Here two publications have to be mentioned—the UNESCO-sponsored study, *Television Traffic—A One-Way Street?,* published in cooperation with Tapio Varis (Nordenstreng and Varis 1974), and the reader, *National Sovereignty and International Communication,* with Herbert Schiller (Nordenstreng and Schiller 1979). The UNESCO report challenged the established theory of the free flow of information, called for "a more balanced flow of information," and became a central resource document in the beginning discussions on the New International Information Order. The reader gave a unique overview of different theoretical approaches to international communication, and it produced a multidimensional concept for the NIIO discussion by pushing the idea of "information sovereignty" into the center of the debate.

In the second period, from the mid-1970s until the late 1980s, Nordenstreng became an active player in international communication negotiations—both as a governmental adviser and as president of the International Organization of Journalists, where he tried to translate some of his theoretical ideas into practice. With his arguments, he inspired numerous international governmental and nongovernmental conferences, and his name is linked directly to at least two crucial instruments seen as cornerstones in the debate on the NIIO: the UNESCO Mass Media Declaration, adopted by consensus by the Twentieth General Assembly in Paris in 1978, after more than five years of controversial negotiations between East and West and North and South; and the "International Principles of Professional Ethics in Journalism," a statement of ethical and moral norms, adopted again in Paris by a group of organizations of professional journalists (Nordenstreng, Gonzalez-Manet, and Kleinwächter 1986:371f).

The third dimension of his scientific and political oeuvre started in the early 1980s, when Nordenstreng, still active in international communication diplomacy, began to describe and summarize his own personal experiences from the numerous international conferences in which he participated. Among others, two books are the main results of those efforts. *The Mass Media Declaration of UNESCO* gives an insight into the real background of the building of an unbelievable consensus that produced an illusion about the possibility of bridging the gap between the enemies of the cold war. The book is an important reference for understanding the rise and fall of the NIIO debate (Nordenstreng 1984). The other book was published as *Useful Recollections,* with Jiri Kubka, and covered in two volumes the history of professional organizations in the journalism sphere. *Useful Recollections* shows the deep roots of the international movement of professional journalists and its efforts to constitute an independent political power, independent both from governmental and commercial control (Nordenstreng and Kubka 1988).

Rather than theoretical analyses of multilateral governmental and nongovernmental negotiations, both books are more practice-oriented, detailed descriptions of the history of international communication diplomacy. They do not constitute a new theory of international communication policy but deal with very political initiatives that determined more than two decades of controversial international discussions and negotiations in the media field that finally failed: the NIIO was not established and the "World Union of Professional Journalists" was not founded. The failures and the reasons for them are not the subject of these books, but the insights into international media diplomacy behind closed doors that are provided give some clues.

Nordenstreng's approach is in parts naturally one-sided—he was in many instances an insider—and perhaps less critical than needed with regard to the East and South. But regardless of the subjective evaluation, based on individual practical (and sometimes also negative) experiences, both books explain, like no other publication, why the two projects appeared on the agenda of international assemblies and why they did not work. With the distance of a decade, today's reader discovers the tremendous gulf between Nordenstreng's idealism and the realities of international communication policies.

The UNESCO Study: Television Traffic—A One-Way Street?

Nordenstreng's profile as a widely known researcher in the field of international communication is first of all linked to this study, one of the first international analyses of television program flow. Its main finding, reflected in the title, was that the international flow is a one-way proposition; its main conclusion, that the flow had to be in both directions. The study became one of the most quoted sources in the debate on NIIO.

The publication summarizes the results of a UNESCO-sponsored research project carried out by the University of Tampere in the early 1970s. The first of its kind, the study was a compilation and comparison of empirical data from North America, Latin America and the Caribbean, Western Europe, Eastern Europe, Asia and the Pacific, and the Near East and Africa.

The results confirmed the argument—already used in multilateral communication negotiations since the early 1960s, when UNESCO organized a series of seminars on communication development in Asia, Africa, and Latin America, and the United Nations had a draft of a "Declaration on Freedom of Information" on its General Assembly agendas—that the free flow of information is very unbalanced and that television programming is dominated by a small group of major media corporations.

Discussing the collected data, Nordenstreng and Varis concluded that "there are two indisputable trends to be discovered in the international flow: (1) a one-way traffic from the big exporting countries to the rest of the world and (2) dominancy of entertainment material in the flow" (Nordenstreng and Varis 1974:40). They stated that the international flow of television programs relates to overall economic structures within and between nations and that "these aspects together represent what might be called a tendency towards concentration."

According to the figures Nordenstreng and Varis collected for the late 1960s, nearly 90 percent of the international flow of television programs was dominated by the United States, United Kingdom, France, and the Federal Republic of Germany. From about 250,000 hours of annual television programs exchange worldwide, the United States alone exported more than 150,000 (Nordenstreng and Varis 1974:30). The authors observed that the way television programs moved globally followed traditional political and economic routes—from North to South, as well as West to East—and that entertainment, not news, was the chief content of internationally exchanged shows.

The central conclusion, formulated during a symposium held in Tampere in May 1973, was to recommend to the international community that "efforts should be made to redress the imbalances" (Nordenstreng and Varis 1974:59). The final statement of the symposium urged that "those who have few opportunities presently may require special assistance, subsidies or protection to permit them an enlarged role in the communication process." It added that "all nations should have the possibility to produce their own cultural-communications material," that "each nation has the right and duty to determine its own cultural destiny," and that "it is the responsibility of the world community and the obligation of the media institutions to ensure that this right is respected" (Nordenstreng and Varis 1974:59).

The Reader on National Sovereignty and International Communication

Against the background of the main conclusion of the UNESCO study, it was only logical that Nordenstreng in his research work would move to the political and legal framework for the international information exchange. It should not come as a surprise that in his efforts to "balance" the international flow of information, he "rediscovered" the principle of sovereign equality.

Sovereign equality was enshrined as a fundamental principle of international law in the Charter of the United Nations, but it was seldom linked to the international communication flow. The reader, *National Sovereignty and International Communication* (Nordenstreng and Schiller 1979), although not producing a new theory on "information sovereignty," did provide a program for further practical actions.

"It seems to us," Nordenstreng and Schiller wrote in the preface, "that the concept of national sovereignty will increasingly emerge as a point of reflection for the most fundamental issues of international communication and related national questions. Like 'domination' and 'dependence,' this concept has become an integral part of the debate around the so-called 'new international information order,'" which is "ultimately aiming at the 'decolonization' of information conditions in the developing countries, and, in general, advocating respect for the cultural and political sovereignty of all nations. However, sovereignty as such has so far received hardly any attention in the scholarly work in this field. Thus the present collection may only indirectly contribute to its comprehensive analysis—mainly by suggesting that this concept be placed high on the agenda of further research" (Nordenstreng and Schiller 1979:xiv).

Fourteen well-known authors—Dallas W. Smythe, Ithiel de Sola Pool, Edward Ploman, Hilding Eek, Leo Gross, John B. Whitton, Mort Rosenblum, Tran Van Dinh, Elihu Katz, Raquel Salinas, Leena Paldan, Karl P. Sauvant, Luis Ramiro Beltran, and Elizabeth Fox—were brought together to discuss different aspects of the implications of national sovereignty for international communication within four major sections: Communication and Development, Direct Satellite Broadcasting, International Law, and International Communication in Transition.

The reader offered a unique combination of progressive and conservative thinkers, providing a stimulating overview about the diversity of ideas concerning a basic principle under international law and encouraging thinking about an undefined concept.

Driven by their dreams for a just world order in which all nations, small or big, powerful or powerless, would be equal in their sovereign rights, Nordenstreng and Schiller hoped that "the concept of national sovereignty" could become "the springboard for a unifying perspective" (Nordenstreng and Schiller 1979:xiv). Obviously, this did not take place.

A second version of the national sovereignty book was compiled by these authors and released in 1993. It included contributions by Andre Gunder Frank, Johann Galtung, Immanuel Wallerstein, Chakravarthi Raghavan, Edward Herman, Omar S. Oliveira, Jesús Martín Barbero, Ullamaija Kivikuru, Oliver Boyd-Barrett, Vincent Mosco, Dan Schiller, John A. Lent, William J. Drake, Eileen Mahoney, Laurien Alexandre, Cees J. Hamelink, Hamid Mowlana, Richard Falk, Leonard Sussman, and Robert G. Meadow.

The Gaps Between Idealism and Realities

Although the description of the international flow of information was very realistic, the conclusion "to balance" the "unbalanced" information flow and to overcome the deficiencies of the world communication order by introducing the principle of information sovereignty was unrealistic, partly naive, and at least politically counterproductive. The theoretical concept, based on noble intentions convincing to critical intellectuals, was misunderstood by the main actors in the West and misused by more than a few governments in the South and East.

Transnational media institutions and the governments of the main Western countries ignored the intention to promote communication development by strengthening the sovereign rights of states in underdeveloped regions. They saw in the introduction of a principle of information sovereignty the "justification of censorship" and, in particular, an attack against their own fundamental interests, which had been best protected in the past by the free-flow principle, ignoring sovereign rights of independent governments.

At the same time, totalitarian governments in the South and East discovered the principle of information sovereignty as a useful instrument to justify censorship of unwanted criticism both from inside and outside the country and to blame the legitimate criticism of the West of the undemocratic practices in these countries as illegal interference into internal affairs.

Information sovereignty, originally introduced to promote justice, equality, and communication development in Southern countries, was turned into a controversial issue that, if anything, tended to make things worse for those countries. Western countries saw behind all the legitimate efforts to improve Third World media an illegitimate attack on press freedom and disregard for the negative tendencies of information colonialism or irresponsible news reporting. Dictatorships in the East and South rejected all international criticism of violations of the right to freedom of expression and against restrictive media practices by referring to their "information sovereignty."

Against the background of such a fundamental controversy, the possibility of bridging different approaches and opinions and of building a global consensus became a utopian task. Simple practical questions of the world communication order, historical challenges of the new information technologies, and global problems in the media field, such as underdevelopment in the telecommunication infrastructure, imbalances in information flow, or biased and distorting news reporting (issues raised also by the report of the International Commission for the Study of Communication Problems under the chairmanship of Sean MacBride) became extremely ideologized in a controversial political debate where power was at stake, not the real information and communication needs of people.

The Mass Media Declaration of UNESCO

The political consequences of the theoretical concepts developed by Nordenstreng, among others, became visible first of all in the negotiations around UNESCO's Mass Media Declaration.

The declaration was initiated by the Soviet Union in the late 1960s. Originally, it was intended to "oblige" the mass media "to contribute to peace and international understanding" and "to combat war propaganda, racism and apartheid" (UNESCO 1982). Later, and here Nordenstreng was one of the main driving forces behind the scene, communication development in Third World countries became one of the central issues.

The first serious draft, designed by Swedish professor of international law Hilding Eek, was discussed at several "experts" meetings in the early 1970s and later at the Eighteenth UNESCO General Conference in 1974 (Nordenstreng 1984:289f). The Eek draft included neither an article in favor of a "balanced flow" of information nor one on the "new world information and communication order," but other controversial issues, such as the "role of the governments," prevented its adoption in 1974.

After an intergovernmental conference on the draft of the declaration in 1975, which ended in an unsettled dispute (the United States and some other delegations left the conference under protest), the Nineteenth General Assembly of UNESCO, which took place in 1976 in Nairobi, was again unable to find a consensus (Nordenstreng 1984:300f). Regardless of the basic differences between the West on the one hand and the East and South on the other, however, the Nairobi conference adopted a remarkable compromise. The postponement of the declaration's adoption was accompanied by a decision to establish an International Commission for the Study of Communication Problems and to encourage thinking about practical assistance for developing countries.

Nordenstreng, who participated in the Nairobi meetings, was an active player in building this "agree-to-disagree consensus." The Nairobi compromise opened the possibility to redraft the agenda of international communication negotiations and to find a way to prevent the justification of governmental interference and yet stimulate measures in favor of a more balanced flow in information.

In the intervening two years between UNESCO assemblies, the Nairobi compromise was translated into the language of a political statement. Nordenstreng, as the president of the International Organization of Journalists, had a certain impact on the different drafts of the declaration. A redrafted version of the Mass Media Declaration, avoiding restrictive language, was finally adopted unanimously by acclamation at the Twentieth General Assembly of UNESCO in Paris in 1978 (Nordenstreng 1984:271f). Even the United States, under the Carter administration, joined the consensus.

The declaration, which was not legally binding, did not introduce a system of media control but recommended that the "free flow of information" be linked to "a wider and better balanced dissemination of information," that "freedom of opinion, expression and information" should be combined with "professional ethics in journalism," and that "a new, more just and more effective world information and communication order" should be established.

Two articles in the declaration reflect Nordenstreng's basic ideas: Article 6 calls for overcoming the imbalances in the global communication flow; Article 8 refers to the role of the professional journalists and their code of ethics. Article 6 specifically states,

> For the establishment of a new equilibrium and greater reciprocity in the flow of information, which will be conducive to the institution of a just and lasting peace and to the economic and political independence of the developing countries, it is necessary to correct the inequalities in the flow of information to and from developing countries, and between those countries. To this end, it is essential that their mass media should have conditions and resources enabling them to gain strength and expand,

> and to co-operate both among themselves and with the mass media in developed countries. (Nordenstreng 1984:274)

The wording of Article 6 follows closely the ideas expressed in the final statement of the 1973 Tampere Symposium. The article reflects both the ideas of the "balanced flow of information" and the sovereign rights of developing countries in the field of information.

The other Nordenstreng contribution is Article 8, which states, "Professional organizations and people, who participate in the professional training of journalists and other agents of the mass media and who assist them in performing their functions in a responsible manner, should attach special importance to the principles of the declaration when drawing up and ensuring applications of their codes of ethics" (Nordenstreng 1984:275). Nordenstreng was at this time both a representative of an international professional organization—he was elected president of the International Organization of Journalists in 1976—and a professor involved in the training of journalists. His theoretical concept, developed *inter alia* in the UNESCO study on television traffic, included the basic thesis that it is not enough to balance the information flow; it is also necessary to look at the content of media messages and to strengthen responsible news reporting.

When Nordenstreng drew the conclusion that on the governmental level information sovereignty could be a useful practical idea, he concluded in the professional field that the elaboration of a code of ethics for working journalists would be helpful in overcoming deficiencies of the present world information and communication order. Neither issue—communication development and the code of ethics—was a major hot issue in the final negotiations. But in the context of other controversial issues—duties of the media, content of information, state responsibility, information sovereignty, and so on—these two articles later became part of a growing ideological dispute that prevented real progress in the follow-up of the declaration. A planned intergovernmental meeting of "experts" at the fifth anniversary of the declaration in 1983, which was to investigate the implementation of the declaration, did not take place. A scientific symposium on the effects of the declaration, scheduled for 1987, was blocked by a group of influential international publisher organizations.

International Principles of Professional Ethics in Journalism

On the basis of Article 8 of the Mass Media Declaration, Nordenstreng immediately started an initiative aimed at the elaboration of a universal set of ethical and moral principles for professional journalists.

The idea of an "International Code of Conduct for Journalists" has a long history. Already in the 1920s and 1930s, the idea of such a code was broached both inside and outside the League of Nations. Later, in the 1950s, the United Nations and UNESCO had a "Draft of an International Code of Ethics" on their agendas (Jones 1980).

As president of the International Organization of Journalists (IOJ), Nordenstreng revitalized the code of ethics debate in the late 1970s and early 1980s when he initiated regular consultative meetings between the main international and regional nongovernmental organizations of working journalists. Besides the IOJ, the International Catholic Union of the Press (UCIP), the Latin American Federation of Journalists (FELAP), the Latin American Federation of Press Workers (FELATRAP), the Federation of Arab Journalists (FAJ), the Union of African Journalists (UAJ), the Confederation of ASEAN Journalists (CAJ), and the International Federation of Journalists (FIJ) participated in the annual meetings, which started in 1979.

Sponsored by UNESCO, the meetings discussed a wide range of political, economic, and cultural topics, from social problems of working journalists to the consequences of media technology. But it was Nordenstreng again and again who raised the question of professional ethics in journalism. The elaboration of a common ground of ethical and moral norms for professional journalists, so Nordenstreng reasoned, could also pave the way for the establishment of a "World Union of Working Journalists."

Although his original proposal—to continue the 1950s' discussion and to draft a universal code of conduct for working journalists—did not receive a majority, the participants at the consultative meetings agreed to elaborate a loose framework of moral and ethical principles. A first draft, the so-called Mexico Declaration (Nordenstreng, Gonzalez-Manet, and Kleinwächter 1986:365f) from 1980, inspired by the FELAP Latin American Code of Journalist Ethics formulated in Caracas in 1979, and adopted by the third consultative meeting, paved the way for the International Principles of Professional Ethics in Journalism, issued by the fifth consultative meeting in Paris in November 1983 (Nordenstreng, Gonzalez-Manet, and Kleinwächter 1986:371f).

The International Principles were not an "international code of conduct"; instead, they were seen by participants in the consultative meeting as "an international common ground and as a source of inspiration" for the adoption of codes of ethics on national and regional levels.

The statement included these ten principles: the people's right to true information; the journalist's dedication to objective reality; the journalist's social responsibility; the journalist's professional integrity; public access and participation; respect for privacy and human dignity; respect for public interest; respect for universal values and diversity of cultures; elimination of war and other great evils confronting humanity; and promotion of a New World Information and Communication Order (Nordenstreng, Gonzalez-Manet, and Kleinwächter 1986:371f).

Comparing these points with Nordenstreng's theoretical framework, put forth in early writings in the 1970s, makes the strong spillover evident. But again, his intention, to contribute to a "more equal and more just NWICO," was overshadowed by an ambiguity, partly misunderstood, and partly misused. By supporting reformist ideas of the new leadership under Gorbachev in the Soviet Union, Nordenstreng did not protest explicitly against restrictive practices in Eastern European countries, and by being silent, he lost some of his credibility. The FIJ, more on the side of the dissidents in the East, withdrew partly from the consensus of the consultative club, and the image of the IOJ as an "arm of the Soviets" also prevented the establishment of a "World Union of Working Journalists."

Theoretical Reflections on Practical Actions

Still active in international media diplomacy, Nordenstreng began writing the history of multilateral communication negotiations. His book, *The Mass Media Declaration of UNESCO,* summarized his main personal experiences in diplomatic maneuvering. The book gives a unique insight into the ups and downs of the diplomatic gamble and into Nordenstreng's own philosophy and illusions.

Nordenstreng believed in the "unbelievable consensus" of UNESCO's Mass Media Declaration, and he underestimated the unbridgeable positions of ideological enemies. In the preface of his book, he calls the Mass Media Declaration "a landmark in the history of journalism and mass communication" (Nordenstreng 1984:xi). He quotes UNESCO Director General M'Bow, who saw the declaration as "a new set of principles" for "creators and distributors," as an instrument with which "for the first time in history the international community has at its disposal a body of principles and ideals such as can provide guidance for the action and practice of all those whose hearts are set on justice and peace." Nordenstreng sees the final success of the declaration as a political and professional triumph. "Politically, it was a triumph of detente, peaceful coexistence between different social systems—so-called East and West, North and South. Professionally, it was a reminder of the fact that journalism and mass communication, however ideological in nature, has a common ground of universal values on which an international code can be constructed" (Nordenstreng 1984:xi).

Nordenstreng's dreams remained unfulfilled. In fact, the contrary was the case. Politically, the adoption of the declaration marked the starting point for a growing controversy in international media policy; professionally, the "unification" of the professional community was nothing more than a utopian vision, unrealistic in a media world determined by conflicting ideologies and a growing domination of commercial interests.

Maybe Nordenstreng already saw the failure of his ambitious plans when he wrote *Useful Recollections* (Nordenstreng and Kubka 1988:part 1, 84). In the two volumes, he rediscovered the history of the professional organizations in journalism. Nordenstreng started his historical journey at the end of the nineteenth century. He showed that all attempts to unite the community of professional journalists before World War I, in the 1920s, and before World War II failed. "It was World War II which wrote in bloody letters the first and fundamental article of the statute of the journalist's profession. The journalist is a citizen who has as many freedoms and rights as have citizens of his country, as a professional, he has only much greater responsibility" (Nordenstreng and Kubka 1988:part 1, 84). As Nordenstreng said in *Useful Recollections,* even on the eve of World War II, the professional community of working journalists failed "to create a union of the truth against the lies of the Nazis."

Obviously, Nordenstreng has asked the right questions. What remains questionable are his practical answers. The experience of the NIIO debate has shown that "information sovereignty" does not help to make the unjust and unequal world communication order more just and more equal. On the contrary, the practice has shown that such concepts help totalitarian regimes to justify restrictions against fundamental rights and freedoms in the field of information and communication, more than it aids small countries in protecting their legitimate interests against foreign domination. It also remains doubtful whether in a time of growing pluralism and diversity, of growing commercialization and privatization in the media field, a "unification" of the world community of journalists under one umbrella is realistic and would help to overcome the deficiencies of the global communication system. But while the answers did not fit, the questions remain on the agenda.

So these right questions of the early 1970s are unanswered in the early 1990s. Lessons from history, Nordenstreng himself has written about. It is no surprise then, that Nordenstreng has moved back to theory. The project of a textbook for Third World journalism students which presents different approaches to communication theory, and his efforts to establish an annual global media discussion, a "MacBride Roundtable on Communication," signal that Kaarle Nordenstreng is looking ahead.

REFERENCES

Jones, C. (1980). *Mass Media Codes of Ethics and Councils.* Reports and Papers on Mass Communication. Paris: UNESCO.

Nordenstreng, K. (1984). *The Mass Media Declaration of UNESCO.* Norwood, NJ: Ablex.

Nordenstreng, K., and J. Kubka. (1988). *Useful Recollections, Part I and Part II.* Prague: International Organization of Journalists.

Nordenstreng, K., and H. I. Schiller, eds. (1979). *National Sovereignty and International Communication.* Norwood, NJ: Ablex.

———. eds. (1993) *Beyond National Sovereignty: International Communication in the 1990s.* Norwood, NJ: Ablex.

Nordenstreng, K., and T. Varis (1974). *Television Traffic—A One-Way Street? A Survey and Analysis of the International Flow of Television Programme Material.* Reports and Papers on Mass Communication No. 70. Paris: UNESCO.

Nordenstreng, K., E. Gonzalez-Manet, and W. Kleinwächter. (1986). *New International Information and Communication Order: A Sourcebook.* Prague: International Organization of Journalists.

UNESCO. (1982). *The Mass Media Declaration, New Communication Order.* Paris: UNESCO.

16

Political Versus Cultural in Critical Broadcasting Research and Policy: A Reevaluation of the Finnish Radical Experiment in Broadcasting in the Late 1960s

TAISTO HUJANEN

This chapter offers a reevaluation of the Finnish radical experiment in broadcasting in the late 1960s known as informational broadcasting, focusing on the relationship between the key ideas of informational broadcasting and critical research in mass communication. In the history of Finnish broadcasting, the period of the late 1960s represents a unique combination of critical research and policy. As such, it offers a useful point of reflection when considering the development of critical research in mass communication, the basis for the first two questions we were asked to address here. For today's critics and reformers, its failure is a good reminder of the problems implied in the rational humanism of the critical tradition. This is why informational broadcasting, even through its failure, can teach an important lesson, not only for broadcasters, but also for critical scholars of communication.

Impact of Ahmavaara's Work

What matters in mass communication and mass media is information. That was the lesson readily adopted in the late 1960s by my generation of students in mass communication theory and research. In Finland, the hot topic of the day was Y. Ahmavaara's book on information (1969) in which he launched his semantic information theory. Together with Nordenstreng's (1968) critique of the empiricism in American mass communication research, Ahmavaara's book became a basic text for critical communication scholarship in Finland and remained a textbook in communication studies until the 1980s. In the context of this chapter, what is even more important is how the ideas of the book affected broadcasting planning and practice in the late 1960s and early 1970s.

As a form of scholarship, Ahmavaara's book was a pure theoretical statement; much of it was even written in the language of formal logic. The paradox of the time was that it was the book's theoretical emphasis that was of the greatest practical value. Ahmavaara, who had been a professor in theoretical physics and had a Ph.D. in psychology, was invited as an expert to a working group that was set up by the National Broadcasting Company (YLE) to define the long-range goals of its policy. At the time, Kaarle Nordenstreng, a professor of journalism and mass communication at the University of Tampere since 1971, was the head of research at YLE (1967–71). He also worked with Ahmavaara on another important expert group that was later created to reform the news policy of the company. The results of the latter group are reported by Nordenstreng in his much-cited article in McQuail's (1972) reader, *Sociology of Mass Communications.* The Finnish experiment of informational program policy, as it was called, is reviewed as a whole in a collection of essays edited by Nordenstreng (1973b).[1]

In Ahmavaara's theory, information was defined in terms of so-called intellectual activation, a form of critical cognition free from the social conditioning of learning.[2] The theory resulted in a distinction between information and ideology: information referred to those contents of mass communication that were neglected by the hegemonistic structures of communication; the rest served the status quo and, accordingly, turned to ideology. In its application to broadcasting policy, the theory was used to define an idealization of an audience that was to be active, participatory, and rational and whose individual members were ever ready to change their beliefs of the world in accordance with increasing information.

YLE's Informational Program Policy

In Finland, the 1960s are known as a decade of great social change. As Nordenstreng (1972) pointed out, broadcasters should not remain passive "mirrors" of society, rather, they should actively participate in it. In political terms, such a viewpoint was an argument against the status quo; culturally, it favored transformation over tradition. The political project incorporated in the informational program policy was that of democratization; objective and accurate information was seen as a resource of democratic participation. The cultural project stressed modernization, the development of individual identities based on rational humanism.

Nordenstreng adopted the combination of research and policy, basic in the development of informational program policy, as an argument in the critique of mass communication research. In his article on policy for news transmission, he concluded:

> What is needed is not only empirical research into the practical aspects of broadcasting at different stages of the communication process (production, programs, audience) but also theoretical advance toward a systematic explication of the ultimate goals of activity, i.e. a careful re-evaluation of policy. This can be carried quite far without any new data, merely by means of systematic discussion and thinking. . . . It should also be remembered that a theoretical emphasis by no means rules out the importance of accumulating empirical evidence of the operation in practice. (Nordenstreng 1972:388)

The methodological program formulated by Nordenstreng stressed theory and goal-oriented normative action, although the need for empirical research was also acknowledged. In such a combination of research and policy, the methodological individualism of mass communication research was complemented with theory and policy (see Nordenstreng 1968, 1970a). The important point here is the idea of complementarity; that is, Nordenstreng's critique emphasized theory and policy over the empirical but did not reject the methodological individualism of the empiricism as such. For example, an empirical application of Ahmavaara's information theory depended, first of all, on a general theory (and psychology) of cognition. In an important way, Ahmavaara's theory on information was doomed to remain individualistic. Because intellectual activation was understood in terms of critical cognition of individuals, it led to a conflict between individual and social subjectivities. The individual symbolized progress and transformation; the social (and cultural) was attached to tradition and the status quo.

The ethnomethodological and constructionist (Berger and Luckmann 1967) critiques of positivism were well known in Finland in the late 1960s; through Jürgen Habermas, hermeneutics was also studied. But that hardly affected empirically oriented mainstream social sciences. In the empirical mass communication research on comprehension inspired by Ahmavaara, there was reference to Berger and Luckmann, but its emphasis on the social remained misunderstood because of focus on the individual and rational. Ahmavaara himself launched a critique of positivism in his other important book of the time (1970), introducing what he called the cybernetic methodology of social sciences. The main and much-cited thesis of his methodology was that objective knowledge was also possible concerning the values of human action. Although Ahmavaara's approach was dominantly epistemological, it fit well the growing interest in Marxism among social scientists.[3] Later in the 1970s, Marxism became the dominant point of departure for critical research in Finnish mass communication, and its methodological monism was adopted as an alternative to positivism.

This contextualization gives a hint to understanding Nordenstreng's emphasis on theory and normative action in relation to the general critique of mainstream social sciences. The paradox of Nordenstreng's critical approach was that it was developed as a rationalization of broadcasting policy, but at the same time the broadcaster's definition of that policy was to become a major failure of the approach. The rational humanism of the approach became a symbol of political and cultural radicalism and led to a conflict, not only between modernists and traditionalists but also between broadcasters and politicians. Through politicization, the democratic potential of the informational program policy died out, and the broadcasters became more and more involved in a direct power struggle with (and within) the political elite.

Public service broadcasting in Europe is historically linked with the development of nation-states. In Finland, the national broadcasting company was created in 1926, less than a decade after the birth of the country as an independent state (1917). The newly created broadcasting company received de facto monopoly status in 1934, which lasted until the introduction of television in the mid-1950s. The monopoly was reestablished in 1965, when YLE bought its private competitors. However, one of the commercial TV companies continued broadcasting within YLE's concession in a duopoly that still exists (on this and later development, see Hujanen and Jyrkiäinen 1991). Cable and satellite television in the late 1970s and local commercial radio in the mid-1980s started a development that led to increasing competition and commercialization of broadcasting (*Finnish Mass Media 1989* 1990).

Although the modernist undertone of the informational program policy was a challenge to the old nationalism of YLE, in the minds of the reformers, YLE was a national institution. Through the politicization of the everyday lives of individual citizens, radio and television were supposed to turn to a national public sphere that would be open to anyone, including ordinary people, marginalized groups, and regions. For the reformers, the nation was, first of all, a democratic community of modern citizens based on equal opportunity and active participation. In the minds of reformers, the old YLE became a symbol of escapism and manipulation; its nationalism was an ideological plot based on nonpoliticization (in the sense of conservatism) and blind loyalty to national values.

Whose side are we on? That is the known question linked with critical research. With its democratic ethos, the informational program policy, as formulated by researchers and broadcasters, tried clearly to be on the side of the audience. However, I would argue that it lost out in this key area; for example, the politicians managed better than the broadcasters in the long run to mobilize the audience. From the present-day perspective, the most probable reason for their failure was that they misunderstood the role of the social and the cultural in the constitution of audiences and subjectivity in general. Emancipation is not only cognitive and political; it is also social and cultural. This is why Nordenstreng's critique of empiricism stayed halfway; because of his rationalistic emphasis, he neglected the significance of the social and cultural in the constitution of subjectivities.

The empirical research on audience inspired by informational program policy offers interesting evidence concerning the problematic nature of the reformers' view of the audience. Nordenstreng (1972) refers to empirical findings of his collaborators which showed that audiences were indifferent to the contents of the news. Nordenstreng said that following the news was for many Finns "a mere ritual, a way of dividing up the daily rhythm, and a manifestation of alienation" (Nordenstreng 1972:391).[4] The news offered essential information only to a small minority of people; most people hardly recalled anything of the news the day after the transmission. The main thing retained from the news was that nothing special happened.

These empirical conclusions were later interpreted by Morley (1980:8) as a reevaluation of "effects" studies (see Jensen 1986:58; Lewis 1991:78). This assessment was correct as these and similar findings contributed to the reevaluation of "effects" studies, and the interest turned from short-term to long-term effects, for example, in terms of manipulation, hegemony, and ideology (Pietilä 1977). In the context of this chapter, however, what is more important is that the reevaluation took place within the dominant emphasis on information and rational cognition. In the recent Finnish discussion concerning the early critical research on broadcasting, Alasuutari (1992) describes the above kind of findings as anomalies of the "public sphere paradigm." They did not fit the dominant view of the mass media, focusing as they did on democracy, information, and rational cognition; consequently, their meaning was misunderstood.

A Cure for Alienation: Information

For Nordenstreng and his collaborators at YLE, the empirical findings of the audience studies demonstrated that the main part of the audience was indifferent and passive. All that, as Nordenstreng pointed out, was a manifestation of alienation, a social condition expressing the powerlessness of the people. What was offered as a cure for alienation was more information; for example, expansion of television news transmissions with more emphasis on background commentary, "to arouse even the most passive viewer" (Nordenstreng 1972:392). In another connection, Nordenstreng (1970b) defines the informational program policy as "a policy of the painful truth." In relation to the alienated audience, this would mean that the structural alienation of the society would be made visible, and as a result people would be able to see their social position. In other words, broadcasting would "offer man the means of conquering his state of alienation by providing facts about society and about ways of participating in the political and economic process" (Nordenstreng 1973a:88).

Although broadcasting had potential for reducing alienation, the key issue, according to Nordenstreng (1973a:87), was the relationship between the audience and the society, not between the audience and broadcasting. Changing society was the number one issue, and broadcasters' relationship with the audience was secondary. Parallel to that, Nordenstreng concluded that the fundamental question of communication policy could not be solved by appealing to the audience:

> This question cannot be settled by appealing to the audience concerned, since people attach importance both to entertainment which reinforces the feeling of security and new information which gnaws away at the old world view. The right decision, in fact, is not to be found in the needs of the individual but in those of the whole society; we must think of what is best for the entire community formed by the media audience. (Nordenstreng 1973a:84–85)

When considering these and similar rationalizations of the informational program policy from today's perspective, it seems that audience itself remained, in fact, an anomaly for the broadcasters.[5] The policy and research focused on either the audience–society relationship or the broadcasting–society relationship, and the relationship between the audience and broadcasting remained a "blindspot."[6] The empirical findings concerning the micro-cosmos of the audience were interpreted in terms of a macro theory of society and mass communication or of a general theory of information and rational cognition. As a result, research and policy failed to cast a critical look at the audience–broadcasting relationship and, in particular, at broadcasters' view of their audience. From this perspective, alienation was a fitting explanation of indifference and passivity among the audience; it showed that society was to be blamed and not the broadcasters.

The overall emphasis on macro theories resulted in conflicting views concerning the role of broadcasting. A logical consequence from the alienation argument is that broadcasting does not matter; instead, one should turn to society. By the same token, the protagonists of the informational program policy were convinced that broadcasting was an important agent of social change. The question was how would broadcasting contribute to social change without power to affect the audience. This paradox of the reformers' thinking and action demonstrates how important a valid micro theory is in any effort to democratize communication. Otherwise, the individual people in their micro worlds remain a pure object of empowerment, an abstraction that only serves the goal setting and legitimation of policy. In this sense, the reformers' view of the audience did not differ from the old YLE, in which, as was typical of European public service broadcasting in general, the audience was considered a "thing" (Ang 1991), a pure object of research and policy.

For YLE's informational program policy, the audience was, first of all, a *public* constituted of modern and rational citizens. From such a perspective, most people looked powerless and isolated in their domestic sphere, passive and indifferent. Nordenstreng and the other reformers would have agreed with Neil Postman's later phrase that people wanted to amuse themselves to death. The audience's seemingly active (!) interest in entertainment, sports, and popular music in radio, old movies, and popular television series was interpreted either politically as manipulation and ideology or sociologically as alienation. Intellectual activation as the overall goal of the policy was attached also to entertainment. The ultimate goal of drama and fiction should be to arouse "new ways of thinking," "new ways of seeing the reality"; also emotions should serve the transmission of information (Ahmavaara 1975:31–39).

YLE's "Normalization" and Failure

The liberal radicalism of the informational program policy aroused a wave of protest in which the bourgeois newspapers took the lead. After the parliamentary election in 1970, Eino S. Repo, the symbol of the new policy, lost his position as the director general of YLE and the situation was "normalized," resulting in a tougher parliamentary control of broadcasting. However, a couple of years later, in 1972, the new administrative council of YLE, representing parliamentary control of broadcasting, accepted a collection of program regulations that made the basic ideas of the informational program policy the official norm. This is a significant and often neglected historical detail, because it shows that the politicians agreed in principle with the broadcasters' reformist goals. Through normalization, however, they demonstrated for the broadcasters and the public that they wanted to maintain their position as the primary definers of the political agenda.

Nordenstreng and his collaborators in YLE and the academic world experienced the normalization as a failure. In a collection of essays presenting the Finnish radical experiment for the international audience, Nordenstreng and his coauthors considered the "failure" as follows:

> . . . the "failure" of the informational broadcasting policy may hardly be attributed to the substance of programme content, i.e. topics covered; instead, obviously, *the way of expression in these programmes was often considered too shocking or abstract or highbrow.* In practice the new policy seems to have gone only halfway towards the democratic principles "for the people" and "by the people." No serious attention was given in the beginning to the proposition that the more active, critical, and informational the orientation of a communications policy, the more the organisational structure to carry out this policy should be changed towards a participatory communications network. (Nordenstreng, et al. 1973:183–84; emphasis in the original)

In this postscript to the "Finnish experiment," the new emphasis on "by the people" opens the way for the critique of paternalism and elitism of the informational broadcasting policy. The audience's point of view matters more than in earlier formulations, and now the question is participation and the audience's direct control over the production. Despite such a critical self-reflection, no suspicion of the information paradigm itself is evident. Otherwise, it would be hard to understand why Nordenstreng and his colleagues did not stop thinking the most revealing contradiction of their conclusions, namely, that the "failure" of the informational program policy was obviously to be attributed to the way of expression in the programs and not to the substance of program content. Their conclusion was based on empirical audience research carried out by one of Nordenstreng's doctoral students, Tapio Varis (1971).

Form vs. Content

This contraction of Nordenstreng and his colleagues raises the general question about the relationship between form and content in communication. In this respect, the earlier example on entertainment is revealing; drama and fiction served as a means of expression, having no value of their own. The transmission view of communication (Carey 1989), typical of the information paradigm, resulted in a technical view of the forms of communication. Radio and television, the media themselves, were regarded as information technology enabling the transmission of accurate and relevant information. The media in their specificity were secondary to information, that is, to the contents of communication.

If we, from our present-day perspective, consider communication as a cultural form, the empirical finding to which Nordenstreng and his colleagues refer is a significant one. It demonstrated that, for the audience, the form perhaps mattered more than the content. The forms were not only means of expression; they were the message as much as the transmitted contents. The fact that Nordenstreng and his colleagues passed by this key contradiction in their conclusions shows that the reformers lacked not only a micro theory on audience, but also a micro theory on the media. The result of the overall fixation on information was that the protagonists of informational broadcasting overlooked the significance of radio and television as media of communication and, even more, the nature of radio and television programs as forms of communication.

Through cultural studies, the ethnography of reception, and the textual analysis of programs, the present-day critical research on broadcasting is much better equipped to understand the audience-broadcasting relationship—the "failure" of the Finnish radical experiment of the late 1960s. However, since then, the political and technological context of public service broadcasting has changed radically. Privatization and deregulation linked with technological innovations have contributed to increased commercialization of broadcasting also in the European context.

Insecure Future

A reasonable question in the light of the new competitive environment of broadcasting is whether the present-day situation opens up any possibility for radical experiments. I would agree with James Curran's (1990:157) conclusion that public service broadcasting is more open to popular opposition movements than the more "closed" organizations of the popular press. Drawing from the British experience, Curran also argues that liberal and radical researchers have found more common ground with each other under the attack from the new right. This reminds one of the Finnish radical experiment in broadcasting, when the radical researchers found a common ground with liberal broadcasters.

The future of the European public service broadcasting is in many ways insecure.[7] If broadcasting institutions are not able to free themselves from their historical burden, nationalism, elitism, and paternalism, they are doomed to become marginalized. Today, and even more in the future, their legitimation is based on direct popular support and involvement. In this sense, "public demand" needs to be taken seriously by the public service broadcasters as well. However, instead of the commodification of their audiences in terms of the market, they must be able to offer something different. This is why public service broadcasting opens up a potential for new insights and new forms of cooperation, not only by broadcasters themselves but also by audiences and—why not?—critical scholars in communication.

NOTES

1. The broadcasting experiment of the late 1960s contributed to the establishment of mass communication research as an academic discipline in Finland (Pietilä, Malmberg, and Nordenstreng 1990:169–74). For an additional contextualization, see Slade and Barchak (1989).

2. The basics of Ahmavaara's (1969) theory are presented in English in a conference report, *Report on a Round Table "Communication 1980" on Mass Communication Research and Policy* (1970). The report includes two papers by Ahmavaara, "Cognition and Its Manipulation" (pp. 28–33), and "The Process of Mass Communication" (pp. 33–38). The conference was organized by the Finnish National Commission for UNESCO within UNESCO's Participation Programme. Nordenstreng (1993) links the conference with the "panel of experts" that UNESCO convened in 1971 and the later discussion on the New World Information and Communication Order (NWICO). According to Nordenstreng, besides thirty Finnish media professionals, cultural critics, and social scientists, two foreign visitors participated in the conference: Lewis Nkosi (a South African author and critic residing in London) and Dallas W. Smythe. The latter contributed a paper, "Toward Goal-Oriented Critical Research for Communications Media" (pp. 7–19).

3. Ahmavaara himself adopted Marxism's dialectical materialism as an element of his later "social cybernetics" (Ahmavaara 1976; see Ahmavaara 1973, 1977). However, he was against Marxism as a political dogma, and that made him later a fierce critic of the Marxist impact on social sciences (see, for example, his book on cybernetic laws of social progress, published in English as Aulin [1982]).

4. Nordenstreng's conclusions point to empirical audience research during two media strikes: TV in 1965, and newspapers in 1967. The research was carried out by Kauko Pietilä, Veikko Pietilä, and Pertti Tiihonen at the Research Institute of Social Sciences, University of Tampere.

5. In his comments on "gratifications research," Nordenstreng (1970a) points to the notion of public demand as an ultimate aim in broadcasting and considers it naive. In Finland, he emphasized, the goal of satisfaction was set in a peripheral position and the goals of information and comprehension in a central position.

6. The term "blindspot" refers to Smythe (1977). According to him, political economy was a blindspot for critical research in communications, which, at the time, was focused on ideology. For a recent reference to the "blindspot" debate, see Budd and Steinman (1989) and Fiske (1989).

7. On this discussion, see, for example, *Public Service Broadcasting: The End?* (1983), MacCabe and Stewart (1986), Dyson and Humphreys (1988), Sepstrup (1989), Syvertsen (1990), and Tracey and Rowland (1990).

REFERENCES

Ahmavaara, I. (1969). *Informaatio* (Information; in Finnish). Tapiola: Weilin-Göös.

———. (1970). *Yhteiskuntatieteen Kyberneettinen Metodologia* (The Cybernetic Methodology of Social Science; in Finnish). Helsinki: Tammi.

———. (1973). A theoretical commentary. In *Informational Mass Communication*, edited by K. Nordenstreng. Helsinki: Tammi.

———. (1975). *Informaatio*. 3rd renewed ed. Tapiola: Weilín-Göös.

———. (1976). *Yhteiskuntakybernetiikka* (Social Cybernetics; in Finnish). Tapiola: Weilin-Göös.

———. (1977). What is intellectual activation, as distinguished from cognitive manipulation? In *Current Theories in Scandinavian Mass Communication Research*, edited by M. Breg, et al., pp. 181–97. Grenaa: GMT.

Alasuutari, P. (1992). Tori vai levykauppa? (A marketplace or a record shop?; in Finnish). *Tiedotustutkimus*, 15(1):53–57.

Ang. I. (1991). *Desperately Seeking the Audience*. London: Routledge.

Aulin, A. (1982). *The Cybernetic Laws of Social Progress*. Oxford: Pergamon Press.

Berger, P., and T. Luckmann. (1967). *The Social Construction of Reality*. London: Penguin.

Budd, M., and C. Steinman. (1989). Television, cultural studies, and the "blind spot" debate in critical communications research. *In Television Studies: Textual Analysis*, edited by G. Burns and R. J. Thompson, pp. 9–20. New York: Praeger.

Carey, J. W. (1989). *Communication as Culture*. London: Unwin Hyman.

Curran, J. (1990). The new revisionism in mass communication research: A reappraisal. *European Journal of Communication*, 5(2–3):135–64.

Dyson, K., and P. Humphreys. (1988). *Broadcasting and New Media Policies in Western Europe.* Guildford and King's Lynn: Routledge.

Finnish Mass Media 1989. (1990). Helsinki: Central Statistical Office of Finland, Culture and the Media.

Fiske, J. (1989). Popular television and commercial culture: Beyond political economy. In *Television Studies: Textual Analysis,* edited by G. Burns and R. J. Thompson, pp. 21–37. New York: Praeger.

Hujanen, T., and J. Jyrkiäinen. (1991). The Finnish media system in transition. *Nordicom Review,* 2:63–79.

Jensen, K. B. (1986). *Making Sense of the News.* Viborg: Aarhus University Press.

Lewis, J. (1991). *The Ideological Octopus.* New York and London: Routledge. MacCabe, C., and O. Stewart, eds. (1986). *The BBC and Public Service Broadcasting.* Oxford: Manchester University Press.

McQuail, D., ed. (1972). *Sociology of Mass Communications.* Bungay, Suffolk: Penguin.

Morley, D. (1980). *The Nationwide Audience: Structure and Decoding.* London: British Film Institute.

Nordenstreng, K. (1968). Communication research in the United States: A critical perspective. *Gazette,* 14(3):207–16.

———. (1970a). Comments on "gratifications research" in broadcasting. *Public Opinion Quarterly,* 34(1):130–32.

———. (1970b). Kuka on vieraantunut ja mistä? (Who is alienated and from which?; in Finnish). Special Printing, Linkki.

———. (1972). Policy for news transmission. In *Sociology of Mass Communication,* edited by D. McQuail, pp. 386–405. Bungay, Suffolk: Penguin.

———. (1973a). Extension of the senses: An audience point of view. In *Informational Mass Communication,* edited by K. Nordenstreng, pp. 81–90. Helsinki: Tammi.

———. (ed.). (1973b). *Informational Mass Communication.* Helsinki: Tammi.

———. (1993). New Information order and communication scholarship: Reflections on a delicate relationship. In *Illuminating the Blindspots: Essays Honoring Dallas W. Smythe,* edited by J. Wasko, V. Mosco, and M. Pendakur, pp. 251–73. Norwood, NJ: Ablex.

Nordenstreng, K., et al. (1973). Lessons of the past and potentials for the future. In *Informational Mass Communication,* edited by K. Nordenstreng, pp. 178–95. Helsinki: Tammi.

Pietilä, V. (1977). On the effects of mass media: Some conceptual viewpoints. In *Current Theories in Scandinavian Mass Communication Research,* edited by M. Berg, et al., pp. 116–46. Grenaa: GMT.

Pietilä, V., T. Malmberg, and K. Nordenstreng. (1990). Theoretical convergences and contrasts: A view from Finland. *European Journal of Communication,* 5(2–3):165–85.

Public Service Broadcasting: The End? (1983). Special issue, *Media, Culture and Society,* 5(3–4).

Report on a Round Table "Communication 1980" on Mass Communication Research and Policy. (1970). Hanko, Finland, April 9–11, 1970. Helsinki: Finnish National Commission for UNESCO and the Finnish Broadcasting Company.

Sepstrup, P. (1989). Implications of current developments in West European broadcasting. *Media, Culture and Society,* 11(1):29–54.

Slade, J. W., and L. J. Barchak. (1989). Public broadcasting in Finland: Inventing a national television programming policy. *Journal of Broadcasting and Electronic Media,* 33(4):355–73.

Smythe, D. W. (1977). Communications: Blindspot of Western Marxism. *Canadian Journal of Political and Social Theory,* 1:3.

Syvertsen, T. (1990). Public service television in pursuit of a new consensus. In *Developments of Communications and Democracy: Main Papers and Abstracts for the 17th IAMCR Conference,* edited by S. Splichal, pp. 13–22. Ljubljana: University of Ljubljana, Faculty of Sociology, Political Science, and Journalism.

Tracey, M., and W. D. Rowland. (1990). Worldwide challenges to public service broadcasting. *Journal of Communication,* 40(2):8–27.

Varis, T. (1971). *Ideologia ja Tiedonvälityksen Loukkaavuus* (Ideology and Offensiveness of Mass Communication; in Finnish). Institute of Journalism and Mass Communication Publication Series, no. 7. Tampere: University of Tampere.

Bibliographies of Featured Scholars

Dallas W. Smythe

Books, Monographs, Invited Papers

Los Angeles Television. With Angus Campbell. Ann Arbor, MI: Edwards Brothers, 1951. 93 pp.

"Television: Boon or Bane for Our Youth." Illinois Council on Motion Pictures, Radio, Television and Publications, Chicago, April 19, 1951. Unpublished.

"A Problem in Content Macroanalysis in the NAEB Monitoring Study of New York Television." Institute for Education by Radio, Columbus, Ohio, May 5, 1951.

New York Television, January 4–10, 1951–52. Urbana, IL: National Association of Educational Broadcasters, 1952. 108 pp.

"Television and Education" (Panel discussion). *The New Republic* (Special Issue), February 26, 1951.

New Haven Television, May 15–21, 1952. Urbana, IL: National Association of Educational Broadcasters, 1952. 161 pp.

"What Mass Communications Do for Us and to Us." Convocation address, Bowling Green State University, Bowling Green, Ohio, June 20, 1952.

"Civilian TV Research: 1952 Model." Institutional media seminar, New York, 1952. 28 pp.

Three Years of New York Television, 1951–1953. Urbana, IL: National Association of Educational Broadcasters, 1953. 161 pp.

"Who Can Speak to My Condition?" Report on New Haven study of religious use of radio and TV, before the Broadcasting and Film Commission, National Council of Churches of Christ, New York, April 8, 1954. 11 pp.

The Television-Radio Audience and Religion. With Everett C. Parker and David W. Barry. New York: Harper, 1955, 464 pp.

"The Meaning of Television for America." Methodist Radio and Film Commission, Dallas, Texas, January 16, 1956.

"A Program Research Plan for the Broadcasting and Film Commission." National Council of Churches of Christ, March 29, 1956.

Report. Royal Commission on Broadcasting, March 15, 1957. Chapter II, "The Programme Fare," and three appendices. Ottawa: Queen's Printer, 1957. 518 pp.

Canadian Television and Sound Radio Programmes: An Analysis. Royal Commission on Broadcasting. Ottawa: Queen's Printer, 1957.

Basic Tables: Report of Television and Radio Programme Analysis. Royal Commission on Broadcasting. Ottawa: Queen's Printer, 1957. 267 pp.

The Structure and Policy of Electronic Communication. Urbana: University of Illinois Press, 1957. 103 pp. Republished in *Documents in American Telecommunications Policy,* edited by J. M. Kittross. New York: Arno Press, 1975.

Toward More Effective Educational TV: A Pilot Study of the Effects of Commercial TV on Verbal Behaviour of Pre-School Children. With Evelyn Walker. Urbana: Institute of Communications Research, University of Illinois, 1958.

"American Culture in the Shadow of the Satellites." Address to the Broadcasting and Film Commission, National Council of Churches of Christ, February 18, 1958. 11 pp.

Attitudes Towards the Frontiers of Faith: "Conversation Piece." TV series, June–July 1958. 55 pp.

"The Cultural Context of Religion and the Mass Media." Study Commission on the Role of Radio, Television, and Films in Religion, August 1958. 11 pp.

Space Satellite Communications and Public Opinion. New York: American Sociological Association, August 1960. 39 pp.

"The Spiral of Terror and the Mass Media." Public lecture, University of Pennsylvania, Philadelphia, September 1960. 29 pp. Also published by Institute of Communications Research, University of Illinois, Urbana.

"The Modern Media Man and the Political Process." Address, Adult Educational Council, Chattanooga, Tennessee, November 17, 1960. Also published by Institute of Communications Research, University of Illinois, Urbana.

"The Mass Media and Foreign Policy-Making in the Cold War." Public lecture, Michigan State University, March 9, 1961.

"Let's Live in the World." Congregational Church, Urbana, Illinois, April 30, 1961.

"Persuasion as a Cultural Phenomenon." American Psychiatric Association national conference, May 11, 1961.

"The Serviceability of the Mass Media and Other Arts in a Nuclear Age." University lecture, University of Maryland, College Park, June 29, 1961. Also published by Institute of Communications Research, University of Illinois, Urbana.

"Statement on Communications." Athens Conference on World Order and Freedom, Athens, Greece, October 25, 1961. 15 pp.

"Mass Media and the Churches." United Church of Canada national meeting, Toronto, Ontario, March 22, 1961; also at Biblical Seminary, New York, January 9, 1962.

"Breaking Through the Thought Barrier to Survival." YMCA-YWCA Forum, University of Illinois, Urbana, April 21, 1962.

"How to Start a Peace Race." University lecture, Kalamazoo College, Kalamazoo, Michigan, May 4, 1962.

"Cuban Crisis: A Failure in Our Definition of Reality." Students for Peace, University of Illinois, Urbana, October 24, 1962.

"The Mass Media." In *Christianity and World Revolution,* edited by Edwin H. Rian. New York: Harper & Row, 1963.

"Peace in a Shrinking World." Voters for Peace, mass meeting, Chicago, Illinois, February 5, 1963.

"Institutional Factors in Cold War Policy." American Ortho-psychiatric Association, Washington, D.C., March 7, 1963. 14 pp.

"The Mass Media Today and Tomorrow." University lecture, University of Pennsylvania, Philadelphia, September 17, 1963.

"Change and the Mass Media of Communication." Saskatchewan Farmers' Union, Saskatoon, December 5, 1963. 42 pp.

"Mass Media and the Cold War." In *Seeds of Liberation,* edited by Paul Goodman, pp. 455–70. New York: Braziller, 1964.
"Adult Education Begins in the First Grade." Conference on Adult Education, Regina, Saskatchewan, June 4, 1964.
"On Thinking About the Effects of Communication Satellites." American Institute of Aeronautics and Astronautics, Washington, D.C., June 30, 1964. 36 pp.
The Citizen and the Mass Media of Communications. Report of the 25th Annual Meeting and 1965 Conference of the Canadian Citizenship Council, 1965.
"On the Effects of Communications Satellites." In *Communications Explosion.* Paper No. 9. Washington, D.C.: George Washington University, Program of Policy Studies in Science and Technology, June 1965. 25 pp.
"Alcoholism as a Symptom of Social Disorder: An Ecological View." School of Alcohol Studies, University of North Dakota, June 13, 1965. 36 pp.
"The Political and Economic Conditions of Freedom of Information." International Consultation of "The Christian Mission and Communications Revolution," Celigny, Switzerland, February 21–28, 1966. 48 pp.
"The Language of the Moving Image." Canadian Education Association, Regina, Saskatchewan, September 1967.
"Cold-War Mindedness and the Mass Media." With H. H. Wilson. In *Struggle Against History,* edited by Neal D. Houghton, pp. 59–78. New York: Washington Square Press, 1968.
"The U.S. and Us." In *Culture and Communications,* edited by G. McCaffrey, pp. 121–24. Geneva Park, Ontario, 1968.
"Comments on 'The Church and the Media of Mass Communications.'" World Council of Churches of Christ, Upsala, Sweden, January 1968.
"Conflict, Co-operation and Communications Satellites." In *Mass Media and International Understanding,* edited by School of Sociology, Political Science and Journalism, pp. 51–73. Ljubljana: Department of Journalism, School of Sociology, Political Science and Journalism, 1969.
Canadian Representative, UNESCO Meeting of Experts on Mass Communication and Society, Montreal, 1969; coauthor of *Final Report.*
"The Legal Problems of International Telecommunications with Special Reference to INTELSAT." Panel of International Law Association, Ottawa, October 1969. Published in *University of Toronto Law Journal,* 20:287 (1970).
"The Orbital Parking Slot Syndrome and Radio Frequency Management." Conference on International Communication by Satellite, Stanford University School of Law and American Society of International Law, Stanford University, California, April 2–3, 1970. 11 pp.
"Toward Goal-Oriented Critical Research for Communications Media." Round Table, "Communications 1980," on Mass Communication Research and Policy, Hanko, Finland, April 9–11, 1970. Finnish National Commission for UNESCO and Finnish Broadcasting Company. Published as part of *Report,* Helsinki, 1970.
The Relevance of United States Legislative-Regulatory Experience to the Canadian Telecommunications Situation. Study for the Telecommission, Department of Communications, Ottawa, June 1970. 211 pp.
The International Telecommunications Union: Issues and Next Steps. Report by the panel on International Telecommunications Policy of the American Society of International Law. Occasional Paper No. 10. New York: Carnegie Endowment for International Peace, 1971. (Smythe was one of the panel member authors.)

"The Political Character of Science (Including Communication Science), or, Science Is Not Ecumenical." Colloquium, Annenberg School of Communications, University of Pennsylvania, Philadelphia, February 2, 1971. 23 pp. Published in Finnish as a monograph by University of Tampere, 1972.

"Cultural Realism and Cultural Screens." International Symposium on "New Frontiers of Television," Lake Bled, Yugoslavia, June 1971. 32 pp.

"Problems of Regulating Public Utilities," Discussant on panel, Canadian Economics Association meeting, Winnipeg, Summer 1971.

"Reflections on Proposals for an International Programme of Communications Research." International Association for Mass Communication Research General Assembly, Buenos Aires, Argentina, September 1972. 14 pp.

"Comment on 'Behavior of the Firm Under Regulatory Constraint: A Reassessment,' by L. L. Johnson, and 'Entry as a Substitute for Regulation,' by W. G. Shepherd." Panel on regulated industries, American Economic Association meeting, Toronto, December 29, 1972. Published by American Economic Association.

"Mass Communications and Cultural Revolution: The Experience of China." International Symposium on Communication, "Technology, Impact and Policy," University of Pennsylvania, Philadelphia, March 23–25, 1972. 41 pp. Published in *Communications Technology and Social Policy,* edited by George Gerbner, Larry P. Gross, and William H. Melody, pp. 441–66. New York: Wiley, 1973.

"Memorandum on Some Questions Regarding Telecommunications Development in British Columbia." For Department of Transportation and Communications, Province of British Columbia, November 1973.

Participant, UNESCO Symposium on the International Flow of Television Programmes, Tampere, Finland, May 21–23, 1973. Report published in *Television Traffic—A One-Way Street?,* by Kaarle Nordenstreng and Tapio Varis, pp. 50–51. Paris: UNESCO, 1974.

A Study of Saskatchewan Telecommunications. Ottawa: Department of Communications, July 1974. 65 pp.

The Role of Mass Media and Popular Culture in Defining Development. International Association for Mass Communication Research Congress, Leipzig, GDR, September 1974. 28 pp.

"Foreword." In *Cable Television and Telecommunication in Canada,* edited by R. E. Babe, pp. viii–xxi. Lansing: Michigan State University Press, 1975.

"Communications." In The *Non-Aligned Movement in World Politics,* edited by Archie Singham, pp. 46–47. New York: Lawrence Hill, 1978.

"The Political Character of Science." In *Communication and Class Struggle,* edited by Armand Mattelart and Seth Siegelaub, pp. 171–76. New York: International General, 1978.

Opportunity Cost and Radio Spectrum Allocation. With W. H. Melody. Ottawa: Department of Communications, March 1978. 66 pp.

"Realism in the Arts and Sciences: A Systematic Overview of Capitalism and Socialism." In *National Sovereignty and International Communication,* edited by Kaarle Nordenstreng and H. I. Schiller. Norwood, NJ: Ablex, 1979.

Economic Analysis and Radio Spectrum Licence Fees: The Microwave Band. With W. H. Melody. Ottawa: Department of Communications, March 1979. 102 pp.

"Issues in International Communications: Peoples, Commodities and Political Processes." George A. Miller Lecture, University of Illinois, Urbana, April 2, 1979. 18 pp.

"Interview at Shanghai Advertising Corporation." With Jennie Smythe and others. Shanghai, China, May 23, 1979.

The Level and Structure of Licence Fees in the Microwave Band. With W. H. Melody. Ottawa: Department of Communications, March 1980. 106 pp.

"Changing Role of the Market in Utilities Regulation: Comment." Papers and Proceedings, American Economic Association, Atlanta, Georgia, December 1979. *American Economic Review,* 70:2 (May 1980):382–404.

The Electronic Information Tiger, or the Political Economy of the Radio Spectrum and the Third World Interest, World Communications, Decisions for the Eighties. Philadelphia: Annenberg School of Communications, University of Pennsylvania, May 1980. 26 pp.

"Statement in Support of Comments of the Office of Communications, United Church of Christ." In *FCC Inquiry on Deregulating Radio,* June 30, 1980. 46 pp.

Panel participant, Plenary Session, "Analysis of *Many Voices, One World,* Report of the UNESCO MacBride Commission." International Association for Mass Communication Research Congress, Caracas, Venezuela, August 28, 1980.

Organizer and program chair, Communication Satellite and Technology Committee, and presented "The Electronic Information Tiger," International Association for Mass Communication Research, Caracas, Venezuela, August 1980.

"Policy on Information and Ideology: The Spiral of Terror, Part 2." San Diego Conference on Culture and Communication, February 19–21, 1981. 10 pp.

"Communications: Blindspot of Economics." In *Culture, Communication and Dependency: The Tradition of H. A. Innis,* edited by W. H. Melody, L. Salter, and P. Heyer, pp. 111–25. Norwood, NJ: Ablex, 1981.

Dependency Road: Communications, Capitalism, Consciousness and Canada. Norwood, NJ: Ablex, 1981. 347 pp.

"Democratization and Integration in International Communication: A Skeptical View." International Studies Association, Philadelphia, March 18–21, 1981.

"Canadian Communications: Media of Cultural Submission." Conference on Culture and Communication, Temple University, Philadelphia, Pennsylvania, April 9–11, 1981. 73 pp.

Organizer and panel chair, "Communications and Ideology," Conference on Culture and Communication, Temple University, Philadelphia, Pennsylvania, April 9–11, 1981.

"On Rationalizing the Relation of the Private and Public Sectors: Deregulation of Radio in the 1980s." Invited paper, Ninth Telecommunications Policy Conference, Annapolis, Maryland, April 1981. 15 pp.

"On Thinking the Unthinkable About Nuclear War and Its Consequences for the Peace Movement." International Peace Research Association, Orillia, Ontario, June 1981. 40 pp. Published in *Key Issues of Peace Research,* edited by Sakamoto and Klaasen, pp. 1–9. Dundas: Ontario Peace Research Institute, 1983. Republished in *The Critical Communication Review, vol. II: Changing Patterns of Communication Control,* edited by Vincent Mosco and Janet Wasko, pp. 32–56. Norwood, NJ: Ablex, 1984.

"Der Elektronische Datentiger oder die politische Okonomie des Radiowellenspektrums und das Interesse der Dritten Welt." In *Informationstechnologie und Internationale Politik,* edited by Jorg Becker, et al., pp. 97–112. Bonn: Friedrich-Ebert-Stiftung, 1983. (Revision of appendix to *Dependency Road.*)

"On Critical and Administrative Research: A New Critical Analysis." With Tran Van Dinh.

In *Ferment in the Field,* edited by George Gerbner, pp. 117–27. Special issue of *Journal of Communication,* 33:3 (1983).

"Radio: Deregulation and the Relation of the Private and Public Sectors," In *Mass Communication Review Yearbook,* vol. 4, edited by Ellen Wartella and D. Charles Whitney, pp. 611–19. Beverly Hills, CA: Sage, 1983.

"New Directions for Critical Communications Research." Invited principal paper, Communications, Mass Media and Development Conference, Chicago, Illinois, October 14, 1983. 26 pp. Published in *Mass Media, Culture and Society,* 6 (July 1984): 205–18.

Comment on five papers on "Adjusting to New Market Structures in Telecommunications"; comment on four papers on "Universal Service and the Access Charge Debate," Institute of Public Utilities, Graduate School of Business Administration, Michigan State University, and 15th Annual Conference, "Changing Patterns in Regulation, Markets and Technology: The Impact of Public Utility Pricing," Williamsburg, Virginia, December 12–14, 1983. 12 pp. and 7 pp.

"The Electronic Information Tiger, Radio Spectrum and the Third World Interest." In *Politics of News: Third World Perspectives,* edited by Jaswant S. Yadava, pp. 272–96. New Delhi: Concept, 1984. Spanish translation in *Analisi* (Barcelona), 10–11 (1987):183–201.

"Ideological Aspects of the Concept 'the State.'" Invited paper, International Association for Mass Communication Research, Prague, Czechoslovakia, August 1984. 37 pp.

"National Policy on Public and Private Sectors." Invited paper, Transportation and Public Utility Group, Allied Social Science Associations, Dallas, Texas, December 1984. 31 pp.

"The Radio Spectrum." For *Encyclopedia of Communications,* University of Pennsylvania, Philadelphia, 1984. 19 pp. *Encyclopedia* published in 1989.

"An Historical Perspective on Equity: National Policy on Public and Private Sectors in the USA." Plenary session address, 13th Annual Telecommunications Policy Research Conference, Airlie House, Virginia, April 1985. 18 pp. Published in *Telecommunications and Equity: Policy Research Issues,* edited by James Miller, pp. 21–30. New York: Elsevier, 1986.

"Needs Before Tools? The Illusions of Electronic Democracy." International Communication Association, Honolulu, Hawaii, May 1985. Published in *Media Development,* No. 4 (1985):8–17.

Communication, Information and Culture: Annotated Bibliography. With William H. Melody, Robin E. Mansell, and Ursel Koebberling. August 1985. 213 pp.

"On the Political Economy of C³I." In *Communication and Domination: Essays to Honor Herbert I. Schiller,* edited by Jorg Becker, Goran Hedebro, and Leena Paldan, pp. 66–75. Norwood, NJ: Ablex, 1986.

"Ideology, Culture and 'Technology.'" Queen's University, Kingston, Ontario, April 1986. 21 pp.

"Culture, Communication 'Technology' and Canadian Policy." The Southam Lecture, Canadian Communication Association, Winnipeg, June 6, 1986. 26 pp. French translation in *Communication,* 8(3):11–29.

"International Communication in the International Year of Peace." First Canberra Conference on International Communication, Canberra, Australia, December 1986. 26 pp.

"Radio Spectrum Policy and World Needs." First Canberra Conference on International Communication, Canberra, Australia, December 1986. 27 pp. In *Prometheus,* 5:2 (December 1987): 263–83.

"Europe for Europeans: A Conspectus." Keynote paper, East-West Conference on Internaional Information Flows, Frankfurt, Federal Republic of Germany, February 1988. 24 pp. Published in *Europe Speaks to Europe,* edited by Jorg Becker and Tamás Szecskö, pp. 3–17. Oxford: Pergamon Press, 1989.

"Freedom Is the Act of Resisting Necessity." Response to "How Free Is the Free Flow of Information?" by Leonard R. Sussman, ICASIETAR, Montreal, April 20, 1987. 17 pp. Published in abridged form as "Unsaintly Alliance Against NICCO." *The Democratic Journalist* (March 1988):10–12.

"The Information Society: What and Whose Choices and Culture? Or on to Globalization." Australia/New Zealand Association for the Advancement of Science, Sydney, Australia, May 1988. 48 pp.

Testimony and Reports for Government Bodies

Report on Effects of De-intermixture in Peoria, Springfield and Related Markets of Illinois. In the Matter of Fostering Expanded Use of UHF Television Channels, Docket No. 14229, Federal Communications Commission, 1962. 81 pp.

Economics of TV Station WTTV. In the Matter of Amendment of Section 3.606, Indiana, Docket No. 14420, Federal Communications Commission, 1962. 26 pp.

Testimony before the (Long) Subcommittee on Monopoly of the Select Committee on Small Business, U.S. Senate, 86th Congress, 1st Session on Communications Satellite Policy, *Hearings,* August 3, 1961, pp. 95–119.

Testimony before the (Kefauver) Subcommittee on Anti-Trust and Monopoly of the Committee on the Judiciary, U.S. Senate, 86th Congress, 1st Session on Communications Satellite Policy, *Hearings,* April 5, 1962, pp. 183–228, 595–601.

Memorandum on Audience Studies Submitted by Atlas Broadcasting Company and Grand Broadcasting Company. Prepared for FCC hearing for West Michigan Telecasters, Inc., with Thomas H. Guback, May 11, 1962. 25 pp.

Testimony before the Federal Communications Commission, Docket No. 14650. Special Investigation of the Telegraph Industry, November 1963. 79 pp. Transcript of Hearings, November 4–5, 1964, pp. 7222–7390.

Comments on Report of the Common Carrier Bureau of the Federal Communications Commission in the Domestic Telegraph Investigation, on Behalf of American Communications Association. Docket No. 14650, February 25, 1966. 23 pp.

The "Rate Adjustment Formula" as Proposed for Telecommunications Carriers by the Canadian Transport Commission. With Michael Bradfield and Rodney D. Peterson. Burnaby, Canada: Simon Fraser University, 1975.

"Report on Financial Disclosures by Cable Television Broadcasting Undertakings as It Relates to Rate Applications." Study for the Canadian Radio-Television Commission, June 1975. 45 pp.

Opportunity Cost and Radio Spectrum Allocation: A Study of the Feasibility of Applying the Opportunity Cost Concept to the Spectrum Allocation Process. With William H. Melody. DOC Contract No. OSU77-00368. March 1978.

Economic Analysis and Radio Spectrum Licence Fees: The Microwave Band. With William H. Melody and Angus Oliver. DOC Contract No. O2SU-36100-809528. March 1979.

Factors Affecting the Canadian and U.S. Spectrum Management Processes: A Preliminary Evaluation. With William H. Melody. DOC Contract No. 36100-4-4259. March 1985. 62 pp.

Journal Articles

"Television: Position and Outlook." *Current Economic Comment,* 2 (February 1949):15–33.

"Television and Its Educational Implications." *Elementary English,* 27 (January 1950):41–52.

"Television in Relation to Other Media and Recreation in American Life." *Hollywood Quarterly,* 4 (Spring 1950):256–61.

"People and Television: The Natural History of an Unfinished Study." Mimeo. June 1950. 360 pp.

"A National Policy on Television?" *Public Opinion Quarterly* (Fall 1950):461–75.

"Use of Surveys by Government Agencies." *Public Opinion Quarterly* (Winter 1950–51):830–40.

"An Analysis of Television Programs." *Scientific American* (June 1951):15–17.

"The Consumer's Stake in Radio and Television." *Consumer Problems in a Period of International Tension: A 15th Anniversary Report from Consumers Union* (November 1951):58–71. Also published in *Quarterly Review of Film, Radio and Television,* 6 (Winter 1951):109–28.

"A Mid-Century View of Competition in the Broadcasting Business." *Current Economic Comment* (May 1952):31–46.

"What TV Programming Is Like." *Quarterly Review of Film, Radio and Television,* 3 (Summer 1952):25–31.

"Facing the Facts About the Broadcasting Business." *University of Chicago Law Review* (Autumn 1952):96–106.

"Civilian TV Research, 1952 Model." In *Proceedings,* Research and Development Board.

"Portrait of an Art Theatre Audience." With P. B. Lusk and C. A. Lewis. *Quarterly Review of Film, Radio and Television,* 8 (1953):28–50.

"Some Observations on Communications Theory." *Audio-Visual Communication Review* (Winter 1954):24–37. Also published as "Aprocci Teoretici Sugli Effetti della Communicazioni di Massi." *Lo Spettacolo* (January–March 1953):1–15.

"The Content and Effects of Broadcasting." Chapter 9, pp. 192–217, in *Mass Media and Education.* National Society for the Study of Education, 53rd Yearbook. 1954.

"Basic Issues in Communication in the Education of Protestant Ministers."*Religious Education,* 49 (1954):428–30.

"The Role of the Film in Educational Television." *Journal of the University Film Producers Association,* 6:3 (Spring 1954):11–13.

"Recent Books on Freedom of Speech." *Audio-Visual Communication Review,* 2 (1954):304–14.

"Reality as Presented by TV." *Public Opinion Quarterly,* 18:2 (Summer 1954):143–56.

"Color Television." *Illinois Business Review* (October 1954):8–9.

"Portrait of a First-run Audience." With J. R. Gregory, A. Ostrin, P. O. Colvin, and W. Monroney. *Quarterly Review of Film, Radio and Television,* 9:4 (Summer 1955):390–409.

"TV Programs We Haven't Seen." *Audio-Visual Communication Review,* 3:3 (Summer 1955):220–28.

"Dimensions of Violence." *Audio-Visual Communication Review* (Winter 1955):58–63.

"Commercial TV Programming in Champaign-Urbana, 1955." *Audio-Visual Communication Review,* 3:2 (1955):220–28.

"The Position of Pay-TV." *Illinois Business Review* (August 1957):6–8.

"Pay TV: An Attempted Revolution Within Cultural Industry." *Current Economic Comment* (November 1957):49–66.

"The Menace of Pay-TV." With Jennie N. Smythe. *The Nation* (January 4, 1958):5–9.
"The Meaning of the Communications Revolution." *Social Action* (April 1958):16–23.
"The Review of Literature on Mass Culture: A Comment." *Social Problems,* 6:3 (Winter 1958–59):476–77.
"Der Zeitfactor in der Massenkommunikation." *Rundfunk und Fernsehen,* 7 (Fall 1959):259.
"Space Satellite Broadcasting: Threat or Promise?" *Journal of Broadcasting,* 6:3 (Summer 1960):191–98; and *Illinois Business Review* (June 1960):6–8.
"Space Satellite Broadcasting." *NAEB Journal* (July–August 1960):71–78.
"On the Political Economy of Communication." *Journalism Quarterly,* 37:4 (Autumn 1960):563–72.
"Responsibilities of Mass Media in the Cold War." *Sekai* (January 1961):128–38.
"Communications Satellites." *Bulletin of the Atomic Scientists,* 17:2 (February 1961):65–70.
"Les Mass Media et la Politique Etrangère." *Les Cahiers de la République,* No. 30 (March 1961):40–50.
"Das Bild des Politikers in den Massenmedien." *Rundfunk und Fernsehen,* 9 (1961):250–61.
"The Space Giveaway: Public Benefit or Private Privilege." *The Nation* (October 14 and 21, 1961):242–45; 264–68.
"Review of *Antitrust in the Motion Picture Industry,* by Michael Conant; and *Broadcast Regulation and Joint Ownership of Media,* by Harvey J. Levin." *Quarterly Review of Economics and Business,* 1 (November 1961):109–11.
"Out-thinking Ourselves: Review of *Civil Defence in the Soviet Union,* with foreword by William F. Libby." *Liberation,* 7:4 (June 1962).
"Considerations on a Worldwide Communication Satellite System." *Telecommunication Journal* (September 1962):3–14.
"Time, Market and Space Factors in Communications Economics." *Journalism Quarterly,* 39:1(Winter 1962):3–14.
"Review of *The Decline of the Cinema,* by John Spraos." *Audio-Visual Communication Review,* 2:3 (May–June 1963):63–64.
"The Churches, the Mass Media and Peace." *Continuum,* 1:2 (Summer 1963):165–78.
"Brainrinsing, Bipartisanship and Dictatorship Versus Peace." *NorthWest Review,* 6:4 (Fall 1963):111–20.
"Review of *The Improper Opinion: Mass Media and the Christian Faith,* by Martin E. Marty." *Review of Religious Research,* 4:2 (Winter 1963):119–21.
"Mass Media and the Cold War." *Liberation,* 8:10 (December 1963):18–23. Reprinted in *Seeds of Liberation,* edited by Paul Goodman, pp. 455–70. New York: Braziller, 1964.
"Die Massenmedien Hute und Morgen," *Rundfunk und Fernesehen,* 12:1 (1964):1–12.
"Orbiting Bombs and the MOL." *Bulletin of the Atomic Scientists* (October 1964):37–38.
"Freedom of Information: Some Analysis and a Proposal for Satellite Broadcasting." *Quarterly Review of Economics and Business,* 6:3 (Autumn 1966):7–24.
"Review of *Television and Society,* by Harry J. Skornia." *Quarterly Review of Economics and Business,* 6:3 (Autumn 1966):7–24.
"Alcoholism as a Symptom of Social Disorder: An Ecological View." *Social Psychiatry,* 1:3 (1966):144–51.
"The Political and Economic Conditions of Freedom of Information," *Study Encounter,* 3:1 (1967):2–20. In French and German by World Council of Churches.
"Conflict, Co-operation and Communications Satellites," *Estudios de Informacion,* No. 9 (October–December 1968):31–73.

"Manufacturing Public Opinion." With W. H. Melody. *The Bill of Rights Journal* (December 1968):17–19.

"Five Myths of Consumership." *The Nation* (January 20, 1969):82–84. Also published in *Mass Media: A Case Book*, edited by Richard F. Hixson, pp. 250–55. New York: Cromwell, 1973.

"Popular Culture: Mythmaker and Brainwasher." *Democratic Journalist*, No. 2 (1969):49–52.

"Cultura Popular: Fabricante de Mitos y Lavado de Corebro." *Estudios de Informacion*, No. 9 (March 20, 1969).

"The Legal Problems of International Telecommunications with Special Reference to INTELSAT," and "International Legal Problems of Direct Satellite Broadcasting." Reports based on two panel discussions of Canadian Society of International Law. *University of Toronto Law Journal*, 20:3 (1970):287–313; 314–32.

"Review of *The Medium Is the Rear View Mirror: Understanding McLuhan*, by Donald F. Theall." *Queen's Quarterly* (Summer 1971).

"Realisms Culturale e Defese Culturali." *Lo Spettacolo*, 22 (January–March 1972):1–18.

"Socijalna Transfomacija i Sredstva Javnog Komuniciranja—Cile, prva Codina." With H. I. Schiller. *Mase Teme* (Zagreb) (February–March 1972):349–67.

"Chile: An End to Cultural Colonialism." With Herbert I. Schiller. *Transaction-Society*, 9:5 (March 1972):35–39, 61.

"China: A Visit to 800 Million People." *Newsletter* of the International Broadcast Institute, No. 6 (Summer 1972):9–10.

"The Orbital Parking Slot Syndrome and Radio Frequency Management." *Quarterly Review of Economics and Business*, 12 (Summer 1972):7–18.

"Analysis and Discussion of the International Flow of TV Material." In *Television Traffic—A One-Way Street?*, by Kaarle Nordenstreng and Tapio Varis, pp. 43–58. Paris: UNESCO, 1973.

"Whom Are You Neutral Against?" *China Notes* (National Council of Churches, New York), 3:1 (Winter 1973–74):7–10.

"The Role of Mass Media and Popular Culture in Defining Development." In *Der Anteil Massenmedien bei der Herausbildung des Bewusstseins in der sich wandelnden Welt*, pp. 367–74. Leipzig: Karl Marx University, 1974.

"Agenda Setting (The Role of Mass Media and Popular Culture in Defining Development)." *Journal of the Centre for Advanced Television Studies*, 3:2 (1975):34–39.

"Communications: Blindspot of Western Marxism." *Canadian Journal of Political and Society Theory*, 1:3 (1977):1–28. Published as "Comunicaciones: 'Agujero Negro' del Marxismo Occidental." In *La Television: Entre Servicio Publico y Negocio*, edited by G. Richeri, pp. 71–103. Mexico: G. Gill, 1983.

"Critique of the Consciousness Industry." *Journal of Communication*, 27:1 (Winter 1977):198–202.

"Rejoinder to Graham Murdock." *Canadian Journal of Political and Society Theory*, 2:2 (Spring–Summer 1978):120–26.

"Review of *The Media Are American*, by Jeremy Tunstall." *Media, Culture and Society*, 1:1(January 1979):107–14.

"Review of *The Public Eye: Television and the Politics of Canadian Broadcasting*, by Frank W. Peers." *Canadian Journal of Sociology*, 5:1 (Winter 1980):79–80.

"Review of *Does Mass Communication Change Public Opinion After All? A New Approach to Effects Analysis*, by James B. Lemert." *Journal of Communication*, 31:3 (Summer 1981): 217–20.

"Radio: Deregulation and the Relation of the Private and Public Sectors." *Journal of Communication,* 32:1 (Winter 1982):192–200. Republished in *Mass Communication Review Yearbook,* Vol. 4, edited by Ellen Wartella and D. Charles Whitney. Beverly Hills, CA: Sage, 1983.

"Review of *Mass Media, Ideologies and the Revolutionary Movement,* by Armand Mattelart; and *Marx and Engels on the Means of Communication,* by Yves de la Haye." Abridged form in *Journal of Communication,* 33:2 (Spring 1983):168–72.

"Tecnología de los comunicaciones y Tercer Mundo." *Chasqui,* No. 6 (January–June 1983):22–27.

"World Communications Year: Reality and Theory on the Information Age." *Directions,* 1:1 (1983):1–3.

"Capitalism, Advertising and the Consciousness Industry." *Media Information Australia,* No. 31 (February 1984):20–25.

"Review of *Communication and Class Struggle, Vol. 2: Liberation, Socialism,* edited by Armand Mattelart and Seth Siegelaub." *Journal of Communication,* 35:1 (Winter 1985):218–23.

"Needs Before Tools: The Illusions of Technology." *Media Development,* 23:4 (1985):6–17.

"One Canadian View: 'Clear Across Australia.'" *Prometheus,* 3:2 (December 1985):431–53.

"A Pillar of Systemic Ignorance: 'The State.'" April 1986. 30 pp. Unpublished.

"Foreword." In *Independence, Liberation, Revolution,* by Tran Van Dinh. Norwood, NJ: Ablex, 1987.

"Radio Spectrum Policy and World Needs?" *Prometheus,* 5:2 (December 1987):263–83.

"El Perill de la Informacio Electronica o L'Economie Politica de les Frequencies de Radio i L'Interes del Terre Mon." *Analisi,* 10:11 (December 1987):183–202.

"Television Deregulation and the Public." *Journal of Communication,* 39:4 (Autumn 1989):133–38.

"Foreword." In *Canadian Dreams and American Control: The Political Economy of the Canadian Film Industry,* by Manjunath Pendakur, pp. 15–26. Detroit: Wayne State University Press, 1990.

George Gerbner

Books

The Analysis of Communications Content: Developments in Scientific Theories and Computer Techniques. Edited with Ole R. Holsti, Klaus Krippendorff, William J. Paisley, and Phillip Stone. New York: Wiley, 1969.

Communication Technology and Social Policy. Edited with Larry P. Gross and William H. Melody. New York: Wiley, 1973.

Editor. *Mass Media Policies in Changing Cultures.* New York: Wiley Interscience, 1977. Translated into Italian in De Donato (ed.). *Le Politiche dei Mass Media.* Bari: S.P.A., 1980.

Child Abuse: An Agenda for Action. Edited with Catherine J. Ross and Edward Zigler. New York: Oxford University Press, 1980.

Communications in the Twenty-First Century. Edited with Robert W. Haigh and Richard B. Byrne. New York: Wiley, 1981.

World Communications: A Handbook. Edited with Marsha Siefert. New York and London: Annenberg/Longman Communication Books, 1984.

International Encyclopedia of Communications. 4 volumes. (Chair, editorial board). New York and London: Oxford University Press, 1988.

Violence and Terror in the Media: An Annotated Bibliography. With Nancy Signorielli. Westport, CT: Greenwood Press, 1988.

The Information Gap: How Computers and Other Communication Technologies Affect the Distribution of Power. Edited with Marsha Siefert and Janice Fisher. New York and London: Oxford University Press, 1989.

Beyond the Cold War: Soviet and American Media Images. Edited with Everette E. Dennis and Yassen N. Zassoursky. Newbury Park, CA: Sage, 1991.

Triumph of the Image: The Media's War in the Persian Gulf. An International Perspective. Edited with Hamid Mowlana and Herbert Schiller. Boulder, CO: Westview Press, 1993.

The Global Media Debate: Its Rise, Fall, and Renewal. Edited with Hamid Mowlana and Kaarle Nordenstreng. Norwood, NJ: Ablex, forthcoming.

Papers, Reports, Chapters, Articles

"A Study of Audience 'Involvement' or 'Interest' in a Training Film." With Lester F. Beck. Air Force Personnel and Training Research Center, 1954.

"Toward a General Model of Communication." *Audio-Visual Communication Review,* 4 (Summer 1956):171–99.

"Content Analysis and Critical Research in Mass Communication." *Audio-Visual Communication Review,* 6 (Spring 1958):85–108. Reprinted in *People, Society and Mass Communications,* edited by L. A. Dexter and D. M. White. Glencoe, IL: Free Press, 1964.

"The Social Anatomy of the Romance-Confession Cover Girl." *Journalism Quarterly,* 35 (Summer 1958):299–306.

"The Social Role of the Confession Magazine." *Social Problems,* 6 (Summer 1958): 29–40.

"Education and the Challenge of Mass Culture." *Audio-Visual Communication Review,* 7 (Fall 1959):264–78.

"Mental Illness on Television: A Study of Censorship." *Journal of Broadcasting,* 3 (Fall 1959):292–303.

"Popular Culture and Images of the Family." *Chicago Theological Seminary Register,* 49 (November 1959):31–37.

"The Interaction Model: Perception and Communication." In *Research, Principles, and Practices in Visual Communication,* edited by John Ball and Francis Byrnes, pp. 4–15. East Lansing, MI: National Project in Agricultural Communications, 1960.

"Mass Communications and the Citizenship of Secondary School Youth." In *The Adolescent Citizen,* edited by Franklin Patterson, et al., pp. 179–205. Glencoe, IL: Free Press, 1960.

"Visual Communication Training: Philosophy and Principles." In *Communication Training,*pp. 29–34. East Lansing, MI: National Project in Agricultural Communications, 1960.

"Social Science and the Professional Education of the Audio-Visual Communication Specialist." *Audio-Visual Communication Review,* 8 (September–October 1960):50–58.

"The Individual in a Mass Culture." *Saturday Review,* 43 (June 18, 1960):11–13, 36–37. Abridged version in *The Executive,* 4 (1960):14–16, and *The National Elementary Principal,* 40 (February 1961):49–54.

"Psychology, Psychiatry and Mental Illness in the Mass Media: A Study of Trends, 1900–1959." *Mental Hygiene,* 45 (January 1961):89–93.

"Regulation of Mental Illness Content in Motion Pictures and Television." With Percy H. Tannenbaum. *Gazette,* 6 (1961):365–85.

"Press Perspectives in World Communications: A Pilot Study." *Journalism Quarterly,* 38 (Summer 1961):313–22.

"Instructional Technology and the Press: A Case Study." Occasional Paper No. 4. Washington, D.C.: National Education Association, Technological Development Project, 1962.

"Mass Media Censorship and the Portrayal of Mental Illness: Some Effects of Industry-Wide Controls in Motion Pictures and Television." With Percy H. Tannenbaum. In *Studies of Innovation and of Communication to the Public,* edited by Wilbur Schramm. Stanford, CA: Stanford University Press, 1962.

"Technology, Communication, and Education: A Social Perspective." In *Tomorrow's Teaching.* Oklahoma City, OK: Frontiers of Science Foundation, 1962.

"How Teachers Can Respond to the Challenge of Video." *Professional Growth for Teachers,* 6 (1962).

"A Theory of Communication and Its Implications for Teaching." In *The Nature of Teaching.* Milwaukee: University of Wisconsin-Milwaukee, School of Education, 1963. Reprinted in *Teaching: Vantage Points for Study,* edited by Ronald T. Hyman. Philadelphia and New York: Lippincott, 1968.

"Smaller Than Life: Teachers and Schools in the Mass Media." *Phi Delta Kappan,* 44 (February 1963):202–5.

"Mass Communication and the 'Humanization' of Homo Sapiens." *AAUW Journal* (March 1963).

"Un Modèle de la Communication." *Etudes de Radio-Television,* 1 (Spring 1963):13–19.

"Teachers vs. the Machine: The Headline Battle of Atlantic City." *Audio-Visual Communication Review,* 11 (May–June 1963):10–18.

"'Mr. Novak'—Young Man to Watch." *Phi Delta Kappan,* 45 (October 1963):13–19.

"A Communication Approach." In *The Content and Pattern for the Professional Training of Audiovisual Communication Specialists,* edited by Robert O. Hall. Washington, D.C.: Educational Media Branch, Office of Education, Department of Health, Education and Welfare, 1964.

"Mass Communications and Popular Conceptions of Education: A Cross-Cultural Study." Cooperative Research Project No. 876. Report of a 10-nation international research project. Washington, D.C.: Office of Education, 1964.

"The Role of Media in Communicating Results of Research." In *Media and Educational Innovation,* edited by W. C. Meierhenry. Lincoln: University of Nebraska Press, 1964.

"Ideological Perspectives and Political Tendencies in News Reporting." *Journalism Quarterly,* 41 (Autumn 1964):495–509.

"Education in Newspaper Advertisements." *School and Society,* 92 (November 28, 1964):363–65.

"Communication and Social Science: A 'Strategic' Approach." *Japanese Annals of Social Psychology,* 6 (1965):161–74.

"An Institutional Approach to Mass Communications Research." In *Communication: Theory and Research,* edited by Lee Thayer. Springfield, IL: Charles C. Thomas, 1966.

"Mass Media and the Crisis in Education." In *Technology and Education.* Syracuse, NY: School of Education, Syracuse University, 1966.

"On Defining Communication: Still Another View." *Journal of Communication,* 103.

"Images Across Cultures: Teachers in Mass Media Fiction and Drama." *School Review,* 74 (Summer 1966):212–29.

"Education About Education by Mass Media." *Educational Forum,* 31 (November 1966):7–15. Also in *Criticism and Mass Communications,* edited by Ralph A. Smith. Urbana: University of Illinois Press, 1966.

"Mass Media and Human Communication Theory." In *Human Communication Theory,* edited by Frank E. X. Dance. New York: Holt, Rinehart and Winston, 1967. Reprinted in *Sociology of Mass Communications,* edited by Denis McQuail. New York: Penguin Books, 1972.

"Newsmen and Schoolmen: The State and Problems of Education Reporting." *Journalism Quarterly,* 44 (Summer 1967):211–24.

"The Press and the Dialogue in Education: A Case Study of a National Educational Convention and Its Depiction in America's Daily Newspapers." *Journalism Monographs,* 5 (1967).

"Communication." *The Encyclopedia Americana,* 1968.

"McLuhan, Herbert Marshall." *The Encyclopedia Americana,* 1968.

"Bibliography of Studies on the Representation of Education and Educators in the Mass Media." *Audio-Visual Communication Review,* 16 (Summer 1968):210–17.

"Dimensions of Violence in Television Drama." Chapter 15 in *Violence and the Media.* Staff report to the National Commission on the Causes and Prevention of Violence, edited by Robert K. Baker and Sandra J. Ball. Washington, D.C.: Government Printing Office, 1969.

"Institutional Pressures Upon Mass Communicators." In *The Sociology of Mass Media Communicators,* edited by Paul Halmos, pp. 205–48. Sociological Review Monograph No. 13. University of Keele, England, 1969.

"Toward 'Cultural Indicators': The Analysis of Mass Mediated Message Systems." *Audio-Visual Communication Review,* 17 (Summer 1969):137–48. Also Chapter 5 in *The Analysis of Communications Content,* edited by George Gerbner, Ole R. Holsti, Klaus Krippendorff, William J. Paisley, and Phillip Stone. New York: Wiley, 1969.

"Pouvoir Institutionnalisé et Systèmes de Messages." *Communications* (Paris), 14 (1969):116–28.

"The Film Hero: A Cross-Cultural Study." *Journalism Monographs,* No. 13 (1969).

"La Politica Culturale e lo Studio delle Communicaziona de Massa." In *Politica Culturale? Studi, Materiali, Ipotesi,* edited by Giovanni Bechelloni. Bologna: Guaraldi, 1970.

"Cultural Indicators: The Case of Violence in Television Drama." *Annals of the American Academy of Political and Social Science,* 388 (March 1970):69–81.

"The Structure and Process of Television Program Content Regulation in the U.S." In *Television and Social Behavior 1: Content and Control,* edited by G. A. Comstock and E. A. Rubinstein. Washington, D.C.: Government Printing Office, 1972.

"Violence in Television Drama: Trends and Symbolic Functions." In *Television and Social Behavior 1: Content and Control,* edited by G. A. Comstock and E. A. Rubinstein. Washington, D.C.: Government Printing Office, 1972.

"The Violence Profile: Some Indicators of Trends in and the Symbolic Structure of Network Television Drama 1967–1971." In *Surgeon General's Report by the Scientific Advisory Committee on Television and Social Behavior, Appendix A* (Hearings before the

Subcommittee on Communications of the Committee on Commerce, U.S. Senate, Serial No. 92–52), pp. 453–526. Washington, D.C. Government Printing Office, 1972.
"Communication and Social Environment." *Scientific American* (September 1972): 153–60. Reprinted in *Communication: A Scientific American Book.* San Francisco: W. H. Freeman, 1972.
"Apples, Oranges, and the Kitchen Sink: An Analysis and Guide to the Comparison of Violence Ratings." With Michael F. Eleey and Nancy Signorielli [Tedesco]. *Journal of Broadcasting,* 17 (Winter 1972–73):21–35.
"Cultural Indicators: The Third Voice." In *Communication Technology and Social Policy,* edited by George Gerbner, Larry P. Gross, and William H. Melody. New York: Wiley, 1973.
"Violence Profile No. 5: Trends in Network Television Drama and Viewer Conceptions of Social Reality." With Larry P. Gross, and with assistance of Michael R. Eleey and Nancy Signorielli [Tedesco]. Philadelphia: Annenberg School of Communications, University of Pennsylvania, June 1973.
"Teacher Image and the Hidden Curriculum." *American Scholar,* (Winter 1973). Also in *Communication Technology and Social Policy,* edited by George Gerbner, Larry P. Gross, and William H. Melody. New York: Wiley, 1973.
"The New Media Environment." In *New Perspectives in Communication.* Boston: Boston University, School of Public Communication, 1974.
"Statement of Violence Profile." Hearings before the Subcommittee on Communications of the Committee of Commerce, U.S. Senate, Serial No. 93-76, pp. 56–105. Washington, D.C.: Government Printing Office, 1974.
"Teacher Image in Mass Culture: Symbolic Functions of the 'Hidden Curriculum.'" In *Media and Symbols: The Forms of Expression, Communication, and Education,* edited by David R. Olson. Chicago: University of Chicago Press, 1974.
"Communication: Society Is the Message." *Communication,* 1 (June 1974):57–64.
"Symbolic Functions of 'Drug Abuse': A Mass Communication Approach." *Studies in the Anthropology of Visual Communication,* 1:1 (Fall 1974).
"Violence Profile No. 6: Trends in Network Television Drama and Viewer Conceptions of Social Reality." With Larry P. Gross, and with assistance of Michael F. Eleey, Nancy Signorielli [Tedesco], and Suzanne Fox. Philadelphia: Annenberg School of Communications, University of Pennsylvania, December 1974.
"Scenario for Violence." *Human Behavior* (1975). Reprinted in *American Mass Media: Industry and Issues,* edited by Robert Atwin, Barry Orton, and William Vesterman. New York: Random House, 1978.
"Violence Trends in Television." With Larry Gross. *Journal of the Producers Guild of America* (March 1975).
"The World of Television: Towards Cultural Indicators." With Larry Gross. *Intermedia,* 3:3 (December 1975).
"The Scary World of TV's Heavy Viewer." With Larry Gross. *Psychology Today* (April 1976). Reprinted in *Mirror of American Life,* edited by David Manning White and John Pendleton. Del Mar, CA: Publications, 1977; and in *Writing the Research Paper,* edited by M. Cummins and C. Slade, forthcoming.
"Violence Profile No. 7: Trends in Network Television Drama and Viewer Conceptions of Social Reality, 1967–1975." With Larry Gross, Michael F. Eleey, Suzanne Fox, Marilyn

Jackson-Beeck, and Nancy Signorielli. Philadelphia: Annenberg School of Communications, University of Pennsylvania, April 1976.

"Living with Television: The Violence Profile." With Larry Gross. *Journal of Communication* (Spring 1976). Reprinted in *Television: The Critical View,* edited by Horace Newcomb. 2nd ed. New York: Oxford University Press, 1979.

"IAMCR Assembly." *Intermedia* (October 1976).

"The Family Hour and Beyond." *Human Behavior* (November 1976).

"Television Violence: Measuring the Climate of Fear." *Impact, American Medical News* (December 13, 1976).

"Comparative Cultural Indicators." Chapter 18 in *Mass Media Policies in Changing Cultures,* New York: Wiley Interscience, 1977.

"Institutional Forces and the Mass Media." In *The Social Uses of Mass Communication,* edited by Mary B. Cassata and Molefi K. Asante. Buffalo: State University of New York at Buffalo, Department of Communication, Communication Research Center, 1977.

"Popular Culture: Who Pays?" *Popular Culture* ("Courses by Newspaper," University of California, San Diego, distributed by United Press International). Del Mar, CA: Publishers, 1977.

"The Real Threat of Television Violence." In *TV Book: The Ultimate Television Book,* edited by Judy Fireman. New York: Workman, 1977.

"Violence Profile No. 8: Trends in Network Television Drama and Viewer Conceptions of Social Reality, 1967–1976." Testimony and Report printed in *Sex and Violence on TV,* Hearing before the Subcommittee on Communications of the Committee on Interstate and Foreign Commerce, House of Representatives, Serial No. 95-103. Washington, D.C.: Government Printing Office, 1977.

"TV Violence Profile No. 8: The Highlights." With Larry Gross, Marilyn Jackson-Beeck, Suzanne Jeffries-Fox, and Nancy Signorielli. *Journal of Communication* (Spring 1977).

"Television: The New State Religion?" *Et cetera* (June 1977). Reprinted in *Philosophy, Technology, and Human Affairs,* edited by Larry Hickman. College Station, TX: Ibis Press, 1985.

"'The Gerbner Violence Profile'—An Analysis of the CBS Report," and "'One More Time': An Analysis of the CBS 'Final Comments on the Violence Profile.'" With Larry Gross, Marilyn Jackson-Beeck, Suzanne Jeffries-Fox, and Nancy Signorielli. *Journal of Broadcasting* (Summer 1977).

"Controller of Our Fears." In a symposium on "The War Against Television Violence." *Business and Society Review* (Fall 1977).

"Proliferating Violence." *Society* (September–October 1977).

"The Many Worlds of the World's Press." With George Marvanyi. *Journal of Communication* (Winter 1977). Reprinted in *Crisis in International News: Policies and Prospects,* edited by Jim Richstad and Michael H. Anderson. New York: Columbia University Press, 1981.

"Fernsehen und Familie." With Suzanne Jeffries-Fox. *Fernsehen und Bildung,* 11 (1977):-222–34.

"Deviance and Power: Symbolic Functions of 'Drug Abuse.'" In *Deviance and Mass Media,* edited by Charles Winick. Beverly Hills, CA: Sage, 1978.

"The Dynamics of Cultural Resistance." Chapter 1 in *Hearth and Home: Images of Women in Mass Media,* edited by Gaye Tuchman, Arlene Kaplan Daniels, and James Benet. New York: Oxford University Press, 1978.

"Television's Influence on Values and Behavior." *Weekly Psychiatry Update Series,* Lesson 24, Vol. 2. New York: Biomedia, 1978.

"Women in Public Broadcasting: A Progress Report." With Nancy Signorielli. Philadelphia: Institute for Applied Communication Sciences, Annenberg School of Communications, University of Pennsylvania, 1978.

"The World of Television News." With Nancy Signorielli. In *Television News Archives: A Guide to Research,* edited by W. Adams and F. Schreibman. Washington, D.C.: George Washington University Press, 1978.

"Violence Profile No. 9: Trends in Network Television Drama and Viewer Conceptions of Social Reality 1967–1977." With Larry Gross, Marilyn Jackson-Beeck, Suzanne Jeffries-Fox, and Nancy Signorielli. Philadelphia: Annenberg School of Communications, University of Pennsylvania, March 1978.

"Television as New Religion." With Kathleen Connolly. *New Catholic World* (March–April 1978).

"Cultural Indicators: Violence Profile No. 9." With Larry Gross, Marilyn Jackson-Beeck, Suzanne Jeffries-Fox, and Nancy Signorielli. *Journal of Communication* (Summer 1978).

"The Image of the Elderly in Prime-Time Television Drama." With Nancy Signorielli. *Generations* (Fall 1978):10–11.

"Über die Angstlichkeit von Vielsehern" (About the Anxiousness of Heavy Viewers). *Fernsehen und Bildung,* 12:1–2 (1978).

"The Role of Media in Citizen Perception of Crime." In *Crime and People: Fears and Realities.* Forum proceedings. Baltimore: Maryland Conference of Social Concern, 1979.

"On Wober's 'Televised Violence and Paranoid Perception: The View from Great Britain.'" With Larry Gross, Michael Morgan, and Nancy Signorielli. *Public Opinion Quarterly* (Spring 1979).

"Violence Profile No. 10: Trends in Network Television Drama and Viewer Conceptions of Social Reality 1967–1978." With Larry Gross, Nancy Signorielli, Michael Morgan, and Marilyn Jackson-Beeck. Philadelphia: Annenberg School of Communications, University of Pennsylvania, March 1979.

"Editorial Response: A Reply to Newcomb's Humanistic Critique." With Larry Gross. *Communication Research* (April 1979):223–29.

"The Demonstration of Power: Violence Profile No. 10." With Larry Gross, Nancy Signorielli, Michael Morgan, and Marilyn Jackson-Beeck. *Journal of Communication* (Summer 1979). Reprinted in *Mass Communication Review Yearbook I.* Beverly Hills, CA: Sage, 1980.

"Women and Minorities in Television Drama 1969–1978." With Nancy Signorielli. Philadelphia: Annenberg School of Communications, University of Pennsylvania, October 29, 1979.

"Children and Power on Television: The Other Side of the Picture." In *Child Abuse: An Agenda for Action,* edited by George Gerbner, Catherine J. Ross, and Edward Zigler. New York: Oxford University Press, 1980.

"Electronic Children: Will the New Generation Be Different?" In *Democracy—Technology. . . Collision!* edited by Al Klose. Indianapolis: Bobbs-Merrill, 1980.

"Stigma: Social Functions of the Portrayal of Mental Illness in the Mass Media." In *Attitudes Toward the Mentally Ill: Research Perspectives,* edited by J. Rabkin, L. Gelb, and J. B. Lazar. Washington, D.C.: Government Printing Office, 1980.

"The Violent Face of Television and Its Lessons." With Larry Gross. In *Children and the Faces of Television: Teaching, Violence Selling,* edited by Edward L. Palmer and Aimee Dorr. New York: Academic Press, 1980.

"Aging with Television: Images on Television Drama and Conceptions of Social Reality." With Larry Gross, Nancy Signorielli, and Michael Morgan. *Journal of Communication* (Winter 1980).

"Death in Prime Time: Notes on the Symbolic Functions of Dying in the Mass Media." *Annals of the American Academy of Political and Social Science,* 447 (January 1980).

"Sex on Television and What Viewers Learn from It." Prepared for the National Association of Television Program Executives Annual Conference, San Francisco, California, February 19, 1980.

"Interpreting the TV World," *Irish Broadcasting Review* (Spring 1980).

"Trial by Television: Are We at the Point of No Return?" *Judicature* (April 1980). Winner of the Media Award of the Philadelphia Bar Association, 1981. Reprinted in *National Shorthand Reporter* (June 1980). Also published in two parts in a somewhat different version in *Louisville Law Examiner,* the "Brandeis Brief" series of "Emerging Legal Issues" (Louisville: University of Kentucky), March 6, and April 14, 1980.

"Violence Profile No. 11: Trends in Network Television Drama and Viewer Conceptions of Social Reality 1967–1979." With Larry Gross, Michael Morgan, and Nancy Signorielli. Philadelphia: Annenberg School of Communications, University of Pennsylvania, April 1980.

"Media and the Family: Images and Impact." With Larry Gross, Michael Morgan, and Nancy Signorielli. For the National Research Forum on Family Issues, sponsored by the White House Conference on Families, Washington, D.C., April 11, 1980.

"Media Portrayal of the Elderly," Statement in *Hearing Before the Select Committee on Aging,* House of Representatives, Los Angeles, California, April 26, 1980. Washington, D.C.: Government Printing Office, Comm. Pub. No. 96-231.

"Television Violence, Victimization and Power." With Larry Gross, Michael Morgan, and Nancy Signorielli. *American Behavioral Scientist* (May 1980).

"The 'Mainstreaming' of America: Violence Profile No. 11." With Larry Gross, Michael Morgan, and Nancy Signorielli. *Journal of Communication* (Summer 1980). Reprinted in *Mass Communication Review Yearbook II.* Beverly Hills, CA: Sage, April 1981.

"Television's Contributions to Public Understanding of Science: A Pilot Project." With Larry Gross, Michael Morgan, and Nancy Signorielli. Report to the National Science Foundation. Philadelphia: Annenberg School of Communications, University of Pennsylvania, October 1980.

"TV: The New Religion Controlling Us." *Long Island Newsday,* November 9, 1980. Also published as "TV as the New Religion," in *The Miami Herald,* November 30, 1980, and *Free Press* (London, Ontario, Canada) (November 1980).

"Education for the Age of Television." In *Education for the Television Age,* edited by Milton E. Ploghoft and James A. Anderson. Athens: Cooperative Center for Social Science Education, College of Education, Ohio University, 1981.

"A Curious Journey into the Scary World of Paul Hirsch." With Larry Gross, Michael Morgan, and Nancy Signorielli. *Communication Research* (January 1981):39–72.

"Television: The American Schoolchild's National Curriculum Day In and Day Out." *PTA Today* (April 1981).

"Scientists on the TV Screen." With Larry Gross, Michael Morgan, and Nancy Signorelli. *Society* (May/June 1981).
"Aging with Television Commercials: Images on Television Commercials and Dramatic Programming, 1977–1979." With Larry Gross, Michael Morgan, and Nancy Signorielli. Philadelphia: Annenberg School of Communications, University of Pennsylvania, June 1981.
"Final Reply to Paul Hirsch." With Larry Gross, Michael Morgan, and Nancy Signorielli. *Communication Research,* (July 1981).
"Television as Religion," *Media & Values* (Fall 1981):1–3.
"Health and Medicine on Television," With Larry Gross, Michael Morgan, and Nancy Signorielli. *New England Journal of Medicine* (October 8, 1981).
"Programming Health Portrayals: What Viewers See, Say and Do." With Michael Morgan and Nancy Signorielli. In *Television and Behavior: Ten Years of Scientific Progress and Implications for the 80's,* edited by David Pearl, Lorraine Bouthilet, and Joyce Lazar. Publication No. (ADM) 82-1196. Washington, D.C.: U.S. Department of Health and Human Resources, 1982.
"Television in the Courtroom." In *Americana Annual/Encyclopedia Year Book.* Danbury, CT: Grolier, 1982.
"TV Professions." With Michael Morgan. In *TV and Teens: Experts Look at the Issues,* edited by Meg Schwartz. Reading, MA: Action for Children's Television, Addison-Wesley, 1982.
"TV's Changing Our Lives." *Presbyterian Survey* (January 1982):11–13.
"Charting the Mainstream: Television's Contributions to Political Orientations." With Larry Gross, Michael Morgan, and Nancy Signorielli. *Journal of Communication* (Spring 1982):100–126.
"The Gospel of Instant Gratification." *Business and Society Review* (Spring 1982). A symposium on advertising.
"What Television Teaches About Doctors and Health." With Larry Gross, Michael Morgan, and Nancy Signorielli. *Mobius: A Journal for Continuing Education Professionals in Health Sciences* (April 1982).
"The World According to Television." With Nancy Signorielli. *American Demographics* (October 1982).
"The American Press Coverage of the Fourth Extraordinary Session of the UNESCO General Conference, Paris, 1982." Study conducted under contract with UNESCO. Philadelphia: Annenberg School of Communications, University of Pennsylvania, August 1983.
"The Importance of Being Critical—in One's Own Fashion." *Journal of Communication* (Summer 1983).
"Political Functions of Television Viewing: A Cultivation Analysis." In *Cultural Indicators: An International Symposium,* edited by Gabriele Melischek, Karl Erik Rosengren, and James Stappers. Vienna: Österreichischen Akademie der Wissenschaften, 1984.
"Liberal Education in the Information Age." *Current Issues in Higher Education,* 1983–84.
"Political Correlates of Television Viewing." With Larry Gross, Michael Morgan, and Nancy Signorielli. *Public Opinion Quarterly* (Spring 1984).
"Health, Medicine, and Violence on TV." *Transactions and Studies of the College of Physicians* (Philadelphia) (March 1984).
"Religion on Television." With Harry E. Cotugno, Larry Gross, Stewart Hoover, Michael Morgan, Nancy Signorielli, and Robert Wuthnow. A Research Report by the Annenberg

School of Communications, University of Pennsylvania, and the Gallup Organization, Inc. (April 1984).

"Defining the Field of Communication." *ACA Bulletin* (April 1984).

"The Impact of the 'Electronic Church' on the Local Church." With Larry Gross, Michael Morgan, and Nancy Signorielli. *Ministries* (Fall 1984):58–61.

"Gratuitous Violence and Exploitive Sex: What Are the Lessons? (Including Violence Profile No. 13)." Statement prepared for a hearing of the Study Committee of the Communications Commission of the National Council of Churches, New York, September 21, 1984.

"Defending the Indefensible." With Steven H. Chaffee, Beatrix A. Hamburg, Chester M. Pierce, Eli A Rubinstein, Alberta E. Siegel, and Jerome L. Singer. *Society* (September–October 1984).

"Facts, Fantasies and Schools." With Larry Gross, Michael Morgan, and Nancy Signorielli *Society* (September–October 1984).

"The Mainstreaming of America: Television Makes Strange Bedfellows." *TV Guide* (October 20, 1984):20–23.

"Le Colonialisme de la Télévision: Les Fonctions Symboliques de la Violence." In *TViolence: Actes du Colloque.* Montreal: Association Nationale des Téléspectateurs, 1985.

"Mass Media Discourse: Message System Analysis as a Component of Cultural Indicators." In *Discourse and Communication,* edited by Teun A. van Dijk. Berlin: Walter de Guyter, 1985.

"Television Entertainment and Viewers' Conceptions of Science." With Larry Gross, Michael Morgan, and Nancy Signorielli. A Research Report to the National Science Foundation. Philadelphia: Annenberg School of Communications, University of Pennsylvania, July 1985.

"Dreams That Hurt: Mental Illness in the Mass Media." First Rosalynn Carter Symposium on Mental Health Policy, Emory University, School of Medicine, Atlanta, Georgia, November 15, 1985.

"Children's Television: A National Disgrace." *Pediatric Annals* (December 1985):822–27. Reprinted in *The Reference Shelf: Representative American Speeches, 1985–1986,* edited by Owen Peterson, pp. 142–48. New York: H. W. Wilson, 1986.

"Living with Television: The Dynamics of the Cultivation Process." With Larry Gross, Michael Morgan, and Nancy Signorielli. In *Perspectives on Media Effects,* edited by Jennings Bryant and Dolf Zillman. Hillsdale, NJ: Lawrence Erlbaum Associates, 1986. Reprinted in *Social Psychology Readings: A Century of Research,* edited by Amy G. Halberstadt and Steve L. Ellyson. New York: McGraw-Hill, 1990.

"The Symbolic Context of Action and Communication." In *Contextualism and Understanding in Behavioral Science,* edited by Ralph L. Rosnow and Marianthi Georgoudi. New York: Praeger, 1986.

"Television's Mean World: Violence Profile No. 14–15." With Larry Gross, Michael Morgan, and Nancy Signorielli. Philadelphia: Annenberg School of Communications, University of Pennsylvania, September 1986.

"Televised Trials—Historic Juncture for Our Courts?" Introduction to *News Cameras in the Courtroom,* edited by Susanna Barber. Norwood, NJ: Ablex, 1987.

"Science on Television: How It Affects Public Conceptions." *Issues in Science and Technology* (Spring 1987):109–15.

"Television's Populist Brew: The Three Bs." *Et cetera,* 1:44 (Spring 1987):3–7.

"The Electronic Church in American Culture." *New Catholic World* (May–June 1987):133–35.

"Ministry of Culture, the USA, and the Free Marketplace of Ideas." *National Forum* (Fall 1987).

"Telling Stories in the Information Age." In *Information and Behavior,* edited by Brent D. Rubin. New Brunswick, NJ:Transaction Books, 1988.

"Symbolic Functions of Violence and Terror." *The Terrorism and the News Media Research Project.* Boston: Mass Communication and Society Division, AEJMC, Emerson College, July 1988.

"Television's Cultural Mainstream: Which Way Does It Run?" *Directions in Psychiatry,* 8:9 (Summer 1988).

"Violence and Terror in the Mass Media." Paris: UNESCO, *Reports and Papers in Mass Communication,* No. 102 (1988).

"Cross-Cultural Communications Research in the Age of Telecommunications." In *Continuity and Change in Communications in Post-Industrial Society. Volume 2 in The World Community in Post-Industrial Society,* edited by the Christian Academy. Seoul: Wooseok, 1989.

"Media Coverage of the Declaration." In *Aspects of the Mass Media Declaration of Unesco,* edited by Hamid Mowlana. International Association for Mass Communication Research Occasional Papers No. 9. Budapest: Hungarian Institute for Public Opinion Research, 1989.

"Waiting for Prime Time: The Outlook for Women in TV News." *New Choices,* 29:3 (March 1989).

"Communications, Study of." With Wilbur Schramm. *International Encyclopedia of Communications.* New York: Oxford University Press, February 1989. Reprinted as "The International Development of Communication Studies." *Communicatio,* 16:1 (1990).

"Epilogue: Advancing on the Path of Righteousness (Maybe)." In *Cultivation Analysis: New Directions in Media Effects Research,* edited by Nancy Signorielli and Michael Morgan. Newbury Park, CA: Sage, 1990.

"Stories That Hurt: Tobacco, Alcohol, and Other Drugs in the Mass Media." In *Youth and Drugs: Society's Mixed Messages.* OSAP Prevention Monograph No. 6. Washington, D.C.: U.S. Department of Health and Human Services, 1990.

"Violence Profile 1967 Through 1988–89: Enduring Patterns." With Nancy Signorielli. Philadelphia: Annenberg School of Communications, University of Pennsylvania, January 1990.

"A New Environmental Movement in Communication and Culture." *Media Development* (April 1990).

"The Crack in the Tobacco Curtain, or the Bill of Rights Disinformation Campaign." In *Free Speech* (Speech Communications Association). (Spring 1990).

"Füehrt Kanalfüelle zu mehr Programmvielfalt?" (Does Channel Proliferation Promote Program Diversity?) *Media Perspectiven* (Frankfurt a.M.) (January 1991).

"Violence in the Mass Media." In *Dictionnaire Critique de la Communication,* edited by Lucien Sfez and Francis Balle. Paris: forthcoming.

"Unesco in the U.S. Press." In *The Global Media Debate; Its Rise, Fall, and Renewal.* Edited by George Gerbner, Hamid Mowlana, and Kaarle Nordenstreng. New York: Ablex, forthcoming.

"The Image of Russians on American Media and 'The New Epoch.'" In *Beyond the Cold War; Soviet and American Media Images.* Edited by George Gerbner, Everette E. Dennis, and Yassen N. Zassoursky. Newbury Park, CA: Sage, 1991.

"Violence and Terror in and by the Media." In *Media Crisis and Democracy,* edited by Marc Raboy and Bernard Dagenais. London: Sage, 1992.

"Persian Gulf War: The Movie." In *Triumph of the Image: The Media's War in the Persian Gulf. An International Perspective.* Edited by George Gerbner, Hamid Mowlana, and Herbert Schiller. Boulder, CO: Westview Press, 1993. A previous short version was delivered as the first Wayne A. Danielson Award for Distinguished Achievement in Communication Scholarship Lecture at the University of Texas, Austin, and published in *Representative American Speeches.* H. W. Wilson, 1992.

"The Politics of Media Violence: Some Reflections." In *Mass Communication Research: On Problems and Policies,* edited by Cees Hamelink and Olga Linne. Norwood, NJ: Ablex, 1994.

"Television Violence: The Art of Asking the Wrong Question." *The World and I* (July 1994):385–97.

"The Risk of Playing to the Cameras." *Legal Times* (July 25, 1994): 21, 23.

"Cultural Indicators and Public Policy." In *Television: Signification and Interpretation,* edited by Chad Gordon and Kenneth H. Tucker, Jr., forthcoming.

"Growing up with Television: The Cultivation Perspective." With Larry Gross, Michael Morgan, and Nancy Signorielli. In *Media Effects: Advances in Theory and Research,* edited by Jennings Bryant and Dolf Zillmann. Hillsdale, NJ: Lawrence Erlbaum Associates, forthcoming.

"Instant History/Image History: Lessons from the Persian Gulf War." In *Images in Language, Media and Mind,* edited by Roy F. Fox. National Council of Teachers of English, forthcoming.

"Learning Productive Aging as a Social Role: The Lessons of Television." In *Achieving a Productive Aging Society,* edited by Scott A. Bass, Francis G. Caro, and Yung-Ping Chen. Westport, CT: Greenwood, forthcoming.

"'Miracles' of Communication Technology: Powerful Audiences, Diverse Choices and Other Fairy Tales." Norwood, NJ: Ablex, forthcoming.

Herbert I. Schiller

Books

Mass Communications and American Empire. New York: Augustus M. Kelley, 1969. 170 pp. Paperback ed., Beacon Press, 1971; Swedish ed., 1977; Portuguese and Spanish eds., 1976; new ed., Westview, 1993.

Superstate: Readings in the Military-Industrial Complex. Urbana: University of Illinois Press, 1970. 353. Paperback ed., 1972.

The Mind Managers. Boston: Beacon Press, 1973. 214 pp. Paperback ed., 1974; Spanish ed. 1974, 1979; Polish ed. 1976; German ed. 1976; Swedish ed. 1977; Hungarian ed., 1977; Japanese ed. 1979;

Communications and Cultural Domination. New York: International Arts and Sciences Press, 1976. 127 pp. Paperback ed., M. E. Sharpe, 1977; Portuguese ed., 1979; Russian ed., 1980; Korean ed., 1983; New ed., M. E. Sharpe, 1984; Persian ed., forthcoming.

National Sovereignty and International Communications. Edited with K. Nordenstreng. Norwood, NJ: Ablex, 1979. 286 pp.

Who Knows: Information in the Age of the Fortune 500. Norwood, NJ: Ablex, 1981. 187 pp. Paperback ed. 1982; Spanish ed., 1983; German ed. 1983. Chapter entitled "The

Privatization of Information" reprinted in *Mass Communication Review Yearbook,* Vol. 4, edited by E. Wartella and D. Charles Whitney, pp. 537–68. Beverly Hills, CA: Sage, 1983.

Information and the Crisis Economy. Norwood, NJ: Ablex, 1984. 133 pp. Paperback ed., Oxford University Press, 1986; Spanish ed., Madrid: Fundesco, 1986.

Hope and Folly: The U.S. and UNESCO, 1949–1985. With Edward Herman and William Preston. Minneapolis: University of Minnesota Press, 1989.

Culture Inc.: The Corporate Enclosure of American Public Expression. New York: Oxford University Press, 1989. Paperback ed., Oxford University Press, 1991.

Other Publications

"Some Effects of the Cold War on United States Foreign Trade." *Review of Economics and Statistics* (November 1955):428–30.

"Economic Factors in Anti-Americanism in Great Britain Since World War II." *Social Science* (January 1956):36–42.

"The Adequacy of Raw Materials." *Illinois Business Review,* 18:8 (September 1961).

"The United States and the Educational Needs of the Developing Economies." *Quarterly Review of Economics and Business,* 2:1 (February 1962):31–38.

"The First Kennedy Budget." *Illinois Business Review,* 19:3 (March 1962).

"The American Right-Wing and the United Nations." *Les Cahiers de la République,* No. 44 (May 1962).

"Review of *American Capital and Canadian Resources.*" *Quarterly Review of Economics and Business,* 2 (May 1962).

"Access to Raw Materials." *Bulletin of the Atomic Scientists* (October 1962):16–19.

"A Natural Resources Policy?" *Illinois Business Review* (October 1963).

"An Inward Look at Foreign Aid." *Challenge* (July 1964):7–10. Reprinted in *Current* (November 1964), and *Front Lines,* U.S. A.I.D.

"The Natural Resources Base—Where Do We Stand?" *World Politics* (July 1964).

"International Resource Relationships in a Changing World." *Social Research* (Autumn 1964):280–95.

"Current Problems in Raw Materials Supply." *Land Economics* (November 1964):361–69.

"The Sovereign State of Comsat." *The Nation* (January 25, 1965).

"Review of *Culture Against Man,* by Jules Henry." *Audio-Visual Communication Review* (Spring 1965):75–77.

"Review of *Mass Media and National Development,* by Wilbur Schramm."*Audio-Visual Communication Review,* 13:2 (Summer 1965):205–7.

"America Rules the Air Waves." *Progressive,* 30:3 (March 1966): 26–29.

"The Dirty Business of School Magazines." *Focus/Midwest,* 55:7–8 (March 1966):10–13.

"Communications and the Third World." *Illinois Political,* 1:1 (April 1966).

"Communications for the Status Quo." *Focus/Midwest* (May 1966).

"Review of *Studies in a Dying Colonialism,* by Frantz Fanon." *Audio-Visual Communication Review* (Summer 1966).

"New of Last Chance in Space Communications." *Illinois Business Review* (December 1966).

"Introduction" to chapter in *As We Saw the Thirties,* edited by Rita J. Simon, pp. 216–18. Urbana: University of Illinois Press, 1967.

"The Slide to International Violence in the Hungering World." *Bulletin of the Atomic Scientists* (January 1967):4–6.

"National Development Requires Some Social Distance." *Antioch Review* (Spring 1967): 63–75.

"Review of *World Television.*" *Audio-Visual Communication Review* (Spring 1967):122–24.

"Communications Satellites: A New Institutional Setting." *Bulletin of the Atomic Scientists* (April 1967):4–8. Reprinted in *Communication Satellites in Political Orbit,* edited by Lloyd D. Musolf, pp. 151–95. San Francisco: Chandler, 1968.

"The Increasing Military Influence in the Governmental Sector of Communications in the United States." *Administrative Law Review,* 19:3 (May 1967):303–18.

"Comment." *Bulletin of the Atomic Scientists* (June 1967):63–64.

"Economics." In *Good Reading,* edited by J. Sherwood Weber. New York: New American Library, 1968.

"Social Control and Individual Freedom." *Bulletin of the Atomic Scientists* (May 1968):16–21.

"Review of *The First Freedom,* by Bryce W. Rucker." *The Nation* (June 24, 1968):835–36.

"Review of *Radio Television: Broadcasting on the European Continent.*" *Audio-Visual Communication Review* (Fall 1968):326–29.

"The Use of American Power in the Post-Colonial World." *Massachusetts Review* (Autumn 1968):631–50.

Program review of "The National Conventions." *Educational Broadcasting Review* (December 1968).

"International Communications, National Sovereignty and Domestic Insurgency." In *Mass Media and International Understanding,* edited by School of Sociology, Political Science and Journalism, pp. 92–100. Ljubljana: Department of Journalism, School of Sociology, Political Science and Journalism, 1969.

"The Mass Media and the Public Interest." In *Television Today: The End of Communications and the Death of Community,* pp. 53–69. Washington, D.C.: Institute for Policy Studies, 1969.

"Public Education Under Siege." *The Progressive* (May 1969).

"Television Comes to Israel." *Educational Broadcasting Review,* 3:4 (August 1969):45–52.

"Review of *The Information Machines,* by Ben H. Bagdikian." *Audio-Visual Communication Review* (Autumn 1969):331–33.

"Review of *Western Economic Warfare 1947–1967: A Case Study of Foreign Policy,* by Gunnar Adler-Carlson." *Bulletin of the Atomic Scientists* (October 1969):44–46.

"Who Owns the Air." *Comment, the Center Magazine,* 3:3 (May 1970):90–91.

"Mind Management: Mass Media in the Advanced Industrial State." *Quarterly Review of Economics and Business* (Spring 1971):39–52. Reprinted in *Mass Media and Society,* by Alan Wells. Palo Alto, CA: National Press, 1972.

"Review of *The Adversaries: Politics and the Press,* by William Rivers." *Science and Society* (Spring 1971):115–17.

"Review of *The Press and the Cold War,* by James Aronson." *Journalism Quarterly* (Spring 1971):139–41.

"Madison Avenue Imperialism." *Transaction-Society* (March–April 1971):52–58. Reprinted in *Communications in International Politics,* edited by Richard L. Merritt, Urbana: University of Illinois Press, 1972; *Sociological Realities,* by I. L. Horowitz and C. Nanry, New York: Harper & Row, 1975.

"Review of *The Pentagon Propaganda Machine,* by William Fulbright." *Bulletin of the Atomic Scientists* (April 1971):43–44.

"Review of *The Age of Imperialism*, by Harry Magdoff." *Journal of Economic History* (June 1971):507–10.

Guest editorial on *War and Peace and the American University. College and University Business* (August 1971):28–29.

"Review of *Communications and National Integration in Communist China*, by Alan P.L. Liu." *Quarterly Review of Economics and Business* (Autumn 1971):93–95.

"Chile: An End to Cultural Colonialism." *Transaction-Society* (March 1972):35–39.

"Review of *Television, the Business Behind the Box*, by Les Brown." *Journalism Quarterly* (Spring 1972):189–90.

"The Polling Industry: The Measurement and Manufacture of Opinion." *Psychology Today* (July 1972).

"Feedback 4: Broadcast Journalism." *Performance*, No. 3 (July–August 1972):57–70.

"Review of *The Public Persuader*." *Journal of Economic Issues* (September 1972):156–58.

"Review of *Picture Tube Imperialism?* by Alan Wells." *Journalism Quarterly* (Winter 1972–73).

"Review of *The Universal Eye*, by Timothy Green." *Journalism Quarterly* (Winter 1972–73).

"Authentic National Development Versus the Free Flow of Information." In *Communication Technology and Social Policy*, edited by George Gerbner, Larry Gross, and William Melody. New York: Wiley Interscience, 1973.

"The Electronic Invaders." *The Progressive* (August 1973). Reprinted as "Satellite Broadcasting and Cultural Imperialism," *Washington Star*, July 29, 1973.

"Review of *The Politics and Technology of Satellite Communications*." *Journalism Quarterly* (Summer 1973).

"Statement." In *Television Traffic—A One-Way Street?* pp. 49–50. Reports and Papers on Mass Communication No. 70. Paris: UNESCO, 1974.

"The Mechanics of International Cultural Domination." *Le Monde Diplomatique* (December 1974).

"Don't Answer That Questionnaire." *Kontext* (Amsterdam) (May 8, 1974):10–11.

"Review of *The Politics of Communication*, by Claus Mueller." *Journalism Quarterly* (Summer 1974):348–49.

"Waiting for Orders: Mass Communications Research in the United States." *Gazette*, 20:1 (1974):11–21.

"Freedom for the Free Flow of Information." *Journal of Communication*, 24:1 (Winter 1974).

"Genesis of the Free Flow of Information Principle: The Imposition of Communication Domination." *Instant Research on Peace and Violence* (Tampere, Finland), 5:1 (1975): 75–86. Reprinted in French as "Libre Circulation et Domination Mondiale," *Le Monde Diplomatique* (September 1975):18–19; in Russian, in *Soviet Russia*, October 17, 1975; and in *Crisis in International News: Policies and Prospects*, edited by Jim Richstad and Michael Anderson, New York: Columbia University Press, 1981.

"Introduction." Special issue, *Kroniek van Afrika*. Leiden: Afrika-Studien-Centrum, Leiden University, 1975.

"The Material Side of Consciousness." In *Der Anteil der Massenmedien bei der Herausbildung des Bewusstseins in der sich wandelnden Welt*, edited by International Association for Mass Communications Research, pp. 24–30. Leipzig: Karl Marx Universität, 1975. Reprinted in *The Democratic Journalist* (June 1976): *Journal of the Centre for Advanced TV Studies* (London) (1976).

"The Appearance of National-Communications Policies: A New Arena for Social Struggle." *Gazette,* 21:2 (1975):82–94.
"The Balance of Power and the Ecology of Ideas." Society for General Systems Research, Annual AAAS meetings, Denver, Colorado, February 1975.
"Review of *Who Controls the Mass Media.*" *Journal of Communication* (Summer 1975): 206–8.
"Review of *Intelsat: Politics and Functionalism.*" *Journal of Communication* (Winter 1975):213–17.
"Review of *Radio Power,* by Julian Hale." *Journalism Quarterly* (1976).
"Transnational Media and National Development." In *Fair Communication Policy Conference,* edited by Jim Richstad. Honolulu: East-West Center, 1976.
"Fabricated Culture." *Lier en Boog* (Holland), No. 4 (July 1976).
"An Effort to Achieve a Delicate Balance." Reply to comment on "Helsinki: The New Equation." With Kaarle Nordenstreng. *Journal of Communication,* 26:3 (Summer 1976):237–38.
"International Advertising and International Communications." *Instant Research on Peace and Violence,* No. 4 (1976).
"Helsinki: The New Equation (On Free Flow of Information)." With Kaarle Nordenstreng. *Journal of Communication* (Winter 1976).
"Review of *Captains of Consciousness: The Social Roots of Advertising,* by Stuart Ewen." *Journal of Communication,* 26:4 (Autumn 1976):227–28.
"Mind Managing the Food and Energy Crisis." In *The Political Economy of Food and Energy,* edited by Louis Junker. Michigan Business Papers No. 62. Ann Arbor: University of Michigan, 1977.
"Now: A New International Information Order?" *Intellect,* 106:2386 (August 1977):42.
"Who's Managing Your Minds?" Interview with Jack Wintz, O.F.M. *St. Anthony's Messenger* (September 1977):12–17.
"Review of *Mass Media: Systems and Effects,* by W. Phillips Davison and James Boyland." *Contemporary Sociology* (September 1977):548.
"Review of *The Manipulators,* by Robert Sobel." *Science and Society,* 41:3 (Fall 1977):346–49.
"Review of *The Media Are American,* by Jeremy Tunstall." *Journal of Communication,* 27:4 (Autumn 1977):226–29.
"Review of *Media, Politics and Democracy,* by Bernard Rubin, and *Snap, Crackle and Popular Taste,* by Jeffrey Schrank." *The Nation* (October 29, 1977):439–42.
"Review of *Media World: Programming the Public.*" *Journalism Quarterly,* 54:4 (Winter 1977):812–13.
"In Search of a New World Information Order." *Baltimore Sun,* December 4, 1977:K-2.
"New Modes of Cultural Domination." *Conradh na Galilge* (Dublin) (1978).
"U.S. Information Policy After Nairobi." *Le Monde Diplomatique* (March 1978). Longer version in English and Spanish published by ILET (Latin American Institute for Transnational Studies), September 1979.
"'Free' Communications Under the Re-Write." *Los Angeles Times,* Opinion Section, August 20, 1978.
"Computer Communications for Whom and for What?" *Journal of Communication,* 28:4 (Autumn 1978). Longer version in *Computer World* (February 12, 1979).
"Review of *The Politics of Propaganda: The Office of War Propaganda, 1942–1945,* by Allan M. Winkler." *Journalism Quarterly,* 55:3 (Autumn 1978).

"Media and Imperialism." *Revue Française d'Etudes Americaines* (Paris) (October 1978). Reprinted in *Tabloid* (November 1979).
"Decolonization of Information: Steps Toward a New World Information Order." *Latin American Perspectives,* 16 (Winter 1978):35–48.
"Transnational Business, the Free Flow of Information, and the Question of Regulation." In *Telecommunications Policy and the Citizen,* edited by Tim Haight. New York: Praeger, 1979.
"The Transnational Corporation and the International Flow of Information." *Current Research on Peace and Violence* (Tampere) (1979).
"Communication Accompanies Capital Flows." In *International Commission for the Study of Communication Problems, The MacBride Commission.* Paris: UNESCO, May 1979.
"Resistances a la Suprematie Americaine dans le Domaine de l'Information." *Communication et Information,* 3:1.
"Review of *The Sponsor,* by Eric Barnouw." *Journal of Communication,* 29:1 (Winter 1979).
"Free Flow and Regulation." *Follies: A Journal of the Arts and Opinion* (December 1979).
"Electronic Utopias and Structural Realities." In *A Reader on the MacBride Report,* edited by Cees Hamelink. Rome: IDOC, 1980. Reprinted in *Mass Communication Review Yearbook,* Vol. 3. Beverly Hills, CA: Sage, 1982.
"Whose New International Economic and Information Order?" *Communication,* 5:4 (1980):299–314.
"Will Advanced Communication Technology Create a New International Information Order?" *WACC Journal,* 27:4 (1980). Reprinted in *Media Information Australia* (February 1981).
"Communications in the 1980s: A Global Perspective." *Equal Opportunity Forum* (January 1980):18–19.
"Review of *Friendly Fascism,* by Bertram Gross." *Journal of Communication,* 30:4 (Autumn 1980):194–98.
"Transnational Communication and Self-Reliance." *Third World* (Mexico) (November–December 1980):64–66.
"Foreword." In *Dependency Road,* by Dallas W. Smythe. Norwood, NJ: Ablex, 1981.
"The Free Flow Doctrine: Will It Last Into the 21st Century?" In *Communications in the 21st Century,* edited by R. W. Haigh, George Gerbner, and R. B. Byrne. New York: Wiley, 1981.
"The War of Words Heats Up." *In These Times* (March 4–10, 1981).
"Information for What Kind of a Society?" Edward R. Murrow Symposium, Washington State University, April 17, 1981. Reprinted in *Telecommunication Issues,* edited by J. Salvaggio. New York: Longman, 1983; *Current Research on Peace and Violence* (March 1981).
"Perspectives on Communication Research: An Exchange." *Journal of Communication,* 31:3 (Summer 1981):15–23.
"The Privatizing of Information: Who Can Own What America Knows?" With Anita Schiller. *The Nation* (April 17, 1982):461–63. Awarded Gold Pen prize, best magazine article for 1982 on freedom of information, Los Angeles PEN, May 28, 1982.
"Information: America's New Global Empire." *Channels of Communication* (September 1982):30–33. Reprinted in *Global Issues,* annual edition, edited by Robert Jackson, 1985.
"Foreword." In *Cultural Autonomy in Global Communications,* by Cees Hamelink. New York: Longman, 1983.
"The Communication Revolution: Who Benefits." *Media Development,* 30 (1983):18–21.
"New Technologies of Communication." *Chasqui,* No. 6 (January–June 1983):46–53.

"Review of *To Inform or to Control,* by Oswald Ganley and Gladys Ganley." *Journal of Communication,* 33:2 (Spring):182–84.

"The World Crisis and the New Information Technologies." *Columbia Journal of World Business,* 18:1 (Spring 1983).

"Critical Research in the Information Age." *Journal of Communication,* 33:3 (Summer 1983):249–57.

"The Language of Science and Science of Domination." *Enjeu,* No. 40 (October 1983): 39–41.

"Information: America's New Global Empire." *Transnational Data Report,* 6:7 (October–November 1983):360–61.

"Corrientes de Informacion Electronica y el Creciente Ataque a la Soberania Nacional." In *Video, Cultural Nacional y Subdesarrollo,* pp. 125–37. Havana, 1984.

"Informatics and Information Flows: The Underpinnings of Transnational Capitalism." In *Critical Communication Review,* Vol. 2, edited by Vincent Mosco and Janet Wasko. Norwood, NJ: Ablex, 1984.

"Remote Sensing by Satellite: Global Hegemony or Social Utility." In *World Communications: A Handbook,* edited by George Gerbner and Marsha Siefert. New York: Longman, 1984.

"L'Atout Informatique: Des Trusts a L'Assaut du Ciel." *Le Monde Diplomatique* (March 1984):6–7.

"Scrapping the International System: The U.S. Withdrawal from UNESCO." *Journal of Communication,* 34:4 (Fall 1984).

"New Information Technologies and Old Objectives." *Science and Public Policy,* 1:6 (December 1984):382–83.

"Beneficiaries and Victims of the Information Age: The Systematic Diminution of the Public's Supply of Meaningful Information." *Vision and Reality,* special edition of *Papers in Comparative Studies,* 4 (1985):185–92.

"Electronic Information Flows: New Basis for Global Domination?" In *Television in Transition,* edited by Richard Collins, Phillip Drummond, and Richard Paterson. London: British Film Institute, 1985.

"Expanding the Club—New Vistas for TDF." In *International Information Economy Handbook,* edited by G. Russell Pipe and Chris Brown, pp. 31–32. Springfield, VA: Transnational Data Reporting Service, 1985.

"Privatizing the Public Section: The Information Connection." *Information and Behavior,* 1:1 (1985).

"Behind the Media Merger Movement." *The Nation* (June 8, 1985):696–98. Reprinted in the *Cleveland Plain-Dealer,* June 23, 1985.

"Breaking the West's Media Monopoly: The U.N. and Information." *The Nation* (September 21, 1985):248–51.

"Review of *Keeping American Uninformed: Government Secrecy in the 1980's,* by Donna Demac." *Telecommunications Policy* (September 1985).

"Review of *The New Politics of Science,* by David Dickson." *Journal of Communication,* 35:1 (Winter 1985):194–96.

"Information—A Shrinking Resource." *The Nation* (December 28, 1985–January 4, 1986): 708–10.

"Democracy in an Information Society." Comment on article by Theodore Sterling. *The Information Society,* 4:1/2 (1986):123–26.

"The Erosion of National Sovereignty by the World Business System." In *The Myth of the Information Revolution,* edited by Michael Traber, pp. 21–34. London: Sage, 1986.

"Strengths and Weaknesses of the New International Information Empire." In *Communication for All,* edited by Philip Lee, 17–32. Maryknoll, NY: Orbis, 1986.

"Review of *Television and the Red Menace: The Video Road to Vietnam,* edited by J. Fred MacDonald." *Contemporary Sociology,* 15:1 (January 1986):77–79.

"Commercializing Information." With Anita R. Schiller. *The Nation* (October 4, 1986):306–9.

"The New Information Technologies: New Means of Creating Cultural Dependency?" In *Dependency Issues in Korean Development,* edited by Kyong Dong Kim. Seoul: Seoul National University Press, 1987.

"Old Foundations for a New (Information) Age." In *Competing Visions, Complex Realities,* edited by Jorge Reina Schement and Leah Lievrouw, pp. 23–31. Norwood, NJ: Ablex, 1987.

"Review of *Exporting the First Amendment: The Press-Government Crusade of 1945–1952,* by Margaret A. Blanchard." *Journal of Communication* (Summer 1987):155–60.

"Information: Important Issue for '88." *The Nation* (July 4–11, 1987):1, 6.

Excerpt from *Who Knows.* In *Questioning Technology,* edited by John Zerzan and Alice Carnes, pp. 170–76. London: Freedom Press, 1988.

"Libraries, Public Access to Information and Commerce." With Anita R. Schiller. In *The Political Economy of Information,* edited by Vincent Mosco, pp. 146–66. Madison: University of Wisconsin Press, 1988.

"Preface." In *The Hidden War of Information,* by Enrique Gonzalez-Manet. Norwood, NJ: Ablex, 1988.

"Corporate Speech, Power Politics and the First Amendment." *The Independent* (July 1988):10–13.

"Computers and the World Economy." In *The Encyclopedia of Communications.* New York: Oxford University Press, 1989.

"The Privatization of Culture." In *Cultural Politics in Contemporary America,* edited by Sut Jhally and Ian Angus, pp. 317–32. New York: Routledge, 1980.

"Review of *United States and the Direct Broadcast Satellite,* by Sarah Fletcher Luther." *Socialism and Democracy* (Spring–Summer 1989):236–39.

"Communication of Knowledge in an Information Society." With Bernard Miege. In *The Information Society: Evolving Landscapes,* edited by Jacques Berleur, Andrew Clement, Richard Sizer, and Diane Whitehouse, pp. 161–67. New York: Springer, 1990.

"Forgetful and Short-Sighted—What Hope for the Future." *Media Development,* 3 (1990): 26–27.

"Kultursponsoring in den USA." *Media Perspektiven,* 11 (1990):730–36.

"Television Is a Social—Not a Biological or Technological—Problem." Comment on article, "The First Amendment in an Age of Paratroopers." *Texas Law Review,* 68:6 (May 1990):1169–78.

"Democratic Illusions." *Multinational Monitor,* 11:6 (June 1990):19–22.

"Sayonara MCA." *The Nation* (December 31, 1990):828–29.

"The Global Commercialization of Culture." *The Progressive Librarian,* No. 2 (Winter 1990–91):15–22.

"My Graduate Education (1946–1948), Sponsored by the U.S. Military Government of Germany." In *Medien/Kultur,* edited by Knut Hickethier and Siegfried Zielinski, pp. 23–29. Berlin: Volker Spiess, 1991.

"Gulf War Forum Interviews." *Propaganda Review,* No. 7 (1991).

"An Interview with Herbert I. Schiller." (Lai-si Tsui). *Media Development,* 27:1 (1991):50–52.

"Le Citoyen sous le Rouleau Compresseur des Firmes de la Communication." *Le Monde Diplomatique* (February 1991):26–27.

"Whose New World Order?" *Lies of Our Times* (February 1991):12–13.

"Not Yet a Post-Imperialist Era." *Critical Studies in Mass Communication,* 8:1 (March 1991):13–28.

"Manipuler et Controler les Coeurs et les Esprits." *Le Monde Diplomatique* (May 1991):14–15.

"Nuestros Medios de Comunicacion Parecen Apendices del Pentagono." *El Independiente* (Madrid) (May 26, 1991):40–41.

"Read This." (Deborah Baldwin). *Common Cause Magazine* (May–June 1991):3036.

"Corporate Sponsorship: Institutionalized Censorship of the Cultural Realm." *Art Journal* (Fall 1991).

"Anticipating the Next Radical Moment: An Unexpected Locale." In *Illuminating the Blindspots: Essays in Honor of Dallas Smythe,* edited by Janet Wasko, Vincent Mosco, and Manjunath Pendakur. Norwood, NJ: Ablex, 1993.

"Communication, Technology and Ecology." In *Mass Communication Research: On Problems and Policies,* edited by Cees J. Hamelink and Olga Linne. Norwood, NJ: Ablex, 1994.

James D. Halloran

A Selection from His Publications

Control or Consent: A Study of the Challenge of Mass Communication. London: Sheed and Ward, 1963. 246 pp.

The Effects of Mass Communication with Special Reference to Television. Leicester: Leicester University Press, 1964. 83 pp.

Attitude Formation and Change. Leicester: Leicester University Press, 1966. 167 pp.

Television and Delinquency. With R. Brown and D. Chaney. Leicester: Leicester University Press, 1970. 221 p.

The Effects of Television. London: Panther Books, 1970. 224 pp.

Demonstrations and Communication: A Case Study. With P. Elliott and G. Murdock. Harmondsworth: Penguin, 1970. 319 pp.

Mass Media in Society: The Need for Research. Reports and Papers on Mass Communication No. 59. Paris: UNESCO, Department of Mass Communication, 1970. 33 pp.

Editor. *Broadcaster/Researcher Cooperation in Mass Communication Research.* Report on an international seminar, University of Leicester, England, December 1970. 183 pp.

Television Programmes in Great Britain: Content and Control, with Special Reference to Violence and Sex. With P. Croll. Washington, D.C.: Government Printing Office, 1971, pp. 415–92.

"Research in Forbidden Territory." In *Communications Technology and Social Policy: Understanding the New "Cultural Revolution,"* edited by George Gerbner, Larry Gross, and William H. Melody, pp. 547–53. New York: Wiley, 1973.

"Communication and Change." In *WACC Journal No. 4/74: Political Access to the Media,* edited by Hans-Wolfgang Hessler, pp. 34–44. Witten/Ruhr, Germany: Eckart, 1974.

"'Mass Media and Race: A Research Approach." Introduction to *Race as News,* pp. 9–34. Paris: UNESCO Press, 1974.

Mass Media and Society: The Challenge of Research. Leicester: Leicester University Press, 1974. 30 pp.

"The Media and Communication in a Developing Country." In *Mass Media Research: Report on International Workshop in Hilversum, November 1973,* pp. 63–70. Geneva: Lutheran World Federation, 1974.

Training in the Critical Reading of Television Language. Report on an International Colloquy in Leicester, September 1973. Strasbourg: Council of Europe, 1974. 25 pp.

"Understanding Television." In *Education and Change* (Strasbourg, Council of Europe) No. 25 (Summer 1974):15–20.

The Development of Cable Television in the UK: Problems and Possibilities. Strasbourg: Council of Europe, 1975. 31 pp.

Editor. *Mass Media and Socialization.* Leicester: International Association for Mass Communication Research, 1976. 130 pp.

"Broadcasting and Continuing Education." In *The Japan Prize Symposium,* supplement to the report of the 11th Japan Prize Contest, pp. 7–18. Tokyo: Nippon Hoso Kyokai, 1977.

"An Exploratory Study of Some Factors That Influence the Production of Drama in an Independent Television Company in the United Kingdom." In *Organisation and Structure of Fiction Production in Television,* pp. 9–50. Turin: Editizione RAI, 1977. Italian and French translations, pp. 51–140.

"Introduction." In *Ethnicity and the Media,* pp. 9–24. Paris: UNESCO, 1977.

Understanding Television: Research and the Broadcaster—Cooperation-Conflict-Compromise. Strasbourg: Council for Cultural Cooperation, Council of Europe, 1977. 31 pp.

"Mass Communication: Symptom or Cause of Violence?" *International Social Science Journal,* 30:4 (1978):816–33

"Mass Communication Research: State of the Art. Where Are We, and Where We Should Be Going." In *Mass Media and Man's View of Society,* pp. 7–30.

"Studying Violence and the Mass Media: A Sociological Approach." In *Deviance and Mass Media,* edited by Charles Winick, pp. 287–305. Sage Annual Reviews in Studies in Deviance, Vol. 2. Beverly Hills, CA: Sage, 1978.

"Social Research in Broadcasting: Further Developments, or Turning the Clock Back?" *Journal of Communication,* 28:2 (Spring 1978):120–32.

"Introduction." In *What Do TV Producers Know About the Young Viewers?* pp. 7–29. Munich: Stiftung Prix Jeunesse, 1979.

"Information and Communication." *Aslib Proceedings,* 31:1 (January 1979):21–28.

"Television in Focus." *Unesco Courier* (March 1979):4–9. In 20 languages.

"New Information and Economic Orders: Need for Research-Based Information." *Communicator,* 14:4 (October 1979):13–14.

"Communication Needs and Communication Policies." *Massa Communicatie,* 8:3/4 (1980)):152–57.

"The Need for Communication Research in Developing Countries." *Media Asia,* 7:3 (1980):137–44.

"The Context of Mass Communication Research." In *Communication and Social Structure: Critical Studies in Mass Media Research,* edited by Emile G. McAnany, Jorge Schnitmann, Noreene Janus, pp. 21–57. New York: Praeger, 1981.

"I Bambini e la Televisione." In *Documenti,* 4:22/23 (May–August 1981):7–13.

"Mass Media Involvement and Social Action." In *Veerstichting,* Proceedings, pp. 41–55, of Symposium, September 2–3, 1981, Leiden, Netherlands.

"Introduction and Background." In *Communication in the Community: An International Study on the Role of the Mass Media in Seven Communities,* pp. 5–14. Paris: UNESCO, 1982.

"The New Communication Technologies and Research." In *Communication Manual,* pp. 50–58. Bonn: Friedrich-Ebert-Stiftung, 1982.

Young TV Viewers and Their Images of Foreigners: A Summary and Interpretation from a Four-Nation Study, pp.1–22. Munich: Stiftung Prix Jeunesse, 1982.

"Freeing the Media from Market Forces." *UNESCO Features,* No. 783 (1983):6–9.

"Information and Communication: Information Is the Answer but What Is the Question?" *Journal of Information Science,* 7 (1983):158–67.

"Research Considerations, Possibilities and Proposals, Introduction." In *The Media Coverage of Disarmament and Related Issues,* Report to UNESCO, pp. i–xvi. Leicester: International Association for Mass Communication Research, 1983.

"A Case for Critical Eclecticism." *Journal of Communication,* 33:3 (Summer 1983):270–78.

"Introduction." In *Television and the Images of the Family,* pp. vii–xxiii. Munich: Stiftung Prix Jeunesse, 1984.

"Coping with Information." In *A Geography of Public Relations Trends,* edited by E. Denig and A. van der Meiden, pp. 23–36. Dordrecht: Martinus Nijhoff, 1985.

"La Famille a la Télévision: Le Portrait de la Famille a la Télévision Britannique." With Marsha Jones. In *Les Enfants et la Télévision—Etudes de Radio-Télévision,* pp. 151–77. Belgium: RTBF, 1985.

"Trendsetters or Trendfollowers: The Contribution of Research." *Massa Communicatie '85* (Netherlands) (1985):157–65.

"What Can Research Tell Us?" Australian Children's Television Foundation, International Conference on "The Challenge of Kids' TV," Melbourne, Australia. Conference Paper No. 9. 1985. 9 pp.

"International Democratization of Communication: The Challenge of Research." In *Communication and Domination: Essays to Honor Herbert I. Schiller,* edited by Jorg Becker, Goran Hedebro, and Leena Paldan, pp. 241–48. Norwood, NJ: Ablex, 1986.

"The Social Implications of Technological Innovations in Communication." In *The Myth of the Information Revolution,* edited by Michael Traber, pp. 46–63. London: Sage, 1986.

"The International Research Experience." In *Rethinking Development Communication,* edited by Neville Jayaweera and Sarath Amunugama, pp. 129–48. Singapore: Asian Mass Communication Research and Information Centre, 1987.

"Learning About the Media: Media Education and Communication Research." With Marsha Jones. In *Communication and Society,* 16. Paris: UNESCO, 1987. 183 pp.

"Television and the Family: A Summary and Interpretation." With Olga Linne. In *Television and the Family in Three Countries,* pp. 5–30. Munich: Stiftung Prix Jeunesse, 1988.

"Asking the Right Questions." *Airwaves*, Winter 1988/1989:15–16.
"Foreword." In *The Mass Media and Village Life: An Indian Study*, pp. 11–14. London: Sage, 1989.
"Ethics and Broadcasting." In *Foundation for Broadcast Culture*, pp. 11–21. Seoul, December 1989.
"Mass Media and Violence." In *Principles and Practice of Forensic Psychiatry*, edited by R. Bluglass and P. Bowden, pp. 571–75. Churchill Livingstone, 1990.
A Quarter of a Century of Prix Jeunesse Research. Munich: Stiftung Prix Jeunesse, 1990. 127 pp.

Kaarle Nordenstreng

Books

Joukkotiedotus ja yleisö (Mass Communication and the Audience). Tapiola: Weilin + Göös, 1969. 278 pp.
Toward Quantification of Meaning: An Evaluation of the Semantic Differential Technique. Helsinki: Annales Academiae Scientiarum Fennicae, 1969. Dissertation summary 35 pp.; four published articles 62 pp.
Joukkotiedotus yhteiskunnassa (Mass Communication in Society). With Yrjö Ahmavaara, et al. Helsinki: Tammi, 1971. 247 pp.
Editor. *Informational Mass Communication*. Helsinki: 1973. 198 pp.
Tajuntateollisuus; viestintäpolitiikan näköaloja (Consciousness Industry: Perspectives on Communication Policy). Tapiola: Weilin + Göös, 1974. 164 pp.
Television Traffic—A One-Way Street? A Survey and Analysis of the International Flow of Television Programme Material. With Tapio Varis. Reports and Papers on Mass Communication No. 70. Paris: UNESCO, 1974. 62 pp.
Joukkotiedotus (Mass Communication). with Sirkka Minkkinene, et al. Helsinki: Tammi, 1975. 327 pp.
Tiedotusoppi; johdatus yhteiskunnallisten viestintäprosessien tutkimukseen (Communication: Introduction to the Study of Social Communication Processes). Helsinki: Otava, 1975. 333 pp. Swedish ed., 1978; Danish ed., 1979; Hungarian ed., 1979.
National Sovereignty and International Communication. Edited with Herbert I. Schiller. Norwood, NJ: Ablex, 1979. 286 pp.
The Mass Media Declaration of UNESCO. Norwood, NJ: Ablex, 1984. 475 pp.
Foreign News in the Media: International Reporting in 29 Countries. Edited with Annabelle Sreberny-Mohammadi, et al. Reports and Papers on Mass Communication No. 93. Paris: UNESCO, 1985. 95 pp.
New International Information and Communication Order: Sourcebook. With Enrique Gonzalez-Manet and Wolfgang Kleinwächter. Prague: International Organizatuon of Journalists, 1986. 392 pp.
Suomen viestintäjärjestelmä (Finland's Communication System). Edited with Osmo A. Wiio. Tapiola: Weilin + Göös, 1986. 299 pp.
Useful Recollections: Excursions to History of the International Movement of Journalists, Parts 1, 2. With Jiri Kubka. Prague: International Organization of Journalists, 1986–88. 121 pp.; 193 pp.

Journalist: Status, Rights and Responsibilities. Edited with Hifzi Topuz. Prague: International Organization of Journalists, 1989. 317 pp.

The Global Media Debate. Edited with George Gerbner and Hamid Mowlana. Norwood, NJ: Ablex, 1992. 200 pp.

Beyond National Sovereignty: International Communication in the 1990s. Edited with Herbert I. Schiller. Norwood, NJ: Ablex, 1993.

Articles, Reports, Papers

(Those issued in English; comprehensive since 1986. Those issued earlier are included selectively.)

"American and Finnish Journalists Look at World Leaders." *Scandinavian Political Studies* (Norway), 3 (1968):167–85.

"Communication Research in the United States: A Critical Perspective." *Gazette,* 3 (1968): 207–16.

"Comments on 'Gratifications Research' in Broadcasting." *Public Opinion Quarterly* (Spring 1970):130–32.

"Comprehension and Interest in Radio Programs." With Osmo A. Wiio. *Journalism Quarterly* (Autumn 1970):564–66.

"A Policy of News Transmission." *Educational Broadcasting Review,* 5 (1971):20–30.

"Communication Research in the Framework of Policy and Planning." International Association for Mass Communication Research, Buenos Aires, Argentina, September 1972. 17 pp.

"Who Determines Public Opinion? A Critical View of the Individual and the Mass Media in Democracy." *EBU Review,* 5 (1973):22–24.

"Mass Media and Developing Nations: A Global Perspective of the Present State of Mass Communication and Its Research." Keynote paper, International Association for Mass Communication Research, Leipzig, September 1974. 9 pp. Published in conference proceedings and in *The Democratic Journalist,* 1 (1975):6–9.

"Recent Developments in European Communications Theory." In *International and Intercultural Communication,* edited by H. D. Fischer and John Merrill, pp. 457–65. New York: Hastings House, 1976. Also in *Communication Yearbook I,* edited by Brent Rubin, pp. 73–78. New Brunswick, NJ: Transaction Books and International Communication Association, 1977.

"Detente and Exchange of Information Between East and West." In *Yearbook of Finnish Foreign Policy 1975,* pp. 57–65. Helsinki: Finnish Institute of International Relations, 1976.

"Free Flow of Information: The Rise and Fall of a Doctrine." *Review of International Affairs* (Yugoslavia), 640 (1976):12, 25–27.

"Helsinki: The New Equation." With Herbert I. Schiller. *Journal of Communication* (Winter 1976):130–34.

"From Mass Media to Mass Consciousness." In *Mass Communication Policies in Changing Cultures,* edited by George Gerbner, pp. 269–83. New York: Wiley, 1977.

"Roles and Functions of a Communication Policy Council." With Osmo A. Wiio. In *National Communication Policy Councils: Principles and Experiences,* pp. 18–26. Reports and Papers on Mass Communication No. 83. Paris: UNESCO, 1979.

"The Paradigm of a Totality." In *Communication in the Eighties: A Reader on the MacBride Report,* edited by Cees Hamelink, pp. 8–16. Rome: IDOC International, 1980.

"A Call for More Democratic Structures in Communication." *Media Development,* 4 (1980):12–14.
"Idealism, Aggression, Apology and Criticism: The Four Traditions of Research on 'International Communication.'" With Heikki Hellman and Tapio Varis. International Association for Mass Communication Research, Caracas, Venezuela, August 1980. 15 pp.
"Journalistic Ethics and International Relations." With Antti Alanen. *Communication* (1981):225–54.
"New International Directions: A Nonaligned Viewpoint." In *Communication in Twenty-First Century,* edited by R. W. Haigh, George Gerbner, and R. B. Byrne, pp. 192–99. New York: Wiley, 1981.
"The Media—Backstopping Official Policy?" In *International Perspectives on the News,* edited by Erwin Atwood, Stuart Bullion, and Sharon Murphy, pp. 145–56. Carbondale: Southern Illinois University Press, 1982.
"The Struggle Around the New International Information Order." *Communicator,* 2:3 (1982):6–8, 43.
"U.S. Policy and the Third World: A Critique." *Journal of Communication* (Summer 1982):54–59.
"The Wider Implications of NWICO in Relation to the Major Issues of Our Times."Address at NAMEDIA Conference of the Non-Aligned, New Delhi, December 1983. 11 pp. Published in abridged form in *The Democratic Journalist,* 2 (1984):7–8.
"Defining the New International Information Order." In *World Communications: A Handbook,* edited by George Gerbner and Marsha Siefert, pp. 28–36. New York: Longman, 1984.
"Three Theses on the Imbalance Debate." In *Politics of News: Third World Perspectives,* edited by J. S. Yadava, pp. 24–39. New Delhi: Concept, 1984.
"World Forum: The U.S. Decision to Withdraw from UNESCO." *Journal of Communication* (Autumn 1984):93–95.
"The Content and Principles of Mass Communication." In *Journalists and Detente,* edited by H. Karkkolainen, pp. 68–97. Helsinki: Union of Journalists in Finland, 1985.
International Communication and Confidence-Building in Europe: Report of the First Leipzig-Tampere Seminar on Confidence-Building in the Non-Military Field, May 14–15, 1986. Edited with Wolfgang Kleinwächter. Reports of the Department of Journalism and Mass Communication, B 20. Tampere: University of Tampere, 1986. 131 pp.
"Professionalism in Transition: Journalistic Ethics." In *Approaches to International Communication,* edited by Ullamaija Kivikuru and Tapio Varis, pp. 311–24. Report No. 35. Finnish National Commission for UNESCO, Helsinki: 1986. Also in *Communication Ethics and Global Change,* edited by Tom Cooper, pp. 277–83. White Plains, NY: Longman, 1989.
"Tanzania and the New Information Order: A Case Study of Africa's Second Struggle." In *Communication and Domination: Essays to Honor Herbert I. Schiller,* edited by Jorg Becker, Goran Hedebro, and Leena Paldan, pp. 177–91. Norwood, NJ: Ablex, 1986.
"The IOJ Is 40 Years Old." *Democratic Journalist,* 5 (1986):3–5.
"The League of Nations and the Mass Media: The Rediscovery of a Forgotten Story." With Tarja Seppä. International Association for Mass Communication Research, New Delhi, India, August 1986. 32 pp.
"UNESCO at Crossroad." *OANA Newsletter* (October 1986–March 1987):51–53.

"UNESCO Departing from Its Constitutional Line." *Democratic Journalist,* 11 (1987):6–7.

"On the Nature and Significance of the Declaration." "Incorporation of the Mass Media Declaration, the MacBride Report and NWICO in the Curricula of Communication Education." Two reports for International Symposium on the Mass Media Declaration of UNESCO, June 1987. Latter with Bhatia, et al. *IAMCR Occasional Papers,* 9 (1989):11–14, 26–37.

"Promotion of Textbooks for the Training of Journalists in Anglophone Africa: Final Report of an IPDC Project." With Kwame Boafo. *IAMCR Occasional Papers* (Hungary), 5 (1988). 45 pp.

Editor. *Nordic/SADCC Media Seminar Proceedings.* Reports of the Department of Journalism and Mass Communication, B 26. Tampere: University of Tampere, 1988. 209 pp.

"International Symposium on the Mass Media Declaration of Unesco: What Happened and What Is to Be Learned?" International Association for Mass Communication Research, Barcelona, Spain, July 1988. 9 pp. and appendix. Published in abridged form in *Democratic Journalist,* 11 (1988):8–9.

Human Rights, Communication and Culture: Report of the Second Leipzig-Tampere Seminar on Confidence-Building in the Non-Military Field, Tampere 1988. Edited with Wolfgang Kleinwächter. Reports of the Department of Journalism and Mass Communication, B 28. Tampere: University of Tampere, 1989. 113 pp.

"The New International Information and Communication Order." With Wolfgang Kleinwächter. In *Handbook of International and Intercultural Communication,* edited by Molefi Asante and William Gudykunst, pp. 87–113. Newbury Park, CA: Sage, 1989.

"The Worldwide Movement for Democratic Communications." Conference on Media Accountability Under International Law, Los Angeles, California, July 1989. 10 pp.

"From Compromise to Compromise." *Media Development,* 3 (1990):36–37.

"Theoretical Convergences and Contrasts: A View from Finland." With Veikko Pietilä and Tarmo Malmberg. *European Journal of Communication,* 2–3 (1990): 165–85.

International Security and Humanitarian Cooperation in the Reunited Europe: Report of the Third Leipzig-Tampere Seminar on Confidence-Building in the Non-Military Field, Leipzig 1990. Edited with Wolfgang Kleinwächter. Reports of the Department of Journalism and Mass Communication, B 32. Tampere: University of Tampere, 1991. 134 pp.

Promotion of Educational Materials for Communication Studies: Report of Phase I of a UNESCO/IPDC Project. Edited with Michael Traber. Reports of the Department of Journalism and Mass Communication, B 34. Tampere: University of Tampere, 1991. 100 pp.

"The New Information Order and Communication Scholarship: Reflections on a Delicate Relationship." In *Illuminating the Blindspots: Essays in Honor of Dallas Smythe,* edited by Janet Wasko, Vincent Mosco, and Manjunath Pendakur. Norwood, NJ: Ablex, 1993.

"The UNESCO Expert Panel with the Benefit of Hindsight." In *Mass Communication Research: In Honor of James D. Halloran,* edited by Cees Hamelink and Olga Linne. Norwood, NJ: Ablex, 1994.

About the Book and Editor

Dallas Smythe, George Gerbner, Herbert Schiller, James Halloran, Kaarle Nordenstreng—these five seminal figures form the backbone of current scholarship in critical communication. From policy research to television demographics and from economic globalization to cultural imperialism, their insights and discoveries have given both scholars and the general public new means of understanding ourselves as we all try to live in the Information Age.

Through interviews with each scholar and essays evaluating their work, John A. Lent has compiled a sparkling introduction not only to the different roads taken by these scholars en route to their discoveries but also to the critical byways that they have opened for others. Whereas the personal memories of each figure give insight to the lives and works that led to their groundbreaking theories, the commissioned essays by leading lights in critical communication demonstrate how those ideas profoundly affect current scholarship. Extensive bibliographies of each of the five scholars provide a springboard for further exploration of their influence on the field. *A Different Road Taken* is an important primer to the works of these five founders and a must-read for all students of critical communication.

John A. Lent has been writing about mass communications, often with a critical perspective, since the early 1960s. The nearly 50 books and monographs he has authored or edited and more than 350 articles under his byline have dealt with media ownership, press freedom, media imperialism, NIIO, women in communications, transnationalization, Third World mass communication, and development communication, as well as Asian newspapers, broadcasting, film, video, popular culture, and comics and Caribbean mass media and popular culture. He is a professor in a Philadelphia "academic factory."

About the Contributors

Robin Mansell has been a Reader in Communication and Information Technology Policy, Science Policy Research Unit, University of Sussex, since 1988. She has experience as a researcher and communication policy analyst with OECD, ESRC Programme on Information and Communication Technologies, and Simon Fraser University, where she received her doctorate in 1984. Her research focuses on European Community and international telecommunication policy and regulation, networking and industrial restructuring, and the development of advanced communication services.

Manjunath Pendakur is Professor and Director of the Program on Communication and Development Studies at Northwestern University. He is the author of *Canadian Dreams and American Control: The Political Economy of Canadian Film Industry,* and coeditor of *Illuminating the Blindspots,* a collection of essays honoring Dallas W. Smythe. His latest work is *Indian Cinema: Industry, Ideology, and Consciousness.* Pendakur concentrates on television and rural culture in India, Tanzanian communications policies and privatization, and film/TV production and "flexible" unions.

Michael Morgan is Associate Professor of Communication at the University of Massachusetts–Amherst. Much of his work has been identified with television, especially in regard to cultivation analysis; some of it has been of a comparative nature. He, with Nancy Signorielli, edited *Cultivation Analysis: New Directions in Media Effects Research.*

Janet Wasko is Professor of Communication at the University of Oregon. She has been active in the Union for Democratic Communication since its beginnings and has served as an officer of that organization as well as of the International Association for Mass Communication Research. Her most recent publications include *Illuminating the Blindspots,* edited with Vincent Mosco and Manjunath Pendakur; *Communication and Democracy,* edited with Slavko Splichal; and *Democratic Communications in the Information Age,* edited with Mosco.

Lai-si Tsui is a doctoral candidate in the sociology–urban affairs program at Michigan State University, where, for her master's degree, she studied international telecommunications. In the period 1986–88, she worked as a researcher for the Asian Regional Exchange for New Alternatives, an NGO in Hong Kong. Among her writings is a three-part series about communication researchers in *Media Development.*

Vincent Mosco is Professor of Communication at Carleton University, Ottawa. His most recent books include *The Pay-Per Society* and *Democratic Communications in the Information Age,* edited with Janet Wasko. He has just finished a three-year leave, during which time he worked on a project concerning the political economy of communication and culture.

Tamás Szecskö is the founder and director (1969–91) of the Mass Communication Research Center and its successor, the Hungarian Institute for Public Opinion Research. From 1984 to 1992, he was general secretary of the International Association for Mass

Communication Research; at other times he has been a trustee of the International Institute of Communication and Chairman of the European Group of Audience Researchers. Besides research into the theory of human communication and sociological/economic aspects of communication policies, he has taught at the Budapest University of Economics, European Extension of St. John's University, and Budapest School of Journalism.

Annabelle Sreberny-Mohammadi succeeded Jim Halloran as Director of the Centre for Mass Communication Research, University of Leicester. Before that she was in the communications program at Queen's College, New York. Among her publications is *Small Media, Big Revolution: Communications, Culture and the Iranian Revolution* (with A. Mohammadi).

Wolfgang Kleinwächter served as a Deputy Director of the Institute for International Studies, Karl Marx University, in Leipzig, where he taught after receiving his doctorate in 1981. He was Director of the Scientific Working Group on Communication of the German Democratic Republic UNESCO Commission, and served on his country's delegations to UNESCO and the Conference on Security and Cooperation in Europe. He is the author of books and scores of articles, mainly dealing with international law of communications and information and the New International Information Order.

Taisto Hujanen is a professor in the Department of Journalism and Mass Communication, University of Tampere. He has written on a number of topics, including democratization of communication, the Gulf War in television news, and the Finnish mass media system.

Index